Lecture Notes in Computer Science

Vol. 1: GI-Gesellschaft für Informatik e.V. 3. Jahrestagung, Hamburg, 8.–10. Oktober 1973. Herausgegeben im Auftrag der Gesellschaft für Informatik von W. Brauer. XI, 508 Seiten. 1973.

Vol. 2: GI-Gesellschaft für Informatik e.V. 1. Fachtagung über Automatentheorie und Formale Sprachen, Bonn, 9.–12. Juli 1973. Herausgegeben im Auftrag der Gesellschaft für Informatik von K.-H. Böhling und K. Indermark. VII, 322 Seiten. 1973.

Vol. 3: 5th Conference on Optimization Techniques, Part I. (Series: I.F.I.P. TC7 Optimization Conferences.) Edited by R. Conti and A. Ruberti. XIII, 565 pages. 1973.

Vol. 4: 5th Conference on Optimization Techniques, Part II. (Series: I.F.I.P. TC7 Optimization Conferences.) Edited by R. Conti and A. Ruberti. XIII, 389 pages. 1973.

Vol. 5: International Symposium on Theoretical Programming. Edited by A. Ershov and V. A. Nepomniaschy. VI, 407 pages. 1974.

Vol. 6: B. T. Smith, J. M. Boyle, J. J. Dongarra, B. S. Garbow, Y. Ikebe, V. C. Klema, and C. B. Moler, Matrix Eigensaystem Routines – EISPACK Guide. XI, 551 pages. 2nd Edition 1974, 1976.

Vol. 7: 3. Fachtagung über Programmiersprachen, Kiel, 5.–7. März 1974. Herausgegeben von B. Schlender und W. Frielinghaus. VI, 225 Seiten. 1974.

Vol. 8: GI-NTG Fachtagung über Struktur und Betrieb von Rechensystemen, Braunschweig, 20.–22. März 1974. Herausgegeben im Auftrag der GI und der NTG von H.-O. Leilich. VI, 340 Seiten. 1974.

Vol. 9: GI-BIFOA Internationale Fachtagung: Informationszentren in Wirtschaft und Verwaltung. Köln, 17./18. Sept. 1973. Herausgegeben im Auftrag der GI und dem BIFOA von P. Schmitz. VI, 259 Seiten. 1974.

Vol. 10: Computing Methods in Applied Sciences and Engineering, Part 1. International Symposium, Versailles, December 17–21, 1973. Edited by R. Glowinski and J. L. Lions. X, 497 pages. 1974.

Vol. 11: Computing Methods in Applied Sciences and Engineering, Part 2. International Symposium, Versailles, December 17–21, 1973. Edited by R. Glowinski and J. L. Lions. X, 434 pages. 1974.

Vol. 12: GFK-GI-GMR Fachtagung Prozessrechner 1974. Karlsruhe, 10.–11. Juni 1974. Herausgegeben von G. Krüger und R. Friehmelt. XI, 620 Seiten. 1974.

Vol. 13: Rechnerstrukturen und Betriebsprogrammierung, Erlangen, 1970. (GI-Gesellschaft für Informatik e.V.) Herausgegeben von W. Händler und P. P. Spies. VII, 333 Seiten. 1974.

Vol. 14: Automata, Languages and Programming – 2nd Colloquium, University of Saarbrücken, July 29–August 2, 1974. Edited by J. Loeckx. VIII, 611 pages. 1974.

Vol. 15: L Systems. Edited by A. Salomaa and G. Rozenberg. VI, 338 pages. 1974.

Vol. 16: Operating Systems, International Symposium, Rocquencourt 1974. Edited by E. Gelenbe and C. Kaiser. VIII, 310 pages. 1974.

Vol. 17: Rechner-Gestützter Unterricht RGU '74, Fachtagung, Hamburg, 12.–14. August 1974, ACU-Arbeitskreis Computer-Unterstützter Unterricht. Herausgegeben im Auftrag der GI von K. Brunnstein, K. Haefner und W. Händler. X, 417 Seiten. 1974.

Vol. 18: K. Jensen and N. E. Wirth, PASCAL – User Manual and Report. VII, 170 pages. Corrected Reprint of the 2nd Edition 1976.

Vol. 19: Programming Symposium. Proceedings 1974. V, 425 pages. 1974.

Vol. 20: J. Engelfriet, Simple Program Schemes and Formal Languages. VII, 254 pages. 1974.

Vol. 21: Compiler Construction, An Advanced Course. Edited by F. L. Bauer and J. Eickel. XIV. 621 pages. 1974.

Vol. 22: Formal Aspects of Cognitive Processes. Proceedings 1972. Edited by T. Storer and D. Winter. V, 214 pages. 1975.

Vol. 23: Programming Methodology. 4th Informatik Symposium, IBM Germany Wildbad, September 25–27, 1974. Edited by C. E. Hackl. VI, 501 pages. 1975.

Vol. 24: Parallel Processing. Proceedings 1974. Edited by T. Feng. VI, 433 pages. 1975.

Vol. 25: Category Theory Applied to Computation and Control. Proceedings 1974. Edited by E. G. Manes. X, 245 pages. 1975.

Vol. 26: GI- 4. Jahrestagung, Berlin, 9.–12. Oktober 1974. Herausgegeben im Auftrag der GI von D. Siefkes. IX, 748 Seiten. 1975.

Vol. 27: Optimization Techniques. IFIP Technical Conference. Novosibirsk, July 1–7, 1974. (Series: I.F.I.P. TC7 Optimization Conferences.) Edited by G. I. Marchuk. VIII, 507 pages. 1975.

Vol. 28: Mathematical Foundations of Computer Science. 3rd Symposium at Jadwisin near Warsaw, June 17–22, 1974. Edited by A. Blikle. VII, 484 pages. 1975.

Vol. 29: Interval Mathematics. Procedings 1975. Edited by K. Nickel. VI, 331 pages. 1975.

Vol. 30: Software Engineering. An Advanced Course. Edited by F. L. Bauer. (Formerly published 1973 as Lecture Notes in Economics and Mathematical Systems, Vol. 81) XII, 545 pages. 1975.

Vol. 31: S. H. Fuller, Analysis of Drum and Disk Storage Units. IX, 283 pages. 1975.

Vol. 32: Mathematical Foundations of Computer Science 1975. Proceedings 1975. Edited by J. Bečvář. X, 476 pages. 1975.

Vol. 33: Automata Theory and Formal Languages, Kaiserslautern, May 20–23, 1975. Edited by H. Brakhage on behalf of GI. VIII, 292 Seiten. 1975.

Vol. 34: GI – 5. Jahrestagung, Dortmund 8.–10. Oktober 1975. Herausgegeben im Auftrag der GI von J. Mühlbacher. X, 755 Seiten. 1975.

Vol. 35: W. Everling, Exercises in Computer Systems Analysis. (Formerly published 1972 as Lecture Notes in Economics and Mathematical Systems, Vol. 65) VIII, 184 pages. 1975.

Vol. 36: S. A. Greibach, Theory of Program Structures: Schemes, Semantics, Verification. XV, 364 pages. 1975.

Vol. 37: C. Böhm, λ-Calculus and Computer Science Theory. Proceedings 1975. XII, 370 pages. 1975.

Vol. 38: P. Branquart, J.-P. Cardinael, J. Lewi, J.-P. Delescaille, M. Vanbegin. An Optimized Translation Process and Its Application to ALGOL 68. IX, 334 pages. 1976.

Informatik-Fachberichte

Herausgegeben von W. Brauer
im Auftrag der Gesellschaft für Informatik (GI)

8

Digitale Bildverarbeitung
Digital Image Processing

GI/NTG Fachtagung
München, 28.– 30. März 1977

Herausgegeben von H.-H. Nagel

Springer-Verlag
Berlin Heidelberg New York 1977

Herausgeber
Prof. Dr. Hans-Hellmut Nagel
Institut für Informatik
Universität Hamburg
Schlüterstraße 70
2000 Hamburg 13/BRD

Library of Congress Cataloging in Publication Data
Main entry under title:

Digitale Bildverarbeitung = Digital image processing.

  (Informatik-Fachberichte ; 8)
  German or English.
  1. Image processing--Congresses. I. Nagel,
Hans-Hellmut. II. Gesellschaft für Informatik.
III. Nachrichtentechnische Gesellschaft. IV. Title:
Digital image processing. V. Series.
TA1632.D54   621.3815'42   77-1670

CR Subject Classifications (1974): 3.63.

ISBN-13:978-3-540-08169-2   e-ISBN-13:978-3-642-95298-2
DOI: 10.1007/978-3-642-95298-2

Preface/Vorwort

Since several years, methods and entire systems have been developped
to evaluate digitized picture data from rather different problem areas
such as medicine, geological and earth resource investigations, sa-
tellite applications, and industrial automation to name but a few. As
is to be expected, methodical approaches are usually first published
in the context of the special application for which they have been developped.

To intensify the exchange of know-how regarding the various methods
across the boundaries of special application areas, the Technical Committee 6 of the Gesellschaft für Informatik in cooperation with the
Technical Committee 6 of the Nachrichtentechnische Gesellschaft in the
VDE have organized a conference on Digitized Image Processing at Munich,
March 28-30, 1977, the proceedings of which are presented in this volume.

It is a pleasure to thank my colleagues

> J. Bodechtel, München
> R. Dierstein, Oberpfaffenhofen
> Th. Einsele, München
> P. Heintzen, Kiel
> H. Kazmierczak, Karlsruhe
> A. Schief, Karlsruhe
> J. Schürmann, Ulm

for their willingness to offer their time and cooperation under somewhat stringent boundary conditions in selecting the program for this
conference. My special thanks are due to Prof. Bodechtel for his or-
ganizational effort to host the conference at his institute.

May I mention that Munich with its world renown treasures of paintings
provides the opportunity to experience some individual picture processing of a kind which in my opinion is worth the effort even it is not
digital.

> H.-H. Nagel

<u>AUTORENVERZEICHNIS</u>

Abele, L.;   TU München, Institut für Nachrichtentechnik, Arcisstr. 21, 8000 München 2

Abmayr, W.;   Gesellschaft für Strahlen- und Umweltforschung mbH., Institut für Strahlenschutz, Ingolstädter Landstr. 1, 8042 Neuherberg, Post Oberschleißheim

Apostolico, A.;   Università di Salerno, Istituto di Scienze dell' Informazione, Via Vernieri, 42, 84100 Salerno

Bertelsmeier, R.;   Institut für Informatik der Universität Hamburg, Schlüterstraße 70, 2000 Hamburg 13

Bodechtel, J.;   Zentralstelle für Geo-Photogrammetrie und Fernerkundung, Luisenstr. 37, 8000 München 2

Böhm, M.;   Universitätskrankenhaus Eppendorf, Radiologische Klinik, Martinistr. 52, 2000 Hamburg 20

Borst, H.;   Gesellschaft für Strahlen- und Umweltforschung mbH., Institut für Strahlenschutz, Ingolstädter Landstraße 1, 8042 Neuherberg, Post Oberschleißheim

Brennecke, R.   Klinikum der Christian-Albrechts-Universität Kiel, Abt. Kinderkardiologie, Fröbelstr. 15, 2300 Kiel

Brown, T.K.;   Klinikum der Christian-Albrechts-Universität Kiel, Abt. Kinderkardiologie, Fröbelstr. 15, 2300 Kiel

Bücheler, E.;   Universitätskrankenhaus Eppendorf, Radiologische Klinik, Martinistr. 52, 2000 Hamburg 20

Bürsch, J.H.;   Klinikum der Christian-Albrechts-Universität Kiel, Abt. Kinderkardiologie, Fröbelstr. 15, 2300 Kiel

Cantoni, V.;   L.A.N. - C.N.R. - C.so Carlo Alberto, 5, 27100 Pavia

De Lotto, I.;   Pavia University, Clinica del Lavoro, Via Boezio, no. 23, 27100 Pavia/Italien

Dittel, R.H.;   Deutsche Forschungs- und Versuchsanstalt für Luft- und Raumfahrt e.V., Institut für Flugfunk und Mikrowellen, 8031 Oberpfaffenhofen Post Weßling/Obb.

Dix, W.-R.;   Deutsches Elektronen-Synchrotron, Notkestieg 1, 2000 Hamburg 52

Ebenritter, W.;   Deutsches Elektronen-Synchrotron, Notkestieg 1, 2000 Hamburg 52

Ehrich, R.W.;   Department of Electrical & Computer Engineering, University of Massachusetts, Amherst / USA

Engel, H.;   Deutsche Forschungs- und Versuchsanstalt für Luft- und Raumfahrt e.V., GSOC, 8031 Oberpfaffenhofen Post Weßling/Obb.

Erhardsberger, X.;   Gesellschaft für Strahlen- und Umweltforschung
                      mbH., Institut für Strahlenschutz, Ingolstädter
                      Landstraße 1, 8042 Neuherberg Post Oberschleiß-
                      heim

Favino, A.;   Pavia University, Clinica del Lavoro, Via Boezio,
                      no. 23, 27100 Pavia/Italien

Fernandez, S.;   Zentralstelle für Geo-Photogrammetrie und Fern-
                      erkundung, Luisenstr. 37, 8000 München 2

Foith, J.P.;   Fraunhofer Gesellschaft, Institut für Informa-
                      tionsverarbeitung in Technik und Biologie, Seba-
                      stian-Kneipp-Str. 12-14, 7500 Karlsruhe

Gais, P.;   Gesellschaft für Strahlen- und Umweltforschung
                      mbH., Institut für Strahlenschutz, Ingolstädter
                      Landstraße 1, 8042 Neuherberg Post Oberschleiß-
                      heim

Good, W.;   Eidg. Institut für Schnee- und Lawinenforschung,
                      CH-7260 Weißfluhjoch/Davos

Gredel, J.;   Deutsche Forschungs- und Versuchsanstalt für
                      Luft- und Raumfahrt e.V., GSOC, 8031 Oberpfaffen-
                      hofen Post Weßling/Obb.

Groen, F.C.A.;   Pattern Recognition Group, Department of Applied
                      Physics, Delft University of Technology/Nether-
                      lands

Guichet, P.;   Université de Besançon, Institut universitaire
                      de technologie de Belfort, Départment d'Informa-
                      tique, Rue Engel-Gros, F-90016 Belfort

Haberäcker, P.;   Deutsche Forschungs- und Versuchsanstalt für
                      Luft- und Raumfahrt e.V., Institut für Nachrich-
                      tentechnik, 8031 Oberpfaffenhofen Post Weßling/
                      Obb.

Haydn, R.,   Zentralstelle für Geo-Photogrammetrie und Fern-
                      erkundung, Luisenstr. 37, 8000 München 2

Heintzen, P.H.;   Klinikum der Christian-Albrechts-Universität Kiel,
                      Abt. Kinderkardiologie, Fröbelstr. 15, 2300 Kiel

Höhne, K.H.;   Deutsches Elektronen-Synchrotron, Notkestieg 1,
                      2000 Hamburg 52

Hoyer, A.;   Philips GmbH., Forschungslaboratorium Hamburg,
                      Postfach 540840, 2000 Hamburg 54

Huang, T.S.;   Lab. for Field Archaeology, Rheinisches Landes-
                      Museum, 5300 Bonn

Kitahashi, T.;   TU München, Institut für Nachrichtentechnik,
                      Arcisstr. 21, 8000 München 2

Kreifelts, Th.;   Gesellschaft für Mathematik und Datenverarbeitung
                      mbH. Bonn, Institut für Grafische Datenverarbei-
                      tung und Strukturerkennung, Postfach 12400,
                      5205 St. Augustin

Langham, E.J.;	Eidg. Institut für Schnee- und Lawinenforschung,
CH-7260 Weißfluhjoch/Davos

Magee, M.J.;	The University of Wyoming, Department of Computer
Science, Laramie, Wyoming 82071, USA

Märgner, V.;	TU Braunschweig, Institut für Nachrichtentechnik,
Schleinitzstraße 23, 3300 Braunschweig

Neuhoff, V.;	Max-Planck-Institut für experimentelle Medizin,
Forschungsstelle Neurochemie, Hermann-Rein-Str.3,
3400 Göttingen

Nicolae, G.;	Deutsches Elektronen-Synchrotron, Notkestieg 1,
2000 Hamburg 52

Nowak, D.;	Städt. Krankenanstalten, Ludwigshafen

Nowak, P.;	Deutsche Forschungs- und Versuchsanstalt für
Luft- und Raumfahrt e.V., Institut für Nachrich-
tentechnik, 8031 Oberpfaffenhofen Post Weßling/
Obb.

Pfeiffer, G.;	Deutsches Elektronen-Synchrotron, Notkestieg 1,
2000 Hamburg 52

Ploeg, M. van der;	Department of Histochemistry and Cytochemistry,
State University Leyden/Netherlands

Radig, B.;	Institut für Informatik der Universität Hamburg,
Schlüterstraße 70, 2000 Hamburg 13

Rattei, W.;	Deutsche Forschungs- und Versuchsanstalt für
Luft- und Raumfahrt e.V., GSOC, 8031 Oberpfaffenhofen Post Weßling/Obb.

Rosenfeld, A.;	University of Maryland, Computer Science Center,
College Park, Maryland 20742, USA

Scollar, I.;	Lab. for Field Archaeology, Rheinisches Landes-
museum, 5300 Bonn

Seiderer, M.;	Zentralstelle für Geo-Photogrammetrie und Fern-
erkundung, Luisenstr. 37, 8000 München 2

Sonne, B.;	Universitätskrankenhaus Eppendorf, Radiologische
Klinik, Martinistr. 52, 2000 Hamburg 20

Spiesberger, W.;	Philips GmbH., Forschungslaboratorium Hamburg,
Postfach 540840, 2000 Hamburg 54

Schärf, R.;	Forschungsinstitut für Informationsverarbeitung
und Mustererkennung, Breslauer Straße 48,
7500 Karlsruhe

Schwarzkopf, G.;	Gesellschaft für Strahlen- und Umweltforschung
mbH., Institut für Strahlenschutz, Ingolstädter
Landstraße 1, 8042 Neuherberg Post Oberschleißheim

Tang, G.;	School of Electrical Engineering, Purdue Univer-
sity, West Lafayette, Indiana

Valenziano, F.;   Pavia University and C.I.S.E.,cp 3986, Milan

Verbeek, P.W.;   Pattern Recognition Group, Department of Applied
                    Physics, Delft University of Technology/Nether-
                    lands

Vitulano, S.;   Università di Salerno, Istituto di Scienze dell'
                    Informazione, Via Vernieri, 42, I-84100 Salerno

Wahl, Fr.M.;   TU München, Institut für Nachrichtentechnik,
                    Arcisstr. 21, 8000 München 2

Weidner, B.;   Lab. for Field Archaeology, Rheinisches Landes-
                    museum, 5300 Bonn

Zamperoni, P.;   TU Braunschweig, Institut für Nachrichtentechnik,
                    Schleinitzstraße 23, 3300 Braunschweig

Zimmer, H.-G.;   Max-Planck-Institut für experimentelle Medizin,
                    Forschungsstelle Neurochemie, Hermann-Rein-Str.3,
                    3400 Göttingen

<u>INHALTSVERZEICHNIS</u>

+)
   Dieser Beitrag ist nicht rechtzeitig zur Veröffentlichung
eingegangen.

AUSWERTUNG VON ROENTGENBILDERN

ÜBERSICHT UND VERGLEICH EINGESETZTER BILDVERARBEITUNGSSYSTEME

DIGITAL IMAGE PROCESSING
AND RECOGNITION

Azriel Rosenfeld
Computer Science Center
University of Maryland
College Park, MD 20742/USA

Abstract. This paper reviews some of the recent developments in image recognition techniques. Topics discussed include data structures for image analysis; image matching; segmentation; texture analysis; and shape description.

1. Introduction. Image (or picture) processing deals with the computer manipulation and analysis of pictorial information which is input to the computer in array form. This restriction on the input format distinguishes image processing from computer graphics, in which pictorial information is represented in other forms -- e.g., as sets of coordinates of points, as sequences of line segments, or as pieces of mathematically defined surfaces.

In a more restricted sense, image processing refers to operations that transform images into other images, while image recognition maps images into descriptions. Major topics in image processing include digitization and coding (or compression) of image data; enhancement and restoration of degraded images; and reconstruction of images from projections. Image recognition topics include image matching and local feature detection (edges, curves, etc.); segmentation (of an image into significant regions) and texture analysis; and shape representation and description. This paper reviews some of the recent developments in image recognition techniques.

There exist at least four textbooks [1-4] and one journal [5] that deal with various aspects of image processing and recognition. In addition, numerous survey articles, meeting proceedings, paper collections, and journal special issues on the subject have appeared. Books, journals, and meetings on pattern recognition and its applications often also contain much material on image recognition. For further references, the reader may consult a series of bibliographies by the present author [6-12] which cover a large portion of the U. S.

The support of the National Science Foundation under Grant MCS-72-03610 is gratefully acknowledged, as is the help of Mrs. Shelly Rowe in preparing this paper.

literature. A recent review of progress in pattern recognition and
image processing is [13], to which the reader is referred for information on topics not covered in the present paper.

2. <u>Data Structures for Image Analysis</u>. During the past few years
there has been considerable interest in the use of "pyramid" or "cone"
data structures for image analysis. An early example of this approach
was the "recognition cone" model of Uhr [14]. The general idea is as
follows: an image is input into a buffer array called the retina. A
set of operations or transforms is applied to this image, and the results are stored in a second buffer array; these transforms can be
arbitrary functions of the input data. A further set of transforms is
applied to the second array, and the results stored in a third array;
and so on. The general role of the transforms is to abstract or
simplify, i.e., to extract "relevant" information from their inputs;
thus each layer of the system is smaller than the last, so that the
overall structure is cone-like.

A concrete implementation of a cone structure for low-level image
analysis has been developed by Riseman et al. [15-16]. The base of the
"cone" is a 256-by-256 image array. Color mappings, line finders, texture analyzers, and the like are applied to this input. The application can involve overlapping neighborhoods of each point, in which case
the output has the same size as the input; or it can involve nonoverlapping neighborhoods, leading to a size reduction. The intent of the
system is to provide many different low-level analyses that can be co-
ordinated with the aid of higher-level or global knowledge.

One simple type of cone structure constructs each layer from the previous
by averaging nonoverlapping neighborhoods. For example, if we take
2-by-2 averages, then a 256-by-256 input is successively reduced to
128-by-128, 64-by-64, and so on. These reduced-resolution images are
convenient if one wants to apply "coarse" operators to the original
image, e.g., for detection of edges between major regions. (The outputs
of these coarse operators can then be used as "plans" to guide the
application of finer operators in selected locations, as described by
Kelly [17].) Structures of this type have been studied by Tanimoto and
Pavlidis [18-19], who have also analyzed the expected errors in detecting
and locating image features when this approach is used.

Cone or pyramid structures can also be used, in some cases, to provide
compact representations of an image. For example, suppose that we
divide the image into quadrants, then further subdivide the quadrants
into subquadrants, and so on; a quadrant is subdivided unless it has

(say) constant gray level. This process defines an ordered tree structure in which the leaves correspond to quadrants that need not be subdivided further. If we specify this tree, and a gray level at each
leaf, the original image can be exactly reconstructed; and in any case,
the tree can be used to construct approximations to the image. This
approach permits compact storage of images, as well as rapid search for
image features; it is discussed by Klinger and Dyer in [20].

More generally, the use of graph representations provide a convenient
framework for constructing and analyzing decompositions of an image into
regions (which need not be quadrants or subquadrants). The graph of
region adjacencies is a valuable aid in implementing split-and-merge
schemes for image segmentation, as shown by Horowitz and Pavlidis [21].
In particular, this graph facilitates the detection of "noise" regions
(small regions that are holes in much larger ones), since these are
cutnodes of the graph. A graph formulation is also useful in certain
matching problems. Some recent work along these lines is described by
Tanimoto and Pavlidis in [22].

3. _Image Matching_. Another topic of current interest is the development of efficient, distortion-tolerant image matching techniques. An
approach that has advantages in both efficiency and distortion-tolerance
is to use a hierarhical matching scheme. In such a scheme, the template
that is to be matched with the image is broken up into subtemplates.
These subtemplates are matched with the images individually, and one
then looks for combinations of such submatches that correspond to the
presence of the entire template. This approach provides for a degree
of insensitivity to distortion, since the subtemplates (being smaller)
are less affected by distortion than the entire template would be, and
one can check for combinations of subtemplate matches in _approximately_
the correct relative positions, rather than insisting on an exact match.
At the same time, the subtemplate approach yields a potential saving in
computational cost, since the costs of matching the subtemplates are
lower than that of matching the entire template, which need only be done
at those positions in which subtemplate matches were found.

The use of "spring-loaded" template (= combinations of subtemplates in
approximate relative positions) as a means of overcoming distortion was
proposed by Fischler and Elschlager several years ago [23]. They used
a dynamic programming approach to search for optimal combinations of
subtemplate matches. An alternative approach, based on relaxation
techniques (see Section 4), is discussed by Davis and Rosenfeld [24].
In this approach, the strengths of subtemplate matches are increased

or decreased according to whether or not consistent subtemplate matches (in the proper relative positions) exist.

A number of authors have discussed the use of sequential matching techniques to reduce the computational cost of matching. A general heuristic search formulation of the matching problem is given by Gaafar [25]. Hayes-Roth [26] discusses how redundancy among partially matching templates can be used to reduce the combinatorics of the matching process. VanderBrug and Rosenfeld [27-28] discuss two-stage matching processes in which the first stage is either a subtemplate or a reduced-resolution template; they determine the size of subtemplate, or coarseness of reduced-resolution template, that minimizes the expected cost of the two-stage matching process, if the entire (fine) template is used only at positions where the sub(coarse)template gives an above-threshold match. Ramapriyan [29] and Ullmann [30] discuss methods of reducing the cost of matching large sets of templates to an image.

4. <u>Segmentation</u>. Several general approaches can be used to segment an image into distinctive regions. One approach is to regard the individual image points as samples, compute a set of features (e.g., gray level, color, or local property values) for each point, and apply pattern classification techniques to divide the points into classes. Since the classes are usually not known a priori, clustering techniques can be applied to the feature data. This approach is widely used to analyze multispectral images, using the spectral band intensities at each point as feature values for that point. The classical method of threshold selection by histogram analysis can be regarded as a special case of this approach. Here there is only one "spectral band", so that the feature space is one-dimensional; clusters in this space are just histogram peaks, and thresholding at the valley bottoms between such peaks amounts to using one-dimensional discriminant functions to separate the clusters. Ohlander [31] has successfully segmented a variety of color images by detecting sharp histogram peaks, deleting them, rehistogramming (with respect to the other features), and repeating the process. Recently there has been interest in extending these ideas to multidimensional feature spaces in which the features are local property values at each point; see, for example, Leboucher and Lowitz [32], who discuss segmentation based on two-dimensional histograms.

Segmentation by clustering or histogramming feature values has the disadvantage that it does not take into account the spatial relationships among the image points belonging to a given cluster or peak. One could circumvent this by treating a point's coordinates as features; but this means that clusters must be detected in a space of dimension 3 or greater (two coordinate features and at least one other feature), which is computationally expensive. A more practical approach is to detect the clusters by a sequential process of "region growing", in which one starts with a single image point or small neighborhood, and "grows" a region from it by successively adding adjacent points that have similar feature values to the points already chosen. A review of region growing techniques by Zucker can be found in [33]. Some recent references on region growing deal with statistical criteria for feature similarity [34], with the selection of starting points for region growth [35-36], with forced-choice region growing (a region fragment must merge with the most similar adjacent fragment) [37], with one-pass region growing [38], and with the use of minimal spanning trees to define natural groupings of regions [39]. "Intelligent" region growing schemes must make use of models for the images that are to be segmented; several references on such schemes are [40-42]. Unfortunately, space does not permit discussing this subject in greater detail.

Another approach to image segmentation is to label image parts with their possible identifications, and then (iteratively) use local context to eliminate incompatible combinations. The labels can have probabilities associated with them, in which case the context can be used to strengthen or weaken these probabilities. A general introduction to this "relaxation" approach to segmentation can be found in Rosenfeld et al. [43], and further discussions by Zucker can be found in [44-45]. As pointed out earlier, relaxation techniques can be applied to spring-loaded template matching [24]; here the labels are subtemplate matches, the probabilities are related to the strengths of these matches, and these probabilities are adjusted in accordance with the probabilities that the other subtemplates are present in the proper relative positions. In particular, the approach can be applied to smooth curve detection [46]; here the subtemplates represent line segments in various orientations, and the probabilities reinforce if two of these segments continue one another. Many other applications of the relaxation approach to image segmentation are under investigation. At a higher level, regions extracted from an image (say by a region growing scheme) can be labelled with their possible identifications (with respect to a model for the given class of images), and incompatible labels can then be eliminated or weakened; on such "interpretation-guided segmentation" see Tenenbaum and Barrow [47].

5. <u>Texture Analysis</u>. Several different types of features have been used to described and classify textures; among them are features based on the Fourier power spectrum, and features based on second-order gray level probability densities. For example, in a "busy" texture, the power spectrum falls off more slowly with increasing spatial frequency than in a smooth or coarse texture. Similarly, the correlation between the gray levels at a pair of points falls off more rapidly for a busy texture with increasing distance between the points. A comparative study of several types of texture features used for terrain classification is reported by Weszka et al. in [48]. It was found that Fourier features performed more poorly, and that features based on first-order statistics of gray level differences performed just as well as those based on second-order statistics of gray level.

Empirical studies such as [48] are lacking in generality. It would be desirable if one could characterize textures so as to be able to predict which features would be most effective for a given classification task. To this end, a number of approaches to texture modelling have been proposed. McCormick and Jayaramamurthy [49] used seasonal time series to model textures. Further work based on time series is reported by Tou et al. [50]; they classify a texture as generated by moving-average, autoregressive, or mixed processes by examining its (partial) auto-correlations. A texture model proposed by Zucker [51] treats textures as perturbed or distorted periodic patterns, but provides no constructive approach to fitting such a model to a given texture. Under current investigation is the use of random geometry to model textures. Such models assume that the image plane is divided into "cells" by a random process, and gray levels are assigned to the cells probabilistically. The first and second order gray level statistics of a texture generated by such a model can be predicted, and these predictions can be used to fit the models to given textures [52].

6. <u>Shape Description</u>. A general theory of patterns, as composed of combinations of prototypes subject to distortions, has been developed by Grenander and his colleagues; the first in a series of monographs on this theory is [53]. This theory can be applied to various important problems in shape and pattern analysis; for example, if we assume that a shape is a distorted polygon, where the distortion arises from a probabilistic process, we can attempt to find the (most likely) underlying polygon, and in this way classify the given shape (as arising from a particular polygon), or segment it (using the sides of the polygon to define the segments). Several recent examples of this approach can be found in [54-57]; the details are beyond the scope of this paper. This

work is of interest from the standpoint of functional approximation, as well as of pattern recognition. In effect, it uses models for the given class of shapes to define optimal segmentation or recognition schemes.

Another approach to shape analysis, not based on models, attempts to find a "natural" hierarchy of successive approximations to a given shape, by detecting "sides" and "angles" (i.e., low-curvature portions and local curvature maxima) at various resolutions [58]. These approximations define a tree structure which provides access to descriptions of the shape at any desired degree of coarseness. They can be used to detect approximate symmetries, as well as to guide rapid shape matching procedures. The angles and sides can be detected by relatively simple smoothing and slope differencing procedures; or they can be found by a relaxation-like procedure [59] in which points on the shape's border are initially given probabilities of being side or angle points, and these probabilities are increased or decreased in accordance with local evidence (e.g., the side probability at a given point is increased if nearby points have similar slopes).

7. <u>Concluding Remarks</u>. This paper has touched on only a few aspects of current research in image processing and recognition. The area of image processing has been completely ignored, and even in image recognition, many important topics have been omitted. For example, nothing has been said about image recognition applications (character recognition, medicine, remote sensing, industrial automation, etc.), each of which has its own substantial literature. (A recent collection of survey papers on applications of image recognition is [60].) We have also not discussed such topics as edge and curve detection, analysis of line drawings, specific shape properties (convexity, straightness, etc.), three-dimensional shapes, depth cues for analyzing three-dimensional scenes, or the use of syntactic analysis in image recognition. For references on these and many other subjects, see [6-12].

Research in image recognition is progressing strongly, and the field seems to be maturing. There is increasing emphasis on the use of models as a basis for designing image recognition algorithms. In our brief review, we have seen that models are finding greater use in image segmentation (e.g., probabilistic models for feature values can be used to define optimal classifiers), in texture analysis, and in shape segmentation and recognition, aside from the growing use of stochastic syntactic models in structural pattern recognition. As our ability to define such models improves, we may hope that the design of image recognition systems will eventually become more like a science.

References

1. A. Rosenfeld, _Picture Processing by Computer_, Academic Press, New York, 1969.

2. H. C. Andrews, _Computer Techniques in Image Processing_, Academic Press, New York, 1970.

3. R. O. Duda and P. E. Hart, _Pattern Classification and Scene Analysis_, Wiley, New York, 1973.

4. A. Rosenfeld and A. C. Kak, _Digital Picture Processing_, Academic Press, New York, 1976.

5. A. Rosenfeld, H. Freeman, T. S. Huang, and A. van Dam, eds., _Computer Graphics and Image Processing_, Academic Press, New York, 1972ff.

6. A. Rosenfeld, Picture Processing by Computer, _Computing Surveys 1_, 1969, 147-176.

7. A. Rosenfeld, Progress in picture processing: 1969-71: _ibid. 5_, 1973, 81-108.

8. A. Rosenfeld, Picture processing: 1972, _Computer Graphics and Image Processing 1_, 1972, 394-416.

9. ___________, Picture processing: 1973, _ibid. 3_, 1974, 178-194.

10. ___________, Picture processing: 1974, _ibid. 4_, 1975, 133-155.

11. ___________, Picture processing: 1975, _ibid. 5_, 1976, 215-237.

12. ___________, Picture processing: 1976, _ibid. 6_, 1977, in press.

13. K. S. Fu and A. Rosenfeld, Pattern recognition and image processing, _IEEE Trans. on Computers C-25_, 1976, 1336-1346.

14. L. Uhr, Layered "recognition cone" networks that preprocess, classify, and describe, _ibid. C-21_, 1972, 758-768.

15. A. R. Hanson and E. M. Riseman, Design of VISIONS: segmentation and interpretation of images, in Conference Record, 1976 Joint Workshop on Pattern Recognition and Artificial Intelligence (IEEE Publ. 76CH1169-2C), pp. 135-144.

16. M. A. Arbib and E. Riseman, Computational techniques in visual systems, _Proc. IEEE_, to appear.

17. M. D. Kelly, Edge detection by computer using planning, _Machine Intelligence 6_, 1971, 397-409.

18. S. L. Tanimoto and T. Pavlidis, A hierarhical data structure for picture processing, _Computer Graphics and Image Processing 4_, 1975, 104-119.

19. S. L. Tanimoto, Pictorial feature distortion in a pyramid, _ibid. 5_, 1976, 333-352.

20. A. Klinger and C. R. Dyer, Experiments on picture representation using regular decomposition, _ibid._, 68-105.

21. S. L. Horowitz and T. Pavlidis, Picture segmentation by a tree traversal algorithm, J.ACM 23, 1976, 368-388.

22. S. L. Tanimoto and T. Pavlidis, Graph labelling algorithms for picture analysis, in 3IJCPR [Proc. 3rd Intl. Joint Conf. on Pattern Recognition, IEEE Publ. 76CH1140-3C], 1976, 749-752.

23. M. A. Fischler and R. A. Elschlager, The representation and matching of pictorial structures, IEEE Trans. on Computers C-22, 1973, 67-92.

24. L. S. Davis and A. Rosenfeld, An application of relaxation labelling to spring-loaded template matching, in 3IJCPR, 1976, 591-597.

25. M. Gaafar, Visual perception: a search problem?, ibid., 308-311.

26. F. Hayes-Roth, Representation of structured events and efficient procedures for their recognition, Pattern Recognition 8, 1976, 141-150.

27. G. J. VanderBrug and A. Rosenfeld, Two-stage template matching, IEEE Trans. on Computers C-26, 1977, in press.

28. A. Rosenfeld and G. J. VanderBrug, Coarse-fine template matching, IEEE Trans. on Systems, Man, and Cybernetics SMC-7, 1977, in press.

29. H. K. Ramapriyan, A multilevel approach to sequential detection of pictorial features, IEEE Trans. on Computers C-25, 1976, 66-78.

30. J. R. Ullmann, Pattern recognition using degenerate reference data, in C. H. Chen, ed., Pattern Recognition and Artificial Intelligence, Academic Press, New York, 1976, 508-528.

31. R. B. Ohlander, Analysis of natural scenes, Ph.D. Dissertation, Computer Science Department, Carnegie-Mellon University, Pittsburgh, PA, April 1975.

32. G. Leboucher and G. E. Lowitz, What can an histogram really tell the classifier, in 3IJCPR, 1976, 689-695.

33. S. W. Zucker, Region growing: childhood and adolescence, Computer Graphics and Image Processing 5, 1976, 382-399.

34. R. L. Ketting and D. A. Landgrebe, Classification of multispectral image data by extraction and classification of homogeneous objects, IEEE Trans. on Geoscience Electronics GE-14, 1976, 19-26.

35. M. D. Levine and J. Leemet, A method for non-purposive picture segmentation, in 3IJCPR, 1976, 494-498.

36. D. Ernst, B. Bargel, and F. Holdermann, Processing of remote sensing data by a region growing algorithm, ibid., 679-683.

37. E. C. Freuder, Affinity: a relative approach to region finding, Computer Graphics and Image Processing 5, 1976, 254-264.

38. C. Somerville and J. L. Mundy, One pass contouring of images through planar approximation, in 3IJCPR, 1976, 745-748.

39. D. J. Burr and R. T. Chien, The minimal spanning tree in visual data segmentation, ibid., 519-523.

40. Y. Yakimovsky, Boundary and object detection in real world images, J.ACM 23, 1976, 599-618.

41. T. Sakai, T. Kanade, and Y. I. Ohta, Model-based interpretation of outdoor scene, in 3IJCPR, 1976, 581-585.

42. H. H. Nagel, Experiences with Yakimovsky's algorithm for boundary and object detection in real world images, ibid., 753-758.

43. A. Rosenfeld, R. Hummel, and S. W. Zucker, Scene labeling by relaxation operations, IEEE Trans. on Systems, Man, and Cybernetics SMC-6, 1976, 420-433.

44. S. W. Zucker, Relaxation labelling, local ambiguity, and low-level vision, in C. H. Chen, ed., op.cit., 593-616.

45. S. W. Zucker, Relaxation labelling and the reduction of local ambiguities, in 3IJCPR, 1976, 852-861.

46. S. W. Zucker, R. A. Hummel, and A. Rosenfeld, An application of relaxation labelling to line and curve enhancement, IEEE Trans. on Computers C-26, 1977, in press.

47. J. M. Tenenbaum and H. G. Barrow, IGS: a paradigm for integrating image segmentation and interpretation, in 3IJCPR, 1976, 504-513; also in C. H. Chen, op.cit., 472-507.

48. J. S. Weszka, C. R. Dyer, and A. Rosenfeld, A comparative study of texture features for terrain classification, IEEE Trans. on Systems, Man, and Cybernetics SMC-6, 1976, 269-285.

49. B. H. McCormick and S. N. Jayaramamurthy, Time series model for texture synthesis, Intl. J. Computer and Information Sciences 3, 1974, 329-343.

50. J. T. Tou, D. B. Kao, and Y. S. Chang, Pictorial texture analysis and synthesis, in 3IJCPR, 1976, 590-590p.

51. S. W. Zucker, Toward a model of texture, Computer Graphics and Image Processing 5, 1976, 190-202.

52. B. J. Schachter, A. Rosenfeld, and L. S. Davis, Random mosaic models for textures, to appear.

53. U. Grenander, Pattern Synthesis (Lectures in Pattern Theory, Vol. 1), Springer, New York, 1976.

54. D. E. McClure, Nonlinear segmented function approximation and analysis of line patterns, Quarterly of Applied Mathematics 33, 1975, 1-37.

55. D. E. McClure and R. A. Vitale, Polygonal approximation of plane convex bodies, J. Mathematical Analysis and Applications 51, 1975, 326-358.

56. B. T. Ang, A heuristic-adaptive procedure for segmentation of time patterns, Intl. J. Computer and Information Sciences 4, 1975, 329-348.

57. D. B. Cooper, On the recognition of highly variable line drawings through the use of maximum likelihood functions, in C. H. Chen, op.cit., 145-163.

58. L. S. Davis, Understanding shape: angles and sides, _IEEE Trans. on Computers_ C-26, 1977, in press.

59. L. S. Davis and A. Rosenfeld, Curve segmentation by relaxation labelling, _ibid._, in press.

60. A. Rosenfeld, ed., _Digital Picture Analysis_, Springer, New York, 1976.

<u>QUANTITATIVE AUSWERTUNG VON ZWEIDIMENSIONALEN MIKRO-CHROMATOGRAMMEN</u>

Hans-Georg Zimmer, Volker Neuhoff
Max-Planck-Institut für experimentelle Medizin
Forschungsstelle Neurochemie
D 3400 Göttingen, Hermann-Rein-Str. 3

Die Dünnschicht-Chromatographie ist ein Verfahren zur Trennung von Gemischen. Es beruht auf der unterschiedlichen Löslichkeit der gemischten Substanzen in den zur Trennung benutzten Flüssigkeiten, Laufmittel genannt. Unsere Mikro-Chromatogramme haben eine Größe von 3 cm x 3 cm und bestehen aus einer etwa 0,2 mm dicken Schicht Polyamid auf einer Aluminiumfolie als Trägermaterial (Zimmer, Neuhoff, Schulze 1976).

Aminosäuren sind die Bausteine der Eiweiße. Messungen ihrer Konzentrationen an bestimmten Stellen des Organismus sind die Grundlagen für die Erforschung ihrer Funktionen. Eine hohe Nachweisempfindlichkeit und schnelle Messung werden insbesondere gebraucht bei der Untersuchung des Nervensystems, wo bereits wenige Zellen sinngemäß die Funktion eines Organs haben können.

Vor der Chromatographie werden die Aminosäuren dansyliert, d.h. in Verbindungen mit Dansylchlorid überführt, die bei UV-Bestrahlung blau bis orange fluoreszieren und dadurch die Aminosäuren, oder genauer deren Reaktionsprodukte, auf dem Chromatogramm sichtbar machen. Eine ausführliche Beschreibung des hier skizzierten Verfahrens findet man bei Neuhoff 1973, Chapter 2. Die Intensität der Fluoreszenz ist in weiten Grenzen der Menge der dansylierten Aminosäure proportional und erlaubt eine Mengenbestimmung auf optischem Wege.

Für die Chromatographie wird das Substanzgemisch in Lösung in kleinen Tropfen in der linken unteren Ecke der Folie aufgetragen und getrocknet. Durch Lösung in einem ersten Laufmittel (4 % Ameisensäure in Wasser) laufen die Substanzen unterschiedlich weit vom Startpunkt nach rechts und später in einem zweiten Laufmittel (20 % Essigsäure in Toluol) von unten nach oben. So entstehen die unterschiedliche Aminosäuren repräsentierenden Flecke auf dem Quadrat 3 cm x 3 cm, die man nur bei UV-Beleuchtung sieht (Fig. 1a). Ein mittelgroßer Fleck enthält 10^{-12} Mol bis 10^{-10} Mol der Aminosäure. Das sind in der Größenordnung von 10^{-9} g, was etwa der Masse von zehn roten Blutkörperchen entspricht.

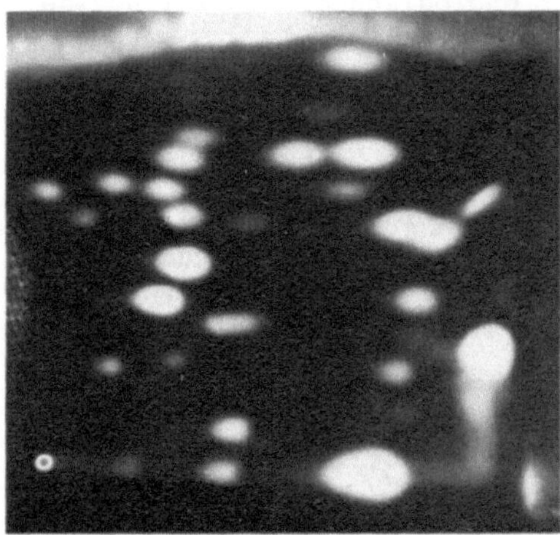

Fig. 1a

Photographie eines Mikro-Chromato-
gramms dansylierter Aminosäuren des
Liquor cerebrospinalis (Mensch).
Originalgröße 3 cm x 3 cm. Starke
Flecke überbelichtet zur Verdeut-
lichung der schwachen Flecke.

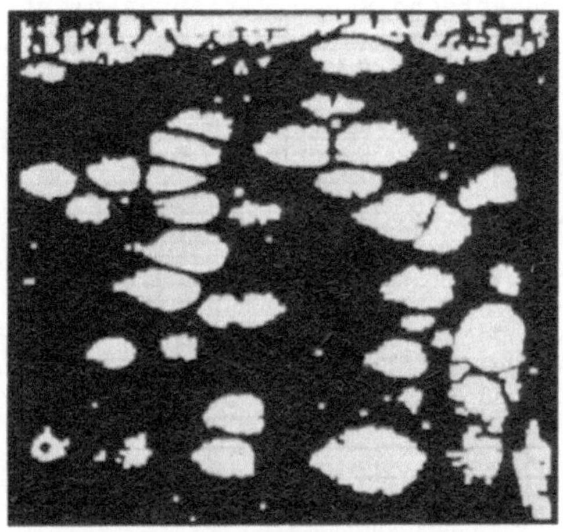

Fig. 1b

Fleckerkennung durch den Computer
für das in Fig. 1a gezeigte Chromatogramm. Photographie vom Bildschirm des Computers. Die als
Teile von Flecken erkannten Meßwerte sind hell dargestellt.

Bei der manuellen quantitativen Auswertung geht man folgendermaßen vor:
Für die Dansylierung nimmt man radioaktives Dansylchlorid, markiert die
Fleckgrenzen unter UV-Beleuchtung, kratzt die Chromatogrammschicht unter
dem Fleck mit feinen Werkzeugen unter dem Stereomikroskop ab und bringt
sie in einen Szintillationszähler zur Auswertung der Radioaktivität
(Neuhoff 1973). Das Verfahren ist kostspielig, zeitraubend und anfällig
für systematische und subjektive Fehler und ungeeignet für die Untersuchung einer großen Anzahl von Proben.

Spivak et al. 1970 haben ein Auflicht-Mikroskop-Photometer beschrieben,
mit dem die Fluoreszenz der Flecke eines Chromatogramms gemessen werden
kann. Der Fleck wird manuell ausgewählt und die Intensität längs zweier
Linien durch das Zentrum des Fleckes registriert. Dieses Verfahren wurde
durch Scanning-Einrichtungen und den Einsatz von Computern weiter auto-
matisiert. Doch beschränken sich die bisher publizierten Verfahren entweder auf den für die Auswertung einfacheren Fall eindimensionaler Chromatogramme (Goodall 1975; Ebel und Hocke 1976) oder auf einzelne Flecke
in zweidimensionalen Chromatogrammen (Franke 1972). Den Einsatz einer
quantitativen Fernsehapparatur für die Auswertung von Chromatogrammpho-
tos beschreibt Giebel 1975.

Da das Auswählen und Abgrenzen einzelner Flecke zeitraubend ist und die
fernsehtechnischen Verfahren nicht die für biologisches Material nötige
Auflösung in der Intensitätsskala besitzen, haben wir zur Auswertung der
zweidimensionalen Mikro-Chromatogramme Scanning-Fluorometrie mit digitaler Bildverarbeitung kombiniert. Der Computer ist eine im Labor vorhandene PDP-12/20 von Digital-Equipment mit einem Kernspeicher für 8k Worte
und einer Wechselplatte für 1600k Worte zu 12 bit. Die Anlage war uns
vorgegeben und nicht für diese Aufgabe angeschafft oder ausgerüstet.

Die Digitalisierung des Bildes besorgt ein rechnergesteuertes Scanning-Mikroskop-Fluorometer (Fig. 2). Das Licht einer stabilisierten Lampe HBO 100 geht durch ein Erregerfilter und ein Mikro-Objektiv und beleuchtet auf dem Chromatogramm einen Kreis mit einem Durchmesser von 0,2 mm. Das Fluoreszenzlicht gelangt durch das Objektiv, Sperrfilter und Meßblende auf einen Photomultiplier, dessen nachfolgender Verstärker ein Signal zwischen 0V und 8V ausgibt. Das geht in den A/D-Wandler des Computers, der neun gültige bit für 1V liefert. Durch programmgesteuerte Bereichsumschaltung bekommen wir zwölf bit für den Bereich von 0V bis 8V, wovon nur die jeweils obersten neun signifikant sind. Jeder Meßwert ist das Mittel aus 16 Einzel-werten, die innerhalb von 0,6 ms über-nommen werden. Die Abtastung des Ob-jekts geschieht durch eine mäander-förmige mechanische Bewegung des Mikroskoptisches, die vom Computer gesteuert wird. Die Schrittweite des

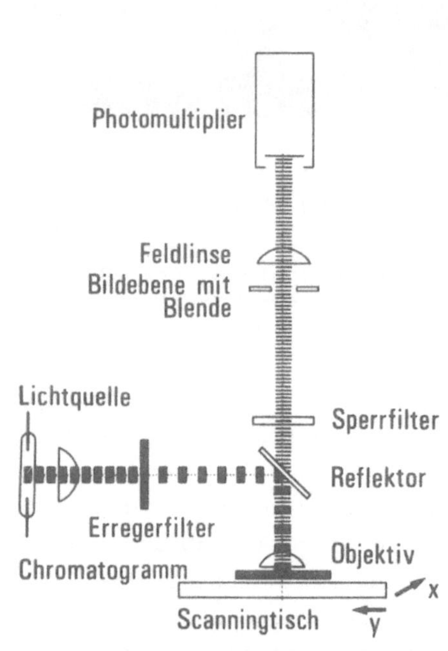

Fig. 2
Prinzipskizze des Scanning-
Mikroskop-Photometers. Erläu-
terungen im Text.

Scanningtisches in X- und Y-Richtung ist 0,1 mm, die maximale Schritt-
frequenz 200 Hz. Dabei läuft der Tisch innerhalb einer Zeile auf Grund
der Trägheit nicht mehr schrittweise, sondern kontinuierlich. Zum Abtasten einer 3 cm langen Zeile braucht der Tisch 300 Schritte oder 1,5 s.
Das Scannen des ganzen Chromatogramms dauert 7,5 min und liefert ein
digitales Bild von 300 x 300 = 90 000 12-bit-Worten im Plattenspeicher
des Rechners.

Jeder Punkt des Chromatogramms wird während des Scannens nur 20 ms lang beleuchtet. Dabei ist das bei langer Bestrahlung deutliche Ausbleichen der Fluoreszenz nicht meßbar.

Die Bildverarbeitung beginnt mit einer digitalen Glättung. Jeder Meßwert $I(x,y)$ eines Bildpunktes mit den Koordinaten x und y wird ersetzt durch den Mittelwert aus sich selbst (mit dem Gewicht 4) und den vier unmittelbar angrenzenden Nachbarn mit dem Gewicht 1, siehe Fig. 3:

$$\tilde{I}(x,y) = \frac{1}{8}\Big\{4\times I(x,y) + I(x,y-1) + I(x-1,y) + I(x,y+1) + I(x+1,y)\Big\}.$$

Aus Zeit- und Platzgründen wird der Mittelwert an seinen ursprünglichen Platz gespeichert. Das bedeutet, daß der untere und der linke Nachbar bereits geglättete Werte sind, während rechts und oben noch rohe Werte stehen. Das Verfahren wird dreimal wiederholt. Die damit verbundene Phasenverschiebung und die Beschneidung der hohen Frequenzen stören unsere Auswertung der Chromatogramme nicht. Die Glättung der Werte gleicht gelegentliche und unvermeidliche Sprünge in der Lampenintensität zwischen verschiedenen Zeilen aus und erleichtert die Berechnungen der Steigungen und Krümmungen der Intensitätsfläche $I(x,y)$, die zur Erkennung der Flecken benutzt werden.

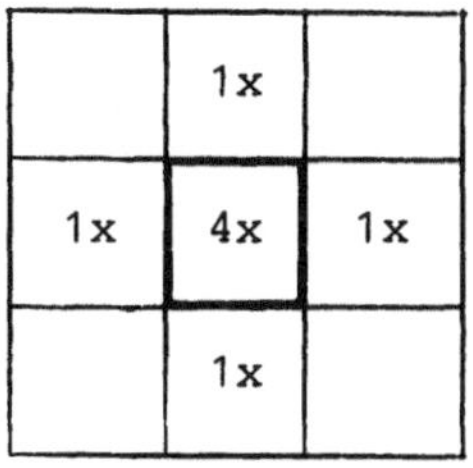

Fig. 3

Skizze zur
digitalen Glättung

Bei der Suche nach Diskriminatoren zur Fleckerkennung haben wir uns auf lokale Operatoren beschränkt, weil uns bei unserem 8k-Speicher praktisch nur 4k für Daten zur Verfügung stehen. Das heißt, wir müssen davon ausgehen, daß nur zwölf Zeilen unseres Bildes im Kernspeicher stehen. Damit nicht nach jeder Zeile ein Zugriff zur Platte nötig wird, benutzen wir nur die Werte aus maximal sechs benachbarten Zeilen für die Berechnung der Diskriminatoren.

Der einfachste lokale Diskriminator ist eine feste Schwelle: Ein Meßwert gehört zu einem Fleck, wenn er über der Schwelle liegt, sonst gehört er zum Untergrund. Das Verfahren ist zwar sehr einfach und schnell, aber auf unser Problem nicht anwendbar. Dazu ist erstens der Untergrund nicht homogen genug, seine Intensität steigt zum oberen Rand hin an. Außerdem fällt die Intensität zwischen zwei Flecken nicht auf die des freien Untergrundes ab. Legt man die Schwelle so tief, daß schwache einzeln liegende Flecke erkannt werden, dann werden benachbarte starke Flecke nicht mehr getrennt. Hebt man die Schwelle an bis zur Trennung benachbarter starker Flecken, dann verschwinden alle schwachen Flecke: Fig. 4.

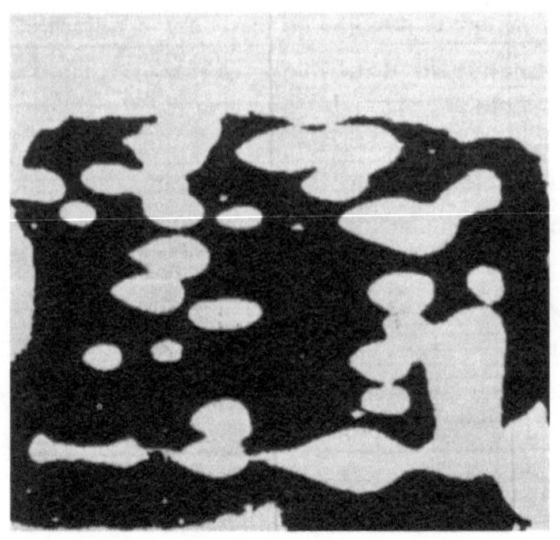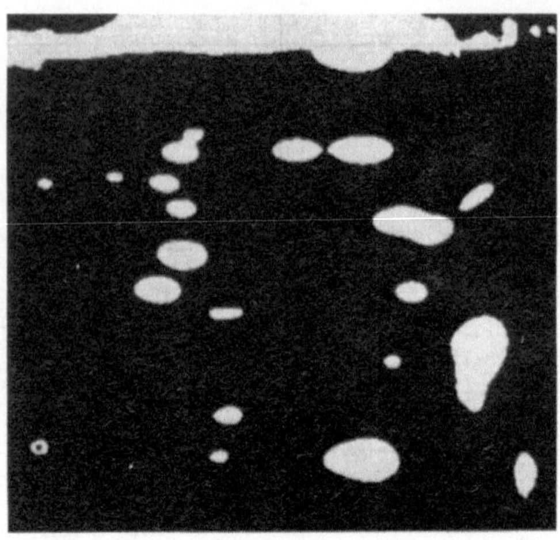

Fig. 4a   Fig. 4b

Fleckerkennung mit einer festen unteren Schwelle. Auf dem Bildschirm werden alle Meßwerte gezeigt, die über der eingestellten Schwelle liegen.

Schwellenwert 112   Schwellenwert 320

Statt der Schwellen für die Funktionswerte I(x,y) kann man in Verallgemeinerung des Verfahrens auch Schwellen für die ersten und zweiten Ableitungen der Funktion (angenähert durch Differenzen) als Diskriminatoren
für die Flecke untersuchen. Wir haben dabei einige nützliche und auch ein
paar überraschende Ergebnisse bekommen, aber keine einfache und über-
sichtliche Bedingung dafür, daß ein Meßwert zu einem Fleck gehört. Dagegen erwies es sich als viel einfacher, einen lokalen Operator zur Erkennung des Untergrundes zu definieren. Da man bei einem Chromatogramm
nur zwischen Flecken und Untergrund zu unterscheiden hat, war damit auch
das Problem der Fleckerkennung für unseren Fall gelöst.

Wir definieren den Untergrund als Orte lokaler Minima. Wäre I(x,y) eine
differenzierbare Funktion, dann liefe das auf die folgenden Bedingungen
hinaus:

Es gibt eine Richtung α durch den Punkt (x,y),
für die $\frac{\partial I}{\partial \alpha} = 0$ und $\frac{\partial^2 I}{\partial \alpha^2} \geqq 0$ ist.

Da I(x,y) nur durch Meßwerte für die diskreten Rasterkoordinaten gegeben
ist, definieren wir den Untergrunddiskriminator auf folgende Weise :
Durch den jeweiligen Meßpunkt (x,y) legen wir acht Richtungen zu den 16
im Raster um zwei Schritte entfernten Punkten, siehe Fig. 5. Für jede
Richtung werden die Intensitätsdifferenzen zwischen den Randpunkten (R)
und dem Zentrum (Z) berechnet. Wenn für wenigstens eine Richtung beide

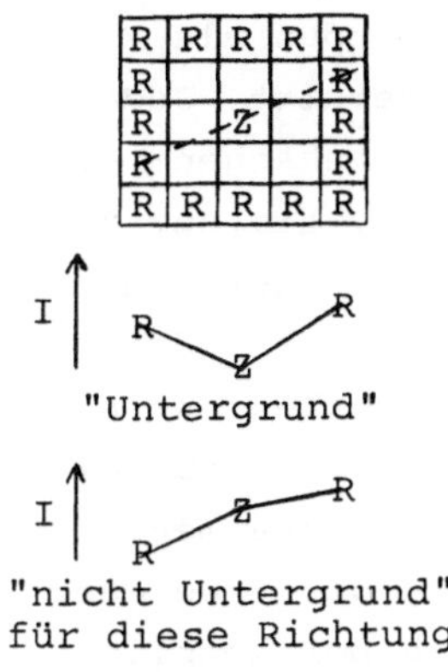

Fig. 5
Definition des
Untergrund-Dis-
kriminators

Differenzen größer sind als eine zweckmäßig ge-
wählte feste Schwelle, dann gehört der Punkt (Z)
mit den Koordinaten (x,y) zum Untergrund, sonst
zu einem Fleck.

In unserem Programm ist die Schwelle -1, wir
lassen also sogar eine schwach konvexe Krümmung
im Untergrund zu. Das ist zweckmäßig im Hinblick
auf Rundungsfehler beim Glätten oder das Rauschen der Meßwerte. Die konvexe Krümmung im Zentrum eines Fleckes ist viel größer, diese Punkte
fallen bei obiger Definition des Diskriminators
nicht heraus.

Der Diskriminator ist ein rein lokaler Operator
und nimmt auf die globalen und topologischen
Eigenschaften der Flecke keine Rücksicht. Bei
der Entscheidung, ob ein Meßpunkt zum Untergrund gehört oder nicht, wird nicht berücksich-
tigt, ob Nachbarpunkte zum Untergrund oder zu Flecken gehören. Trotzdem
erkennt das Verfahren die Flecke in einer für unsere Meßzwecke ausrei-
chenden Weise, wie der Vergleich der Fig. 1b mit Fig. 1a zeigt.

Die Wahl des Diskriminators und insbesondere der darin verwendeten Schwelle hat zur Folge, daß stets eine Anzahl von Punkten des Untergrundes nicht
als solche erkannt werden, weil an dieser Stelle des Chromatogramms ein
kleines, durch Rauschen oder Staub bedingtes lokales Maximum liegt. Solche Störstellen werden in zwei Schritten beseitigt.

Zuerst werden diejenigen Flecken oder Fortsätze von Flecken gelöscht,
d.h. als Untergrund erklärt, die eine Breite (in X-Richtung) oder Höhe
(in Y-Richtung) von weniger als drei Rasterpunkten haben. Dabei spielt
die Größe des Flecks, zu dem die Punkte gehören, keine Rolle. Der nächste
Schritt erfolgt bei der quantitativen Auswertung, wo alle Flecke unter
den Tisch fallen, zu denen weniger als 36 zusammenhängende Meßpunkte gehören. Der zweite Schritt macht den ersten im Prinzip überflüssig. Unser
Vorgehen ergab sich aus der beschränkten Speicherkapazität, weil wir bei
der Auswertung für jeden Fleck einen Speicherbereich zur Akkumulation
der Daten reservieren und deshalb Miniflecke vorher eliminieren müssen.

Bei der quantitativen Auswertung gehen wir von dem diskriminierten Bild
aus, wo der Untergrund die Intensität Null hat, die als Meßwert nicht
vorkommt, und so von den zu Flecken gehörenden Meßwerten unterscheidbar

ist. Das Bild wird zeilenweise ausgewertet. Alle miteinander zusammenhängenden Meßpunkte, die nicht zum Untergrund gehören, werden als Fleck definiert. Dabei ist Zusammenhang als "Kanten-Kontakt" gemeint. Jeder Punkt kann höchstens mit vier Nachbarn unmittelbar zusammenhängen: oben, unten, rechts oder links. Jeder Fleck bekommt eine Nummer, die zur Adressierung seines Speicherbereichs dient. Sobald das Verfahren auf einen Meßpunkt trifft, der nicht mit einem vorher numerierten Fleck (oder Teil eines Fleckes) zusammenhängt, wird eine neue Nummer ausgegeben. Wenn sich später ergibt, daß zwei verschieden numerierte Fleckteile zusammenhängen, werden die bis dahin getrennt akkumulierten Daten zusammengelegt. Der freigewordene Speicher enthält danach einen Hinweis, unter welcher Numerierung die Daten akkumuliert werden. Damit ist auch bei kompliziert verzweigten Fleckgrenzen sichergestellt, daß jeder Fleck genau einmal gezählt wird, wobei der Zusammenhang der Meßpunkte die topologische Definition eines Fleckes ist.

Während der Auswertung des Bildes werden für jeden Fleck berechnet: Anzahl der Meßpunkte, Summe der Meßwerte, kleinster und größter Meßwert, dazu die Summen der Produkte aus Koordinaten und Meßwert zur Berechnung des Schwerpunkts. Mit der Aufstellung dieser Liste ist die Bildverarbeitung beendet. Das anschließende Drucken einer Karte und der normierten Meßwerte und die statistische Auswertung gehören zur normalen Datenverarbeitung. Die Bildverarbeitung und das Drucken der Ergebnisse dauert etwa 6 min.

Das digitale Bild wird noch gebraucht für manuelle Eingriffe, wenn das automatische Verfahren der Fleckerkennung zwei Flecke nicht getrennt hat. Das geschieht bisweilen am Rand der Flecke mit ausgeprägten Schleppen über dem Untergrund. Dort ist kein Minimum zwischen den Flecken, und hier versagt ein lokaler Operator, weil er sich prinzipiell nicht "erinnern" kann, ob er die Zentren getrennt hat oder nicht.

Zur manuellen Trennung benutzen wir den Bildschirm der PDP-12. Er hat 512x512 ansteuerbare Punkte, speichert aber die Information nicht. Wir können deshalb die 90 000 Meßpunkte wegen des Flackerns nicht in einem Bild zeigen. Aus diesem Grunde zeigen wir erst in einer Übersichtskarte die Lage der Flecke (Fig. 6a) und wählen darin einen Ausschnitt von 60 x 60 Punkten. In dieser Ausschnittsvergößerung können wir mit einem Joystick eine Löschmarke bewegen und damit Brücken zwischen zwei Flecken zerstören (Fig. 6b und 6c).

Neben dieser legalen Prozedur erlaubt der manuelle Eingriff auch die "Entfaltung der künstlerischen Freiheit" zur Trennung von Flecken, die

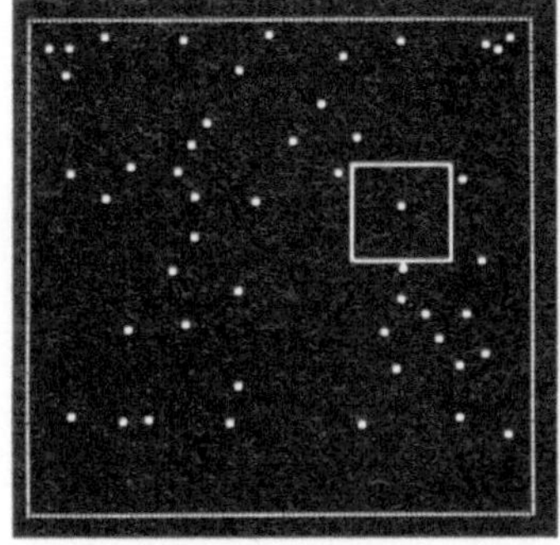

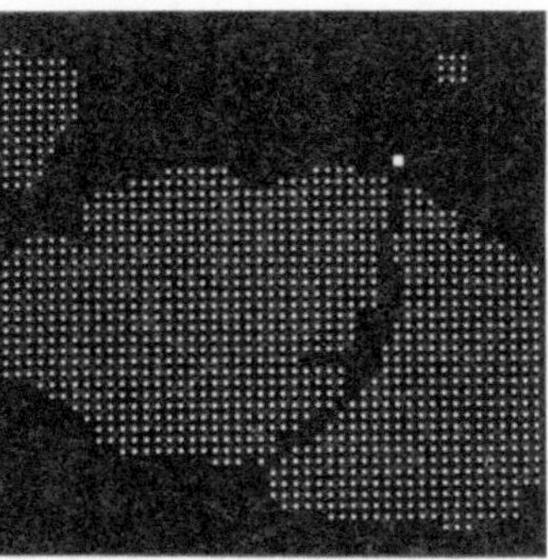

Fig. 6a

Übersichtskarte auf dem
Bildschirm zeigt die
Orte der Flecke und er-
laubt die Wahl eines
Ausschnitts (kleines
Quadrat) für die An-
zeige aller Meßwerte.

Fig. 6b

Anzeige der Meßwerte für den in Fig. 6a
gewählten Ausschnitt. Alle als "Nicht-
Untergrund" erkannten Meßpunkte sind hell
dargestellt. Das kleine helle Quadrat
kann durch einen Joystick bewegt werden
und dient zum Löschen störender Meßwerte.

Anzeige vor
der Löschung.

Fig. 6c

Anzeige nach
der Löschung.

bei der Chromatographie nicht getrennt wurden. Hier zeigt der Bildschirm
viel stärker als das Chromatogramm, welche Willkür in dem Verfahren liegt
und fordert vom Benutzer eine bessere Reproduzierbarkeit bei der Herstel-
lung der Proben als sie bei rein manueller Auswertung üblich war.

Das hier geschilderte Verfahren ist routinemäßig anwendbar im Bereich
von 10^{-12} bis 10^{-10} Mol der einzelnen dansylierten Aminosäuren. Dort
liegt die durch die Fluorometrie und das Verfahren der Fleckerkennung
erreichbare Reproduzierbarkeit der Messung an einem Chromatogramm zwischen 1% und 3% mit einem Mittelwert bei 2% für die einzelnen Flecke.
Die Reproduzierbarkeit für verschiedene Chromatogramme derselben Probe
liegt zwischen 1% und 5% mit einem Mittelwert von 3%. Sie hängt aber
entscheidend ab von der Standardisierung des chromatographischen Verfahrens. Die Geschwindigkeit und Reproduzierbarkeit des Auswerteverfah-
rens hat uns überhaupt erst in die Lage versetzt, Fehlerquellen systematisch zu untersuchen und zu beseitigen. Nach einer Entwicklungszeit
von über einem Jahr wird das Verfahren jetzt in unserem Labor routinemäßig für die Untersuchung biologischen Materials verwendet.

Literaturhinweise:

1   S. Ebel and J. Hocke: Computer-Controlled Evaluation in Thin-Layer
     Chromatography. J. Chromatogr. 126 (1976) 449-456.

2   K. Franke: Laborstudie über den Einsatz von Rechnern in optischen
     Meßgeräten. Zeiss Informationen 20. Jahrg. (1972) Heft 80.

3   W. Giebel: Quantitative Bestimmung von Aminosäuren im Pico-Mol-Be-
     reich durch Densitometrie von Mikro-Dünnschicht-Chromatogrammen.
     Fortschritte der quantitativen Bildanalyse, IMANCO-Symposium 1975,
     295-302.

4   R.R. Goodall: Densitometry of Miniature Thin-Layer Chromatograms.
     J. Chromatogr. 103 (1975) 265-278.

5   V. Neuhoff (editor): Micromethods in Molecular Biology. Berlin,
     Heidelberg, New York; Springer 1973, 428 p.

6   V.A. Spivak, V.M. Orlov, V.V.Shcherbukhin, and Ja.M.Varshavsky:
     Quantitative Ultramicroanalysis of Amino Acids in the Form of their
     DNS-Derivatives. Anal.Biochem. 35 (1970) 227-234.

7   H.-G. Zimmer, V. Neuhoff and E. Schulze: Low-fluoroscence polyamide
     sheets for thin-layer chromatography. J. Chromatogr. 124 (1976)
     120-122.

<u>COMPUTATION OF DNA-BASED PARAMETERS FROM CHROMOSOME SCANS</u>

F.C.A. Groen, P.W. Verbeek
Pattern Recognition Group, Dept. of Applied Physics
Delft University of Technology, Netherlands
and
M. van der Ploeg
Dept. of Histochemistry and Cytochemistry
State University Leyden, Netherlands

<u>Summary</u>

In this paper algorithms are described and evaluated to compute DNA-based parameters of chromosomes in scanned metaphases. Four parameters are investigated: DNA
content, DNA arm ratio, length and centromeric index. The coefficients of variation
introduced by the successive steps are given and it is concluded, that the measuring
errors are smaller than the errors due to preparation and staining procedures. Classification results obtained with these features are given.

<u>Introduction</u>

Individual human chromosomes can be visualized during the mitotic division of cells.
The metaphase is that part of the normal cell cycle that immediately precedes the
division of the cell into two daughter cells. In this phase the chromosomes condense
into discrete objects of different lengths, varying from 2 to 20 μm.

In a normal metaphase 46 chromosomes are present, which can be arranged into 22
homologous pairs of autosomes and two sex chromosomes. A female has two X chromosomes
and a male one X chromosome and one Y chromosome.

Originally the chromosomes were karyotyped by the cytologist according to the
Denver system [2] in seven groups, characterized by length and position of the centromere. However, the result of these length measurements is sensitive to the state of
contraction of the chromosomes. The contraction can differ not only from cell to cell,
but also from chromosome to chromosome and from short arm to long arm.

DNA-based parameters are independent of contraction. To compute these parameters
the DNA of the chromosomes can be stained stoichiometrically (e.g. Feulgen staining)
after which absorbance or fluorescence, resulting from the staining, can be measured.
A more detailed classification can be obtained with a staining procedure developed by
Caspersson [1], who discovered that human metaphase preparations stained with
quinacrine mustard show specific banding patterns along the chromosomes. The importance
of these banding patterns for cytodiagnosis was established at the Paris conference in
1971, where karyotyping of individual chromosomes was based on these patterns. In the

present investigation banding was combined with a DNA specific staining procedure on the same metaphases to investigate the DNA-based parameters of chromosomes, which had been accurately classified according to the banding pattern.

Quantitative measurement of these parameters allow to detect statistically significant aberrations from the normal average chromosome. Therefore the following parameters were computed: DNA content, DNA arm ratio,length of the chromosome and centromeric index. The mean and standard deviation in the parameters were analysed. These parameters were also used to investigate the error rate of classification based on these parameters.

The preparation, staining and photography of the metaphase spreads have been described by Van der Ploeg et al. [7]. The photomicrographic negatives of the metaphases were mechanically scanned and digitized with a Zeiss Cytosan apparatus controlled by a PDP-12 computer. The data are stored on magtape for further processing with an IBM 370/158. Fig. 1 shows the measured optical densities as displayed on the line-printer. A set of modular programs to be described here, was used for the computation of the parameters. The calling of subsequent modules is controlled by a main program. In fig. 2 a block diagram of the row of modules is given.

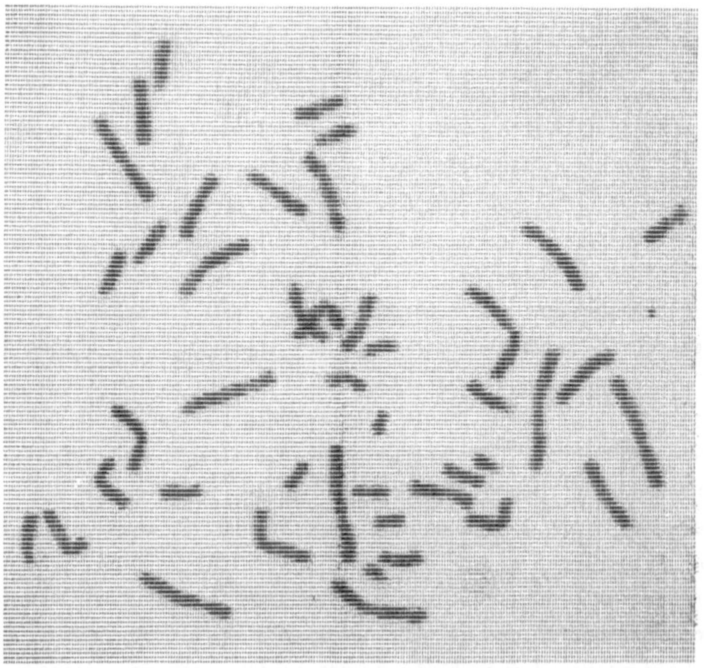

Figure 1 Line-printer picture of a scanned part of a metaphase

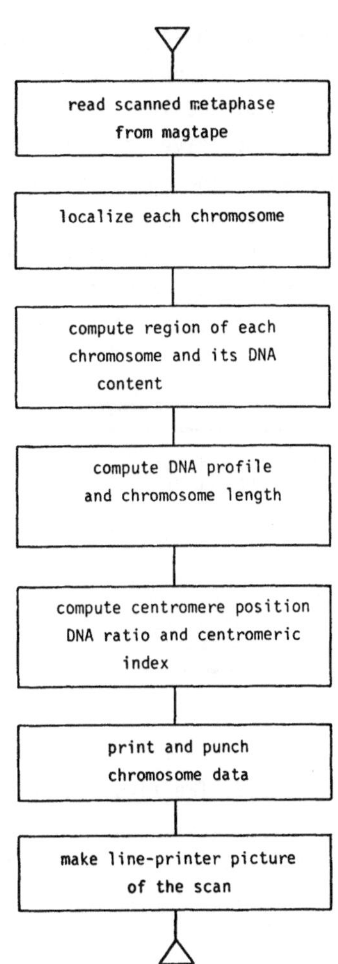

*Figure 2   Block diagram of the program used
to compute DNA-based parameters*

Description of the modules

The first module controls the data input. The second module discriminates between chromosomes and background by a dissection density-level and localizes the chromosomes. The dissection level is obtained from the histogram of density values. This dissection level D_L is

$$D_L = D_{bp} - f(D_{bp} - D_c) \tag{1}$$

in which D_{bp} is the background peak value of the histogram, D_c is a representative minimal density (3% of the cumulative histogram) and f is a certain fraction, heuristically determined. When the density value of a measuring spot position is larger than this dissection level, this spot position is regarded as a background point, otherwise it is regarded as an object point. (Because the data are obtained by scanning of a

photographic negative, the background densities are higher than those of the objects.)
The boundaries of the chromosomes are determined with an eight-neighbour contour-
tracing algorithm. This algorithm scans the eight neighbours of the last found contour-
point in a clockwise direction, until the first one of two successive scanned neighbours is a background point and the next one is an object point. The points inside the
contour are marked to constitute the so-called initial chromosome region.

In the third module this initial chromosome region is expanded. The initial region
cannot be used to compute the DNA content, because of the relative low setting of the
dissection level to separate chromosomes close together, illustrated in fig. 3. There-

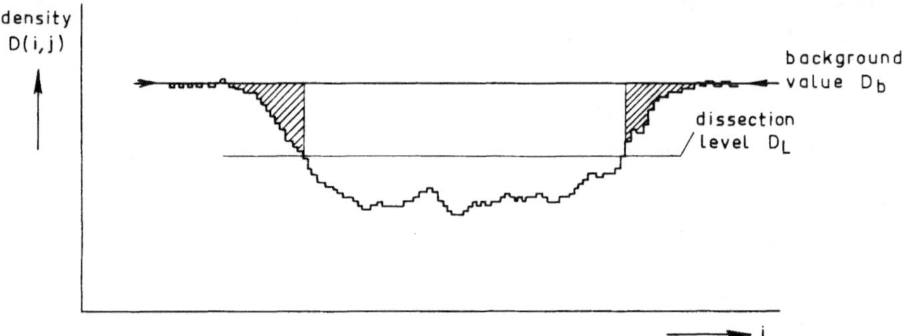

Figure 3 Section along a scanline of the density values

fore the regions of all chromosomes are simultaneously expanded. The first expansion
consists of the points, which have four-neighbour connectivity to a point of the initial region. The following expansions consist of those points, which have four-neighbour connectivity to the previous expansion. Those expansions within 0.7 μm (on the
scale of the specimen) from the chromosome image are henceforth attributed to it, those
between 0.7 μm and 1.4 μm define the 'local background'. Where chromosomes lay close,
these zones may be narrowed by the borders of the initial regions. The DNA content is
now computed as the integral of the density difference with the local background D_b
over the area C of the expanded chromosome as

$$\text{DNA} = ch^2 \sum_{i,j \in C} [D_b - D(i,j)] \tag{2}$$

in which h is the grid constant and c is a constant depending on the specific
absorptivity of the chromophore involved in the staining and the gamma of the photographic film emulsion.

The fourth module starts computing the distribution of DNA along the length of the
chromosome: the DNA-profile. To this end, the density differences are integrated over
narrow slices orthogonal to the chromosome's 'backbone'. When the chromosome is not
bended this backbone is a straight line (principal axis). The angle θ between the
principal axis and the X-axis of the grid is:

$$\theta = \tfrac{1}{2} \arctan \frac{2m_{11}}{m_{20} - m_{02}} \qquad (3)$$

where

$$m_{pq} = h^{p+q} \sum_{i,j \in C} \sum i^p j^q [D_b - D(i,j)]. \qquad (4)$$

The summation stripes perpendicular to the principal axis constitute a new grid (re-quantization grid) rotated an angle θ from the scan grid. The profile is obtained by summation of the requantization grid points, illustrated in fig. 4. For each point

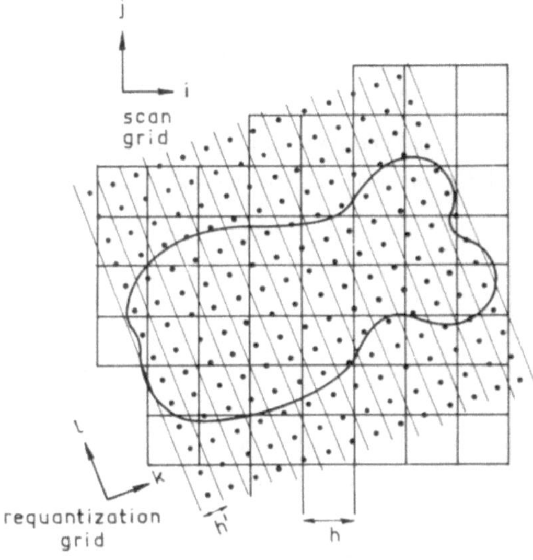

Figure 4   Summation of the requantization grid points

(k,l) of the requantization grid, the nearest point (i,j) in the scan grid is computed. The value of $D(i,j)$ is given to $D(k,l)$. These grid points are summed in the y' direction of the requantization grid to obtain the profile p(k)

$$p(k) = ch'^2 \sum_l [D_b - D(k,l)] \qquad (5a)$$

where $D(k,l) = D(i,j)$
with the restriction that $i,j \in C$ and
$$i = \text{integer } [(kh' \cos \theta - lh' \sin \theta)/h + \tfrac{1}{2}]$$
$$j = \text{integer } [(lh' \cos \theta + kh' \sin \theta)/h + \tfrac{1}{2}]. \qquad (5b)$$

The profile error caused by the requantization can be reduced by interpolating between the corner points of the scan-grid elements. Oosterlinck [6] gives an inter-polation formula in which the density in a grid element $D(x,y)$ is approximated by

$$D(x,y) = c_1 + c_2 x + c_3 y + c_4 xy \tag{6}$$

in which (x,y) is the position of the sample point measured from the centre $(0,0)$ of the scan-grid element. The coefficients of equation (6) are solved from the requirement that the approximation is exact at the four corner points of the grid element, which are actually measured.

When the chromosome is bended, a parabola is fitted to the chromosome (Ledley [4]). The decision for second order fit is made automatically if a certain amount of asymmetry is detected. The parabola in the rotated grid (x',y') determined by the principal axis is

$$g(x') = q_1 x'^2 + q_2 x' + q_3. \tag{7}$$

When the distance between a point (x',y') and the polynomial is measured along the y' axis, this polynomial is the best fit in the RMS sense if it minimizes

$$E = \sum_{i,j \in C} \sum \; [y' - g(x')]^2 \, [D_b - D(i,j)] \tag{8}$$

with
$$\begin{aligned} x' &= ih \cos \theta + jh \sin \theta \\ y' &= jh \cos \theta - ih \sin \theta \; . \end{aligned} \tag{9}$$

The minimum of E is found by differentiation of E with respect to the coefficients of the polynomial q_1, q_2 and q_3 and setting these derivatives to zero.

In order to sum, a new curvilinear grid (x'',y'') with y'' perpendicular to the parabola is sampled. The points (x',y') in the coordinate system of the principal axis corresponding to the points (x'',y'') of the curvilinear grid are computed from the equations

$$\begin{aligned} x' &= s^{-1}(x'') - y'' \sin \varphi \\ y' &= g(s^{-1}(x'')) + y'' \cos \varphi \end{aligned} \tag{10a}$$

in which $\tan \varphi = 2q_1 x' + q_2'$, and s^{-1} is the inverse function corresponding to the arc length function s. This inverse arclength is numerically computed from the arclength s given as

$$s(x') = \frac{1}{4q_1} \left[2q_1(x'-x_o') \sqrt{1+4q_1^2(x'-x_o')^2} + \ln[\, 2q_1(x'-x_o') + \sqrt{1+4q_1^2(x'-x_o')^2}\,] \right] \tag{10b}$$

with $x_o' = -\dfrac{q_2}{2q_1}$.

The sample points are weighed with the grid element area, because this area in a curvilinear coordinate system is not constant. This area a is

$$a = h"[\, 1-2q_1 y"/(1 + \tan^2 \varphi)^{3/2}]\qquad(11)$$

in which h" is the grid constant at the second order polynomial.

At last, the length of the chromosome is computed. The end points of the profile are defined as the points where the density drops below 0.1 of its maximum value.

The fifth module derives the position of the centromere from the density profile. For median and submedian chromosomes the centromere position is given by a minimum in the DNA profile. Generally a minimum is difficult to observe in the profiles of acrocentric chromosomes; the centromere position in that case has to be determined from a shoulder (local change in slope) in the profile (illustrated in fig. 5). The shoulder

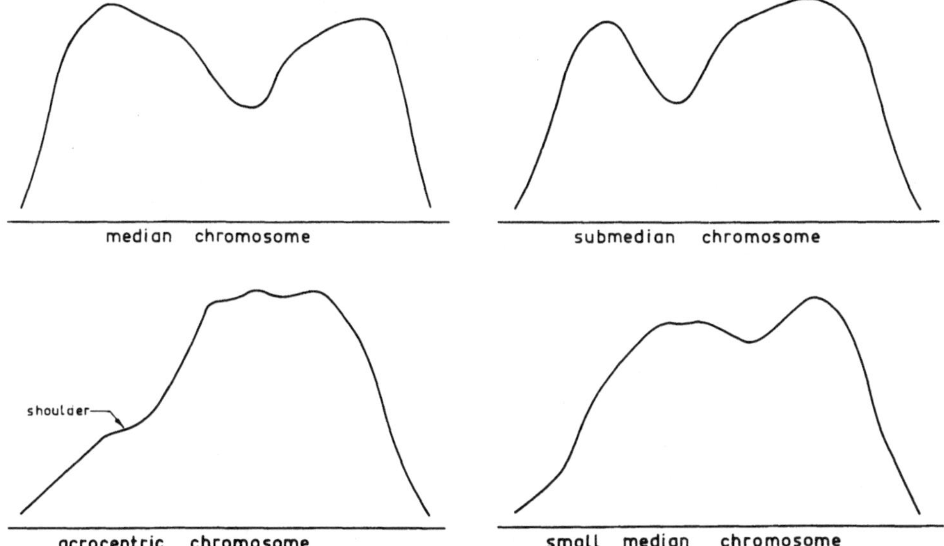

Figure 5 Profiles of different types of chromosomes

in the profile of acrocentric chromosomes is found with the aid of a filter, which gives the first derivative of a profile. Thus the problem is reduced to that encountered in median or submedian chromosomes: to locate a minimum between two maxima. When this minimum is not deep enough, the centromere position was rejected. The DNA arm ratio is calculated as the relative DNA content of the longest arm. The relative length of the longest arm, or centromeric index, is computed as well.

The sixth and seventh module control the output of the results obtained and the display of the input scan respectively.

Performance and accuracy

The performance of the program described has been tested in four successive steps. First one negative was scanned several times. This was repeated for different grid constants (scan-step sizes). The coefficients of variation (standard deviations divided by the means) were found to depend only slightly on the grid constant. The shallow variation minima of DNA content and DNA arm ratio coincided at grid constant values between 0.1 μm and 0.2 μm (at the specimen level). Henceforth the grid constant was chosen according to those values. The coefficients of variation for two negatives at repeated scanning with the optimal grid constant are given in the first two lines of table 1.

Then the influence of the photographic process on the measuring results was investigated. One metaphase was recorded on nine negatives. The errors resulting from the combined effect of photography and scanning are given in the third line of table 1. Apart from the length determination, which seems hardly further deteriorated the other errors have increased by a factor three.

Next the errors due to the preparation and staining technique and to contaminations were estimated. Ten metaphases of one subject were used, hence each type of chromosome could occur twenty times. In this test chromosome-identification is essential as this determines how the groups are composed. For this method the resulting combined errors of preparation, misclassification, photography and scanning are found to be about three times larger than those found from photography and scanning alone. The values are given in the fourth line of table 1.

Table 1 Overall coefficients of variation of some DNA-based parameters

coefficient of variation due to	DNA content	DNA arm ratio	length	centromeric index
scanning negative A	0.6%	0.7%	1.2%	1.1%
scanning negative B	0.9%	1.0%	1.3%	1.0%
scanning and photography	2.2%	3.0%	1.8%	3.0%
scanning, photography, spreading, staining	6.9%	9.2%	8.6%	8.7%

Table 2 Error percentages in the classification

parameters	24 classes of autosomes and sex chromosomes	7 groups of the Denver system
DNA content, DNA arm ratio	48.2%	7.7%
length, C.I.	53.2%	14.6%
DNA content	59.3%	13.3%
length	65.6%	21.2%

At last classification based on these parameters was investigated. In this
experiment 5 subjects were involved. At least six metaphases of each subject were
scanned. A n-1 method was used for the classification. In this method the metaphases
of one subject are used as a test set and the metaphases of the other subjects as a
learning set. This is repeated for all subjects, so the metaphases of all subjects are
used as a testset once. For the classification a parametric method was used, in which
it was assumed that the features are normally distributed (Duda et al. [4]). The
constraint that of each type of chromosome only one pair can be present was taken into
account in the classification. In table 2 the error rates of the classification are
given. The error rate is defined as the percentage of differences between the classification resulting from the program and that by the cytologist. The classification
based on DNA content and DNA arm ratio is better than the classification based on length
and centromeric index. When the chromosomes are classified into the seven groups of the
Denversystem [2], based on DNA content and DNA arm ratio the error rate is 7.7%. The
error rate of classification into the 24 classes of autosomes and sex chromosomes is
large. When the classification is based on DNA content and DNA arm ratio, this error
rate is about 48%. The a priori probability of correct classification is about 4%.
Using all four features gives only a slight improvement of the results. Results
published by Mayall et al. [5] are better, but in his system human interaction is
applied to correct the errors.

The metaphases of the five subjects were also used to compute the mean and
standard deviation of the parameters for the individual subjects. One of the two
chromosomes 1 of one subject had a significantly larger DNA content than the other,
due to the fact that this subject had a polymorphic chromosome number 1.

Conclusions

In this paper it is shown, that the measuring errors in the system described, are
smaller than the variations present between homologous chromosomes due to e.g. preparation and staining procedures. The classification results with DNA-based parameters
so far can only be a first step in an interactive karyotyping system. A more important
application of DNA-based parameters may be the detection of variant chromosomes such
as found in cases of polymorphism, translocation or deletion.

References

1 Caspersson, T., S. Farber, G.E. Foley, J. Kudynowski, E.J. Modest, E. Simonsson,
    U. Wagh, L. Zech, Chemical differentiation along metaphase chromosomes. Exp. Cell
    Res. 49 (1968), pp. 219-222.
2 Denver conference, A proposed standard system of nomenclature of human mitotic
    chromosomes. Am. J. Hum. Gen. 12 (1960), p. 384.

3 Duda, R.O., P.E. Hart, Pattern classification and scene analysis. New York,
   Wiley-Interscience, 1973.
4 Ledley, R.S., Analysis of cells. IEEE Trans. on Computers 21 (1972) 7, pp. 740-753.
5 Mayall, B.H., A.V. Carrano, D.H. Moore II, L.K. Ashworth, D.E. Bennett, E. Bogart,
   J.L. Littlepage, J.L. Minkler, D.L. Piluso, M.L. Mendelsohn, Cytophotometric
   analysis of human chromosomes. In: Proceedings of the Asilomar workshop on
   automation of cytogenetics. Pacific Grove, California (1975) pp. 135-144.
6 Oosterlinck, A., Contribution at the meeting on computer assisted chromosome
   analysis. Delft, April 23-24, 1975.
7 Ploeg, M. van der, P. van Duijn, J.S. Ploem, High-resolution scanning-densitometry
   of photographic negatives of human metaphase chromosomes. I: Instrumentation, II:
   Feulgen DNA measurements. Histochemistry 42 (1974), pp. 9-29, pp. 31-46.

<u>EIN DIGITALES VERFAHREN ZUR KONTURFINDUNG UND STÖRBESEITIGUNG BEI ZELLBILDERN</u>

Ludwig Abele, Tadahiro Kitahashi, Friedrich Wahl

Institut für Nachrichtentechnik
Techn. Universität München

I. Einleitung

In den letzten Jahren wurden von amerikanischen, japanischen und europäischen
Forschungsgruppen große Anstrengungen unternommen, Systeme für die automatische
Auswertung von Präparaten aus Vorsorgeuntersuchungen zur Früherkennung von Ge-
bärmutterkrebs zu entwickeln. Die Nachfrage nach solchen Systemen entstand
durch die große Anzahl der dabei anfallenden Präparate, mit deren Begutachtung
heute noch Zytologen beschäftigt sind.
Ein komplettes Zellanalysesystem gliedert sich, von Durchflußsystemen einmal
abgesehen, üblicherweise in fünf Unterbereiche:

    a) Zytologische Präparations- und Färbetechniken
    b) Auffindung vereinzelter Zellen
    c) Abtastung des Zellbildes (z.B. Scanning- oder Fernsehmikroskop)
    d) Zellbildvorverarbeitung und Merkmalsextraktion
    e) Zellklassifikation

Für die Gewinnung der für die Klassifikation wichtigen Zellparameter ist eine
genaue Kenntnis der Zellkern- und Zytoplasmaumrisse erforderlich. Geometrische
Parameter, wie Umfang, Fläche und Exzentrizität von Kern und Plasma lassen
sich unmittelbar aus diesen Konturen ableiten. Darüberhinaus erlauben die aus
dem Graubild der Zelle gewonnenen Umrisse die Erstellung von Bildmasken, die
zur Strukturuntersuchung der Zelle unter Ausschaltung von Umgebungseinflüssen
benötigt werden. Varianzen der Zellfärbung und benachbarte Störobjekte sollten
sich möglichst wenig auf die ermittelten Parameter auswirken. Die bisher am
meisten verwendeten Verfahren zur Gewinnung von Bildmasken arbeiten mit einer
Grauwertschwelle. Die in dieser Arbeit vorgestellte Methode besteht aus drei
Stufen: Eine nichtlineare Filterung zur Beseitigung hochfrequenter Störungen,
eine Differentiation des Filterergebnisses und eine abschließende Konturex-
traktion, die auch größere Störobjekte in der Zellumgebung eliminiert, sofern
diese bestimmte Voraussetzungen erfüllen. Obwohl dreistufig, läßt sich dieses
Verfahren doch relativ aufwandsgünstig durchführen. Es kann außerdem ohne
Schwierigkeiten auf andere Anwendungsgebiete mit ähnlicher Signalstatistik zugeschnitten werden.

II. Die Median-Filterung

Der bekannte Nachteil der Gradientenfilterung, hochfrequente Störungen im Bild
zu verstärken, kann durch eine vorausgehende "Median-Filterung" umgangen werden. Bild 1 zeigt das Prinzip dieser Operation. Literatur /1/,/2/

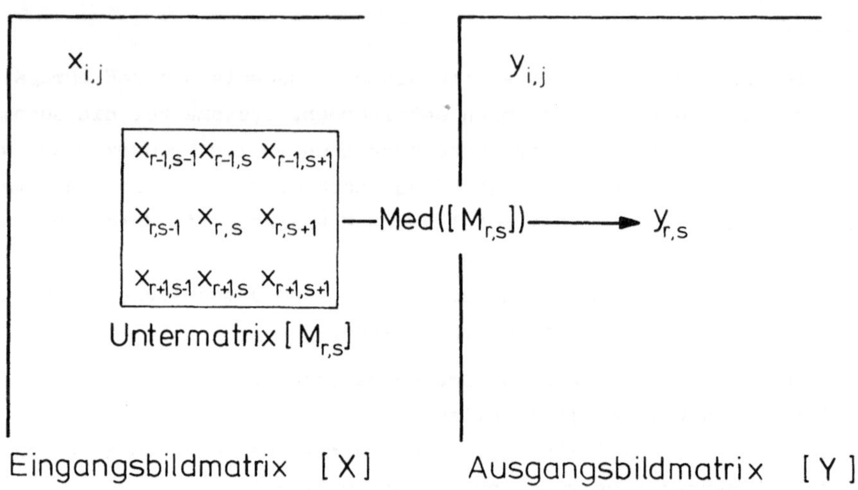

Bild 1: Prinzip der Medianoperation bei Bildsignalen

Gegeben sei ein Objektfeld $[X]$, ein Bildfeld $[Y]$ mit je NxN Bildpunkten und
eine Maske $[M_{rs}]$, die im Objektfeld MxM Bildpunkte überdeckt, wobei der Mit-
telpunkt der Maske x_{rs} ist. Die Maskenpunkte werden mit $m_{11}, m_{12} \ldots m_{MM}$ bezeichnet. Dann ergibt sich die Abbildungsvorschrift folgendermaßen:
Wenn alle $m_{11}, m_{12} \ldots m_{MM}$ dem Betrag nach geordnet werden, daß sich eine Zahlen-
folge $z_1, z_2 \ldots z_M2$ ergibt, für die gilt

$$z_1 \leq z_2 \leq z_3 \ldots \leq z_M2$$

dann errechnet sich y_{rs} zu $y_{rs} = z_F$ mit $F = (M^2 + 1)/2$ und M = 3,5,7 ...

Dieses Verfahren beseitigt alle Strukturen vollständig, deren Ausdehnung innerhalb der Maske nicht mehr als (M - 1)/2 Bildpunkte beträgt (z.B. Linien,
Punkte). Bildkanten dagegen bleiben nach einer Median-Filterung erhalten und
werden nicht verunschärft, wie etwa nach einer Tiefpaßfilterung. Die Bilder
2-9 zeigen deutlich den Effekt dieses Filterverfahrens. Eine Differentiation

ohne Median-Filterung (Bild 6) läßt eine vernünftige Konturfindung nicht zu.

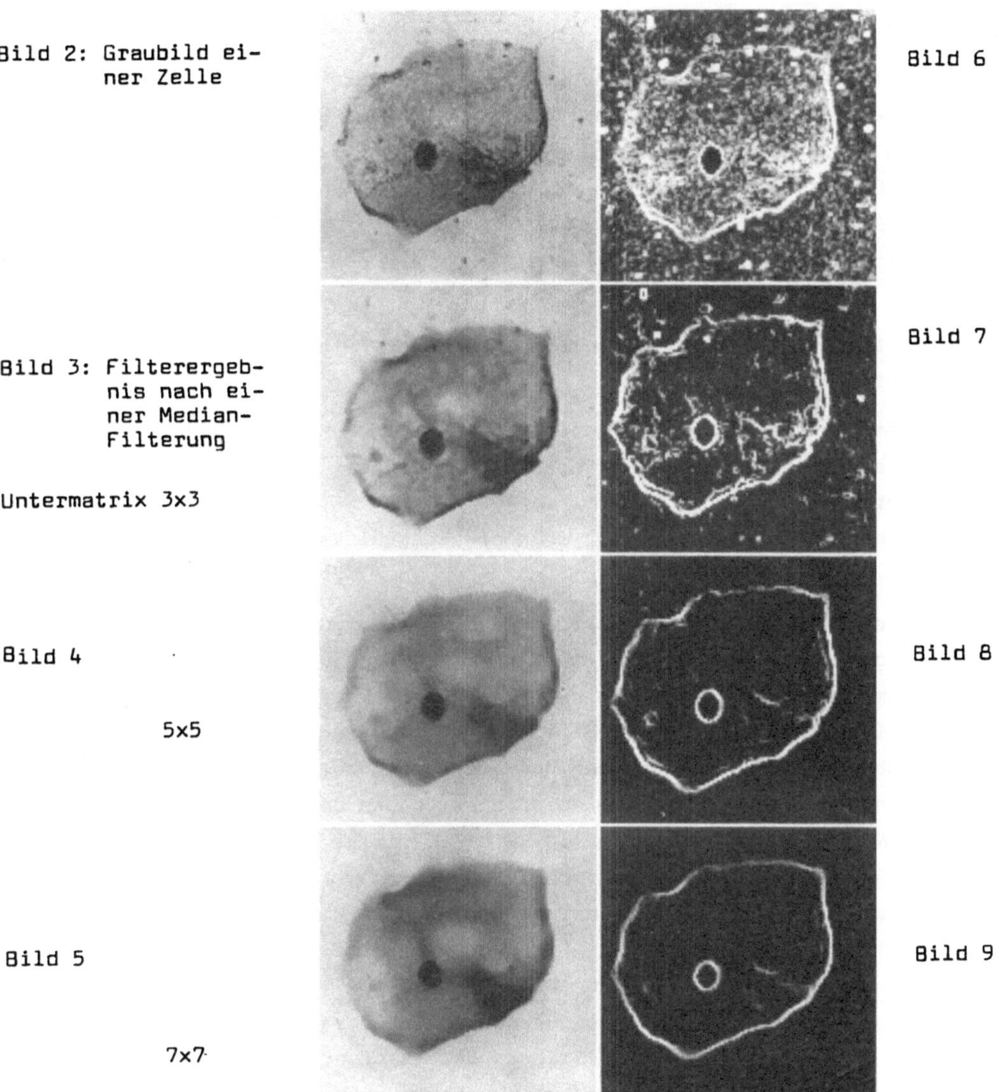

Differenzierte Zellbilder

III. Die Gradientenfilterung

Die Gradientenbilder werden nach folgendem einfachen Algorithmus erstellt -
wobei die Bezeichnungen genauso gewählt wurden, wie in Kapitel II.

$$y_{rs} = MAX\left[\left|x_{r,s}- x_{r-1,s}\right| , \left|x_{r,s}- x_{r,s-1}\right| , \left|x_{r,s}- x_{r-1,s-1}\right|\right]$$

Dieser Algorithmus bewirkt zwar eine weiter keine Rolle spielende Phasenverschiebung um einen Bildpunkt, gewährleistet dafür aber Richtungsinvarianz,glei-
che Bewertung von Ecken und Kanten und vermeidet eine Tiefpaßwirkung wie sie
bei größeren Operationsmatrizen als 2x2 auftritt.

IV. Konturextraktion und Störbeseitigung

Das sequentielle Verfahren zur Konturfindung aus dem Gradientenbild besteht
aus drei Schritten:

- Auffindung je eines Anfangspunktes aus Kern- und Zytoplasmarand.
- Entlanglaufen am Kamm des "Gradientengebirges" unter Vermeidung fal-
  scher Abzweigungen.
- Beendigung des Algorithmus, wenn eine geschlossene Kurve entstanden
  ist.

Störungen, wie benachbarte Zellen werden unter der Voraussetzung beseitigt,
daß die Anfangspunkte richtig gewählt sind. Die Auffindung dieser Punkte kann
nur dann automatisch erfolgen, wenn bestimmte Forderungen bezüglich der Störobjekte erfüllt sind: Es dürfen sich im Bildfeld außer der zu untersuchenden
Zelle keine Objekte mit geschlossenen Konturen befinden, die über einen festgelegten Umfang, nämlich den kleinsten zu erwartenden Umfang eines Zellkerns
hinausgehen. Nachdem das Gradientenbild kein Binärbild, sondern ein Graubild
ist, muß der Ausdruck "geschlossen", definiert werden:
Eine Kontur ist als geschlossen zu betrachten wenn im Verlauf der Konturverfolgung der Bildrand nicht erreicht wird und keine Stelle im Gradientenbild
betragsmäßig unter eine festzulegende Schwelle gerät.
Zur Auffindung von geeigneten Anfangspunkten tastet der Algorithmus das Bildfeld in einem gewissen Abstand mit "Bildschnittvektoren" ab, deren 4 jeweils
maximalen Werte er solange als Zell- und Kernrandpunkte interpretiert, bis
sich eine der daraus durch Konturverfolgung ergebenden Linien als nicht geschlossen erweist - diese Linie wird gelöscht und ein neuer Vektor in der gleichen Zeile erstellt. Wenn nach einigen Löschschritten noch keine zwei verschiedene, geschlossene Konturen erhalten werden, spielt der Algorithmus das gleiche
Verfahren einige Zeilen weiter durch. Auf diese Weise verschwinden immer mehr
Störungen aus dem Bildfeld bis passende Anfangspunkte gefunden sind, die dann

zu den richtigen Konturen führen. Das ganze Bild wird außerhalb dieser Konturen zu Null. Voraussetzung für das sichere Funktionieren dieses Verfahrens ist
allerdings, daß sich keine anderen Zellkerne, und damit auch Zellen im Bildfeld befinden.
Nach der Auffindung zweier Anfangspunkte sucht das Verfahren die betragsmäßig
größten Nachbarpunkte aus dem Gradientenbild, gewinnt daraus eine Richtungsinformation über das weitere Fortschreiten auf dem Gradientenkamm und kann aus
dieser Richtungsinformation die nächsten drei zu untersuchenden Punkte gewinnen.
Bild 10 zeigt dieses Prinzip.

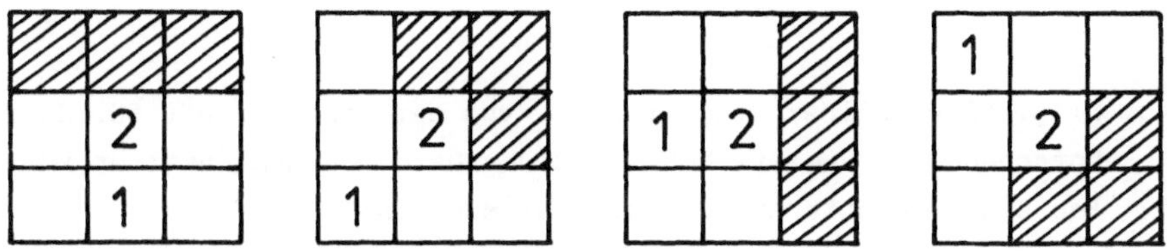

Bild 10: Die Punkte 1 und 2 bezeichnen die beiden zuletzt aufgefundenen Punkte der Kontur, die schraffierten Felder die drei Punkte, deren betragsmäßig größter als nächstes Konturelement genommen wird.

Das Programm ist beendet, wenn die Koordinaten des letzten aufgefundenen Punktes gleich denen des Anfangspunktes der entsprechenden Kontur sind. Bei evtl.
Verzweigungen (siehe Bild 11) werden beide Strecken eine gewisse Anzahl von
Elementen verfolgt und überprüft, welche dieser Strecken in ihrem Verlauf unter eine Schwelle S abfällt um dann die Kontur entlang der richtigen Strecke
weiter zu verfolgen.

Beide Zweige werden n Elemente weit
untersucht

Bild 11: Eine Verzweigung ist dann gegeben, wenn die Betragsdifferenz von zwei
Eckpunkten kleiner als T ist und der mittlere Punkt den Betrag der
beiden Eckpunkte nicht übersteigt.

Die mit diesem Verfahren gewonnene Kontur ist in Bild 12 zu sehen.

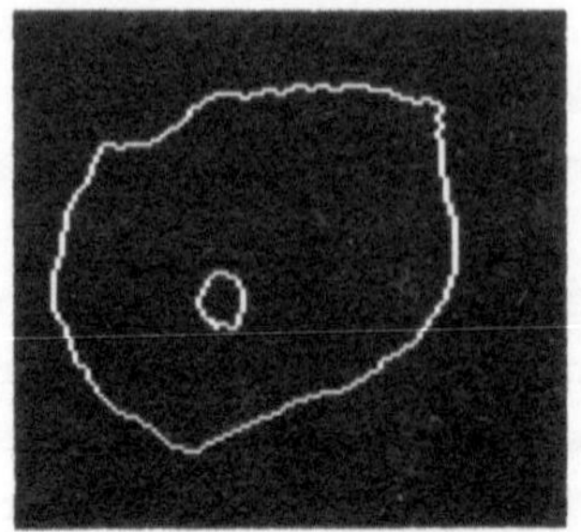

Bild 12: Umrisse von Zellkern und Zytoplasma der Zelle aus Bild 2

Anmerkung: Originalzellbilder erhielten wir von der Gesellschaft für Strahlen-
forschung und Umweltschutz in Neuherberg und dem Institut für Zytologie der Technischen Universität München

Literaturverzeichnis

/1/ B.R. Frieden
"A New Restoring Algorithm for the Preferential Enhancement of Edge Gra-
dients"
J.Opt.Soc.Am., Vol.66, No.3, March 1976
/2/ L.R. Rabiner, M.R.Sambur, C.E.Schmidt
"Applications of a Nonlinear Smoothing Algorithm to Speech Processing"
IEEE Vol. ASSP-23, No.6, Dec.1975
/3/ K.Preston Jr.
"Digital Picture Analysis in Cytology"
Topics in Appl. Physics, Vol.11, 1976, pp.209-294
/4/ G.T.Herman, H.K.Liu
"Dynamic Boundary Surface Detection"
3.Intern. Joint Conference on Pattern Recognition, Coronado 1976
/5/ W. Abmayr, H. Borst
"Untergrundelimination und Merkmalsextraktion an Zellen"
Med. Physik in Forschung und Praxis, de Gruyter 1975
/6/ J.M.S. Prewitt
"Parametric and Nonparametric Recognition by Computer: An Application to
Leukozyte Image Processing"
Adv. in Computers Vol.12, 1972

DIGITALISIERUNG, SPEICHERUNG UND MERKMALSEXTRAKTION VON EPITHELZELLEN DER ZERVIX

W.Abmayr, H.Borst, P.Gais, G.Schwarzkopf und X.Erhardsberger

Gesellschaft für Strahlen- und Umweltforschung mbH, München
Institut für Strahlenschutz
8042 Neuherberg, Ingolstädter Landstr.1

Einleitung

Im Rahmen eines Projekts[+] zur Entwicklung automatischer Verfahren zur Auswertung des bei der Krebsvorsorgeuntersuchung anfallenden Abstrichmaterials wird eine Datenbank von visuell ausgewählten und klassifizierten Einzelzellen aus dem Epithel der Zervix eingerichtet.

Ein Ziel der Entwicklungen ist die Normierung der Diagnostik atypischer Veränderungen durch exakte Vermessung morphologischer Bildmerkmale und Zell- und Präparateklassifikation im Rechner. Die gewonnenen Ergebnisse stellen die informationstheoretischen Voraussetzungen zur Realisierung eines Prescreeninggerätes für zytologische Präparate zur Anwendung in der gynäkologischen Vorsorgeuntersuchung dar.

Die heutigen Entwicklungen für eine Automatisierung auf diesem Gebiet beruhen im wesentlichen auf zwei apparativ verschiedenen Verfahren. Diese sind

a) Durchfluß-Systeme, die von einer Zellemulsion ausgehen; die Zellen werden durch eine enge Kanüle geschickt und an den sich bewegenden Zellen elektrische und optische Messungen vorgenommen /1/;

b) hochauflösende Systeme, bei denen die Zellen auf einem Objektträger deponiert sind /2, 3/.

Beide Verfahren gehen von der Voraussetzung aus, daß die Zellen nicht überlagert sind, was auch in Zukunft noch umfangreiche Anstrengungen auf dem Gebiet der Präparationstechnik erforderlich macht.

[+] Projekt TUDAB, vom BMFT gefördert unter der Nr. RV 12/GfW/1, in Zusammenarbeit mit dem Institut für Klinische Zytologie der TUM, dem Institut für Physikalische Elektronik der Universität Stuttgart, dem Institut für Nachrichtentechnik der TUM und dem Institut für med. Datenverarbeitung der GSF.

Bei unseren Arbeiten verwenden wir ein hochauflösendes System, bei dem die Bilddatendigitalisierung mit einem Scanningmikroskopphotometer oder einer Fernsehkamera und die Auswertung in einem Rechner vorgenommen wird.

Bilddatenerfassung und Speicherung

Die Digitalisierung der Mikroskopbilder mit einem Scanningphotometer (SMP) erfolgt computergesteuert in einem Raster von 0,5/um und einer Grauwertauflösung von > 128 Graustufen. Es treten dabei keine geometrischen Abbildungsfehler auf, weil immer im Linsenmittelpunkt gemessen wird; durch eine Leuchtfeldblende wird der Streulichtanteil stark reduziert. Die Abtastgeschwindigkeit ist jedoch durch die Mechanik des Scanningtisches auf 50 BP/sec beschränkt. Dies ist die genaueste Methode zur Mikroskopbilddigitalisierung und damit zum Aufbau einer Zelldatenbank.

Die Digitalisierung mittels kommerziellem Fernsehabtastsystem (TV) ist wegen ihrer Abtastgeschwindigkeit für Prescreeninggeräte besser geeignet. Mittels kommerziellem TV-System wird heute eine Graustufenauflösung bis zu 64 Graustufen erreicht, wobei allerdings spezielle ausgewählte Plumbikonkameras mit Shadingkorrektor verwendet werden müssen. Eine Linearität der Ablenkung von 0.2% ist erreichbar. Ein Meßvergleich zwischen Zellen, die mit dem SMP und mit dem TV-System erfaßt wurden, ist in Vorbereitung. Das im Rahmen dieses Projekts entwickelte TV-Bilderfassungssystem[+] ist über einen schnellen TV-Bildspeicher mit 300x512 BP an den Rechner gekoppelt.

Um Merkmalsextraktionsmethoden testen sowie eine Merkmalsanalyse durchführen zu können, wird eine Zelldatenbank aufgebaut, wobei zunächst nur visuell ausgewählte und klassifizierte Einzelzellen aus konventionellen PAP[++]-Präparaten verwendet werden. Mikroskopbilder solcher Zellen sind in Abbildung 1 dargestellt. Die Datenbank enthält zur Zeit ca. 1500 Einzelzellen aus 8 verschiedenen Zellklassen, die mittels Scanningphotometer erfaßt wurden. Jeder Zelle wird eine Begleitinformation aus 80 alphanumerischen Zeichen beigegeben, die alle wichtigen Informationen wie Meßparameter, Präparate-Identifikation sowie Diagnose enthält. Weiter wird eine Datenbank mit TV-abgetasteten Zellen erstellt.

[+] Das System wurde im Institut für Physikalische Elektronik in Stuttgart (Leitung Prof.Bloss) entwickelt.

[++] PAPANICOLAOU-Färbung, die sich für die visuelle Routinediagnostik durchgesetzt hat.
Die Zellen wurden vom Institut für Klinische Zytologie (Leitung Prof.Soost) ausgewählt und bereitgestellt.

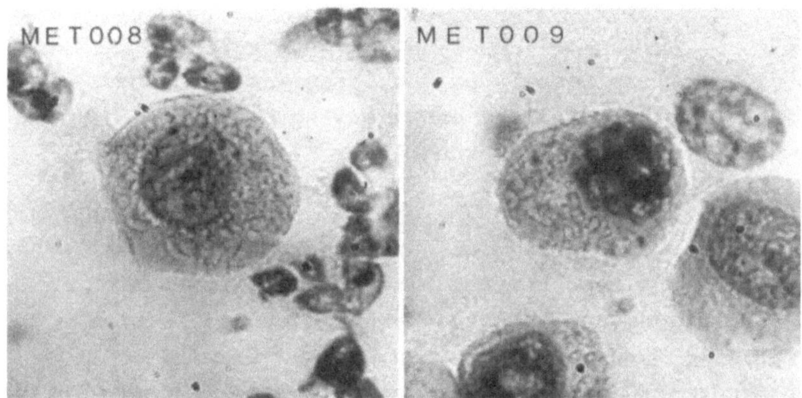

Abb.1 Mikroskopaufnahmen der Zellen MET∅∅8 (Parabasalzelle mit
schleimigem Untergrund) und MET∅∅9 (schwere Dysplasie mit
Detritus) mit Objektiv 100 aufgenommen

<u>Software-System zur Merkmalsextraktion</u>

Das Software-System zur Merkmalsextraktion kann in drei Funktionskomponenten aufgeschlüsselt werden (Abb.2):

- Bestimmung von Extinktionsintervallen zur Objekttrennung
- Erstellung der Objektmasken und
- Berechnung der Zellmerkmale innerhalb der Masken.

Im ersten Schritt werden Extinktionsintervalle ermittelt, die geeignet
sind, die Form von Objekten (Zytoplasma, Zellkern, Ektoplasma, Endo-
plasma, Nucleoli, Fremdobjekte) so wiederzugeben, daß im zweiten
Schritt Objektmasken schnell und sicher ermittelt werden können.

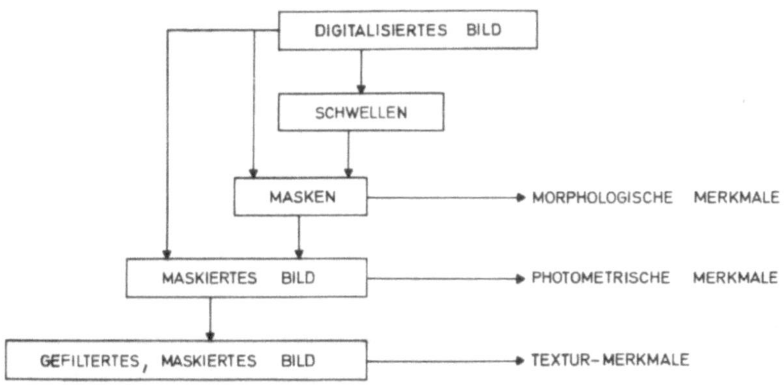

Abb.2 Softwaresystem zur Merkmalsextraktion

Geeignete Schwellen zur Objekttrennung ergeben sich bei den Extinktions-
werten
- mit relativ wenig Bildpunkten/Extinktionsintervall
- bei denen die mittlere Anzahl der dunkleren Nachbarn stark ansteigt
- bei denen der mittlere Gradient besonders hoch ist
- bei denen das Objekt besonders rund ist.

Gegenüber der CYBEST-Methode nach WATANABE /4/ wird somit zusätzlich
die Information über die Anzahl der dunkleren Nachbarn und über die
Rundheit des Objekts verwendet. Beide Merkmale erwiesen sich in der
Mehrzahl der Zellbilder unserer Datenbank als besonders wirkungsvoll.
Gegenüber der TICAS-Methode nach TAYLOR et al. /5/ wird außerdem zusätzlich der Gradient verwendet, der bei kontrastreichen Zellbildern
wesentlich die Schwellensuche bestimmt.

Mittels geeigneter Linearkombination der Extinktionswerte aus den vier
Histogrammen wird ein Kombinationshistogramm berechnet, dessen Maxima
als Schwellen zur Objekttrennung geeignet sind. Durch wiederholte Glät-
tungen dieses Kombinationshistogramms wird eine vorgegebene Anzahl signifikanter Maxima ermittelt.

Zur Zeit werden vier Schwellen angeboten, aus denen dann nach einer vi-
suellen Überprüfung die geeignetste Schwelle für Zytoplasma sowie für
den Zellkern ausgewählt wird. Ein Beispiel für die Schwellwertbestim-
mung nach dieser Methode ist in Abbildung 3 dargestellt. Durch diese
Methode wurden etwa 80% der Zellbilder des Lernsatzes unserer Quellda-
tenbank, die Zellen verschiedenen Reifegrades und eine Vielzahl krankhafter Zellen des Zervixepithels enthält, zufriedenstellend behandelt.

Nachdem geeignete Schwellen für Zytoplasma und Zellkern gefunden sind,
werden in einem zweiten Schritt durch schnelle parallele Bildverarbeitungsprozeduren aus den binären Intervallbildern gereinigte Objektmasken erstellt. Das dafür entwickelte Programm besteht aus einer Reihe
von parallelen und sequentiellen Bildverarbeitungsprozeduren, die eine
schnelle Binärbildverarbeitung erlauben /6/.

Im folgenden wird nur eine spezielle Prozedur für die Maskengenerierung
von PAP-gefärbten Zellen diskutiert. Die einzelnen Schritte und Parameter der Prozedur wurden mittels Dialogprogramm interaktiv optimiert.

Ausgehend von der errechneten Zytoplasmaschwelle wird eine Maske für
den Untergrund (ohne benachbarte Objekte) und eine Maske für die Zelle
ermittelt. Zur Bestimmung der Zellmaske sind 2 Stufen notwendig.

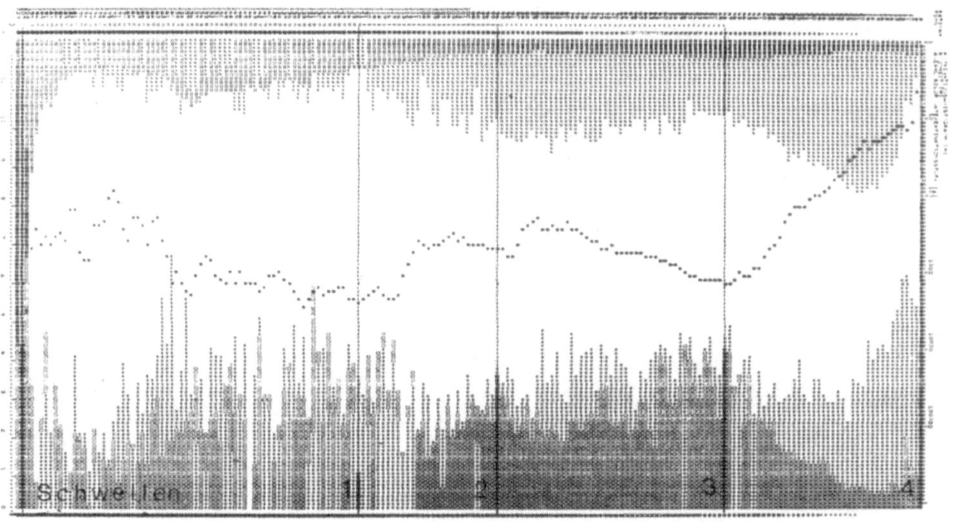

Abb. 3

a) Darstellung der im Schwellwert-
programm verwendeten 4 Histogramme sowie des Kombinationshistogramms am Beispiel der
Zelle METØØ8

b) Schwellwertbild der Zelle
METØØ8 (4 Schwellen)

  · = Schwelle 1
  : = Schwelle 2
     = Schwelle 3
     = Schwelle ´4

In der ersten Stufe wird mittels größerer Lösch- und Füllparameter
eine grobe Maske erzeugt, die größer ist als die gesuchte. In der
zweiten Stufe wird, ausgehend von der groben Maske mit kleineren Lösch-
und Füllparametern, eine feine Maske erstellt und mit der ersten Maske
verglichen. Dadurch werden Strukturen am Maskenrand wenig geglättet.
Die gleiche Prozedur, jedoch mit abgeänderten Parametern, wird auch
zur Erzeugung der Kernmaske angewendet. Weitere Masken werden dann von
der Kernmaske abgeleitet.

In Abbildung 4 sind die Ergebnisse der einzelnen Schritte dieser Prozedur im Beispiel der Zelle METØØ9 dargestellt.

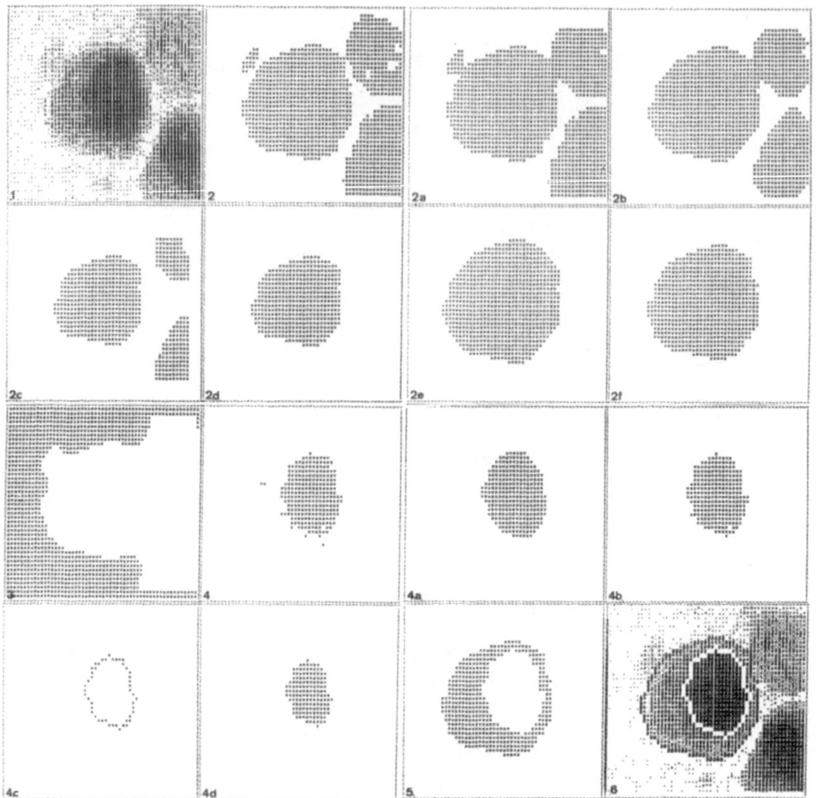

Abb.4   Maskengenerierung am Beispiel der Zelle MET∅∅9

Erläuterungen:

1   Plott der örtlichen Extinktionsverteilung der Zelle MET∅∅9
3   Maske des Untergrundes

Generierung_der_Zellmaske

2   ungereinigtes Binärbild der Zelle
2a Auffüllen von Löchern
2b Punktegruppen richtungsabhängig löschen
2c SHRINK, richtungsabhängig löschen
2d Suchen des maximalen Objekts
2e grobe Maske der Zelle
2f feine Maske der Zelle

Generierung_von_Kernmaske_und_abgeleitete_Masken

4   ungereinigtes Binärbild des Zellkerns
4a grobe Maske des Zellkerns
4b feine Maske des Zellkerns
4c Maske des Kernrandes
4d Maske der Kernmitte

5   Plott der örtlichen Extinktionsvert ilung der Zelle
    MET∅∅9 mit Grenzen für Zytoplasma und Kern

Aus den verschiedenen Ableitungen des Extinktionsbildes der Zellen werden nun die Zellmerkmale berechnet.

Aus den Masken allein werden morphologische Merkmale abgeleitet wie Fläche, Umfang, Schwerpunktkoordinaten, Länge der Sehnen durch den Schwerpunkt sowie Formfaktoren.

Aus dem Extinktionsbild der Zelle und den Maskenbildern werden maskierte Extinktionsbilder erzeugt und photometrische Merkmale abgeleitet. Dazu werden Histogramme der maskierten Extinktionsbilder bestimmt und die Potenzmomente der Extinktionsverteilungen errechnet.

$$\text{Moment 1.Grades} \quad m_1' = \frac{\Sigma\ fi\cdot zi}{n} \quad (\text{Mittelwert})$$

$$\text{Moment 2.Grades} \quad m_2' = \frac{\Sigma\ fi\cdot zi^2}{n} \quad (\text{Streuung})$$

$$\text{Moment 3.Grades} \quad m_3' = \frac{\Sigma\ fi\cdot zi^3}{n} \quad (\text{Schiefe})$$

$$\text{Moment 4.Grades} \quad m_4' = \frac{\Sigma\ fi\cdot zi^4}{n} \quad (\text{Exzess})$$

Mit den Momenten 3 und 4 werden mögliche Abweichungen von der Normalverteilung unterschieden.

In Abbildung 5 ist als Beispiel die Extinktionsverteilung des Kerns einer Parabasalzelle (normal) und einer schweren dysplastischen Zelle (krankhaft verändert) dargestellt. Dabei geht der Wert für den Exzeß bei der Parabasalzelle gegen 0 (Normalverteilung) und bei der dysplastischen Zelle gegen -1 (rechteckförmige Verteilung).

Texturmerkmale werden dadurch gewonnen, daß die Momente der Extinktionsverteilungen gefilterter, maskierter Grautonbilder errechnet werden. Ausgehend von einer gegebenen Nachbarschaft von 3x3 Bildpunkten mit folgender Numerierung

$$\begin{array}{ccc} I1, & I2, & I3 \\ I8, & I\emptyset, & I4 \\ I7, & I6, & I5 \end{array}$$

wurde zur Filterung das Laplace-Filter für 4 Nachbarpunkte der Form

$$LAP4(I\emptyset) = I\emptyset - (I2 + I4 + I6 + I8)/4,$$

sowie das Gradientenfilter für 4 Nachbarpunkte der Form

$$GRA4(I\emptyset) = MAX\ (/I2 - I\emptyset/,\ /I4 - I\emptyset/)$$

verwendet.

Zur Zeit werden mit dem beschriebenen System 19 Kernmerkmale (Kennzeichen KE), 7 Zytoplasma und Zellmerkmale (Kennzeichen ZY, ZE), 4 Merkmale für den Untergrund (Kennzeichen U) sowie 3 abgeleitete Merkmale berechnet.

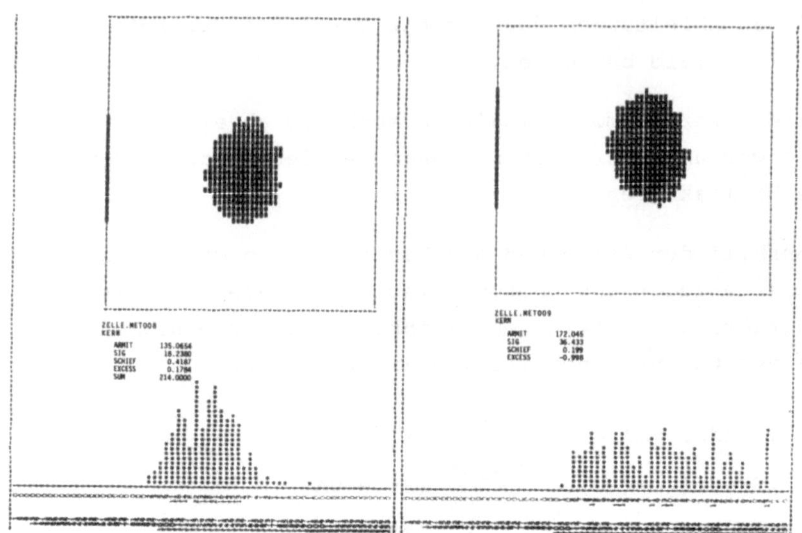

Abb.5 Vergleich der Kernextinktionsverteilung einer
       Parabasalzelle (METØØ8) mit einer schweren dys-
       plastischen Zelle (METØØ9)

Die aus einem Quelldatenfile (örtliche Extinktionsverteilung einer Zelle) errechneten Merkmale werden in ein normiertes Merkmalsdatenfile geschrieben. In den ersten 80 Bytes ist dabei die Begleitformation alpha-
numerisch für jede Zelle enthalten, in den restlichen Bytes sind bis zu
44 Merkmale formatfrei (4 Bytes für eine Realzahl) abgespeichert.

Das beschriebene Softwaresystem läuft auf einem Rechner 4004/151 und
wird zur Zeit auf einem Prozeßrechner Siemens PR330 implementiert.

<u>Schlußfolgerung</u>

Zur Zeit sind die Merkmale von 800 Zellen aus 20 verschiedenen Präparaten und 8 verschiedenen Zellklassen errechnet, woraus 600 als geeignet
für die Merkmalsanalyse verwendet wurden. 200 Zellen konnten nicht verwendet werden, weil sich die Zellen überlappten oder falsche Schwellen
errechnet wurden. Diese Zellen müssen interaktiv gereinigt, sowie
Schwellen gesucht werden. In der Datenbank sind jedoch genug Zellen, um
mittels statistischer Diskriminanzanalyse Zellklassen zu unterscheiden
und eine Aussage über die Signifikanz der mit dieser Methode errechneten Zellmerkmale zu erhalten /7/.

Wir glauben, daß die Erkennungsraten für spezielle Zellklassen durch
weitere Texturmerkmale zum Teil verbessert werden können. Die entschei-
dende Frage ist jedoch, ob nicht durch eine maschinengerechtere Färbung
die Merkmalsextraktionsalgorithmen einfacher und die Erkennungsraten
verbessert werden können.

Literatur

/1/   Mullaney, P.F.: An Introduction to Flow Systems for Cell Analysis
      and Sorting. Proceedings of the International Conference on Auto-
      mation of Uterine Cancer Cytology Chicago, April 1975

/2/   Wied, G.L. and G.F.Bahr (ed.): Automatic Cell Identification and
      Cell Sorting, Academic Press. New York (1970)

/3/   Bartels, H. and G.L.Wied: High Resolution Prescreening Systems
      for Cervical Cancer. Proceedings of the International Conference
      on Automation of Uterine Cancer Cytology Chicago, April 1975

/4/   Watanabe, S.: An Automatic Apparatur for Cancer Prescreening.
      Computer Graphics and Image Processing 3 (1974) 350

/5/   Taylor, J., G.F.Bahr, P.H.Bartels, M.Bibbo, D.L.Richards and
      G.L.Wied: Development and Evaluation of Automatic Nucleous Fin-
      ding Routines: Thresholding of Cervical Cytology Images. Acta
      Cytologica 19 (1975) 289

/6/   Abmayr, W.: Die quantitative Auswertung optischer Information aus
      dem physikalischen und biomedizinischen Forschungsbereich, Dis-
      sertation, TU München (1974)

/7/   Entwicklung und Anwendung eines hybriden Verfahrens zur automa-
      tischen Bildanalyse histologischer und zytologischer Präparate
      zur Früherkennung von Tumoren (Phase II), TUDAB-Projektbericht
      der GSF

<u>Erkennung und Parametrisierung geometrischer Strukturen</u>
von LANDSAT - Bildern

W. Good, E.J. Langham*

Eidgenössisches Institut für Schnee- und Lawinenforschung, Weissfluhjoch,
Davos

*Glaciology Division, Water Resources Branch, Inland Waters Directorate,
Ottawa, Canada

<u>Zusammenfassung</u>

In Anlehnung an die Fähigkeit des menschlichen Auges, durch Formerken-
nung wichtige Information aus redundanter herauszufiltern, benutzt diese Arbeit eine Methode der numerischen Mustererkennung um geographische
Formen - Seen - aus digitalem LANDSAT Bildmaterial zu erfassen. Diese
Strukturen werden nach geometrischen Kriterien parametrisiert. Ein jedes Bild wird so durch einen Satz von Parametern charakterisiert. Der
Parametersatz entspricht einem Zustandsvektor in einem nicht orthonor-
mierten Koordinatensystem. In einem angepassten Koordinatensystem bilden die Endpunkte der Zustandsvektoren von Bildern mit ähnlichen Para-
metersätzen Punkthaufen.
Mit Hilfe der Clusteranalyse können Individuen natürlicher Gruppen ermittelt werden. Weitere Bilder werden mittels Diskriminationsanalyse
einer bestimmten Gruppe zugeordnet. Im Bereich der Geomorphologie erlaubt dieses Verfahren subjektive, willkürliche Klassifizierungen durch
objektive, numerische zu ersetzen.

1. LANDSAT Daten {2}

Von den 4 MSS Bändern wurde das Band 7 im Bereich $0.8 - 1.1 \mu$m gewählt. Die geringe Eindringtiefe dieser Strahlung in Wasser ergibt
eine gute Unterscheidung zwischen Land und Wasser.

2. Formerkennung (Pattern recognition)

2.1 Merkmalsdefinition

Jeder verarbeitete Messpunkt liegt im Intensitätsintervall
$I_{min} \leq I \leq I_{max}$ des Spektralbandes 7. Dem primären Merkmal I
(Intensität) kann ein sekundäres Merkmal M (Wasser) zugeordnet

werden {1}.

2.2 Homogene Rasterpunkte

Homogene Rasterpunkte haben in ihrer nächsten Umgebung 4 Nachbarpunkte, die sich bezüglich Merkmalwert um weniger als einen vorgegebenen Betrag ($\Delta I \leq \varepsilon$) unterscheiden.

2.3 Gebiet und Rand

Das Innere eines Gebietes ist eine zusammenhängende Menge von homogenen Punkten. Der Rand ist eine Kette der dieser Menge am nächsten gelegenen, nicht homogenen Punkte.

2.4 Abschnitt

Das Formerkennungsprogramm M3STER.FTN {3} kann ca. 10'000 Bildpunkte im Kernspeicher haben. Die Verarbeitung eines Bildes mit mehr Rasterpunkten (z.B. 600 x 600) hat deshalb abschnittsweise zu erfolgen. Mit der minimalen Zeilenzahl von 3 (eine obere und untere Ueberlappungszeile, 1 Arbeitszeile) könnte eine Zeile demzufolge ca. 3300 Punkte aufweisen.

2.5 Operationeller Aufbau des Randes

Das Bild der homogenen Gebiete wird ein erstes Mal zeilenweise abgetastet und der erste, nicht homogene Punkt bestimmt (erster Randpunkt). Vom letzten inneren, homogenen Punkt werden im Bereich der 8 nächsten Nachbarn weitere Randpunkte ermittelt.

3. Parametrisierung der berandeten Gebiete

Nun wird das Bild der homogenen, berandeten Gebiete zeilenweise abgetastet und beim Durchlaufen des Randes der Schwerpunktsvektor und der zweidimensionale Trägheitstensor gebildet. Weitere Parameter werden direkt oder mit Hilfe der ersten beiden bestimmt. Für jedes verarbeitete Bild (Individuum j) entsteht so ein Satz von 32 Grössen x_{jk} (k = 1, ...32). Die nicht koordinatenfreien Parameter und diejenigen, die in irgend einer Form die Gebietszahl enthalten, wurden für die weitere Behandlung zugunsten der formbeschreibenden Parameter eliminiert. Die verbleibenden 21 Parameter (siehe Tab. 1) sind teilweise linear abhängig ; Punktdichte, mittlerer Gebietsdurchmesser und freie Weglänge z.B. sind offensichtlich miteinander korreliert.

1 Punkdichte

2 mittlerer Gebietsdurchmesser

3 mittlere freie Weglänge

4 mittlerer konkaver Radius der Berandungskurve

5 mittlerer konvexer Radius der Berandungskurve

6 mittlerer Winkel zwischen Laborkoordinatensystem und Haupt-
   achsensystem des Trägheitstensors
7 Varianz

8 Verhältnis der Hauptachsen des Trägheitstensors
9 Varianz

10 mittlere Elliptizität
11 Varianz

12 mittlere Gebietsfläche
13 Varianz

14 mittlere Berandungslänge
15 Varianz

16 **mittlere** Intensität **der** Gebiete
17 Varianz

18 relative Varianz der Gebietsintensität
19 Varianz

20 mittlere Konvexität der Gebiete
21 Varianz

Tabelle 1 : Auswahl der benützten Parameter

4. Wahl eines optimalen Koordinatensystems

Es liegt nahe, den Abstand zwischen 2 Endpunkten der Ortsvektoren
(Zustandsvektoren) X_i, X_k zu betrachten. Dieser sollte ein Mass für
den Unterschied der beiden Individuen darstellen. Die allgemeine
Abstandsformel

$$d^2(q_i, q_k) = \sum_{i,k} m_{ik} \, dq_i \, dq_k$$

und die zusätzliche Bedingung der Dreiecksungleichung definieren
einen metrischen Tensor M = m_{ik}. Für den Spezialfall eines kartesi-
schen Koordinatensystems wird M = E (Einheitstensor, $m_{ik} = \delta_{ik}$).

4.1 Faktoranalyse

Es kann gezeigt werden {4,5}, dass eine Lösung des Eigenwert-problems

$$u^{-1} P^T P\, u = \Lambda$$

existiert ($P^T P$ ist die Korrelationsmatrix) und diese ein optimales, orthonormiertes Koordinatensystem liefert, das die folgenden Eigenschaften aufweist :

- u_i sind die Eigenvektoren zu den Eigenwerten λ_i
- Die Komponenten von u_i sind Linearkombinationen der Erwartungswerte $\hat{x}_k$ der Parameter x_{jk}.
- Die Elemente der Matrix P sind :

$$P_{jk} = \frac{x_{jk} - \overline{x}_k}{\sigma_{x_k}}$$

- Der erste Eigenvektor ist so gewählt, dass die Quadratsumme der darauf projizierten Zustandsvektoren der Individuen maximal ist (maximale Dispersion).
- Durch verschiedene Skalierung der Achsen (Faktoren) können unterschiedliche Abstandsverhältnisse sichtbar gemacht werden.
- Individuen und Parameter lassen sich in diesen Koordinatensystemen darstellen.

5. Formerkennung (Clusteranalyse)

Mit einem Abstandskriterium, d wird versucht die Frage zu beantworten, ob sich eine "natürliche" Häufung von Individuen in wenige Gruppen (Clusters) anbietet. d^2 ist die Quadratsumme der Abstände der Gruppenindividuen zum Gruppenschwerpunkt

$$d_G^2 = \sum_{j=1}^{N_G} \Delta^2\, (P_j,\, P_s)\,.$$

Die beste (natürliche) Gruppenbildung ist dann erreicht, wenn die Zielfunktion Z minimal wird {6}.

$$Z = \Sigma\, d_G^2 = \min.$$

Z hängt nicht nur von der Zahl der Cluster, sondern auch von der Anfangspartition, das heisst von der ursprünglichen Zuweisung der Individuen in die einzelnen Cluster ab. Durch iterativen Einsatz des Clusteralgorithmus KMEANS {6} bezüglich Anfangspartitionen und Clusterzahl wurde versucht, diesem Umstand Rechnung zu tragen. Die Anfangspartitionen werden durch einen Zufallszahlengenerator bestimmt und von den relativen Minima von Z wird nur das kleinste abgespeichert (Minimalkonfiguration). Es zeigt sich, dass bestimmte Individuen praktisch unabhängig von Clusterzahl und Anfangspartition immer wieder zusammengruppiert werden. Diese stabilen Individuen bilden natürliche Gruppen (Strong pattern), K, GN, GS, ... LN in Tabelle 3.

Eine weitere Möglichkeit die Gruppenzuweisung zu überprüfen, wurde durch verschiedene Normierung der orthogonalen Achsen benutzt. In den definitiven, natürlichen Gruppen wurde der Durchschnitt der Individuen aus obigen Verfahren belassen.

6. Diskriminationsanalyse

Die definitiven, natürlichen Gruppen, ohne lose gebundene Individuen, weisen geringe Parameterstreuungen auf. Für jede Gruppe wurde eine Diskriminationsfunktion F_i und die Koeffizienten c_{ik} für die k Parameter bestimmt {4,7}.

Auf diese Weise lassen sich die übrigen Individuen in eine der definitiven Gruppen zuweisen (1, 2, ... 7 der Tabelle 3) und der Verwandtschaftsgrad zu den andern Gruppen wird ersichtlich.

6.1 Klassierung neuer Individuen

Die Koordinaten des Zustandsvektors des zu klassierenden Individuums werden zentriert und gewichtet

$$X_i \rightarrow P_i \left(\frac{x_{i1} - \bar{x}_1}{\sigma_{x_1}} , \frac{x_{i2} - \bar{x}_2}{\sigma_{x_2}} , ... \right)$$

Der transformierte Zustandsvektor P_i wird auf die bestehenden Eigenvektoren projiziert.

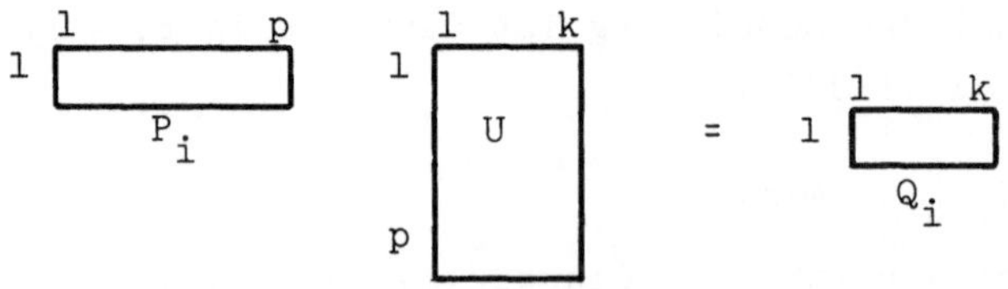

$$\begin{array}{ccc} \underset{P_i}{\boxed{}}^{\,1 \quad\quad p} & \underset{p}{\overset{1 \quad k}{\boxed{ U }}} & = \quad \underset{Q_i}{\boxed{}}^{\,1 \quad k} \end{array}$$

Gemäss 6 wird mit den vorher bestimmten Funktionen und Koeffizienten das Individuum (Q_i) in eine der definitiven, natürlichen Gruppen zugewiesen.

7. Numerische Berechnungen

Die nachstehende Tabelle gibt Auskunft über die benutzten Programme

und Subroutinen und die ausgeführten Berechnungen. Die Kosten für 1
Bild (Subframe 600 x 600 Bildpunkte) gemäss der folgenden Zusammen-
stellung betragen ca. SFr. 300.-.

Name	Maschine	Bibliothek	Berechnung
TAPRED	CDC 6000	SLF	Extraktion von Kanal und Bild
M3STER	CDC 6000	SLF	Formerkennung + Parametrisierung
M.FAC	PDP 11/45	SLF	
Subr.: CORRE		IBM/dec {8,9}	
EIGEN		IBM/dec	
TRACE		IBM/dec	Faktoranalyse
LOAD		IBM/dec	
FACT		SLF	
MCLUST	PDP 11/45	SLF	Clusteranalyse
Subr.: KMEANS		SLF {6}	
MDISCR	PDP 11/45	SLF	
Subr.: DMATX		IBM/dec	Diskriminationsanalyse
MINV		IBM/dec	
DISCR		IBM/dec	
MGRPFL	PDP 11/45	SLF	Zuweisung neuer Individuen

Tabelle 2 : Numerische Berechnungen

8. Diskussion der Resultate

8.1 Geographische Angaben

In der vorliegenden Arbeit wurden vier Gegenden aus Kanada -
Koukdjuak River, Grande Rivière, Rupert River, Laurentides - so
ausgesucht, dass möglichst verschiedene Seentypen miteinander
verglichen werden konnten.
Jedes Gesamtgebiet (frame) wurde in 20 Bilder (Subframes) unterteilt. Die nicht verarbeiteten Bilder sind auf der Tab. 3 durch-
gestrichen. In derselben Tabelle sind auch Angaben über Bildzen-
trum, Aufnahmedatum und -Bedingungen zu finden.

8.2 Natürliche Gruppen

Die natürlichen Gruppen sind aus den stabilen und den zugewie-
senen Individuen oder Bilder zusammengesetzt (Tab. 3). Interes-

sant ist die Feststellung, dass z.B. die Bilder Koukdjuak (2,2)
und Koukdjuak (3,4) mehr gemein haben mit den ca. 2000 km süd-
licher gelegenen Individuen Grande Rivière (1,1) und Grand Rivière (1,2) als mit ihren nächsten Nachbarn.

8.3 Orientierung der Seen

Von den berechneten Parametern sei einer etwas näher erläutert :
Der Parameter Nr. 6 (Tab. 1) ist der mittlere Winkel zwischen
der längeren Hauptachse des Trägheitstensors und der X_1 Richtung
des Laborkoordinatensystems. Die Dichtefunktionen sind in Fig. 1
und die Summenkurven in Fig. 2 dargestellt. Da die Flugbahn von
LANDSAT nicht genau N-S verläuft - sie schneidet die Längenkrei-
se in der Bildmitte von Koukdjuak unter 26°, von Laurentides unter 16° - sind diese Werte von den Zahlen beider Darstellungen
zu subtrahieren, um den Winkel zur W-E-Richtung zu erhalten.
Mit Ausnahme der Seen des Gebietes Laurentides, weichen alle anderen, zum Teil erheblich, von einer Zufallsverteilung - entsprechend der Diagonale in Figur 2 - ab. Das scharfe Maximum zwischen
10 und 20° bildet sich bei der Gruppe R 1 zurück, es erscheint
ein Nebenmaximum bei 40°, das für R 2 zum Hauptmaximum wird (Figur 1).

8.4 Gruppeneinteilung in der Faktordarstellung

In Fig. 3 ist die erste Hauptebene (F_1, F_2) mit den 38 stabilen
Individuen und den Schwerpunkten der natürlichen Gruppen dargestellt. Die wichtigsten Komponenten des Faktors F_1, die Parameter Berandungslänge c, die Varianz von c und die Gebietsfläche a,
sind negativ korreliert. Also liegen Individuen, deren Gebiete
gleichmässig klein sind und eine einfache Berandung aufweisen,
im ersten oder vierten Quadranten. Die Achse F_2 ist positiv mit
der freien Weglänge A korreliert. Die Individuen der Gruppe Grande Rivière Nord (Bild 1), mit der sehr grossen Anzahl Seen und
den kleinen Abständen zwischen ihnen, und ihr Schwerpunkt, sind
deshalb in der unteren Halbebene anzutreffen. In ähnlicher Weise
lassen sich in den anderen Hauptebenen interessante Zusammenhänge aufzeigen. Die Berechnungen wurden mit 6 Faktoren durchgeführt, was einer Beschränkung auf 80% der totalen Information
entspricht.

8.5 Parameter und Gruppen

Nicht nur die weniger eindeutig zu den einzelnen Gruppen gehören-

den Individuen lassen sich mittels Diskriminationsfunktionen
und Koeffizienten zuweisen, auch die Parameter gehören zu gewissen Gruppen und charakterisieren diese.

9. Ausblick

Die hier skizzierte und am Beispiel von LANDSAT-Daten erläuterte
Methode der Erkennung, Parametrisierung und Darstellung relevanter
Strukturinformation scheint allgemein anwendbar zu sein. Sie wurde
beispielsweise schon eingesetzt um Gefüge- (Schnee) Schnitte zu charakterisieren und diese mit mechanischen Messwerten zu verknüpfen
{10}.

10. Verdankung

Wir danken dem Canadian Centre for Remote Sensing, Ottawa für die
Ueberlassung der Datenbänder und der LANDSAT-Informationen, sowie
dem Rechenzentrum der ETH, Zürich für die zur Verfügung gestellte
Rechenzeit.

11. Literaturenangaben

{1}   Fürbringer W. und Haydn R. 1974. Zur Frage der Orientierung
        nordalaskischer Seen mit Hilfe des Satelliten-
        bildes. Polarforschung, $\underline{44}$, p. 47 - 53.

{2}   1975. General LANDSAT Information Kit. Canadian Centre
        for Remote Sensing, Ottawa, Ontario, Canada.

{3}   Crettol R. und Good W. 1974. MSTER- Ein Programm zur Bestim-
        mung von strukturellen Parametern mittels Com-
        puter - kompatibeln Abbildungen von Schneedünn-
        schnitten. Interner Bericht No. 536. Eidg. Ins-
        titut für Schnee- und Lawinenforschung Weiss-
        fluhjoch/Davos.

{4}   Cooley W.W. und Lohnes P.R. 1971. Multivariate Data Analysis.
        John Wiley & Sons, Inc. New York.

{5}   Lebart L. und Fenelon J.P. 1973. Statistique et Informatique
        Appliquées. 2ème édition, Dunod, Paris.

{6}   Späth H.   1975. Cluster-Analyse-Algorithmen. R. Oldenbourg

Verlag, München.

{7}   Romeder J.-M. 1973 Méthodes et Programmes d'Analyse Discri-
                    minante. Dunod, Paris.

{8}   1970. IBM System/360 Scientific Subroutine Package.
                    Version III. 5th edition. IBM Corporation,
                    Technical Publications Department, New York.

{9}   1973. dec-11-SSP Reference Manual. Digital Equipment
                    Corp., Maynard, Mass.

{10}   Good W.   1976. Multivariate Data Analysis to Describ
                    Intra- and Inte -G anular Relations in Thin
                    Sections. Proceedings of the Fourteen. Interna-
                    tional Congress for Stereology, NBS, Gaithers-
                    burg, Maryland, September 1975, p. 75 - 78.

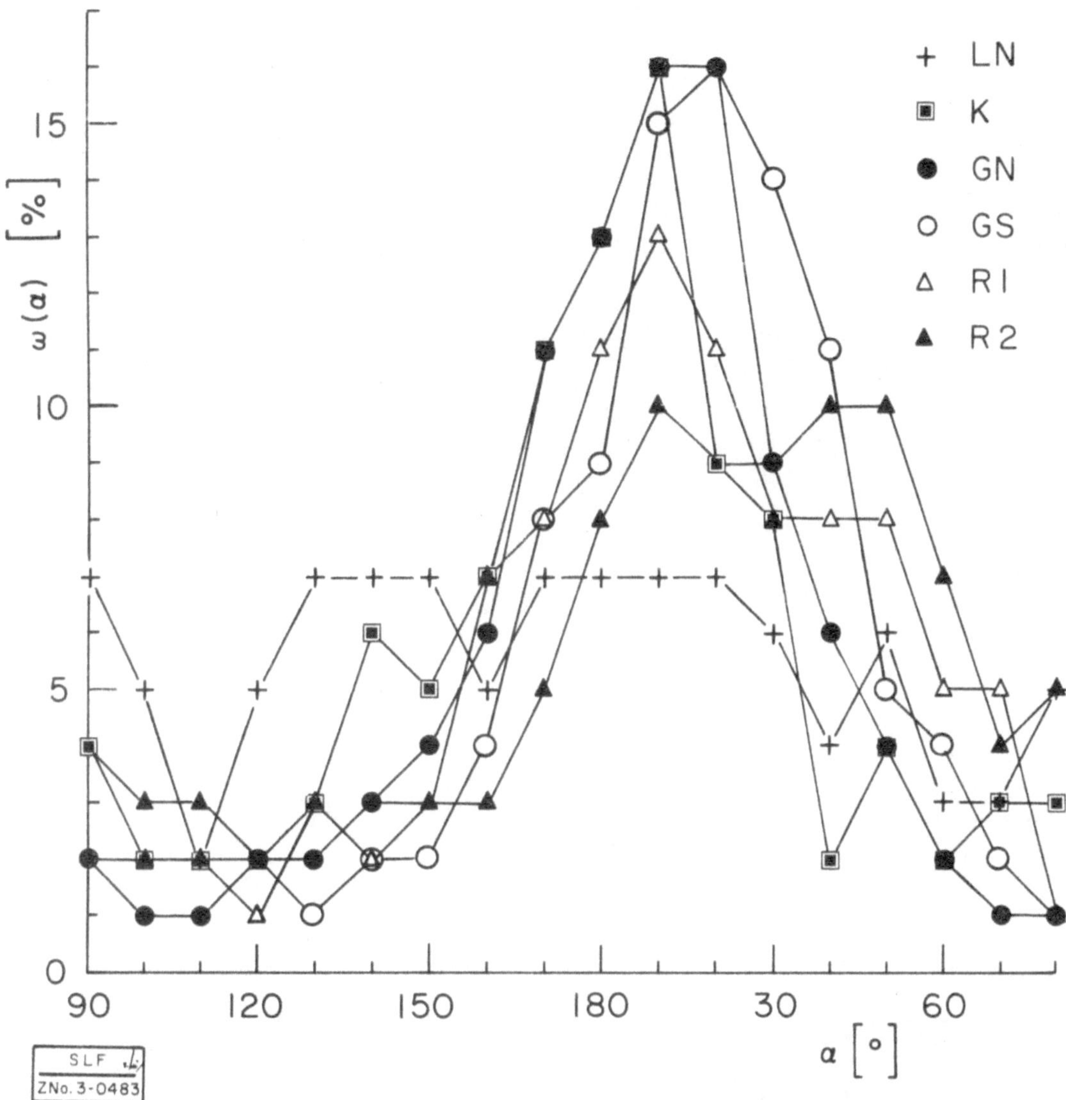

Fig. I   AUSRICHTUNG DER GEBIETE.

α = ∢ (TRÄGHEITSMOMENT I_1, SCANRICHTUNG)

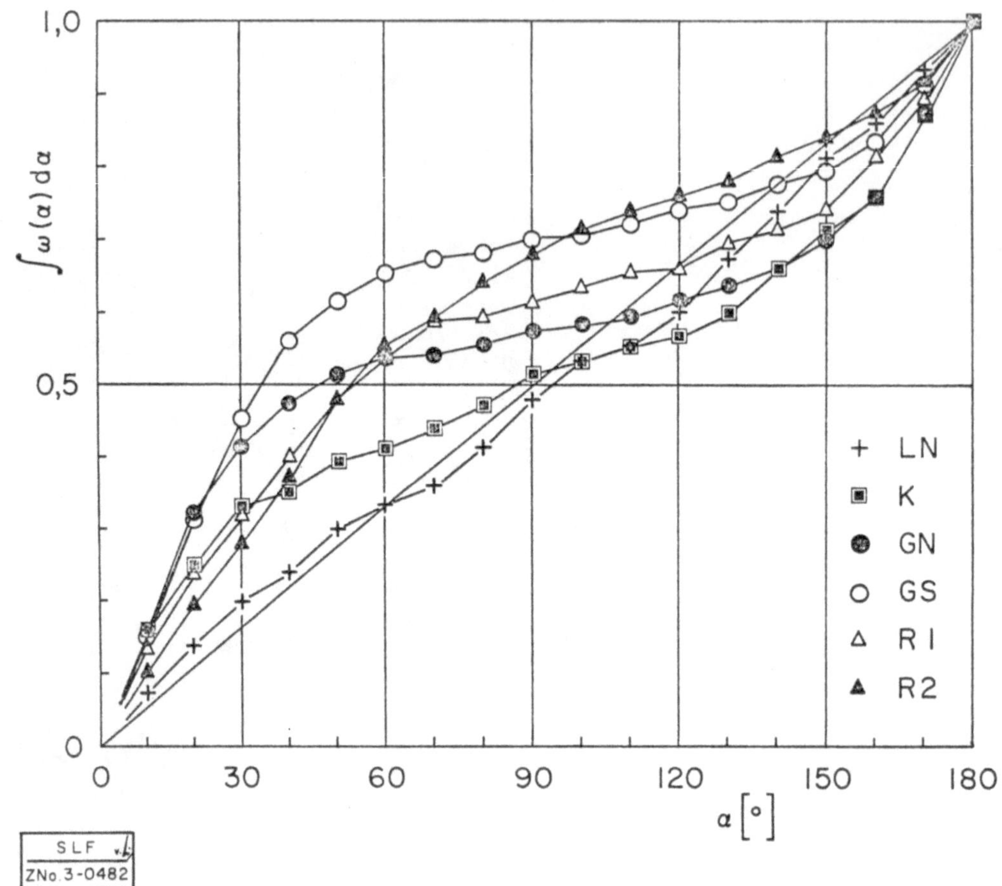

Fig. 2

ABWEICHUNG DER AUSRICHTUNG DER GEBIETE
VON EINER ZUFALLSVERTEILUNG

F₂ (r_, E, A, ...)
F₁ (c, σc, κ, a, ...)
1 K
7 LN
4 RI
6 R3
5 R2
3 GS
2 GN
SLF
ZNo.4-1382
F1 / F2 < 38 , 7 >

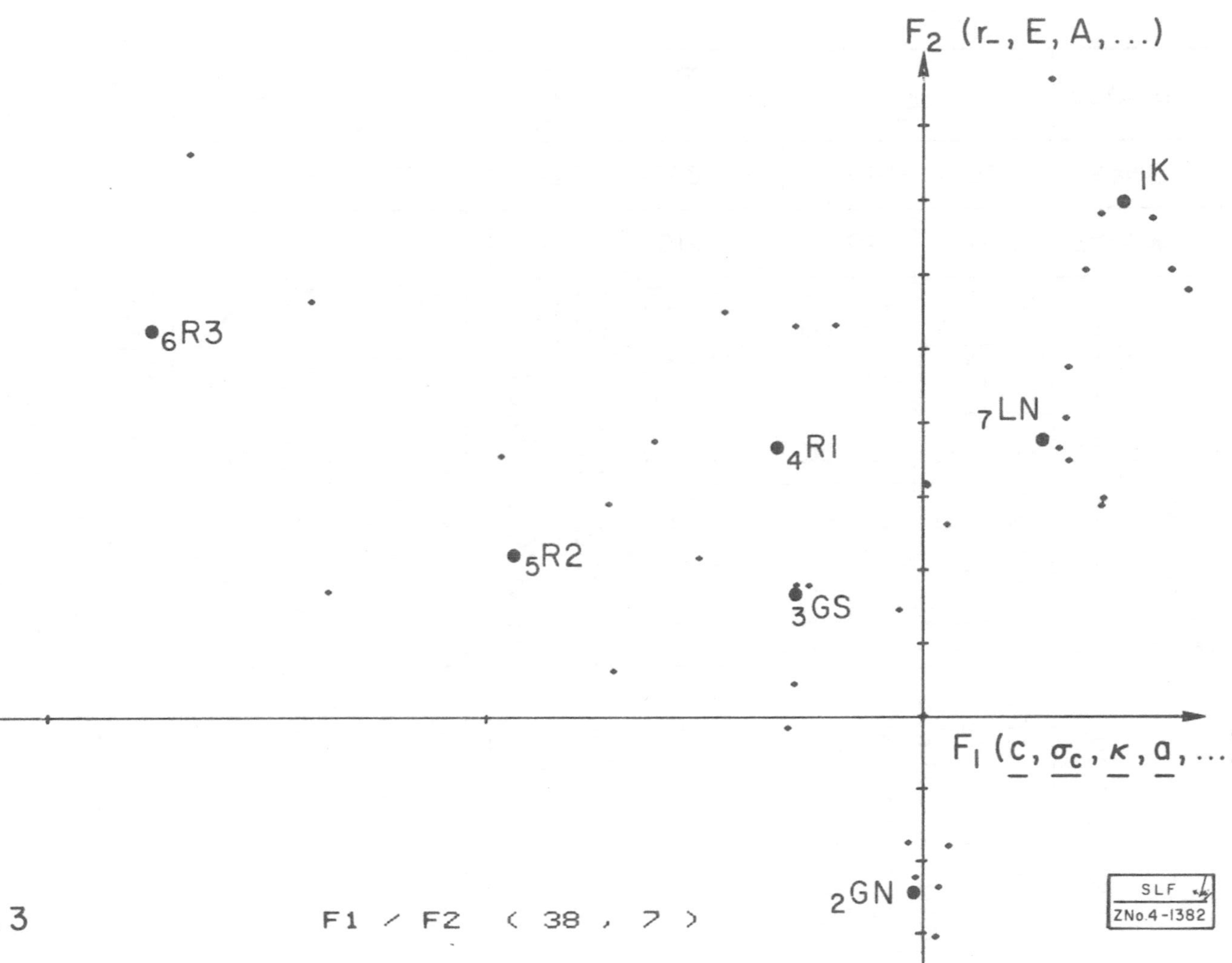

Fig. 3

IDENTIFICATION	SUBFRAME	SUBFRAME (600 × 600 PIXEL)					TAPE #	FRAME	GROUPS
		1	2	3	4	5			
PICTURE CENTRE: 24-13/67N, 72W DATE, CLOUDINESS: 29-07-74, 10% "KOUKDJUAK"	1			1			5147	1736-15482	$_1$K
	2		2	K			5147		
	3		K	K	2		5155		
	4		1	K	7,1	2,7	5155		
PICTURE CENTRE: 20-22/54N, 76W DATE, CLOUDINESS: 25-07-74, 0% "GRDE RIVIERE"	1	GN	2	2	GN	GN	5149	1732-15292	$_2$GN
	2		2	2	2,3	GN	5149		
	3	GN	GN	GS		2,3	5150		$_3$GS
	4	3	GS	GS	GS	2	5150		
PICTURE CENTRE: 19-24/51N, 76W DATE, CLOUDINESS: 11-08-74, 1% "RUPERT RIVER"	1	R1	R1	R1	R1	R3	5156	1749-15235	$_4$R1
	2	6	R3	R3	R2	R2	5156		$_5$R2
	3	R1		2,3	2,3	2,3	5148		
	4	R2	R2	4	3		5148		$_6$R3
14-27/47N, 71W 24-07-73, 30% "LAURENTIDES"	1	LN	LN	LN	LN	7,2	4443	1366-15052	$_7$LN
	2	LN	LN	LN	LN	7,2	4443		

"STABLE
"ATTRIBUTED } INDIVIDUALS" { (K) (I)

TABELLE 3:

RESULTATE DER NUMERISCHEN KLASSIFIZIERUNG

BILD I

<u>MÖGLICHKEITEN DER HAUPTKOMPONENTENANALYSE
FÜR DIE AUFBEREITUNG MULTISPEKTRALER
BILDDATEN ZUM ZWECKE DER KLASSIFIKATION
UND DER BILDVERBESSERUNG</u>

Rudolf H. Dittel
Institut für Flugfunk und Mikrowellen
Deutsche Forschungs- und Versuchsanstalt
für Luft- und Raumfahrt e. V.
8031 Oberpfaffenhofen

Darlegung des Problems

Bei der Bearbeitung multispektraler Bilddaten tritt in zunehmendem
Maße das Problem auf, aus der Gesamtzahl der vorliegenden Spektralbereiche jene Minimalkombination auszuwählen, die für eine nutzerbezogene anlagenunterstützte Auswertung (z. B. Klassifikation) oder
eine bildhafte Darstellung alle in der Szene vorhandenen Klassen
erfaßt und sie auf Grund der spektralen Merkmale auch signifikant
unterscheidbar quantitativ bestimmen läßt. Wesentlich bei dieser
Zielsetzung ist die Tatsache, daß einer entsprechenden Selektion
keine bestimmte nutzerbezogene Aufgabenstellung zugrunde liegt,
und diese auch nicht auf die Hervorhebung nur einiger weniger Klassen ausgerichtet ist. Es soll vielmehr mit einem Minimum an Spektralbereichen ein Maximum der vorliegenden Informationen sichergestellt und verfügbar gemacht werden. Die Erfüllung einer solchen
Forderung hätte den Vorteil, daß durch eine derart <u>einmal</u> vorgenommene Auswahl ein Datensatz bereitgestellt wird, <u>der</u> bezüglich des
Verhältnisses Informationsinhalt/Datenmenge für jede weitere Aufgabenstellung optimale Voraussetzungen böte.

Eine entsprechende Selektion könnte durch versuchsweise Ausführung
aller möglichen Spektralbereichskombinationen erfolgen. Sie stößt
jedoch auf folgende Schwierigkeiten:
a) Anzahl und Ausprägung der mit einer bestimmten Sensorkombination
   erfaßten und in einer Szene vorhandenen Klassen sind nicht bekannt.
b) jeder der verwendeten Spektralbereiche enthält neben den eigentlichen Informationen auch noch statistisch auftretende Meßfehler.
c) es gehen auch jene Spektralbereiche in die ausgewählte Merkmals-
   menge ein, die gegenüber anderen verwendeten Spektralbereichen
   eine hohe lineare Abhängigkeit (hohe Korrelation) aufweisen. Diese Spektralbereiche liefern somit keinen wesentlichen Informati-
   onsbeitrag zur Bestimmung der vorhandenen und zur Differenzierung
   der dargestellten Klassen.

Bei einer solchen Vorgehensweise scheint tatsächlich bei bestimmten
Kombinationen der angestrebte Optimalzustand erreicht zu sein. Die
Tatsache jedoch, daß jeder der dabei verwendeten Spektralbereiche
mit Fehlern behaftet ist, führt durch deren Aufsummierung bereits
bei diesem Zustand zu einer ungenauen Beschreibung der Klassen-
eigenschaften relativ zu der durch die Ausgangsdaten gegebenen möglichen Präzision der Merkmalswerte. Die Folge sind Überlappungen
der die einzelnen Klassen repräsentierenden Datenpopulationen durch
Vergrößerung der Standardabweichung, eine Angleichung der Populati-
onszentren (arithmetische Mittelwerte der Spektralintensitäten),
sowie eine Gleichausrichtung der Populationsellipsoide (Korrelati-
ons- und Kovarianzmatrizen) im Merkmalsraum. Treten in ausgewählten
hochkorrelierten Spektralbereichen gleichzeitig auch statistische
(nicht korrelierte) Fehler auf, dann werden gerade diese fehler-
hafte Merkmale als signifikante Informationen gewertet. Man ent-

fernt sich damit nicht nur von der eigentlichen Zielsetzung, nämlich
der Auswahl einer minimalen Anzahl notwendiger und hinreichender
Spektralbereiche, sondern gleichzeitig werden auch die Klassenkenn-
größen verfälscht.

Eine derart vorgenommene Auswahl geeigneter Spektralbereiche kann
darüberhinaus dazu führen, daß zwar das spektrale Verhalten großflächiger, offensichtlich verschiedener Oberflächentypen genügend
berücksichtigt wird, Unterscheidungsmerkmale für zwar vorhandene,
jedoch nicht so prägnant hervortretende Oberflächen, übersehen werden, weil ihre wesentlichen zusätzlichen Unterscheidungsmerkmale
gerade in einem Spektralbereich auftreten, der nicht selektiert
wurde.

Zu ähnlichen Erkenntnissen gelangt man auch bei der Verwendung von
durch farbliche Überlagerung einzelner Spektralauszüge erzeugten
Bildern. Hierbei ergibt sich bereits die grundlegende Schwierigkeit
einer Differenzierung der erzeugten Mischfarben bei Kombination von
mehr als drei Spektralauszügen.

Prinzip der Hauptkomponentenanalyse (HKA)

Einen Ausweg aus diesem Engpaß bietet die HKA. Sie basiert auf dem
Grundgedanken, daß die Merkmale (spektrale Intensitäten) einzelner
Oberflächentypen für eine bestimmte Szene untereinander definierte,
statistisch reproduzierbare Abhängigkeiten aufweisen. Trägt man die
Merkmalswerte als Koordinatenpunkte im Merkmalsraum mit einer der
Anzahl der Spektralbereiche entsprechenden Dimensionalität auf, so
führt die statistische Reproduzierbarkeit zur Ausbildung bevorzugter
Ausdehnungsrichtungen der so gebildeten Datenpopulation. Mit statistischen Fehlern behaftete Meßwerte werden demgegenüber Zufallsverteilung aufweisen und somit keinen Beitrag zur szenenspezifischen
Gestaltsausbildung leisten. Die Größe der Ausdehnung einer solchen,
auch Cluster genannten, Datenpopulation in bestimmte Richtungen des
Merkmalsraums stellt somit ein Maß für die Reproduzierbarkeit und
damit die Aussagequalität der entsprechenden Merkmalsgrößen dar. Sie
wird quantitativ durch die Varianz beschrieben. (Abb. 1).

Die Gesamtheit des Einzelklassenverhaltens einschließlich der durch
Fehler geprägten Ereignisse bestimmen die Eigenschaften des Szenen-
Clusters. Dieses Gesamt-Cluster wird in seinem Ausgangszustand kaum
parallel zu den Koordinatenachsen des Merkmalsraums ausgerichtet
sein. Seine Lage im Merkmalsraum läßt sich als Winkelfunktion mit
Hilfe der Korrelationsmatrix bestimmen. Projeziert man nun die ermittelten Klassenzentren auf eine von zwei Koordinatenachsen aufge-
spannte Ebene, so stellt man fest, daß die entsprechenden Werte auf
einer Koordinatenachse keine signifikante Unterscheidbarkeit für den
dadurch repräsentierten Spektralbereich ermöglichen. Die Ursache ist
darin zu suchen, daß die Einzelklassen im Merkmalsraum zwar hinreichend großen Abstand aufweisen, jedoch durch die Projektion eine
Annäherung und sogar Gleichheit der Koordinatenwerte eintritt. Die
projezierten Werte stellen dabei die eigentlichen Meßwerte dar.

Eine Steigerung der Differenzierbarkeit kann durch Projektion der
Klassenzentren auf Ebenen erreicht werden, die durch Achsen entlang
der Hauptausdehnungsrichtungen der Datenpopulation aufgespannt werden. Die erste Achse wird dabei so gelegt, daß sie entlang der größten Ausdehnung des Clusters verläuft und die Summe der Abweichungen
von allen Ereignispunkten im Merkmalsraum ein Minimum wird. Die
weiteren Achsen stehen senkrecht auf dieser und bilden somit das
Koordinatensystem eines neuen Merkmalsraums. (Abb. 2)

Im einzelnen wird dabei wie folgt vorgegangen:

a) Beschreibung der spektralen Szeneneigenschaften mit Hilfe der Kovarianzmatrix $\hat{\Sigma}$. Dabei ist wegen der Beziehung $s_{ij} = \sigma_i \, \sigma_j \, r_{ij}$ durch die Standardabweichungen σ_i, σ_j die Abmessung und durch die Korrelationskoeffizienten r_{ij} in ihrer Bedeutung als Cosinuswert des zwischen den Vektoren i und j eingeschlossenen Winkels die Lage des Clusters im Merkmalsraum festgelegt.

b) Feststellung der Hauptausdehnungsrichtungen der Datenpopulation durch Ermittlung der Eigenwerte

$$|\hat{\Sigma} - \lambda I| = 0$$

Die Eigenwerte stellen ein Maß für die Varianz und damit die Größe der Ausdehnung in einer bestimmten Richtung des Merkmalsraums dar.

c) Sortierung der Eigenwerte nach abnehmender Größenordnung mit entsprechend aufsteigender Indizierung

$$\lambda_1 \geq \lambda_2 \geq \lambda_3 \cdots \geq \lambda_s$$

Dadurch wird erreicht, daß im Gegensatz zu den Ausgangsvariablen eine eindeutige Beziehung zwischen dem Rang der Variablen und deren durch die Varianz repräsentierten Anteil an der Gesamtinformation hergestellt wird. Der Beitrag der Varianz entlang einer Achse l zur Gesamtvarianz errechnet sich zu

$$\eta_\ell = \frac{\lambda_\ell}{\Sigma \lambda}$$

d) Bestimmung der Eigenvektoren $\quad (\hat{\Sigma} - \lambda_\ell I) \, V = 0$

deren Komponenten V_{ij} den Cosinuswert des Winkels θ_{ij} angeben, um den das ursprüngliche Koordinatensystem gedreht werden muß, um in die Lage des Koordinatensystems der Datenpopulation zu gelangen. Die Komponenten der Eigenvektoren können auch als Wichtungfunktion der Ursprungsvariablen aufgefaßt werden. Durch die vorhergehende Sortierung wird erreicht, daß die Variablen entsprechend ihrer "Reproduzierbarkeits-Qualität" gewichtet werden.

e) Ausführung der Transformation $\quad Y = X V$

wobei ein neuer Datensatz Y gebildet wird, der den Merkmalswerten X der ursprünglichen Ereigniswerte im neuen Merkmalsraum entspricht. Dabei ist den Variablenwerten Y niederer Indizierung bereits ein höherer Informationsanteil zugewiesen als sie im allgemeinen irgendeine Variable des Ausgangsdatensatzes aufweist.

Beispiel einer HKA

An zwei Bildbeispielen wurde eine HKA durchgeführt. Es handelt sich hierbei um

a) eine LANDSAT-1-Aufnahme (4 Spektralbereiche)
b) einen Szenenausschnitt einer Vorbefliegung des Deutschen Flugzeugmeßprogramms (FMP) (11 Spektralbereiche)

Abb. 3 zeigt die Bildabzüge aller Spektralbereiche für Beispiel a, Abb. 4 die Spektralbereiche 1, 3, 6, 9 für Beispiel b. Die Korrelationsbeziehungen und Varianzanteile sind für a in Abb. 5, für b in Abb. 6 wiedergegeben.

Die Korrelationskoeffizienten geben zwar einen Hinweis auf den Grad der linearen Abhängigkeit der Spektralinformationen, sie erlauben jedoch weder eine Aussage dazu, welche der Variablen hoher Korrelation gegenüber einer anderen bevorzugt werden sollte, noch geben sie einen Hinweis zu den nicht erklärten Varianzanteilen (Fehlerbeitrag) der einzelnen Variablen. Hierzu bedarf es einer faktoranalytischen Betrachtung. Dabei ergibt sich, daß manche Merkmale einen für die vorliegende Aufgabenstellung willkommenen hohen Varianzanteil besitzen, dieser jedoch wegen der gleichzeitig ausge-

prägten linearen Abhängigkeit zu anderen Merkmalen nicht genutzt
werden kann. Bei der Faktorenanalyse wird die Korrelationsmatrix
in Vektoren (Faktoren) zerlegt, deren Produkt wiederum die Ausgangs-
matrix ergibt. Die Komponentenwerte (Faktorenladungen) der einzelnen
Faktoren repräsentieren dabei durch die zwischen O und 1 liegenden
Absolutbeträge der Zahlenwerte die Signifikanz der entsprechenden
Variablen. Berücksichtigt man nun die auf Grund des Bargmann-Tests
(α =0.05) die zufällig erreichbare Anzahl signifikanter Variablen,
und nimmt die ermittelten Absolutbeträge > 0.5 als wesentliche Fak-
torladungen an, so ergeben sich für die einzelnen Spektralbereiche
durchschnittlich gleich große Anteile nicht erklärter Varianz
(Tab. 1). Dabei wird angenommen, daß sich diese Anteile, auch be-
dingt durch Meßfehler, auf alle Klassen gleichmäßig verteilen. Die
Auswahl einer Minimalanzahl von Spektralbereichen, die einen über-
durchschnittlichen Informationsanteil beinhalten, ist somit nicht
eindeutig möglich.

Abb. 7 und Abb. 8 zeigen die Varianzanteile für die einzelnen Variablen nach erfolgter Transformation. Die ausgeprägte Bedeutung der
Merkmale niederer Indizierung ist offensichtlich. In Abb. 9 ist das
Bildergebnis der HKA für die LANDSAT-1-Szene (Abb. 3) und in Abb. 10
die der ersten vier Merkmale (Achsen) der FMP-Szene (Abb. 4) wiedergegeben. Beide Ergebnisse zeigen deutlich den hohen Differenzierungs-
grad der Bilddarstellungen für die Variablen hohen Varianzanteils.

Grenzbedingungen der Anwendung

Bei den bisherigen Betrachtungen wurde davon ausgegangen, daß eine
Differenzierung mit gleicher Güte unabhängig von der Anzahl der vorliegenden Klassen und der Anzahl der Spektralbereiche erfolgen kann.
Sehr oft tritt jedoch der Fall auf, daß bei Vorliegen eines zu
großen Verhältnisses (Anzahl der Klassen/signifikante Informationen
beitragende Spektralbereiche) trotz der Optimallage der Projektions-
ebenen im neuen Merkmalsraum die gestellte Forderung nicht vollständig erfüllt werden kann. In der folgenden Ableitung sollen die
Grenzbedingungen einer HKA-Anwendung untersucht werden.

Es wird dabei von der Kovarianzmatrix der Ursprungsvaraiablen ausgegangen, die die Eigenschaften der s Variablen des Szenen-Clusters
beschreibt. Die Kovarianzmatrix läßt sich in zwei Terme aufgliedern:
Der erste berücksichtigt das Streuverhalten der vorliegenden Klassen,
der zweite das Streuverhalten der Ereignisse innerhalb jeder Klasse.
Vereinfachend wird dabei für jede Klasse gleiche Normalverteilung
der Ereignisdichte angenommen. Damit ergeben sich die Ausdrücke

$$\hat{\Sigma} = \frac{1}{N} \sum_{i=1}^{k} n_i \, (\bar{x}_i - m)(\bar{x}_i - m)^T + \frac{1}{N} \sum_{i=1}^{k} \sum_{\ell=1}^{n_\ell} (x_\ell - \bar{x}_i)(x_\ell - \bar{x}_i)^T$$

$$= \qquad \frac{1}{N} Z(x) \qquad\qquad + \qquad\qquad \frac{1}{N} K(x)$$

Nimmt man nun eine hinreichend große Anzahl von Ereignissen für jede
Klasse an, so läßt sich der Ausdruck K(x) vereinfachend darstellen
zu

$$\frac{1}{N} \sum_{i=1}^{i=k} n_i \, \sigma_i \, I = c\,I$$

wobei N die Gesamtzahl der Ereignisse und c eine Konstante ist.
Für den ersten Term lassen sich die s Eigenwerte $u_1 \geq u_2 \geq \ldots \geq u_s$
und die entsprechenden Eigenvektoren $w_1, w_2, \ldots w_R \ldots w_s$ ermitteln.
Der Rang R der Matris Z(x) wird durch die Minimalbeziehung (Anzahl
der Klassen k; Anzahl der Variablen s) festgelegt. Ist hierbei $k \leq s$,
dann ergibt sich ein Rang $R \leq k-1$; ist $k \geq s$, dann wird der Rang $R \leq s$.
Das bedeutet, daß nur ein R-dimensionaler Unterraum des s-dimensio-
nalen Merkmalsraums für die Projektion zum Zwecke der Klassendiffe-
renzierung zur Verfügung steht, da von den s Eigenvektoren genau R
den Eigenwert $\lambda_i = u_i + c$ annehmen, und die R+1,...,s verbleibenden den

Wert $\lambda_i = c$ annehmen, für die Differenzierung somit nicht mehr nutzbar
sind. Für den Fall k $\leq$ s ist dies nicht weiter nachteilig, da alle
k Klassenzentren auf die R $\leq$ (k-1) von den Eigenvektoren gebildeten
Ebenen projeziert werden. Für den Fall k $\geq$ s tritt jedoch der Fall
ein, daß eine hinreichende Differenzierung selbst bei Verwendung
aller Merkmalswerte nicht gewährleistet werden kann.

Für eine Anwendung der HKA auf Multispektraldaten unter erdwissenschaftlichen Gesichtspunkten hätte dieser Befund weitreichende Folgen. Die von Interpreten festgelegten Klassen unterscheiden sich
jedoch bezüglich ihrer Lage derart stark, daß dieses Problem nur
in untergeordneter Bedeutung zum Tragen kommt. Die mathematisch
trennbaren Klassen gehen zumeist in den nutzerbezogenen Klassen als
zulässige Variationen des Spektralverhaltens unter. Auswirkungen
sind allerdings dann feststellbar, wenn bei der unkontrollierten
Klassifikation der Euklid-Radius der Klassenabstände zu klein
gewählt wird. Hierbei treten eine Vielzahl von Klassen auf, die
selbst bei Anwendung der HKA keine quantitav und phänomenologisch
eindeutige Differenzierung erkennen lassen. Einen Ausweg bietet dabei die Verwendung eines auch das Kovarianzverhalten des Clusters
berücksichtigendes Abstandsmaß, z. B. der Mahalanobis-Abstand

$$D = (x_{K1} - x_{K2})^T \hat{\Sigma}^{-1} (x_{K1} - x_{K2})$$

zur Ermittlung der Distanz zwischen zwei Klassen K1 und K2. Hierbei
konnte für eine Extremfallbetrachtung an einem Ausschnitt der vorliegenden LANDSAT-1-Szene (das Ostersee-Gebiet in der linken oberen
Ecke mit 11760 Bildelementen) bei einem Abstand von 32 Einheiten
und Verwendung aller Spektralbereiche für den Euklid-Abstand
1 Klasse und für den Mahalanobis-Abstand 8 Klassen unterschieden
werden. Ähnliche Ergebnisse erlangt man bei sonst gleichen Voraussetzungen bei Verwendung nur der beiden höchstvariaten Variablen
des transformierten Datensatzes. Der Differenzgewinn bei Verwendung
des Mahalanobis-Abstands gegenüber dem Euklid-Abstand tritt jedoch
nicht so deutlich hervor.

Versuchsweise wurden im Falle der LANDSAT-1-Bilder Zweierkombinati-
onen von Spektralbereichen vorgenommen mit der Zielsetzung, die
Auswirkungen unterschiedlicher Varianzbeiträge und Korrelations-
grade auf das Ergebnis der HKA und die erzeugten Bilder zu untersuchen. Die quantitativen Angaben finden sich in Tab. 2. Die Bilddarstellungen der transformierten Variablen sind in den Abb. 11,
Abb. 12 und Abb. 13 wiedergegeben.

Verwendung beliebiger Kovarianzmatrizen

In Anlehnung an den Grundgedanken der Karhunen-Loève-Transformation
wird oft der Versuch einer   Transformation nach den Eigenvektoren einer bestimmten Oberfläche vorgenommen. Man erhofft sich
dadurch die Hervorhebung - was darunter zu verstehen ist, darüber
sind sich viele Autoren nicht einig - gerade dieser Klassen in der
entsprechenden Szene. Eine Verbesserung soll auch durch die farbliche Überlagerung von in diesem Sinne nach mehreren Oberflächentypen transformierten Bildern einer Szene erzielt werden. Stellt
sich der gewünschte Erfolg nicht ein, dann wird auf ungenügende
Grauwertdifferenzierung oder mangelnde Unterscheidbarkeit der Mischfarben verwiesen.

Theoretische Untersuchungen zeigen jedoch, daß weder eine Verbesserung der Klassentrennbarkeit noch der Bildqualität mit diesem Verfahren möglich ist. Die wesentlichen Gründe hierfür sind:
a) die Hauptachsen der Musterklasse sind denen des Szenen-Clusters
   nicht identisch. Die erste Projektionsebene wird somit in eine
   Position des Merkmalsraums gebracht, die keine optimale Trenn-

barkeit herbeiführt. Eine wesentliche Voraussetzung zur Erreichung
des angestrebten Ziels wir somit nicht geschaffen.
b) Damit werden Überlappungen ansonsten trennbarer Klassen verursacht,
d. h. Oberflächen mit völlig verschiedenen Eigenschaften werden einer
Klasse zugeordnet. Die Folge ist eine Verschlechterung, zumindest
jedoch keine Verbesserung gegenüber der Trennbarkeit, wie sie mit
Hilfe der Originaldaten erzielt werden kann.
c) Da die Lage der ersten Hauptachse nicht durch die Eigenschaften
des Gesamt-Clusters bestimmt wird, ist der sonst gegebene Zusammenhang zwischen dem Variablenindex und dem Varianzanteil nicht gewährleistet: zwischen Variablenindex und Varianzanteil besteht kein
offensichtlicher Zusammenhang.
d) Daraus folgt, daß keine Aussage zum Informationsgehalt und zur
Korrelation einzelner Variablen getroffen werden kann, ebenso wie
dies bei den Ausgangsvariablen der Fall ist. Ein Fortschritt durch
die Anwendung dieses Verfahrens wird somit nicht erzielt.
e) Die scheinbaren Erfolge ausgeprägter Hervorhebung einzelner ange-
strebter Klassen ist darauf zurückzuführen, daß die Eigenschaften
der Musterklasse denen der Clustereigenschaften ähnlich sind. Ein
Vergleich von Klassifizierungsergebnissen (unkontrollierte Klassifikation) mit den Resultaten einer nach der üblichen HKA-Methode
transformierten Datenmenge zeigt, daß die Abweichungen vor allem
an den Grenzen klasseneinheitlicher Areale auftreten.

Aus den durchgeführten Untersuchungen zur Überprüfung dieser Theorie
wird hier die Transformation der LANDSAT-1-Szene nach der Oberfläche
"Wasser" vorgeführt. Die Kenndaten sind in Tab. 3, die bildhafte Darstellung ist in Abb. 14 wiedergegeben.

Methoden der Bildverbesserung

Es ist überflüssig, noch einmal zu beweisen, daß zwischen der Größe
der Eigenwerte und dem Kontrastreichtum des mit Hilfe der entsprechenden Eigenvektoren erzeugten Bildes ein Zusammenhang besteht.
Wesentlicher als der Kontrastreichtum ist hier jedoch die Tatsache,
daß in hochvariaten Bildern eine Vielzahl von Phänomenen vereint
werden, wie sie sonst nur, wegen der annähernden Gleichverteilung der
Differenzierungsmöglichkeiten über alle Spektralbereiche, aus den
Einzeldarstellungen durch vergleichende Betrachtung zu ermitteln sind.
Diese Bilder sind damit den durch Wichtungsfunktionen (z. B. Ratio-
bildern) erzeugten Darstellungen ähnlich, nur daß bei diesen keine
die statistische Reproduzierbarkeit und die lineare Abhängigkeit
wertende Untersuchung vorgenommen wird und diese Ergebnisse entsprechend genutzt werden. Die Intensitätszuordnung für eine Klasse
in einem Spektralbereich ist bei den HKA-Bildern ebenfalls nicht eindeutig; es bedarf deshalb für die Klassifikation eine bestimmte Min-
destzahl an Variablen, die dann jedoch mit einer geringeren Anzahl
von Merkmalswerten als dies mit den Originaldaten der Fall war, zu
eindeutigeren Ergebnissen führen. Ebenfalls eindeutigere Ergebnisse
erhält man bei der farblichen Überlagerung der hochvariaten Bilder.
Die versuchsweise Kombination zur Erzielung des optimalen Differen-
zierungsergebnisses entfällt.

Ein Problem bei mit HKA-Variablen erzeugten Bildern stellen statistisch auftretende, seriell ausgeprägte Bildfehler dar, wie z. B.
fehlerhaft erfaßte Abtastzeilen in einzelnen Spektralbereichen. Diese
Streifen lassen sich bei nichtkorreliertem Auftreten auch nicht aus
den hochvariaten Bilddarstellungen entfernen. Sie verschwinden jedoch
bereits in der der 2. oder 3. Hauptkomponente entsprechenden bildhaften Wiedergabe. In einem solchen Fall ist es angebrachter, die
niedervarianten Darstellungen zu verwenden, da durch die kontrast-
reich abgesetzten Streifen bereits wesentliche Anteile des verfüg-

baren Dynamikbereichs vergeben sind. Ein Beispiel bietet hierzu
die Verwendung der kontrastarmen Spektralbereiche 1 und 10 des
FMP-Pildbeispiels (Abb. 15). In den Ergebnissen der Transformation
treten die Bildzeilenfehler in dem der 1. Hauptkomponente entsprechenden Bild auf, sie fehlen in der Darstellung des Bildes
der 2. Hauptkomponente, das dadurch kontrastreicher und differenzierender hervortritt (Abb. 16). Ein ähnliches Beispiel zur Kon-
trasterhöhung bei Verwendung mehrerer wenig differenzierender Aus-
gangsbilder wird mit Hilfe der in Abb. 4 verwendeten Spektralauszüge demonstriert. Auch hier tritt in der Darstellung der höchsten
Varianz wieder der Zeilenfehler (des Spektralbereichs 6) auf. Die
Auswertung der Bilder niederer Varianz liefert dabei einen Hinweis
auf ein interessantes Phänomen: Stimmt eine Oberfläche in mehreren
Spektralbereichen mit den spektralen Eigenschaften von dort vorhandenen Klassen annähernd gut überein, ohne jedoch die Klassenzu-
gehörigkeit in allen Spektralbereichen streng beizubehalten, so
werden diese Intensitätseigenarten bei der HKA als Datenfehler bei
der Klasse gewertet, mit der größte Übereinstimmung besteht. Diese
konsequente Abweichung äußert sich als Intensitätsextremum in der
eine niedere Varianz repräsentierenden bildhaften Darstellung der
Szene. Durch Zuordnung einer Kontrastfarbe für dieses Bild in Kombination mit anderen Farben für die hoch varianten Abzüge läßt sich
der geometrische Ort solcher Klassen ermitteln. Im vorliegenden
Fall konnte dadurch ein Schilfgürtel an einem See identifiziert
werden; diese Erkenntnis läßt sich jedoch auch für die Entdeckung
getarnter Objekte nutzbringend verwenden. (Abb. 17).

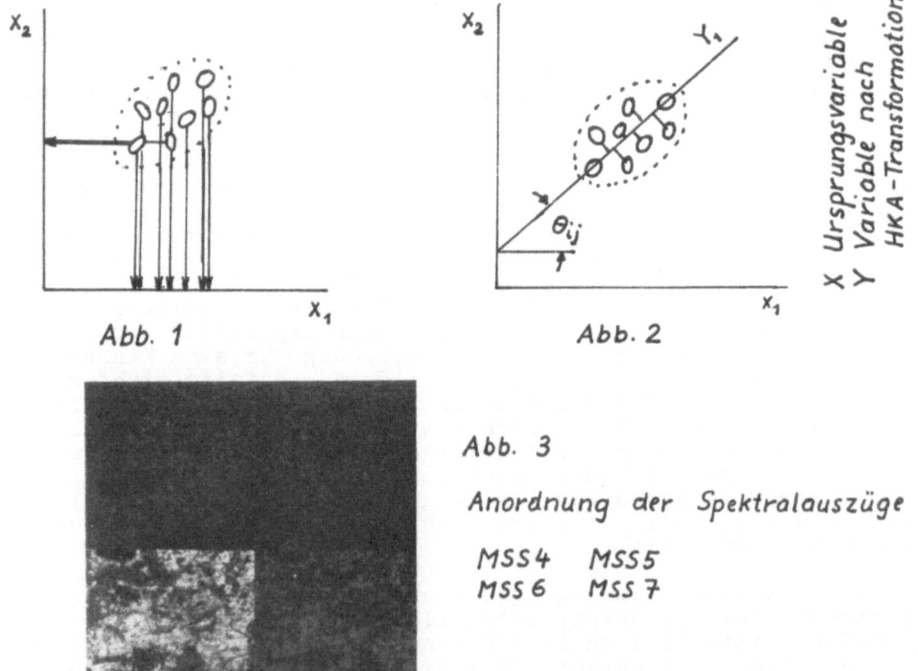

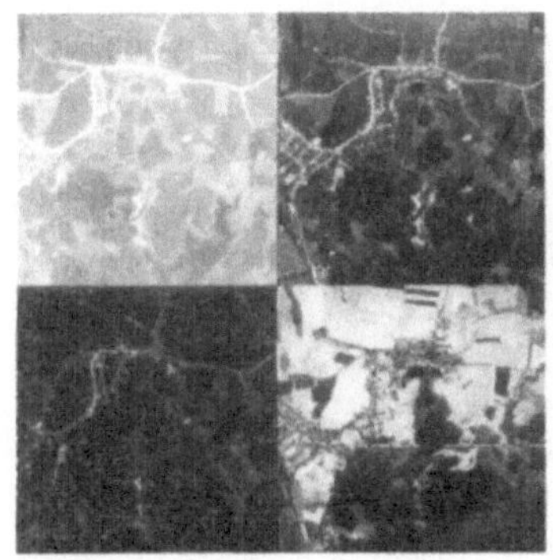

Abb. 4
Anordnung der Spektral-
auszüge

SB1   SB3
SB6   SB9

Abb. 10
Anordnung der Haupt-
Komponenten-Darstellung
HK1   HK2
HK3   HK4

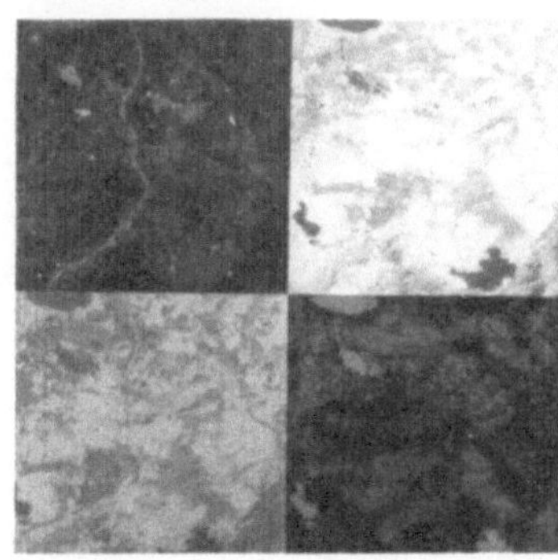

Abb. 14
HK1   HK2
HK3   HK4

Abb. 9
Anordnung der Hauptkomponenten-
Darstellung

HK1   HK2
HK3   HK4

Abb. 11
HK1   HK2

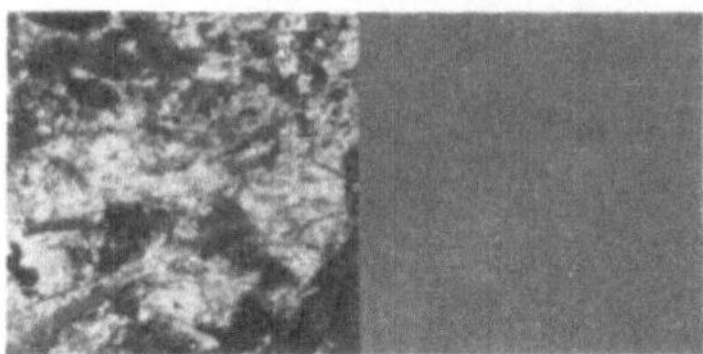

Abb. 12
HK1   HK2

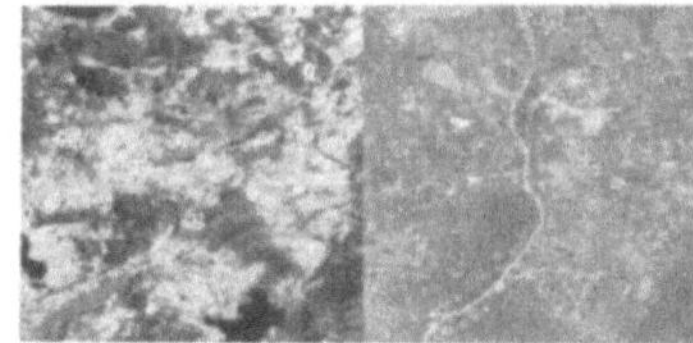

Abb. 13
HK1   HK2

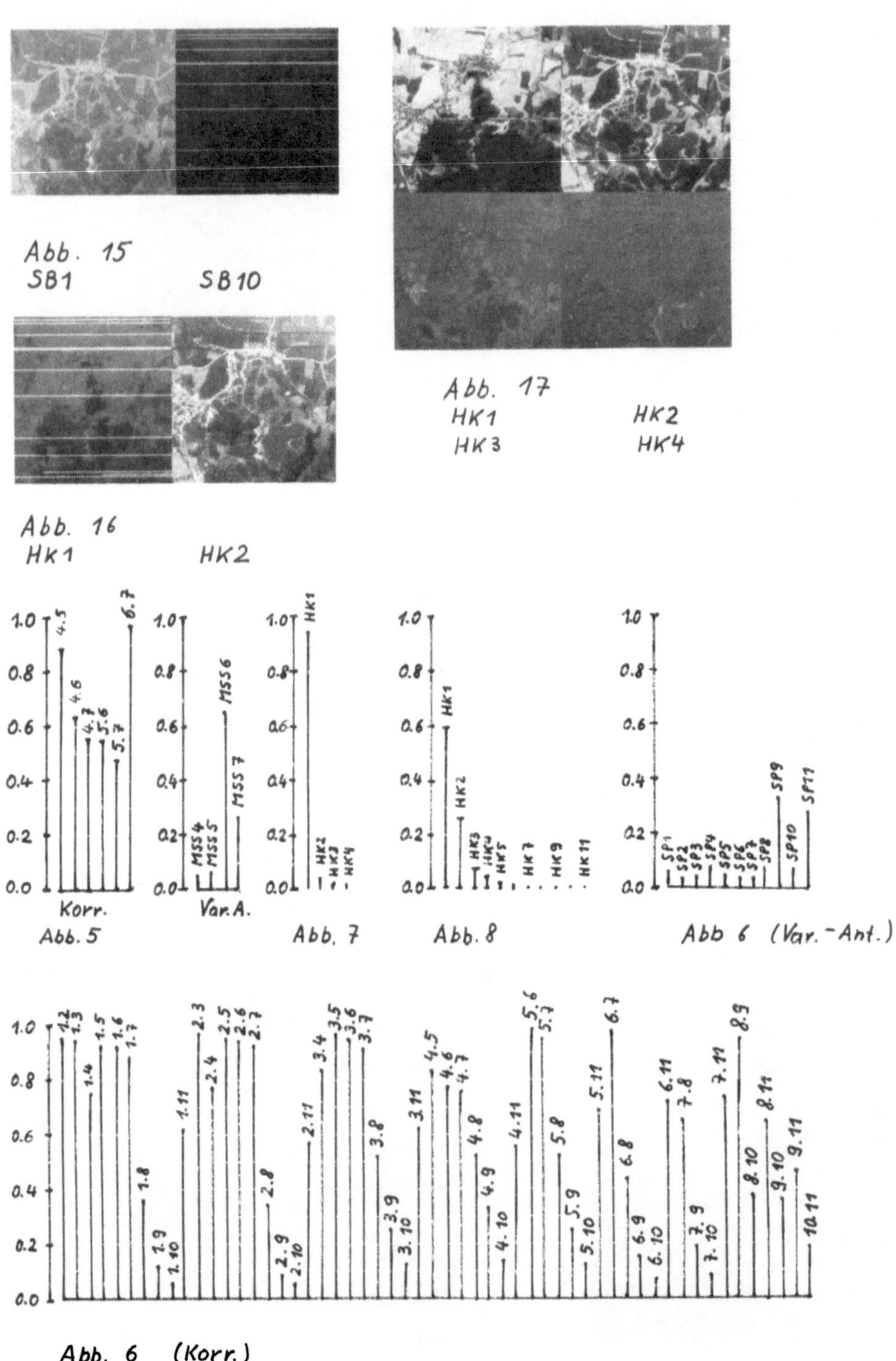

Abb. 15
SB1   SB10
Abb. 16
HK1   HK2
Abb. 17
HK1   HK2
HK3   HK4
Korr.
Abb. 5
Var. A.
Abb. 7
Abb. 8
Abb 6 (Var.-Ant.)
Abb. 6 (Korr.)

		MSS4	MSS5	MSS6*	MSS7	
Faktoren	1	0.65	0.57	1.00	0.99	LANDSAT-1-Szene
	2	0.71	0.80	-0.02	-0.12	
	3	0.28	-0.19	-0.00	0.00	
	4	0.02	0.04	-0.04	0.10	*Rundungsungenauigkeit bei Druckerausgabe
Δ Varianz		0.07	0.04	0.01	0.01	

		SP1	SP2	SP3	SP4	SP5	SP6
Faktoren	1	0.62	0.60	0.71	0.70	0.73	0.69
	2	0.66	0.69	0.56	0.40	0.59	0.67
	3	0.29	0.35	0.38	0.42	0.25	0.18
	4	-0.01	-0.00	-0.02	-0.02	-0.00	0.01
FMP-Szene	5	0.18	0.16	0.13	-0.40	0.12	0.13
	6	-0.23	-0.08	-0.04	-0.00	0.18	0.14
	7	0.09	-0.06	-0.12	0.01	-0.05	0.00
	8	0.02	-0.03	-0.01	0.0	0.00	-0.01
	9	0.02	-0.06	-0.04	0.0	0.06	0.06
	10	-0.01	0.07	-0.04	0.0	-0.02	0.04
	11	-0.00	0.01	-0.01	0.0	0.02	-0.02
Δ Varianz		0.18	0.16	0.18	0.51	0.13	0.09

		SP7	SP8	SP9	SP10	SP11
Faktoren	1	0.71	0.92	0.79	0.34	0.85
	2	0.63	-0.35	-0.60	-0.27	0.31
	3	0.13	0.09	0.07	0.09	-0.42
	4	0.01	-0.05	-0.07	0.90	0.02
FMP-Szene	5	0.14	0.05	0.02	0.00	-0.04
	6	0.21	0.05	-0.01	-0.00	-0.02
	7	0.12	0.00	0.00	0.0	-0.01
	8	-0.05	0.11	-0.02	-0.00	-0.00
	9	-0.06	-0.02	0.00	0.0	-0.00
	10	-0.02	0.00	0.0	0.0	0.0
	11	0.00	0.0	0.0	0.0	0.0
Δ Varianz		0.11	0.16	0.02	0.19	0.17

Tab. 1

Kombination	Korr.	Var. Ant. (Org.Var.)	Var. Ant HK1	HK2	Abb.	Zweck
MSS4 / MSS5	0.882	0.42 / 0.58	0.94	0.06	11	Hohe Korrel., geringe Varianz
MSS6 / MSS7	0.986	0.7 / 0.3	0.999	0.001	12	Hohe Korrel., hohe Varianz
MSS5 / MSS7	0.478	0.15 / 0.85	0.86	0.14	13	Geringe Korrel. Gemischte Var.Ant.

Tab. 2

Eigenvektoren (Gesamt-Szene)

0.135	0.590	0.792	0.078
0.137	0.766	-0.609	0.155
0.830	-0.067	-0.037	-0.552
0.523	-0.247	0.015	0.816

Eigenvektoren (Wasser)

0.927	-0.019	-0.208	0.311
0.303	0.547	0.643	-0.443
-0.103	0.752	-0.646	-0.079
-0.194	0.367	0.356	0.837

Literatur:
1. Überla, K., Faktorenanalyse, Springer, Berlin 1971
2. Bock, H. H., Automatische Klassifikation, Vandenhoeck &
   Ruprecht, Göttingen, 237 - 248
3. Nagy, G., State of the Art in Pattern Recognition, Proc. IEEE,
   Vol. 56, 836-862
4. Fukunaga, K. et al, Application of the Karhunen-Loève
   Expansion to Feature Selection and Ordering, IEEE Trans.
   Computers, Vol. C-19, 311 - 318

Daten:
1. LANDSAT-1, Szene 1021-09380
2. Vorbefliegung FMP, Testgebiet IV vom 29.4.1975

Programme:
1. Sämtliche bilderzeugenden Rechnungen wurden am Bildverarbeitungssystem DIBIAS durchgeführt. Für die Hauptkomponentenanalyse wurde das Modul HK (Autor: Herr Haberäcker) verwendet.
2. Untersuchungen des Datenverhaltens (Hauptkomponentenanalyse,
   Faktorenanalyse, unkontrollierte Klassifikation) wurden mit
   Routinen des Programmpakets IMAGIN (Autor: Dittel) an der
   Anlage TR 440 des Rechenzentrums Oberpfaffenhofen der DFVLR
   durchgeführt.

MULTISPEKTRALE KLASSIFIZIERUNG IN DIBIAS

P. Haberäcker
Institut für Nachrichtentechnik

DEUTSCHE FORSCHUNGS- UND VERSUCHSANSTALT
FÜR LUFT- UND RAUMFAHRT E.V.

8031 Oberpfaffenhofen, BRD

Zusammenfassung:

Es wird das Standardverfahren der Maximum-Likelihood-Klassifizierung, angewendet auf multispektrale Scannerdaten, erläutert. Dieses aufgrund der mathematischen Theorie optimale Verfahren hat den Nachteil, daß bei der Klassifizierung von n Klassen pro Bildpunkt n Matrizenmultiplikationen durchzuführen sind. Dadurch wird das Verfahren sehr rechenzeitintensiv. Es wird der Versuch eines verbesserten Algorithmus vorgestellt, in dem durch die Definition von Kernbereichen der rechnerische Aufwand reduziert wird und somit eine Beschleunigung des Verfahrens erreicht werden kann.

Multispektrale Klassifizierung: Einleitung und Anwendungen

In den Jahren 1975 und 1976 wurde im Institut für Satellitenelektronik der DFVLR, Oberpfaffenhofen, jetzt Institut für Nachrichtentechnik, das interaktive, digitale Bildverarbeitungssystem "DIBIAS" aufgebaut. Im Jahre 1976 wurde DIBIAS hauptsächlich für die Bilddatenauswertung im Erdfernerkundungsprojekt "Flugzeugmeßprogramm (FMP)" des Bundesministeriums für Forschung und Technologie eingesetzt. Dabei lagen die Schwerpunkte der Untersuchungen der sechs Testgebiete in folgenden geowissenschaftlichen Bereichen:

(1) Ostfriesisches Wattengebiet mit Teilen der Nordsee:
Wechselwirkung Land – Wasser im Küstenbereich

(2) Ein Meeresgebiet in der Deutschen Bucht für ozeanographische
Untersuchungen

(3) Ein Meeresgebiet in der Kieler Bucht, ebenfalls für ozeanographische Untersuchungen

(4) Ein Gebiet im Bereich des Untermains mit Taunus und Wetterau

mit der Schwerpunktaufgabe: Biosphäre eines Ballungsgebietes
für Fragen der Regionalplanung und des Umweltschutzes
(5) Oberrheintal-Bruch und Schwarzwald bei Freiburg i.Br.:
Bearbeitung von Vegetations- und Landnutzungsformen
(6) Ein Alpenrandgebiet südlich von München bei Murnau mit der
Schwerpunktaufgabe: Ökologie eines Hochgebirgsrandgebietes.

Bei fast allen dieser Testgebiete wurde sehr bald die Notwendigkeit
einer multispektralen Klassifizierung deutlich. Da sich der Bedarf
schon während der Aufbauphase von DIBIAS abzeichnete, wurde parallel
zur Implementierung von DIBIAS ein in das DIBIAS-System integriertes
Klassifizierungssystem konzipiert. Dieses Klassifizierungssystem
stellt Verfahren aus dem Bereich der überwachten und der selbstlernen-
den Klassifizierung zur Verfügung. Neben den Standardklassifizierungs-
verfahren (z.B. Minimum Distance) und einigen speziellen Algorithmen
wurde auch das Klassifizierungsverfahren nach der Maximum-Likelihood-
Methode implementiert. Dieses Verfahren, das nach der zugrunde liegenden mathematischen Theorie optimale Ergebnisse, d.h. minimalen durchschnittlichen Verlust bei Fehlklassifizierungen liefert, ist jedoch
bei der Verwendung mehrerer Spektralbereiche und Klassen sehr rechenzeitintensiv. In diesem Papier soll nun ein Algorithmus vorgestellt
werden, der bei gleichbleibender Qualität eine erhebliche Rechenzeit-
ersparnis erlaubt.

Das Maximum-Likelihood-Klassifizierungsverfahren

Es sei eine multispektrale Szene

$$S = (S_1, S_2, \ldots, S_n)$$

gegeben, wobei die Matrizen

$$S_k = (s_{ij}^{(k)})$$

den k-ten Spektralbereich der Szene S darstellen. Die Indizies i und j
beschreiben die Zeilen- und die Spaltenanzahl der Szene S.
Ein Bildpunkt $\vec{x}$ ist somit ein n-dimensionaler Vektor der Form:

$$\vec{x} = (s_{ij}^{(1)}, s_{ij}^{(2)}, \ldots, s_{ij}^{(n)}).$$

In der Szene S sind verschiedene Objekte abgebildet. Vermöge der zur
Charakterisierung der abgebildeten Objekte ausgewählten Merkmale, bei
Scannerszenen also der verschiedenen Spektralbereiche, wird jedem Ob-
jekt ein Muster zugeordnet. In der Natur können die Objekte zu ver-

schiedenen Objektklassen zusammengefaßt werden. Dies impliziert in der aufgezeichneten Szene S verschiedene Musterklassen

$$\omega_i, \quad i = 1(1)m.$$

Es ist nun die Aufgabe eines Klassifikators, einen beliebigen Bildpunkt $\vec{x}$ der Szene S, von dem nicht bekannt ist, von welchem der abgebildeten Objekte er erzeugt wurde, einer der Musterklassen zuzuordnen und so die Entscheidung zu treffen, zu welchem Objekt der Bildpunkt gehört.

Bei der Klassifizierung ist eine Verlustmatrix

$$L = (1_{ij})$$

gegeben, die wie folgt interpretiert werden kann:

- der Bildpunkt $\vec{x}$ sei ein Muster der Musterklasse ω_i;
- der Klassifikator ordnet den Bildpunkt $\vec{x}$ jedoch der Musterklasse ω_j zu;
- durch diese Zuordnung tritt der Verlust 1_{ij} auf.

Nehmen wir an, die Bildpunkte der Musterklasse ω_i treten mit einer bestimmten a priori-Wahrscheinlichkeit $p(\omega_i)$ auf. Die Wahrscheinlichkeit, daß ein Bildpunkt $\vec{x}$ zu der Musterklasse ω_i gehört, wird mit $p(\omega_i/\vec{x})$ bezeichnet. Da $\vec{x}$ zu m Musterklassen gehören kann, berechnet sich der bedingte durchschnittliche Verlust gemäß:

$$r_j(\vec{x}) = \sum_{i=1}^{m} 1_{ij} \, p(\omega_i/\vec{x}).$$

Der Klassifikator wird somit $\vec{x}$ derjenigen Musterklasse ω_j zuordnen, für die sich ein minimaler bedingter durchschnittlicher Verlust ergibt. Ein Klassifikator, der nach diesem Kriterium entscheidet, heißt Bayes'scher Klassifikator.
Durch Umformung mit der Bayes'schen Formel

$$p(\omega_i/\vec{x}) = \frac{p(\omega_i) \, p(\vec{x}/\omega_i)}{p(\vec{x})}$$

ergibt sich für $r_j(\vec{x}) = \sum_{i=1}^{m} 1_{ij} p(\vec{x}/\omega_i) \, p(\omega_i).$*

Dabei wird $p(\vec{x}/\omega_i)$ als "Likelihood-Funktion" der Musterklasse ω_i bezeichnet.

*Der konstante Faktor $1/p(\vec{x})$ wurde weggelassen.

In der Praxis wird oft angenommen, daß die Verlustmatrix folgende
Form hat:

$$L = (1_{ij}) = (1-\delta_{ij}), \text{ wobei}$$

$$\delta_{ij} = 1, \text{ für } i = j \text{ und}$$

$$\delta_{ij} = 0, \text{ für } i \neq j.$$

Interpretiert heißt das, daß bei richtiger Klassifizierung kein und
bei unrichtiger Klassifizierung immer derselbe Verlust auftritt. Mit
dieser speziellen Verlustmatrix ergibt sich für den bedingten durchschnittlichen Verlust:

$$r_j(\vec{x}) = \sum_{i=j}^{m} (1-\delta_{ij}) \, p(\vec{x}/\omega_i) \, p(\omega_i) =$$

$$= p(\vec{x}) - p(\vec{x}/\omega_j) \, p(\omega_j).$$

Somit wird das Muster $\vec{x}$ der Musterklasse ω_i zugeordnet, falls für
$j = 1(1)m$, $i \neq j$, gilt:

$$p(\vec{x}) - p(\vec{x}/\omega_i) \, p(\omega_i) < p(\vec{x}) - p(\vec{x}/\omega_j \, p(\omega_j)$$

oder

$$p(\vec{x}/\omega_i) \, p(\omega_i) > p(\vec{x}/\omega_j) \, p(\omega_j).$$

Man erhält dadurch zu jeder Musterklasse ω_i eine Trennungsfunktion

$$(7) \qquad d_i^!(\vec{x}) = p(\vec{x}/\omega_i) \, p(\omega_i), \quad i = 1(1)m.$$

Unbekannt ist nun die Verteilung der bedingten Wahrscheinlichkeiten
$p(\vec{x}/\omega_i)$. Nehmen wir an, daß sie nach einer Gauß'schen Normalverteilung der Form:

$$(8) \qquad p(\vec{x}/\omega_i) =$$

$$= 1/\left\{(2\pi)^{n/2} * /C_i/^{1/2}\right\} * \exp\left\{-1/2(\vec{x}-\vec{m}_i)' \, C_i^{-1} \, (\vec{x}-\vec{m}_i)\right\}$$

$i = 1(1)m$ verteilt sind. dabei ist $\vec{m}_i$ der Mittelwertsvektor und C_i
die Kovarianzmatrix der Musterklasse ω_i.

Durch die Exponentialform der Normalverteilung wird als Trennungsfunktion nicht die Form in (7) sondern der natürliche Logarithmus davon verwendet. Durch Einsetzen von (8) und Weglassen des Terms
$(n/2)\ln 2\pi$ ergibt sich:

$$(9) \quad d_i(\vec{x}) = \ln p(\omega_i) - 1/2 \ln/C_i/ - 1/2 \left\{ (\vec{x}-\vec{m}_i)' \; C_i^{-1} \; (\vec{x}-\vec{m}_i) \right\}$$

$$i = 1(1)m.$$

Ein Klassifikator nach der Maximum-Likelihood-Methode läuft mit
obigem Formalismus etwa wie folgt ab:

(10) Berechnung der Mittelwertsvektoren $\vec{m}_i$, der Kovarianz-

   matrizen C_i, der Determinanten $/C_i/$ und der Inversen C_i^{-1}.

(11) Festlegen der a priori-Wahrscheinlichkeiten $p(\omega_i)$.

(12) Für jeden Bildpunkt $\vec{x}$ der Szene S:

   Für jede Musterklasse ω_i:

      Berechne $d_i(\vec{x})$ gemäß (9).

$$d_j(\vec{x}) = \max. \left\{ d_i(\vec{x}) \right\} ;$$
$$1 \leq i \leq m$$

      Ordne $\vec{x}$ der Musterklasse ω_j zu.

Bei einem Klassifizierungsproblem, bei dem n Klassen unterschieden
werden sollen, sind für jeden Bildpunkt der Szene n Matrizenmultiplikationen gemäß (9) zu berechnen. Die Anzahl der skalaren Multiplika-
tionen nimmt dabei quadratisch mit der Anzahl der verwendeten Spektralbereiche zu. Auf der Rechenanlage des DIBIAS-Systems (Interdata
M85) benötigt eine Maximum-Likelihood-Klassifizierung einer Szene
von 500 x 500 Bildpunkten im sieben-dimensionalen Raum bei sieben
Klassen etwa 90 Minuten. Um einen Zeitvergleich mit anderen Anlagen
zu geben, seien für die oben genannte Rechenanlage folgende Rechenzeiten angegeben.

   Fixpointmultikation: 2.25/usec,
   Floatingpointmultiplikation: 24.00/usec (im Mittel).

Definition der Kerne der Musterklassen

Durch die Trennungsgrenzen in (9) ist zu jeder Musterklasse eine
Schar von n-dimensionalen Ellipsoiden gegeben:

$$(13) \quad (\vec{x}-\vec{m}_i)' \; C_i^{-1} \; (\vec{x}-\vec{m}_i) - 2 \ln p(\omega_i) + \ln/C_i/ = const.$$

Um eine Zurückweisungsklasse zu definieren, wird zu jeder dieser
Scharen dasjenige Ellipsoid ausgewählt, das den $\lambda_z \sigma$ - Grenzen der zugehörigen Normalverteilung entspricht. Alle Bildpunkte, die außerhalb
der $\lambda_z \sigma$ - Grenzen liegen, werden als nicht klassifizierbar eingeord-
net.

Die $\lambda_z \sigma$ -Grenzen der verschiedenen Musterklassen werden sich i.a. teilweise überdecken, so daß nach der Feststellung, daß ein Bildpunkt innerhalb der $\lambda_z \sigma$ -Grenzen einer Musterklasse liegt, daraus noch nicht
gefolgert werden kann, daß dieser Bildpunkt zu der Musterklasse gehört. Zur Klassifizierung muß zu jeder Musterklasse der Funktionswert
der Trennungsfunktion berechnet werden. Liegt dieser außerhalb der
$\lambda_z \sigma$ - Grenzen, so scheidet die Musterklasse aus. Liegt der Bildpunkt
im Überdeckungsbereich von $\lambda_z \sigma$-Ellipsoiden, so wird er der Musterklasse mit minimaler Konstante in (13) zugeordnet. Bei dieser Vorgehensweise muß die Trennungsfunktion nur mehr für jene Musterklassen berechnet werden, die an Überdeckungen beteiligt sind. Es werden nun aus
den Ellipsoidscharen der Musterklassen solche Ellipsoide gesucht, für
die, falls ein Bildpunkt innerhalb des Ellipsoids liegt, damit auch
sofort folgt, daß der Bildpunkt zu der zugehörigen Musterklasse gehört. Dazu wird zu jedem Paar (ω_i, ω_j) von Musterklassen ein Ellipsoid-
paar so bestimmt, daß gilt:

(14) die Ellipsoide berühren sich von außen;
(15) alle Punkte auf der Oberfläche der Ellipsoide ergeben
     denselben Funktionswert der Trennungsfunktion.

Zur Berechnung dieser ausgezeichneten Ellipsoide wird folgender
Algorithmus durchlaufen:

(16) Zu jedem Paar (ω_i, ω_j), $i \neq j$, von Musterklassen wird ge-
    prüft, ob sich die $\lambda_z \sigma$-Ellipsoide schneiden.

(17) Falls sie sich schneiden, werden aus den beiden Scharen diejenigen gemäß (14) und (15) ausgewählt. Der zugehörige Funktionswert von (13) wird in eine Hilfsmatrix eingetragen.

(18) Falls sie sich nicht schneiden, wird der Wert der Konstante in (13) für die $\lambda_z\sigma$-Ellipsoide in die Hilfsmatrix eingetragen.

(19) Nachdem die Schritte (16), (17) und (18) für alle Paare von Musterklassen durchgeführt wurden, wird in jeder Zeile i der Hilfsmatrix der minimale Eintrag gesucht. Das zu diesem Konstantenwert gehörige Ellipsoid aus der Schar der Musterklasse ω_i wird als Kern dieser Musterklasse bezeichnet.

Liegt nun ein Bildpunkt $\vec{x}$ im Kern einer Musterklasse, so folgt daraus sofort, daß er nur zu dieser Musterklasse gehören kann. Dadurch kann sich bei geschickter Wahl einer Prüfreihenfolge der Musterklassen eine wesentliche zeitliche Ersparnis ergeben.

Festlegen einer Prüfreihenfolge

Bei dem in (10), (11) und (12) beschriebenen Algorithmus wird zur Berechnung der Trennungsfunktionen keine ausgezeichnete Reihenfolge eingehalten. Zur weiteren Optimierung der Rechenzeit wird jetzt eine Prüfreihenfolge festgelegt:

- Am Anfang ist die Prüfreihenfolge beliebig.

- Falls der zu klassifizierende Bildpunkt nicht am Anfang einer Bildzeile liegt und der linke Nachbar des Bildpunktes einer Musterklasse zugeordnet wurde, wird die Prüfreihenfolge so geändert, daß die Musterklasse des linken Nachbarn an die erste Stelle tritt.

- Nach jeder Bildzeile wird die Prüfreihenfolge gemäß der Häufigkeitsverteilung der Musterklassen neu aufgestellt.

Algorithmus zur Klassifizierung nach der Maximum-Likelihood-Kern-Methode:

In DIBIAS wurde ein überwacht-lernender Klassifikator nach dem oben beschriebenen Verfahren implementiert. Die einzelnen Schritte des Klassifikators werden im folgenden kurz aufgeführt:

(20) Auswahl der Trainingsgebiete und sequentielles Abspeichern auf ein Hilfsmagnetband.

(21) Berechnung der Mittelwertsvektoren und der Kovarianzmatrizen aus den Trainingsgebieten und Eintrag in eine Hilfsdatei.

(22) Berechnung der $\lambda_z\sigma$-Schalenellipsoide und Eintrag der zugehörigen Konstanten gemäß (13) in eine Tabelle A.

(23) Verarbeitung der Musterklasse ω_i:

(23.1) Verarbeitung des Paares von Musterklassen (ω_i,ω_j):

Falls sich die beiden $\lambda_z\sigma$ - Ellipsoide schneiden: entsprechenden Vermerk in Tabelle B; Berechnung der Ellipsoide gemäß (14) und (15) und Eintrag der zugehörigen Konstanten in eine Hilfsmatrix.

Sonst: Eintrag der Konstanten der $\lambda_z\sigma$ - Ellipsoide in die Hilfsmatrix.

(24) Auswahl der Kerne durch zeilenweise Minimumsuche in der Hilfsmatrix und Eintrag der Kern-Konstanten in Tabelle C.

(25) R = $(\omega_1, \ldots)$: beliebige Prüfreihenfolge der Musterklassen.

(26) Für jede Bildzeile der Szene S:

(26.1) Für jeden Bildpunkt der Zeile:

Falls der Bildpunkt am linken Rand der Zeile oder der linke Nachbar nicht klassifiziert wurde: Die Prüfreihenfolge ist durch R gegeben.

Sonst: An den Anfang der Prüfreihenfolge wird die Musterklasse des linken Nachbarn gestellt.

(26.1.2) MR: = R: momentane Prüfreihenfolge; MIN: = 0.0; KLASSE: = undefiniert.

(26.1.3) Solange MR nicht leer ist: Berechnen des Funktionswertes gemäß (13) zur ersten Musterklasse in MR.

Falls der Bildpunkt im Kern liegt (Tabelle C): der Bildpunkt ist klassifiziert; weiter bei (26.1).

Falls der Bildpunkt außerhalb des Schalenellipsoids liegt (Tabelle A): Streichen der ersten Musterklasse in MR; weiter bei (26.1.3).

Falls der Bildpunkt im Schalenellipsoid liegt (Tabelle A):
Falls der Bildpunkt nicht im Überdeckungsbereich mehrerer
Schalenellipsoide liegt (Tabelle B):
der Bildpunkt ist klassifiziert; weiter bei (26.1).
Sonst: Streichen derjenigen Musterklassen in MR, die nicht
an der Überdeckung beteiligt sind;
Streichen der ersten Musterklasse in MR.
Falls Fkt.-Wert kleiner als MIN:
MIN: = Fkt.-Wert   KLASSE : = zug. Klassenbezeichnung.
weiter bei (26.1.3).
(26.1.4) Falls KLASSE = undef.:
der Bildpunkt ist nicht klassifizierbar; weiter bei (26.1).
Sonst: KLASSE enthält die Klassenbezeichnung der
Musterklasse des Bildpunktes; weiter bei (26.1).
(26.2) Stelle am Ende jeder Bildzeile eine neue Prüfreihenfolge nach der Häufigkeitsverteilung der Musterklassen auf.
(27) Ende.

Abschlußbemerkungen:

Für die fachliche Beratung und die Unterstützung bei der Programmierung
sei den beiden Mitarbeitern der Firma Klein und Stekl, Frau Dipl.-Math.
K. BRICHTA und Herrn Dipl.-Math. H. SCHUMACHER herzlich gedankt.

Literatur

J.T. TOU
R.C. GONZALES

Pattern Recognition Principles
(Addison-Wesley Publishing Company,
Massachusetts, 1974)

W.S. MEISEL

Computer-Oriented Approaches to
Pattern Recognition
(Academic Press, New York and London
1972)

J.R. ULLMANN

Pattern Recognition Techniques
(London Butterworths, 1973)

H. NIEMANN

Methoden der Mustererkennung
(Akademische Verlagsgesellschaft, 1974).

<u>RELATIONAL-BÄUME :</u>
<u>EINE DATENSTRUKTUR ZUR BESCHREIBUNG VON BILDZEILEN IN GRAUWERTBILDERN</u>

Jörgen P. Foith

Institut für
Informationsverarbeitung
in Technik & Biologie (IITB)
Fraunhofer-Gesellschaft
Karlsruhe

Roger W. Ehrich

Dept. of El. & Comp. Eng.
Univ. of Massachusetts
Amherst, Mass.

z.Zt. Virginia Polytechnic
Institute & State University
Blacksburg, Va.

ZUSAMMENFASSUNG :

Bisherige Algorithmen der Szenenanalyse verwenden als Eigangsdaten die
ursprünglichen Grauwerte oder daraus abgeleitete Daten (z.B. Ausgangs-
werte von Filtern,Approximationskoeffizienten, symbolische Marken,Wahr-
scheinlichkeiten,etc.), die in einer Vorverarbeitungsphase gewonnen
werden. Die Art der gewählten Daten beeinflusst die Methoden, die Wirksamkeit und den Aufwand der Verarbeitung. Schwächen und Stärken der
Ansätze liegen als Erfahrungswerte vor. Aus ihnen kristallisieren sich
Auswahlkriterien in Form von intuitiv formulierten Prinzipien.

Hier wird ein neues Verfahren zur Vorverarbeitung von Grauwertbildern
dargestellt, welches einige dieser Prinzipien berücksichtigt. Das Verfahren liefert eine Beschreibung des Bildes mit Merkmalen, die auf
Änderungen der Intensität bzw. ihres Gradienten beruhen. Aus technischen
Grunden erfolgt die Verarbeitung zeilenweise.Der Ansatz beruht auf
"strukturellen" Verfahren, mit denen die Struktur der Intensitätsprofile
von Bildzeilen durch Betrachtungen über Nachbarschaften direkt aus den
Daten ermittelt wird. Bildpunkte werden nach kontext-bedingten Kriterien
gruppiert und in einer hierarchischen Datenstruktur gespeichert,welche
die Relationen dieser Gruppierungen zueinander repräsentiert ("Relational-
Bäume").Die Relational-Bäume werden durch einen Algorithmus erzeugt, der
mit mehreren Stapeln arbeitet und die Datenstruktur on-line aufbaut. Es
werden Eigenschaften und Modifikationen der Relational-Bäume und des
Erzeugungsalgorithmus vorgestellt. Die Darstellung schliesst ab mit einem
Ausblick auf Anwendungen und die weitere Verarbeitung.

1. DIE WAHL DER DATEN

Die Probleme der Szenenanalyse beginnen mit der Wahl derjenigen Daten,
die als Grundelemente ('Primitives') der Verarbeitung dienen. Von ihnen
hängt ab, welche Techniken eingesetzt werden können. Geschickte Wahl der
Daten steigert die Wirksamkeit der Algorihtmen und verringert den Aufwand der Verarbeitung. Bei der Auswahl ist zu beachten, welcher Aufwand
notwendig ist, um die gewünschten Daten aus den ursprünglichen Daten zu
gewinnen. Im Computer liegen die Szenen in einer digitalen Bildmatrix
$I(x,y)$ vor. Als Primitives kann man die ursprünglichen Grau- oder Farb-
werte der Matrixelemente wählen und z.B. durch Histogrammanalysen eine
Segmentation vornehmen /1-3/. Eine andere Möglichkeit besteht darin, den
Inhalt der Matrixelemente in einer Vorverarbeitungsphase in andere Daten
zu überführen. Beispiele solcher Daten sind : die Anwendung von Filtern
/4-5/, Fourier-Analysen /6/, numerische Approximationen /7-8/, oder die
Analyse von Grauwertübergangen /9-10/. Eine dritte Art der Daten sind
solche, die Aussagen uber Zuordnungen zur realen Welt beinhalten, wie
z.B. symbolische Marken /11-12/ oder Wahrscheinlichkeiten von Klassen-
zugehörigkeiten /13-14/.

Allgemein gültige Kriterien für die Auswahl der Daten gibt es nicht.
Durch ihre Erprobung stellen sich jedoch Erfahrungswerte ein, die sich
in intuitiv formulierten Verarbeitungsprinzipien niederschlagen /15-17/.
Diese dienen als Richtlinien fur zukünftige Entwicklungen. Zwei Prinzipien
sind im Zusammenhang mit der Auswahl der Primitives besonders wichtig :
das "Principle of Least Commitment" (PLC) /16/ und das "Prinzip der
heterarchischen Verarbeitung" (PHV) /15/. Das PLC besagt, dass man keine
Interpretation der Daten vornehmen soll, die man später wieder rückgängig
machen muss. Mit anderen Worten : man soll nur soviel Interpretation der
Daten vornehmen, wie notwendig. Das PHV verteilt die Kontrolle über Entscheidungen auf eine Vielzahl von Moduln, die gleichberechtigt auf verschiedenen Kontext-Ebenen miteinander arbeiten. Eine Folge des heterarchischen Informationsflusses ist die Notwendigkeit einer hierachischen
Informationsdarstellung /17/ : nur wenn der Zusammenhang der Informationen
über die Kontext-Ebenen hinweg bekannt ist, können die Moduln sinnvoll
miteinander kommunizieren.

Wählt man die ursprünglichen Daten als Primitives, so tut man zwar dem
PLC Genüge, aber man hat nur wenig spezifische Information für die weitere
Verarbeitung zur Verfügung. Eine hierarchische Informationsdarstellung
ist nur mit grossem Aufwand möglich, etwa durch Pyramidensysteme, in denen

die Szene mit abnehmender Auflösung mehrfach übereinander gespeichert
ist /18-19/. Die Problematik von Daten, die auf Interpretationen der
ursprünglichen Daten beruhen, wird bei der Anwendung von Filtern deutlich.
Ziel der Filterung ist es, bestimmte Eigenschaften hervorzuheben, indem
Teilstrukturen im Intensitätsverlauf auf ihre Übereinstimmung mit vorgegebenen Masken überprüft werden. Zur Detektion aller wichtigen Teilstrukturen muss eine Vielzahl von Masken auf jeden Bildpunkt angewandt
werden, aus deren Ausgabewerten der "beste" ausgewählt wird. Neben der
Schwierigkeit, diesen besten Wert zu finden, tritt das Problem auf, dass
an fast allen Bildpunkten alle Masken Ausgabewerte über Null aufweisen,
da die Filter auch auf den Kontext reagieren, in den die gesuchte Teilstruktur eingebettet ist. Bei der Anwendung von Filtern - wie auch bei
den meisten anderen Verfahren - arbeitet man mit Primitives, die Interpretationen der ursprünglichen Daten sind. Diese werden mit hohem Aufwand erstellt und bergen eine eigene Problematik in sich.

Aus diesem Grund werden hier Verfahren vorgeschlagen, die wir "strukturell
Verfahren" genannt haben : man verwendet die ursprünglichen Daten, indem
man sie durch kontext-bedingte Gruppierungen zu Segmenten zusammenfasst.
Die Segmente entsprechen Teilstrukturen im Intensitätsverlauf und werden
durch rechnerisch günstige Verfahren direkt aus den Daten ermittelt. Da
die Primitives aus Punktmengen bestehen,und nicht mehr aus einzelnen Bildpunkten, lässt sich in natürlicher Weise eine hierarchische Darstellung
einführen.

2. RELATIONAL-BÄUME

In technischen Systemen werden Bilder häufig zeilenweise abgetastet. Es
liegt daher nahe, die ersten Schritte der Bildverarbeitung so zu kon-
zipieren, dass nach Abtasten einer Zeile sofort mit der Verarbeitung an-
gefangen werden kann. Die zeilenweise Verarbeitung bietet den weiteren
Vorteil, dass sie für die heutigen, sequentiell arbeitenden Computer
besonders geeignet ist. Obwohl das Konzept der strukturellen Verfahren
auf zweidimensionalen Strukturen aufbaut, wird der Ansatz aus praktischen
Grunden über die Betrachtung eindimensionaler Grauwertfunktionen durchgeführt. Der Nachteil der eindimensionalen Verarbeitung muss durch eine
zusätzliche Verarbeitung quer zu den Zeilen ausgeglichen werden. Jede
Bildzeile wird als Intensitäts-Profil aufgefasst. Statt also den Hellig-
keitsverlauf der Zeilen zu betrachten, der durch unser eigenes Sehsystem
oft trügerisch einfach aussieht, werden jetzt die Grauwertfunktionen

als Diagramme aufgezeichnet (Bild 1 und 2).

Intuitiv kann ein Intensitäts-Profil (I-Profil) beschrieben werden, indem
man es in Segmente zerlegt und die Segmente zusammen mit ihren gegen-
seitigen Relationen angibt. Die Zerlegung in Segmente erfolgt durch ein
kontext-bedingtes Gruppierungskriterium. Als ursprüngliches Kriterium
war die Relation "PEAK" gewählt worden /20/. Ein PEAK besteht aus Bildpunkten einer lokalen Nachbarschaft δ , die sich um ein lokales Maximum
scharen und die durch das höchste benachbarte lokale Minimum beschränkt
werden. Bild 3a zeigt ein I-Profil und seine Zerlegung in PEAKS : wir
gehen aus von einer I-Verteilung I(x) und betrachten ein lokales Minimum
innerhalb einer Umgebung δ als ein "TAL" V mit Koordinaten $(x^V, I(x^V))$,
wobei :

$$(x^V, I(x^V)) = \min_{I} [\ (x, I(x)\ /\ x\ \epsilon\ [x^V - \frac{\delta}{2},\ x^V + \frac{\delta}{2}]\ ]$$

Zieht man einen waagrechten Strich $y = I(x^V)$ rechts und links von V, so
ergeben sich an den Punkten x, an denen zum ersten Mal $I(x) = I(x^V)$ gilt,
ein rechter Basispunkt R und ein linker Basispunkt L. Für deren
Koordinaten gilt :

$$L = (x^L, I(x^L))\ \ \text{mit}\ \ x^L = \max_{x} [\ x\ /\ I(x) \leq I(x^V)\ \&\ x < x^V\ ]$$

bzw.

$$R = (x^R, I(x^R))\ \ \text{mit}\ \ x^R = \min_{x} [\ x\ /\ I(x) \leq I(x^V)\ \&\ x > x^V\ ]$$

Ein PEAK ist dann die Menge der Bildpunkte, die oberhalb der Basis $[x^L, x^V]$
bzw. $[x^V, x^R]$ liegen :

$$PEAK = \{\ (x, I(x)\ /\ I(x) \geq I(x^V)\ \ \text{f.}\ \ x\ \epsilon\ [x^L, x^V]\ \ \text{bzw.}\ \ x\ \epsilon\ [x^V, x^R]\ \}$$

Ein PEAK hat eine Reihe von Attributen, die leicht berechnet werden können
(Bild 4) :

    (A1)   Die absolute Höhe des I-Maximums, $(x^P, I(x^P))$

    (A2)   Die relative Höhe als : $I(x^P) - I(x^V)$

    (A3)   Die Basisbreite aus : $x^R - x^V$ bzw. $x^V - x^L$

(A4)   Die ausgezeichneten Koordinaten x^L, x^P, x^V bzw. x^V, x^P, x^R

(A5)   Die Fläche des PEAKS :

$$F = \sum_{x^L}^{x^V} I(x) - I(x^V)(x^V - x^L) \quad \text{f. } x^P < x^V$$

(Die Fläche für $x^P > x^V$ berechnet man analog.)

Beim Betrachten des I-Profils in Bild 3a fällt auf, dass PEAKs ineinander verschachtelt sind, wobei bestimmte PEAKs andere "dominieren". Im Beispiel von Bild 3a dominiert P_2 innerhalb der Basis $[x^L 3, x^V 3]$ die PEAKs P_1 und P_3. Die "Dominanz" $D(P_i, P_j)$ - d.h. P_i dominiert P_j - erzeugt eine Ordnung über den PEAKs und führt im Beispiel zu folgendem Ausdruck :

$$D(D(D(P_2, P_3) P_1), D(D(P_5, P_6) P_4)$$

Dieser Klammerausdruck lasst sich unter Berücksichtigung der Reihenfolge der PEAKs durch eine Baumstruktur darstellen, wenn zusätzlich verabredet wird, den dominanten PEAK innerhalb einer Klammer als Repräsentanten der Klammer einzusetzen (siehe Bild 3b). Sonderfälle - wie PEAK-Konfiguratione in denen Dominanz nicht entschieden werden kann - werden durch Zusatz- regeln behandelt. Da die PEAKs durch Relationen der lokalen Maxima und Minima definiert sind und die Baumstruktur Relationen zwischen diesen Relationen wiedergibt, wird der entstehende Baum "Relational-Baum" (R-Baum) genannt. Zusammenfassend kann ein R-Baum folgendermassen definier werden :
"Ein Relational-Baum ist ein Graph, dessen Topologie die Verschachtelung von PEAKs wiedergibt. Diese Verschachtelung wird induziert durch lokale Minima mit zunehmenden Intensitätswerten, die in sich einschliessenden Intervallen des I-Profils liegen. Die Grenzknoten des R-Baumes entspreche PEAKs, die keine weitere Struktur haben und sind durch diese PEAKs markie Nachfolgerknoten entsprechen lokalen Minima und sind mit dem dominanten PEAK des betreffenden Minimums markiert, d.h. mit dem höheren der beiden Vorgänger. Grenz- und Nachfolgerknoten werden entsprechend der Folge der lokalen Minima miteinander verknüpft, bis das absolute Minimum erreicht ist. Der R-Baum kann bottom-up oder top-down konstruiert werden." (Bild 3)

3. EIGENSCHAFTEN VON RELATIONAL-BÄUMEN

Relational-Bäume haben u.a. folgende Eigenschaften :

(E1)   Die Grenzknoten des Baumes stellen eine Beschreibung der PEAKs des I-Profiles von links nach rechts dar, so dass die Topologie des Profiles erhalten bleibt.

(E2)   Obwohl ein PEAK als Marke mehrfach auftreten kann, hat der PEAK-Name bei jedem Auftreten eine andere Bedeutung : jedem Knoten im Baum ist eine "Attributs-Liste" zugeordnet, welche die Attribute A1 - A5 (und eventuell weitere Attribute) enthält. In dieser Liste sind alle notwendigen Informationen über einen PEAK gespeichert.

(E3)   Ein R-Baum induziert eine totale Ordnung über den x-Koordinaten aller Maxima und Minima und eine Halbordnung über den y-Koordinaten derselben. Deshalb zerlegen R-Bäume die Menge der I-Profile in Äquivalenzklassen,deren Elemente sehr unterschiedlicher Form sein können. (Vgl. Bild 5)

(E4)   Wenn man in einem R-Baum von den Grenzknoten in Richtung Wurzel auf einem Weg gleicher Marken läuft, so nehmen die relativen Höhen und die Basisbreiten in den Attributslisten dieser Knoten streng zu. Dadurch sind schnelle Suchverfahren möglich.

4. DER ERZEUGUNGSALGORITHMUS

Durch die Beschränkung auf eindimensionale Grauwertfunktionen ist es möglich, einen schnellen Algorithmus zur Konstruktion der R-Bäume einzusetzen. Der entwickelte Algorithmus arbeitet mit mehreren Stapeln,so dass die Daten on-line ohne aufwendige Zwischenspeicherung verarbeitet werden können. Der Algorithmus durchläuft die Bildzeile von links nach rechts und speichert dabei die Bildpunkte in einem "Punkt"-Stapel, die lokalen Mimima in einem "Tal"-Stapel, und die Maxima in einem "Peak"-Stapel. Durch Vergleiche der jeweils oberen Stapeleintragungen kann der Algorithmus gewissermassen "nach rechts und nach links schauen" und kontextabhangige Entscheidungen treffen. Durch den Einsatz von Stapeln muss nur wenig gerechnet werden. Da sich immer nur wenige Daten in den Stapeln befinden, ist der Aufwand der Zwischenspeicherung gering. Der R-Baum für eine Bildzeile wird während des Zeilendurchlaufes konstruiert. Mit dem

Erreichen des letzten Datenpunktes liegt der R-Baum komplett vor. Die ausführliche Beschreibung des Algorithmus befindet sich in /20/.

Aus dem R-Baum kann mit Hilfe der Baumstruktur und der Information in den Attributslisten der Knoten der Verlauf der Grauwertfunktion rekonstruiert werden. Dies geschieht durch einen Algorithmus, der - von der Wurzel beginnend - die Verschachtelung der PEAKs durch Einsatz eines Stapels auflöst. Nach Auflösung aller Verschachtelungen liegen die ausgezeichneten Punkte x^L, x^P, x^R, sowie x^V aller PEAKs und Täler von links nach rechts geordnet vor. Da die Intensitäten dieser Punkte in der Datenstruktur ge-speichert sind, können alle Grauwerte, die zwischen den gespeicherten Punkten liegen, durch Interpolation gewonnen werden. Dadurch ist es möglich, ein Grauwertbild aus den R-Bäumen aller Bildzeilen zu rekonstru-ieren. Bild 6 und 7 zeigen zwei Beispiele für rekonstruierte Bildzeilen zusammen mit den R-Bäumen der entsprechenden Grauwertfunktionen. Die Ausgabe der R-Bäume auf dem Bildschirm erfolgt ebenfalls durch ein Programm

5. MODIFIKATIONEN

Modifikationen der R-Bäume können in zwei Richtungen vorgenommen werden. Einerseits konnen weitere Strukturen durch zusätzliche Gruppierungs-kriterien berücksichtigt werden, andrerseits kann das Konzept des R-Baumes vereinfacht werden, um den Speicherbedarf zu verringern. Im zweiten Fall kann man zum Beispiel auf die Baumstruktur verzichten und mit einer ein-fachen Liste arbeiten, die die PEAKs und ihre Attribute enthält. In besonderen Fällen reicht dies z.B. für Textur-Analysen aus. Die Erweiterun von R-Bäumen auf andere Strukturen wird exemplarisch am Beispiel von PLATEAUs gezeigt.

Bild 8 zeigt, dass homogene Flächen im I-Profil weniger als PEAK, sondern vielmehr als PLATEAU auftreten. PLATEAUs sind Punktgruppen, die durch einen I-Verlauf mit einem Gradienten nahe Null gekennzeichnet sind. Sie müssen durch Detektion der Änderung des Gradienten bestimmt werden. Zu diesem Zweck wird der Erkennungsmechanismus des Algorithmus durch einen "Gradienten-Sensor" erweitert. Dieser Sensor wird aktiviert und trifft Entscheidungen, solange bis ein lokaler Extremwert erreicht wird. Bei Detektion von Extremwerten durch den "Intensitäts-Sensor" wird der "Gradienten-Sensor" de-aktiviert und nach Überschreiten des Extremwertes neu gestartet. Während seiner aktiven Phase werden Änderungen des Gradien-ten detektiert. Bei Detektion von Knickstellen mit einem Gradienten nahe

Null werden alle folgenden Datenpunkte in einen "PLATEAU-Stapel" geschoben, bis eine weitere Knickstelle detektiert wird. Nach Erreichen
der zweiten Knickstelle werden die entsprechenden Punkte zu einem
PLATEAU zusammengefasst und der "PLATEAU-Stapel" geleert. Gleichzeitig
wird das PLATEAU als virtueller PEAK in den "PEAK-Stapel" eingetragen
und ein entsprechendes virtuelles "Tal" am Rand des PLATEAUs in den
"Tal-Stapel" geschoben. Durch die Einführung von virtuellen PEAKs über
den PLATEAUs ist es möglich, PLATEAUs nahtlos in das Konzept der R-Bäume
einzugliedern. Als absolute Höhe wird die Intensität des PLATEAUs eingetragen, als Basisbreite die Länge des PLATEAUs , während die relative
Höhe und die Fläche gleich Null sind (Bild 9). Durch diese Erweiterung
können neben Änderungen im I-Verlauf auch Änderungen des Gradienten
detektiert und beschrieben werden.

6. ANWENDUNGEN UND DIE WEITERE VERARBEITUNG

Die folgende Erörterung ist nicht um Details bemüht, sondern versucht,
den Stil der weiteren Verarbeitung und die damit verbundenen Möglichkeiten der Anwendungen herauszustellen. Nach Erzeugung der R-Bäume aller
Bildzeilen eines Grauwertbildes liegt eine Repräsentation des Bildes in
symbolischer Form vor. Diese ist Ausgangspunkt aller weiteren Verarbeitungsschritte. Analog zu den eingangs erwähnten Verfahren, die mit den
ursprünglichen Grauwerten arbeiten, können die PEAKs der R-Bäume als
Eingangsdaten von Verarbeitungsalgorithmen aufgefasst werden. Ein Beispiel
hierfür sind Histogramm-Analysen, die ähnliche Ergebnisse wie die
'Gray-Level-Adjacency-Matrices' von HARALICK et al. /9/ liefern (Bild 10).
Aus der hierarchischen Datenstruktur lassen sich sowohl Mikro- als auch
Makro-Texturen und die Zusammenhänge zwischen ihnen herauslesen. Es ist
eines der Ziele dieses Ansatzes, zu modellieren, wie Mikrotextur in
Makrotextur übergeht. Dies läuft auf die Aufgabe hinaus, Bildregionen
mit Textur auf verschiedenen Auflösungsniveaus zu definieren und festzustellen, wie man von einer Auflösungsebene zur anderen gelangt. Elemente
von Mikrotexturen sind in den Grenzknoten des Baumes enthalten, während
Elemente von Makrotexturen sich in den Knoten in der Nähe der Wurzel befinden /21/. Zur Bestimmung dieser Knoten werden wieder Gruppierungs-
mechanismen verwendet. Diese Mechanismen führen zu Transformationen, in
denen benachbarte PEAKs zu PEAK-Gruppen zusammengefasst werden. Ein
Beispiel für eine solche Transformation kann an der Teilstruktur "Stamm"
gezeigt werden : im I-Profil ist ein "Stamm" ein dominanter PEAK, der
einige Neben-PEAKs an den Flanken hat, wobei die Minima nach rechts und

links abnehmende Werte haben. Im R-Baum ist ein "Stamm" dann folgendermassen definiert : "Der 'Weg eines Stammes' ist ein Weg entlang von
Knoten einer identischen Marke. Ein 'Stamm' besteht dann aus allen Knoten
und Kanten, die vom Weg des Stammes bis zur Grenze reichen." (Bild 11)
Histogramm-Analysen dieser Teilstrukturen zeigen dann Textureigenschaften
der entsprechenden Makrotexturelemente (Bild 12). Experimente zeigen,
dass aus den Merkmalen der PEAK-Gruppen brauchbare Textur-Deskriptoren
abgeleitet werden können.

Die Transformationen führen eine Verarbeitung entlang der Zeilen durch.
Zusätzlich bleibt zu erörtern, wie die Verarbeitung quer zu den Zeilen
verläuft. Die Verarbeitung quer zu den Zeilen muss die zwei-dimensionale
Information der Bildregionen erarbeiten. Dies geschieht, indem Teilstrukturen - wie die oben erwähnten PEAKgruppen oder einzelne PEAKs -
über mehrere Zeilen hinweg verfolgt werden. Der Vorgang in dieser Ver-
arbeitungsrichtung wird "Profilverfolgung" genannt. Die Aufgabe der
Profilverfolgung ist, für Elemente in der Datenstruktur einer Zeile den
Anschluss an Elemente der benachbarten Zeilen zu finden und diese Elemente
durch Zeiger miteinander zu verknüpfen. Dabei genügt es, die Verknüpfungen
bis zu einer Kontext-Ebene durchzuführen, die für den betreffenden An-
wendungsfall (z.B. Objektlokalisation) ausreicht. Bevorzugt werden zunächst Knoten in der Nähe der Wurzel, da diese Datenobjekte grossen
Regionen in den Bildzeilen entsprechen und dadurch leicht zu verfolgen
sind. Bei der Profilverfolgung werden - wieder mit Hilfe eines Stapel-
Algorithmus - lokale Minima, Maxima und PLATEAUs beachtet. Die Verzeigerung wird solange fortgesetzt, bis man das Ende eines PLATEAUs oder
ein lokales Minimum erreicht hat. Während der Verzeigerung wird aus den
x^L und x^R der betreffenden Knoten die Umrisslinie der verfolgten Region,
aus den Attributen die Fläche, mittlere Intensität, Kontrast, Textur,etc.
ermittelt. Mit diesen Informationen wird entschieden, ob die Analyse ausreicht oder ob eine Verzeigerung von Knoten notwendig ist, die ferner von
der Wurzel sind - also auf einer niedrigeren Kontext-Ebene liegen. Bild 13
zeigt den Anschluss von PEAKs und "Tälern" zwischen zwei Bildzeilen,
Bild 14 stellt die Verzeigerung von Regionen über mehrere R-Bäume hinweg
dar.

7. DISKUSSION

Die Darstellung von Bildzeilen durch Relational-Bäume führt Grauwert-
bilder in eine symbolische Repräsentation über. Durch das hier vorgestellte Konzept wird die Bildmatrix in Zeilen bzw. Spaltenrichtung
unterschiedlich verarbeitet. In Zeilenrichtung werden Bildpunkte in Abhängigkeit des Kontextes ihrer Grauwerte zu Einheiten zusammengefasst.
Durch den Einsatz kontext-bedingter Gruppierungskriterien unterscheidet
sich der Ansatz von einem anderen Verfahren, bei dem Bäume zur Darstellung
von Konturlinien auf fest vorgegebenen Grauwertstufen benutzt werden /22/.
Durch die Verschachtelung von Punktgruppen - den PEAKs - wird jede Bildzeile in Kontext-Ebenen gegliedert, die von lokaler Information (Grauwert
eines Punktes) bis zu globaler Information (Struktur der Bildzeile) reicht.
Diese Darstellung wird in einem Durchlauf aus den Daten aufgebaut. Die
anschliessende Verarbeitung quer zu den Zeilen berücksichtigt nicht mehr
alle Datenpunkte, sondern nur einen Teil derjenigen Punktgruppen, die in
Zeilenrichtung zusammengefasst werden. Diese Verknüpfung kann auf verschiedenen Kontext-Ebenen arbeiten und dabei lokale und globale Informationen berücksichtigen. In dieser Richtung ist Verarbeitung in einem Durchlauf nicht immer möglich, da es zu Rücksprüngen, neuen Starts und Korrekturen kommen kann. Dass es sich dabei um ein Konzept handelt, das spei-
cheraufwendig ist, liegt in der Natur der Sache : dem PLC folgend werden
auf jeder Verarbeitungsstufe nur vorsichtige Interpretationen vorgenommen
und die Reduktion unwichtiger Information schreitet zuerst langsam und
dann schneller voran. Die strukturelle Betrachtungsweise erlaubt den
Einsatz von rechnerisch günstigen Verfahren.

8. LITERATUR

/1/   CHOW, C.K.   Automatic Boundary Detection Of The Left
      KANEKO, T.   Ventricle From Cineangiograms.
                             J. of Comp. Biomed. Res. $\underline{5}$(1972),388-410

/2/   HANSON, A.R.   Region Growing In Textured Outdoor Scenes.
      RISEMAN, E.M.   COINS TR 75c-2, Univ. of Mass., Amherst,1975
      NAGIN, P.

/3/   OHLANDER, R.B.   Analysis Of Natural Scenes.
                             Dept. of Comp. Sc., Carnegie-Mellon-Univ.,
                             Pittsburg, Ph.D. Thesis, 1975

/4/ ZUCKER, S.W. Picture Segmentation By Texture Discriminatior
     ROSENFELD, A. Picture Processing Lab. TR-356, Univ. of
     DAVIS, L.S. Maryland, College Park, 1975

/5/ MARR, D. The Low-Level Symbolic Representation Of
     Intensity Changes In An Image.
     MIT Artificial Intelligence Memo 325, Cambridç
     Mass., 1974

/6/ BAJCSY, R. Computer Description Of Textured Surfaces.
     Proc. of 3rd IJCAI Aug. 1973,pp. 572-579

/7/ PAVLIDIS, T. Segmentation Of Pictures And Maps Through
     Functional Approximation.
     Computer Graphics & Image Processing $\underline{1}$(1972),
     pp. 360-372

/8/ HOROWITZ, S.L. Picture Segmentation By A Directed Split-And-
     PAVLIDIS, T. Merge Procedure.
     Proc. 2nd IJCPR, Copenhagen, 1974, pp. 497-49ς

/9/ HARALICK, R.M. Textural Features For Image Classification.
     SHANMUGAN, K. IEEE Trans. SMC $\underline{3}$(1973),pp. 610-621
     DINSTEIN, I.

/10/ DEUTSCH, E.S. Texture Description Using Neighborhood
     BELKNAP, N.J. Information.
     Computer Graphics & Image Processing (1972),
     pp. 145-168

/11/ GUZMAN, A. Computer Recognition Of Three-Dimensional
     Objects In A Visual Scene.
     MIT Thesis,AI Lab., Cambridge, Mass, 1968

/12/ WALTZ, D. Understanding Line Drawings Of Scenes With
     Shadows.
     in /15/

/13/ YAKIMOVSKY, Y. A Semantics-Based Decision Theory Region
     FELDMAN, J. Analyzer.
     Proc. 3rd IJCAI 1973, pp.580-588

/14/ ROSENFELD, A. Scene Labelling By Relaxation Operations.
     HUMMEL, R.A. Picture Processing Lab. TR 379, Univ. of
     ZUCKER, S.W. Maryland, College Park, 1975

/15/ WINSTON, P. The Psychology Of Computer Vision.
     (Hrsg.) McGraw-Hill Book Company., N.Y. 1975

/16/ MARR, D. Analyzing Natural Images.
     MIT AI Memo 334, Cambridge, Mass.,1975

/17/ FOITH, J.P. Prinzipien der Szenenanalyse beim Menschen
     und im Computer.
     IITB-Mitteilungen 1976 , IITB, Fraunhofer-
     Gesellschaft, Karlsuhe

/18/ HANSON, A.R. Preprocessing Cones : A Computational
     RISEMAN, E.M. Structure For Scene Analysis.
     COINS TR 74c-7,Univ. of Mass., Amherst, 1974

/19/ TANIMOTO, S.   A Hierarchical Data Structure For Picture
      PAVLIDIS, T.   Processing.
                           Computer Graphics & Image Proc. $\underline{4}$(1975),
                           pp. 104-119

/20/ EHRICH, R.W.   Representation Of Random Waveforms By
      FOITH, J.P.   Relational Trees.
                           IEEE Trans. on Comp. C-25(1976), July,
                           pp. 725-736

/21/ EHRICH, R.W.   A View Of Texture Topology And Texture
      FOITH, J.P.   Description.
                           ECE Report, Univ. of Mass, Amherst, Mass.,1975

/22/ KRAKAUER, L.   Computer Analysis Of Visual Properties Of
                           Curved Objects.
                           MIT Report, AI Lab., Cambridge, Mass. 1971

9. ABBILDUNGEN

BILD 1 : Ein Grauwertbild

BILD 2 : Bildzeilen aus Bild 1 als Intensitäts-Profile

BILD 3 : a) Ein Intensitäts-Profil
          b) Top-Down Konstruktion des entsprechenden R-Baumes

BILD 4 : PEAK-Attribute

BILD 5 : Zwei I-Profile mit identischer Baumstruktur

BILD 6 : a) Original I-Profil
          b) Rekonstruiertes I-Profil aus der Datenstruktur
          c) R-Baum

BILD 7 : wie Bild 6

BILD 8 : I-Profile von Bildzeilen aus Bild 1 : die homogenen Flächen
          der Kondensatoren treten als Plateaus in den I-Profilen auf.

BILD 9 : Die Einführung von virtuellen Peaks über Plateaus

BILD 10: Drei Texturen :
          a) Moos I   b) Moos II   c) Kleiderstoff
          d) Zweidimensionale Histogramme für Grenzknoten der Basisbreite
              3-4 (Der Nullpunkt liegt in der linken oberen Ecke ,
              x-Achse = absolute Höhen, y-Achse = relative Höhen)

BILD 11: "Stamm"-Transformation : (0) original I-Profil
          (1) nach der ersten Anwendung (2) nach der zweiten Anwendung

BILD 12: Zweidimensionale Histogramme von "Stamm-Knoten" (Legende wie
          Bild 10) :   (a) Knoten mit Basisbreite 5-8
                        (b) Konten mit Basisbreiten 17-32

BILD 13: Zeiger zwischen benachbarten Peaks und Tälern

BILD 14: Die Verzeigerung von benachbarten R-Bäumen

BILD 1

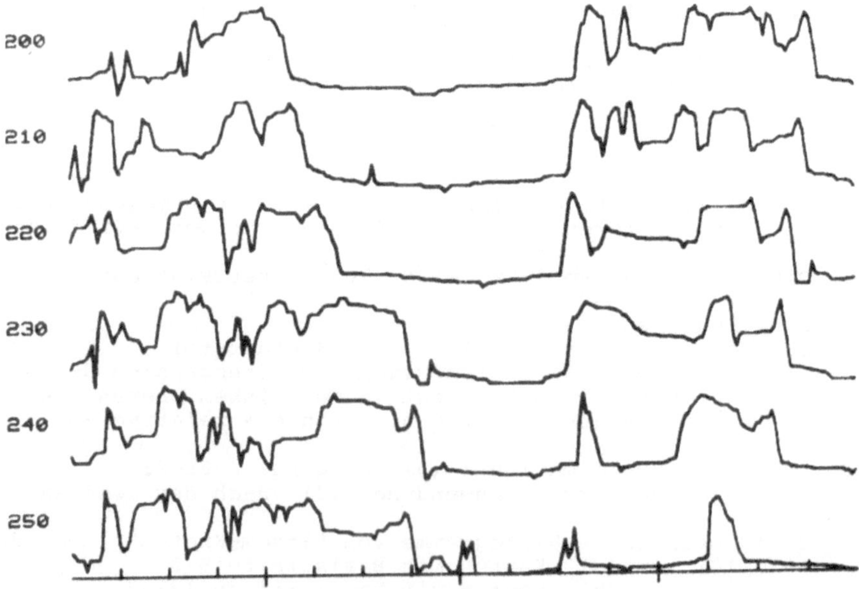

BILD 2

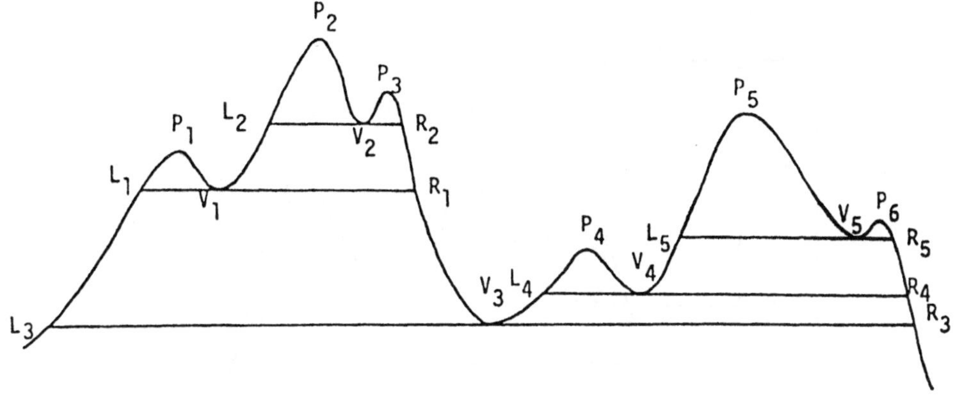

<u>BILD 3a</u>

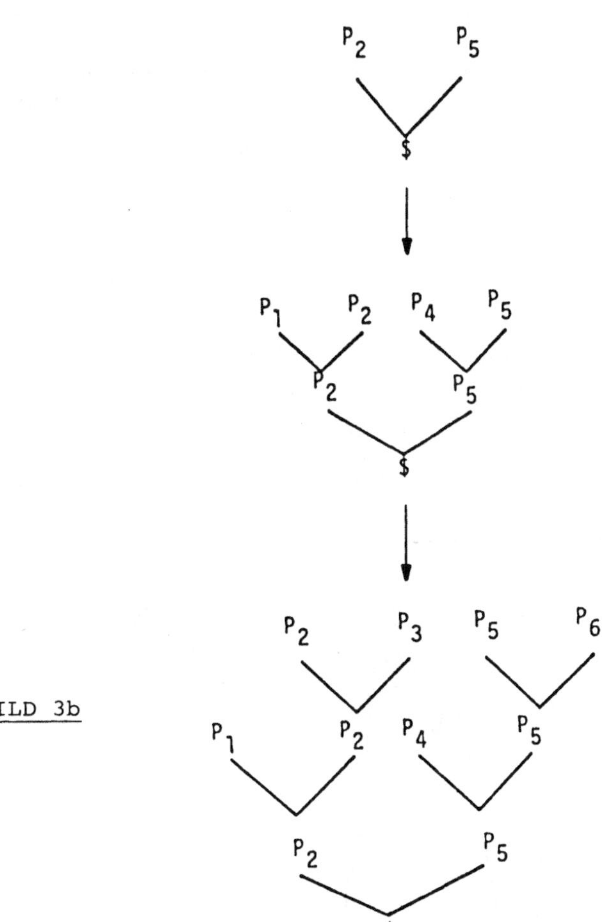

<u>BILD 3b</u>

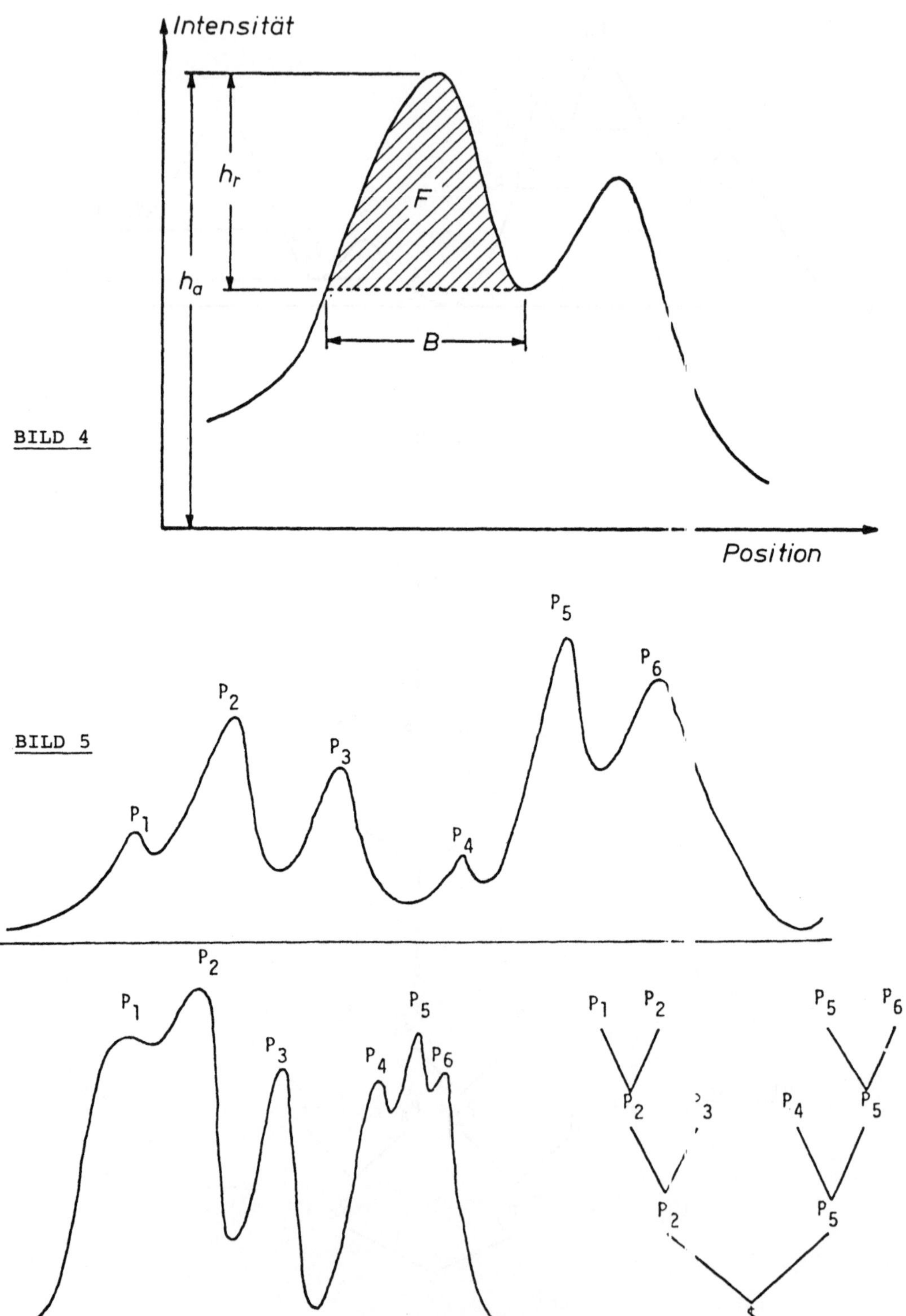

Intensität
h_r
F
h_a
B
Position
BILD 4
BILD 5
P_1
P_2
P_3
P_4
P_5
P_6
P_1
P_2
P_3
P_4
P_5
P_6
P_1
P_2
P_5
P_6
P_2
P_4
P_5
P_2
P_5
$

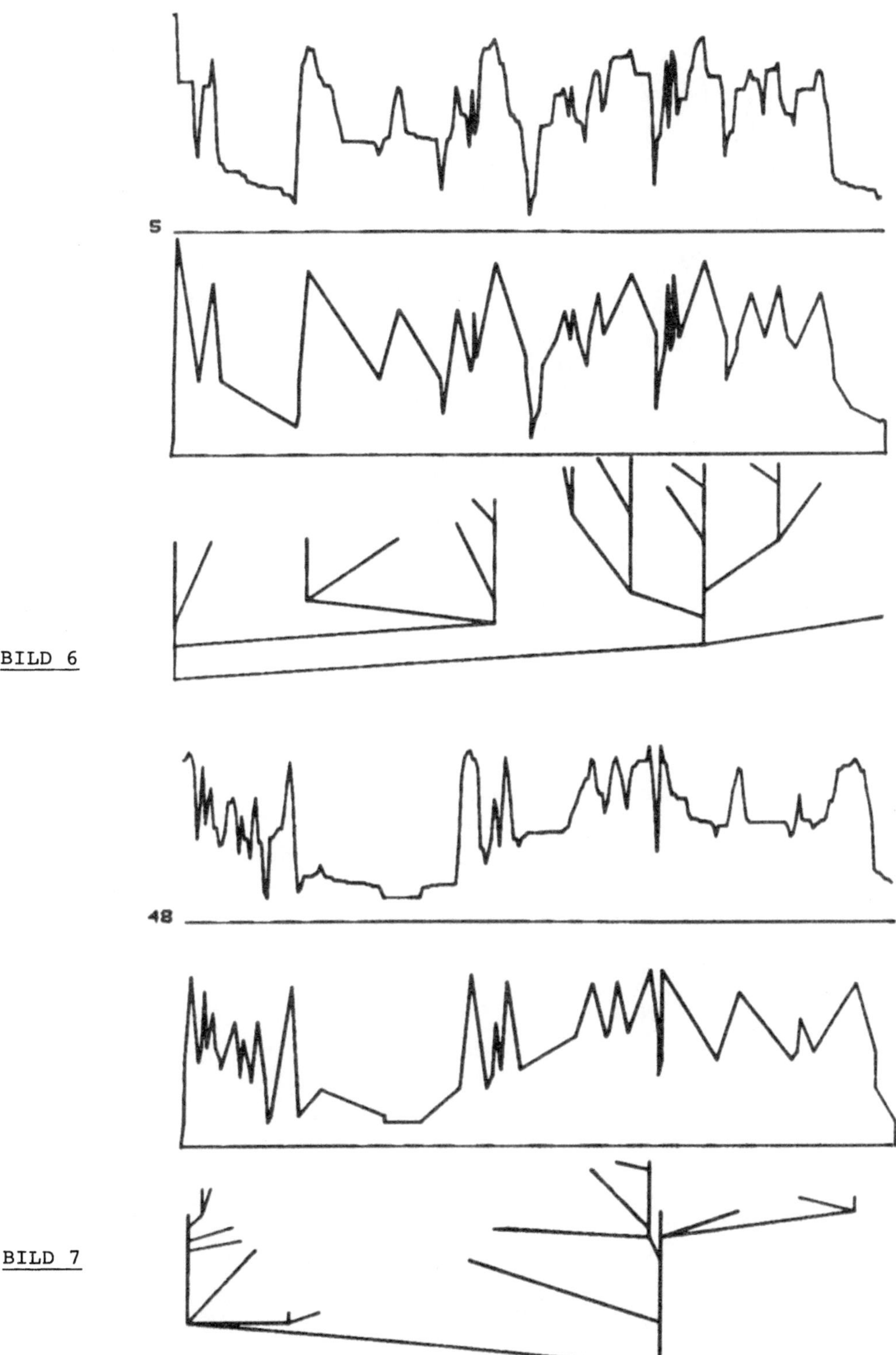
S
48
BILD 6
BILD 7

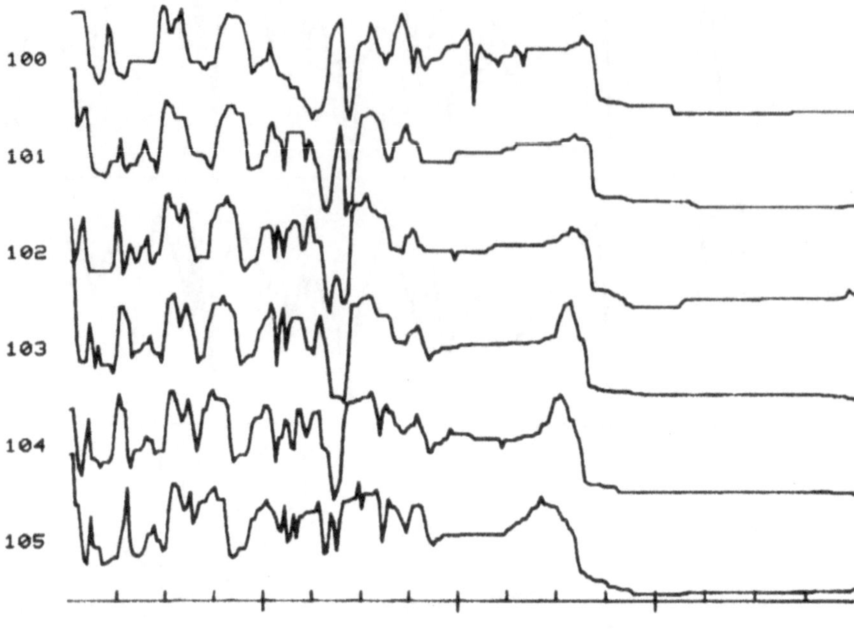

BILD 8

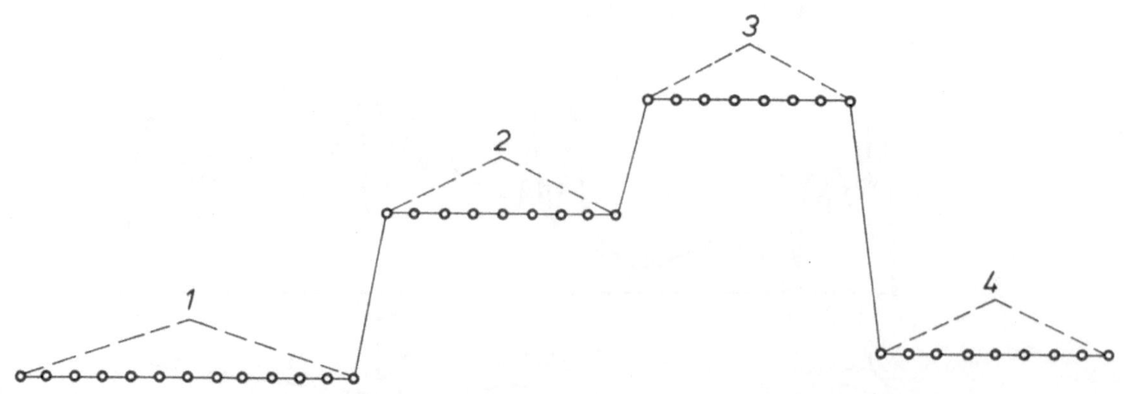

BILD 9

BILD 10a

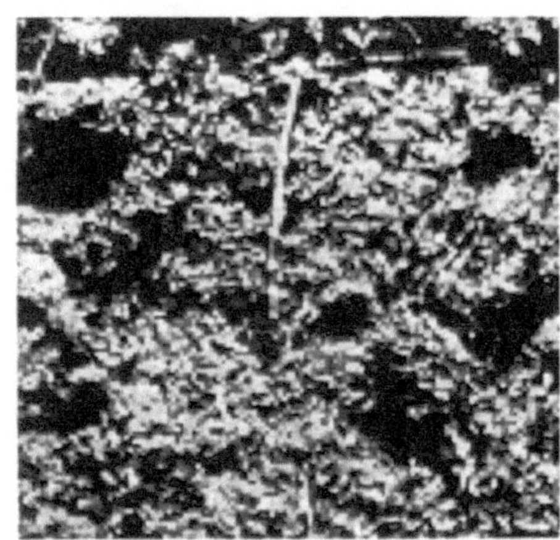

BILD 10b

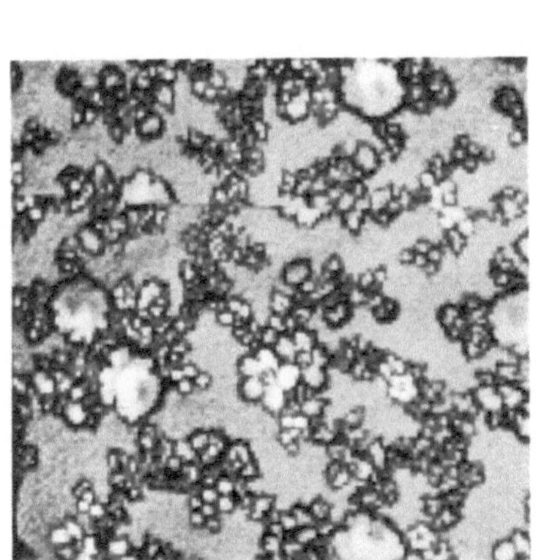

BILD 10c

```
                              LINES AND COLUMNS

    Y-Coordinate Rel Height,    X-Coordinate ABS Height      0-160 In Steps of 16

      148     205      58      43      50      88     114     115      26       1    848
        0      18     108      82     115     160     261     241      92       5   1082
        0       0      19      61      96     140     217     257     107       6    903
        0       0       0       3      57      93     151     175      82      17    578
(a)     0       0       0       0       4      37      71      81      59       5    257
        0       0       0       0       0       2      14      55      25       4    100
        0       0       0       0       0       0       2      13       0       3     26
        0       0       0       0       0       0       0       0       0       0      0
        0       0       0       0       0       0       0       0       0       0      0
        0       0       0       0       0       0       0       0       0       0      0

      148     223     185     189     322     520     830     937     399      41
    Width From 3 to 4            Matrix Sum = 3794

    Y-Coordinate Rel Height,    X-Coordinate ABS Height      0-160 In Steps of 16

       56     112      49      50     105     204     183      54       0       0    813
        0      16      77     100     173     390     433     187       7       0   1303
        0       0       9      60     141     253     356     157       9       0    985
        0       0       0      12      76     116     172      93       7       0    476
(b)     0       0       0       0       6      37      52      43       7       0    145
        0       0       0       0       0       3      24      15       3       0     45
        0       0       0       0       0       0       2       1       0       0      3
        0       0       0       0       0       0       0       0       0       0      0
        0       0       0       0       0       0       0       0       0       0      0
        0       0       0       0       0       0       0       0       0       0      0

       56     128     135     222     501    1003    1222     550      33       0
    Width from 3 to 4            Matrix Sum = 3850

    Y-Coordinate Rel Height,    X-Coordinate ABS Height      0-160 In Steps of 16

        0       0       1      35     156     205     857     905      21      20   2200
        0       0       0       2      94     293     377     142      33      11    952
        0       0       0       0       6      56     264     178      55      20    579
        0       0       0       0       0       4      35      67      61      17    184
(c)     0       0       0       0       0       0       4       8      18       9     39
        0       0       0       0       0       0       0       0       1       0      1
        0       0       0       0       0       0       0       0       0       0      0
        0       0       0       0       0       0       0       0       0       0      0
        0       0       0       0       0       0       0       0       0       0      0
        0       0       0       0       0       0       0       0       0       0      0

        0       0       1      37     256     558    1537    1300     189      77
    Width from 3 to 4            Matrix Sum = 3955
```

BILD 10d

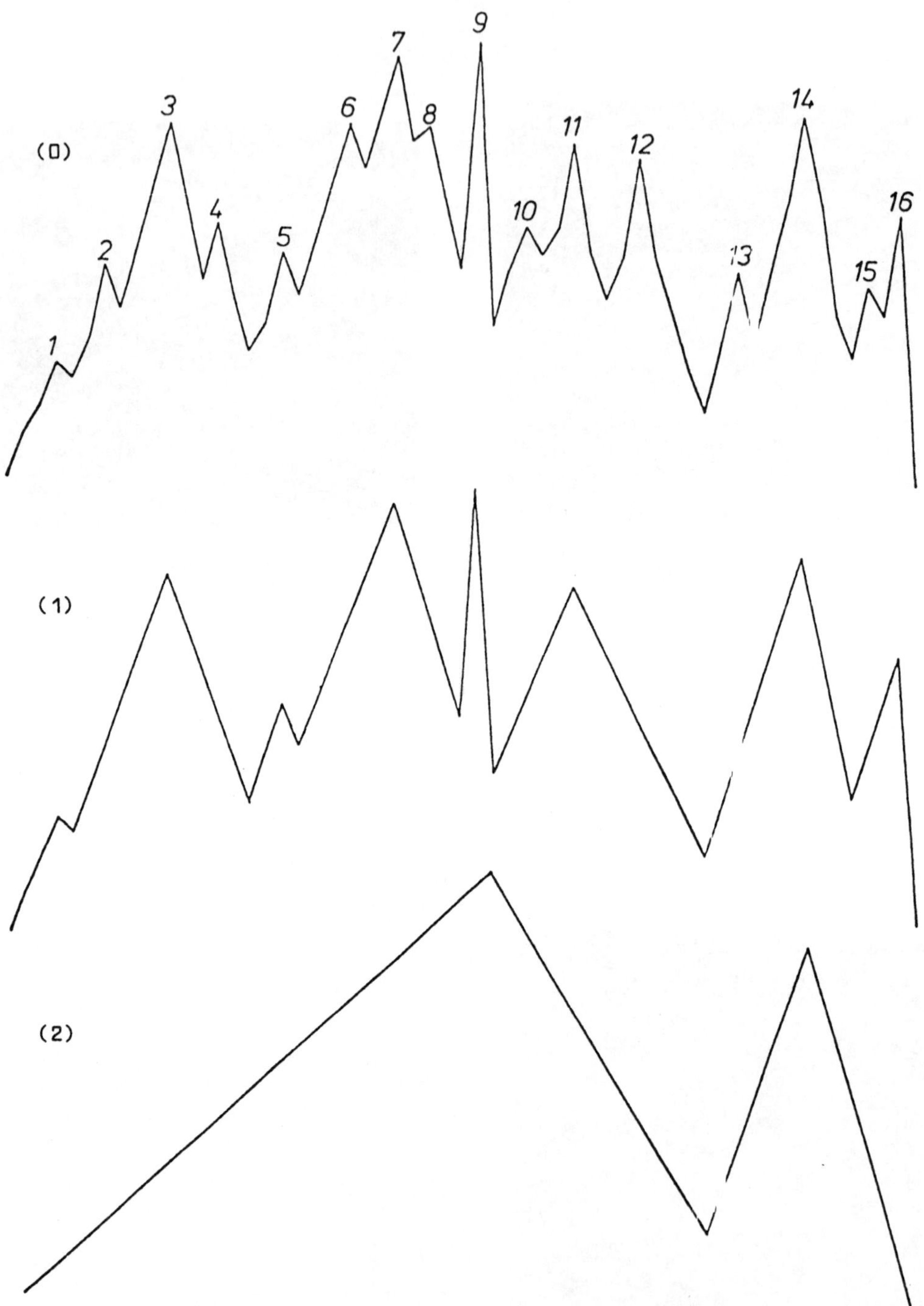

BILD 11

LINES AND COLUMNS

Y-Coordinate Rel Height,   X-Coordinate ABS Height   0-160 In Steps of 16

(a)

										Σ
31	28	3	0	0	5	4	1	0	0	72
0	13	29	8	7	10	29	24	8	0	128
0	0	11	27	21	39	73	56	14	0	241
0	0	0	6	39	49	100	76	15	0	285
0	0	0	0	14	42	94	83	23	0	256
0	0	0	0	0	18	89	119	27	0	253
0	0	0	0	0	0	33	147	45	1	226
0	0	0	0	0	0	0	68	103	0	171
0	0	0	0	0	0	0	0	18	3	21
0	0	0	0	0	0	0	0	0	0	0
31	41	43	41	81	163	422	574	253	4	

Width from 5 to 8   Matrix Sum = 1653

Y-Coordinate Rel Height,   X-Coordinate ABS Height   0-160 In Steps of 16

(b)

										Σ
4	8	1	0	1	3	9	1	0	0	27
0	9	14	10	16	44	68	16	0	0	177
0	0	8	28	45	121	135	26	0	0	363
0	0	0	4	57	105	162	38	1	0	367
0	0	0	0	12	104	172	46	0	0	334
0	0	0	0	0	18	217	82	0	0	317
0	0	0	0	0	0	58	154	2	0	214
0	0	0	0	0	0	0	27	1	0	28
0	0	0	0	0	0	0	0	0	0	0
0	0	0	0	0	0	0	0	0	0	0
4	17	23	42	131	395	821	390	4	0	

Width from 5 to 8   Matrix Sum = 1827

Y-Coordinate Rel Height,   X-Coordinate ABS Height   0-160 In Steps of 16

(c)

										Σ
0	0	0	0	11	13	157	178	0	0	359
0	0	0	0	26	94	103	62	2	3	290
0	0	0	0	2	63	215	141	2	0	423
0	0	0	0	0	10	153	208	10	0	381
0	0	0	0	0	0	26	104	19	1	150
0	0	0	0	0	0	1	13	24	4	42
0	0	0	0	0	0	0	1	4	2	7
0	0	0	0	0	0	0	0	0	0	0
0	0	0	0	0	0	0	0	0	0	2
0	0	0	0	0	0	0	0	0	0	0
0	0	0	0	39	180	655	707	61	10	

Width From 5 to 8   Matrix Sum = 1652

BILD 12a

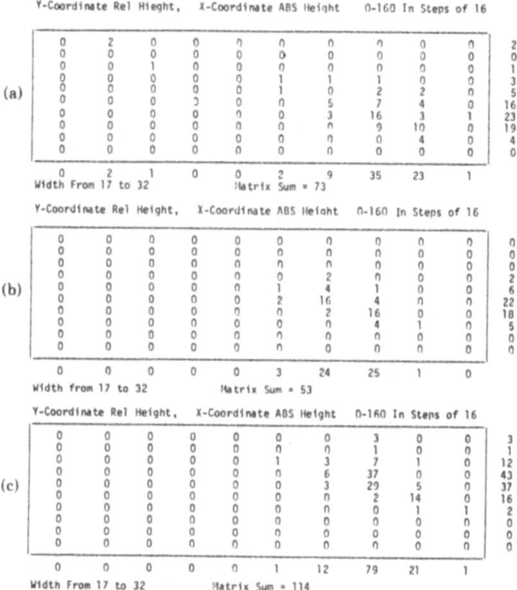

LINES AND COLUMNS

Y-Coordinate Rel Hieght,   X-Coordinate ABS Height   0-160 In Steps of 16

(a)

										Σ
0	2	0	0	0	0	0	0	0	0	2
0	0	0	0	0	0	0	0	0	0	0
0	0	1	0	0	0	0	0	0	0	1
0	0	0	0	0	1	1	1	0	0	3
0	0	0	0	0	1	0	2	2	0	5
0	0	0	0	0	0	5	7	4	0	16
0	0	0	0	0	0	3	16	3	1	23
0	0	0	0	0	0	0	9	10	0	19
0	0	0	0	0	0	0	0	4	0	4
0	0	0	0	0	0	0	0	0	0	0
0	2	1	0	0	2	9	35	23	1	

Width From 17 to 32   Matrix Sum = 73

Y-Coordinate Rel Height,   X-Coordinate ABS Height   0-160 In Steps of 16

(b)

										Σ
0	0	0	0	0	0	0	0	0	0	0
0	0	0	0	0	0	0	0	0	0	0
0	0	0	0	0	0	0	0	0	0	0
0	0	0	0	0	0	2	0	0	0	2
0	0	0	0	0	1	4	1	0	0	6
0	0	0	0	0	2	16	4	0	0	22
0	0	0	0	0	0	2	16	0	0	18
0	0	0	0	0	0	0	4	1	0	5
0	0	0	0	0	0	0	0	0	0	0
0	0	0	0	0	0	0	0	0	0	0
0	0	0	0	0	3	24	25	1	0	

Width from 17 to 32   Matrix Sum = 53

Y-Coordinate Rel Height,   X-Coordinate ABS Height   0-160 In Steps of 16

(c)

										Σ
0	0	0	0	0	0	0	3	0	0	3
0	0	0	0	0	0	0	1	0	0	1
0	0	0	0	0	1	3	7	1	0	12
0	0	0	0	0	0	6	37	0	0	43
0	0	0	0	0	0	3	29	5	0	37
0	0	0	0	0	0	0	2	14	0	16
0	0	0	0	0	0	0	0	1	1	2
0	0	0	0	0	0	0	0	0	0	0
0	0	0	0	0	0	0	0	0	0	0
0	0	0	0	0	0	0	0	0	0	0
0	0	0	0	0	1	12	79	21	1	

Width From 17 to 32   Matrix Sum = 114

BILD 12b

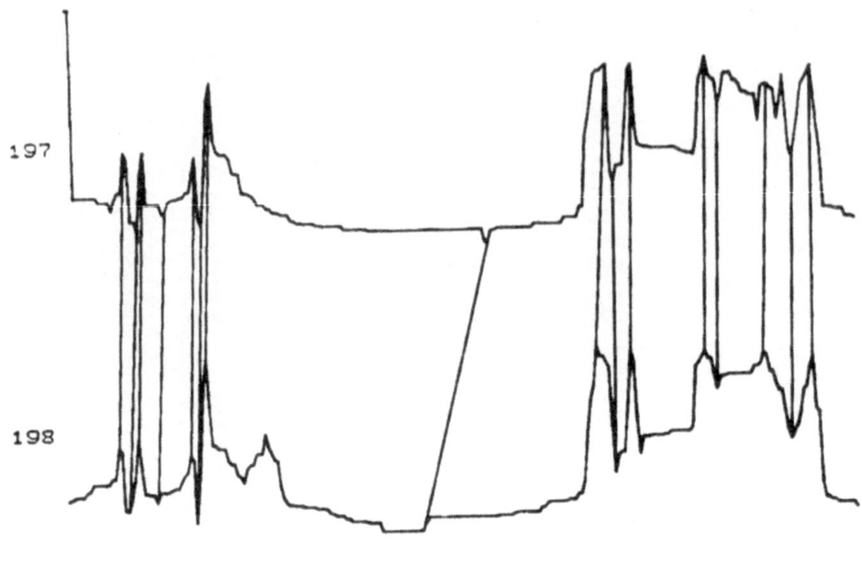

BILD 13

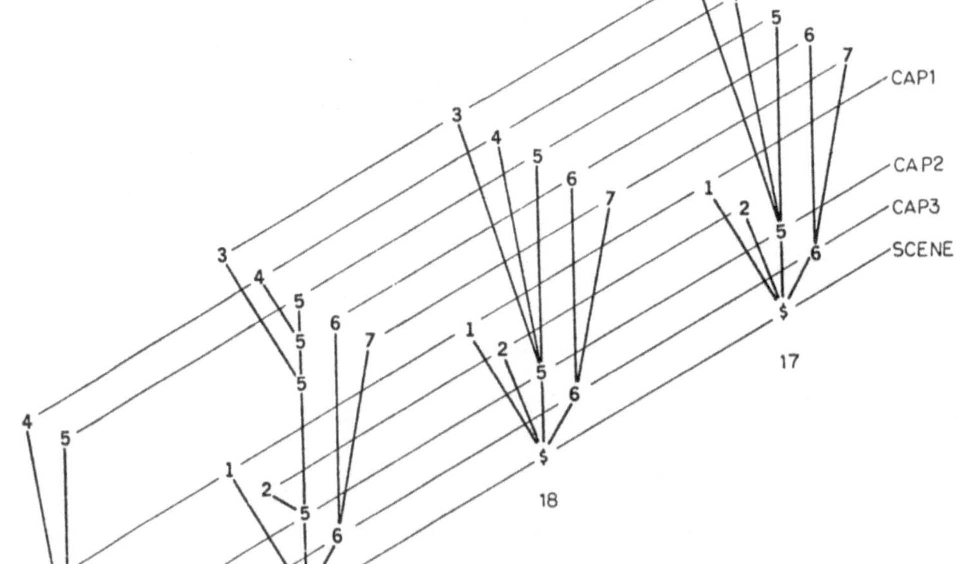

BILD 14

<u>Kontextunterstützte Analyse von Szenen mit bewegten Objekten</u>

R. Bertelsmeier, B. Radig
Institut für Informatik, Universität Hamburg

1. Übersicht

Der Versuch, statische Szenen zu erkennen, begann mit heuristischen Programmen, die auf eine spezielle Klasse von Szenen, die "Blocks-World" zugeschnitten waren /1,2/. Eine Verallgemeinerung dieser heuristischen Ansätze durch Formulierung von graphähnlichen Modellen wurde in /3,4/ dargestellt. Eine Erweiterung der Komplexität der Vorlagen auf natürliche Szenen begann mit den Arbeiten von Yakimovsky, Ohlander und Shirai /5,6,7/. Gleichzeitig vollzog sich der Übergang von heuristischen Programmen zur Formalisierung der Beschreibung von Segmentierung, Modellbildung und Interpretation der Szene /8/.

Die Erkennung bewegter Objekte in Szenenfolgen wurde bisher vernachlässigt. Es sind nur wenige Arbeiten bekannt, die sich auf wenige, vorzugsweise auf einfache Objekte (polygonal begrenzt) /9/, sehr eingeschränkte Szenen /10/ oder auf den Vergleich von Folgebildern beschränken /11, 12/. Eine andere Richtung der Entwicklung verzichtet auf die Interpretation realer Grauwert-Bilder und geht von einer vollständigen symbolischen Beschreibung der Szenenfolge aus. Daraus wird eine zutreffende, sprachliche Beschreibung der Bewegung der Objekte konstruiert /13,14/. Dabei wird die Erzeugung einer vollständigen und exakten symbolischen Objektbeschreibung aus einem digitisierten Bild als nicht lösbar beim gegenwärtigen Stand der Technik eingeschätzt.

Unser Vorschlag versucht, die formalen Ansätze der statischen Szenenanalyse mit den Möglichkeiten, die sich durch die Benutzung von zeitlichem Kontext eröffnen, zu verbinden. Unser Ziel ist weniger, komplexe natürliche Szenenfolgen zu analysieren, als vielmehr erst einmal die Bedeutung von örtlichem und zeitlichem Kontext für die Szenenanalyse aufzuzeigen. Wir halten ihn für besonders wichtig für die Analyse von realen Grauwertbildern, wenn man die Schwierigkeiten betrachtet, die durch die Digitisierung und die damit verbundene beschränkte Auflösung und die nicht ideale Segmentierung entstehen.

2. Definition des Szenenanalyse-Systems

Um unser Szenenanalyse-System zu beschreiben, werden seine Aufgaben
und die vorausgesetzten Annahmen beschrieben /32/.

2.1 Definitionen

<u>Bild</u>: Grauwertmatrix, bestehend aus Pixeln, gewonnen durch die Abbil-
dung der Szene über die Optik einer Kamera auf deren zweidimensionale
Sensorfläche und Digitisieren des Videosignals.

<u>Pixel</u>: Einzelnes Element des Bildes als Meßwert für die Lichtintensi-
tät an einem Ort der Szene; Tripel (G,i,j), das den Grauwert $(0 \leq G \leq 255)$
an der horizontalen Position i $(1 \leq i \leq 512)$ und der vertikalen Position
j $(1 \leq j \leq 573)$ beschreibt.

<u>Sensor</u>: Schwarzweiß-Fernsehkamera (CCIR-Norm), deren Videosignal von
einem an einen Prozeßrechner angeschlossenen Analog-Digital-Wandler
(100 nsec Konversionszeit) zum Bild umgeformt wird. Die Abbildung der
Szene auf das Bild ist in erster Näherung linear bezüglich Lichtinten-
sität und Geometrie, aber vom Bild läßt sich nicht umkehrbar eindeutig
auf die Szene schließen.

<u>Szene</u>: Ausschnitt aus einer Miniwelt, der vom Sensor erfaßt wird.

<u>Miniwelt</u>: Menge aller Konfigurationen einer endlichen Anzahl einfacher
Realobjekte (Abb. 2).

<u>Realobjekt</u>: Undurchsichtiges Objekt mit einfacher Struktur der Kontur
und Oberfläche.

<u>Skizze</u>: Relationalstruktur mit einer Trägermenge, bestehend aus Ort,
Fleck, Kontur, Gerade, Kreisbogen mit einstelligen Relationen (Eigenschaften) und zweistelligen Relationen (geometrischer Kontext).

<u>Bildobjekt</u>: Teilmenge des Bildes (i.a. ein Bereich benachbarter Pixel),
die ein Realobjekt der Szene repräsentiert. Zu ein und demselben Realobjekt können in verschiedenen Bildern verschiedene Bildobjekte gehören (Einfluß von Rauschen und Beleuchtungsschwankungen, Reduktion von
drei auf zwei Dimensionen).

<u>Skizzenobjekt</u>: Die ein Bildobjekt repräsentierende Substruktur der Skizze.

<u>Modellobjekt</u>: Relationalstruktur zur Beschreibung des Prototyps einer Klasse von Skizzenobjekten, die dasselbe Realobjekt repräsentiert.

<u>Modell</u>: Menge von Relationalstrukturen für Modellobjekte zusammen mit einer Hierarchie von monomorphen Abbildungen zwischen Modellobjekten. Die Trägermenge der Modellobjekte ist Teilmenge der Trägermenge der Skizze. Die Relationen der Skizze sind erweitert um solche, die sich aus der Skizze berechnen lassen.

<u>Szenenmodell</u>: Erlaubte Konfigurationen und Bewegungszustände von Realobjekten.

2.2 Aufgaben des Szenenanalyse-Systems

2.2.1 Segmentierung
Das Bild einer Szene wird in Konturen und Flecken zerlegt. Flecke sind disjunkte, zusammenhängende (4-Nachbarschaft) Teilmengen des Bildes, die von einer geschlossenen Kontur berandet sind.

2.2.2 Symbolische Darstellung der Segmentierung
Das Ergebnis der Segmentierung wird in einer relationalen Datenstruktur, der Skizze, dargestellt.

2.2.3 Finden und lokale Interpretation von Skizzenobjekten
Durch Konstruktion von Abbildungen zwischen Skizze und Modell werden den Modellobjekten zugeordnete Skizzenobjekte gruppiert.

2.2.4 Verifikation des geometrischen Kontextes
Durch Abbildung der Skizzenobjekte, die mehreren Modellobjekten im Verlauf der Interpretationsphase zugeordnet worden sein konnten, auf ein Szenenmodell werden kontextverletzende Interpretationen von Skizzenobjekten eliminiert.

2.2.5 Verifikation des zeitlichen Kontextes
Der zeitliche Verlauf des geometrischen Kontextes, also die Bewegung von Objekten gegeneinander oder relativ zum Hintergrund, erlaubt durch Bildung von Bewegungshypothesen die Interpretation von über z.B. Form und Grauwert lokal nicht erkennbaren Skizzenobjekten. Das ist wichtig

für die Analyse von teilweise verdeckten Objekten und zur Unterscheidung von lokal gleichen Objekten.

2.3 Annahmen

2.3.1 Realobjekte haben verschiedene Repräsentation als Bildobjekt
- Die Projektion einer 3-dimensionalen Szene auf eine 2-dimensionale Sensorfläche erzeugt möglicherweise Überdeckungen, perspektivische Verzerrungen und verschiedene Erscheinungsformen durch Rotation von Körpern.
- Die Transformation dieser Projektion in das Bild wird durch Amplituden- und Raster-Rauschen des Sensors gestört.
- Beleuchtungsänderungen beeinflussen den Grauwert des Bildobjektes.
Daher müssen verschiedene Bildobjekte als zugehörig zur Äquivalenzklasse eines Realobjekts erkannt werden können.

2.3.2 Die Transformation des Bildes in die Skizze erfolgt fast bedeutungstreu, d.h. Unterscheidbarkeit und Kontext von Bildobjekten bleiben beim Übergang auf die entsprechenden Skizzenobjekte erhalten. Dann können Aussagen über Bildobjekte auf Aussagen über Skizzenobjekte zurückgeführt werden und die Skizze allein kann als Grundlage der weiteren Analyse dienen.

2.3.3 Erkennen eines Bildobjektes bedeutet, eine Teilmenge des Bildes zu finden, die einem Modellobjekt zugeordnet werden kann. Die Erkennung eines Bildobjektes kann (s. 2.3.2) auf die Erkennung des zugehörigen Skizzenobjektes zurückgeführt werden. Dann kann eine Zuordnung von Skizzenobjekt zu dem ebenfalls relational formulierten Modellobjekt strukturgetreu erfolgen.

2.3.4 Zur Erkennung eines Skizzenobjektes werden benutzt:
- lokale Eigenschaften wie Grauwertverteilung, Kontur, Form, Fläche, Position
- geometrische Beziehungen zu anderen Skizzenobjekten im selben Bild wie Abstand, relative Lage, Nachbarschaft
- zeitliche Entwicklung des geometrischen Kontextes und der lokalen Eigenschaften.
Das Ausnutzen von Kontext erleichtert die Erkennung von Skizzenobjekten, ist notwendig zur Unterscheidung von Skizzenobjekten mit gleichen lokalen Eigenschaften und zur Identifizierung von Bildobjekten mit gestörter Form, wie sie bei einer Überdeckung der projizierten Realob-

jekte entsteht.

2.3.5 Folgebilder einer zeitlich geordneten Szenenfolge sind semantisch
ähnlich, d.h. sie enthalten äquivalente Bildobjekte in nur wenig ver-
änderter Konfiguration, wenn die Abtastrate des Sensors groß gegenüber
der Geschwindigkeit der Bewegung ist.

2.3.6 Folgebilder können trotz ähnlichem Kontext in ihrer Grauwert-
struktur und in ihrer Repräsentation als Skizze sehr verschieden sein.
Das unzuverlässige Segmentierungsverfahren ist empfindlich gegenüber
den in 2.3.1 aufgeführten Einflüssen, zu denen noch die Veränderung
der Reflexion von bewegten Objekten (bei feststehender Lichtquelle)
hinzukommt.

Die Verschiedenheit der Skizzen von Folgebildern ist also nur notwendig für Bewegung in den zugrundeliegenden Szenen, aber nicht hinreichend.

Die in diesem Absatz (2.3) gemachten Bemerkungen über Folgebilder treffen auch auf Bildpaare von Stereoaufnahmen zu, da sich hierbei durch
den verschiedenen Standort der Kameras der Beobachter relativ zur Szene
bewegt.

2.4 Formale Struktur des Szenenanalyse-Systems

Die Abbildung 1 gibt einen Überblick über den Aufbau des Szenenanalyse-
Systems, wie er sich aus den gestellten Aufgaben und den zugrundeliegenden Annahmen ergibt.

2.4.1 Das vom Sensor erzeugte Bild wird durch das Skizzengenerator-Pro-
gramm in die Relationalstruktur der Skizze transformiert. Die so gewonnene symbolische Beschreibung des Bildes dient dem Interpretationsprozeß als Ausgangs-Datenbasis.

2.4.2 Der Interpreter ist ein Algorithmus, der - formal unabhängig vom
Inhalt des Modells und der Skizze - gemeinsame Substrukturen im Modell
und in der Skizze findet, wodurch eine Abbildung zwischen Elementen der
Trägermengen vom Modell und von der Skizze impliziert ist. Der Interpreter kann von der Skizze ausgehend, Skizzenobjekte finden und best-
mögliche Übereinstimmungen mit Modellobjekten suchen ("bottom-up" Arbeitsweise). Er kann auch bei Folgebildern modellgesteuert die Instan-

zen von Modellobjekten verifizieren ("top-down" Richtung).

2.4.3 Das Modell enthält Modellobjekte, Szenenmodelle und Prozeduren zur Berechnung von Relationen. Die Modellobjekte setzen sich hierarchisch aus Teilmodellen zusammen, wobei als Bestandteile der untersten Ebene Elemente aus der Trägermenge der Skizzenrelationalstruktur, nämlich Ort, Gerade, Kreisbogen und Superfleck, gewonnen werden. Der Superfleck ist eine modellgesteuerte Vereinigung von benachbarten Flekken. Die Abbildungen zwischen Relationalstrukturen, die Modell-(Teil-)Objekte in den verschiedenen Hierarchie-Ebenen repräsentieren, sind ebenfalls im Modell enthalten. Das Modell wird bei der Definition des Systems vorgegeben.

3. Aufbau der Skizze

Die Skizze ist als Relationalstruktur formuliert. In Tabelle 1 sind die Elemente der Trägermenge, die einstelligen und die zweistelligen Relationen aufgeführt.

TABELLE 1
___

Trägermenge

O	Ort	⎤
F	Fleck	⎬ Aufbau während der Segmentierung
K	Kontur	⎦
GK	Gerade	⎤ Aufbau durch spezielle Interpretations-
KRS	Kreisbogen	⎬ funktion, die Elementoperatoren
SF	Superfleck	⎦

Eigenschaften

X:	$O \to [0,255]$	⎱ Koordinaten des Ortes
Y:	$O \to [0,190]$	⎰
XS:	$F \to [0,255]$	⎱ Koordinaten des Schwerpunktes eines Flecks
YS:	$F \to [0,190]$	⎰
FL:	$F \to [0,48896]$	Fläche (Zahl der Geo-Pixel)
G:	$F \to [0,255]$	mittlerer Grauwert
GS:	$F \to [0,GSmax]$	Streuung der Grauwerte
KK:	$K \to [Bytekette]$	Ketten-Kode einer Kontur, d.h. die 4 Himmelsrichtungen der vom Anfangs- zum Endpunkt aufeinanderfolgenden Kantenelemente

KS: K   →[0,KSmax]   Kantenstärke einer Kontur

KL: K   →[1,KLmax]   Länge (Zahl der Kantenelemente im Raster)

GPHI: GK →[0,π]   Winkel einer Geraden zur x-Achse

GL: GK →[1,GLmax]   euklidischer Abstand zwischen Anfangs- und
                           Endpunkt

KPHI: KRS→[0,2π]   Zentriwinkel des Kreisbogens

KR: KRS→[0,KRmax]   Radius

MPX: KRS→[0,255]   ⎤
MPY: KRS→[0,190]   ⎦ Koordinaten des Mittelpunktes

zweistellige Relationen (wahr oder falsch)

KF: FxF ⟶ [W,F]   Fleck-Kontakt; zwei Flecken haben ein gemein-
                           sames Konturstück

TV: FxF ⟶ "   Teil von: ein Fleck ist von einem benachbar-
                           ten Fleck vollständig umgeben

RF: KxF ⟶ "   rechter Fleck: ein Fleck liegt rechts von
                           einem Rand-Konturstück

LF: KxF ⟶ "   linker Fleck

AP: KxO ⟶ "   Ort ist Anfangspunkt einer Kontur

EP: KxO ⟶ "   Endpunkt

TK: GKxK ⟶ "   Konturstück ist Teil einer Geraden bzw. Teil
         KRSxK→ "   eines Kreisbogens

TF: SFxF ⟶ "   Fleck ist Teil eines Superflecks

V: GKxO ⟶ "   Ort ist Anfangs- oder Endpunkt einer Geraden
         KRSxO→ "   bzw. eines Kreisbogens

3.1 Segmentierung

Die Berechnung der Skizze setzt die Segmentierung des Bildes voraus.
Die vom Sensor gelieferte Grauwertmatrix hat 512 Spalten und 573 Zeilen. 256 Grauwertstufen (8 bit) werden unterschieden, die Streuung des
Meßwertes ist 2. Die Matrix hat kein geometriegetreues Format, da bei
ihr das Seitenverhältnis 512/573 = 0.89, bei der abgetasteten Sensorfläche jedoch 4/3 = 1.33 ist. Deswegen wird die Ur-Matrix in eine geo-
metriegetreue überführt, indem 2 Spalten und 3 Zeilen zu einem "Geo-"
Pixel zusammengefaßt werden. Das neue Seitenverhältnis ist damit
256/191 = 1.34. Bei diesem Vorgang wird gleichzeitig für horizontal
bzw. vertikal benachbarte Paare von Geo-Pixeln die Wahrscheinlichkeit
geschätzt, die ein Maß dafür angibt, daß die beiden Pixel zu verschiedenen oder zum gleichen Fleck gehören. Es wird nach /21/ das Likeli-
hood-Verhältnis gebildet:

$$LH = \frac{(\sigma_0^2)^{12}}{(\sigma_1^2)^6 \cdot (\sigma_2^2)^6}$$

$$\sigma_1^2 = ((\Sigma G1_i^2)\cdot 6 - (\Sigma G1_i)^2)/36$$

$$\sigma_2^2 = ((\Sigma G2_i^2)\cdot 6 - (\Sigma G2_i)^2)/36$$

$$\sigma_0^2 = ((\Sigma G12_i^2)\cdot 12 - (\Sigma G12_i)^2)/144$$

wobei G1 und G2 die Grauwerte aus dem einen bzw. anderen Geopixel sind
und G12 die Grauwerte aus beiden benachbarten Geopixeln.

Dort, wo LH in horizontaler bzw. vertikaler Richtung ein lokales Maximum
erreicht, das zur Unterdrückung des Rauschens außerdem über einem vorgebbaren Schwellwert liegen muß, wird ein vertikales bzw. horizontales
Kantenelement gesetzt. Aus zusammenhängenden Kantenelementen werden unter Auffüllen kleiner Lücken längere Konturstücke gebildet. Flecke werden dadurch definiert, daß sie von einer geschlossenen Kontur berandet
sind. Die Eigenschaften der Konturen und Flecke sowie die Relationen
AP, EP, LF, RF und KF werden schon in der Segmentierungs-Phase berechnet.

Für die Szene Bild 2 entstehen etwa 1500 Konturstücke und 350 Flecke.
Bild 3 und 4 zeigen das Ergebnis der Segmentierung.

Der Segmentierungsprozeß arbeitet konservativ. Sein Ergebnis wird über-
arbeitet, indem
- alle Konturstücke, die nicht Teil eines Fleck-Randes sind, entfernt
  werden und
- ähnliche Flecke verschmolzen werden.

In die Ähnlichkeit gehen ein
- eine Likelihood-Schätzung über die Grauwertverteilung der Flecke
- die gemeinsame Konturlänge und -stärke
- und die Fläche der beiden Flecke

$$\text{Ä} = \frac{(\sigma_1^2)^{F_1}\cdot(\sigma_2^2)^{F_2}\cdot KL^2}{(\sigma_0^2)^{F_1+F_2}\cdot(F_1+F_2)\cdot KS}$$

Der Verschmelzungsprozeß benutzt eine nach abnehmender Ähnlichkeit ge-
ordnete Liste von benachbarten Flecken. Er verschmilzt die beiden Flek-
ke vom Anfang der Liste, rechnet die Ähnlichkeiten für alle Nachbar-
flecke neu aus und ordnet die Liste, falls notwendig, um. Abgebrochen

wird nach Unterschreiten einer vorgebbaren Mindestähnlichkeit.

Das Resultat Bild 4 enthält etwa 150 Flecke und 350 Konturstücke. Die
Segmentierungs- und Verschmelzungsphase benötigt etwa 5 min CPU-Zeit
auf einer PDP-10 bei einem Speicherbedarf von etwa 60K 36 bit Worten;
der Speicherbedarf der Skizze beträgt 7K 36 bit Worte (zum Vergleich:
Das Rohbild würde 75K benötigen). Ein Beispiel zeigt Abbildung 7.

3.2 Berechnung der Skizze

Die Formbeschreibung von Konturstücken beschränkt sich auf Geraden und
Kreisbögen. Komplexere Formen scheinen uns bei der Detailliertheit und
Auflösung der Bilder sowie der Störanfälligkeit der Segmentierung be-
züglich Raster- und Amplitudenrauschen des Sensors unangemessen.

Zur Analyse einer Kontur wird für jedes Kantenelement in der Kontur
ein Winkel zur Horizontalen berechnet, indem an die Kontur möglichst
lange Geraden angepaßt werden, die einen "Schlauch" um die Kontur mit
der Breite einer Kantenelementlänge nicht verlassen, wobei jedes Kantenelement einmal als Anfangspunkt einer solchen Gerade in Vorwärts-
bzw. Rückwärtsrichtung benutzt wird. Als Winkel für ein Kantenelement
wird der mit der Länge gewichtete mittlere Winkel aller das Element
passierenden Geraden berechnet. Wird der Winkel gegen die Konturlänge
aufgetragen, ergibt sich für gerade Konturstücke ein horizontaler, für
Kreisbögen je nach Drehsinn ein linear ansteigender oder abfallender
Verlauf /33/. Der Verlauf wird durch Geradenstücke angenähert /22/,
aus deren Länge und Steigung Länge und Radius des entsprechenden Kon-
turstücks berechnet werden. Abb. 5 zeigt das Ergebnis der Zerlegung
für die Kontur der Vase aus Bild 4.

Die Formbeschreibung wird erst auf Wunsch des Interpreters vorgenommen
(der also mit einer unvollständigen Skizze beginnen kann), beim ersten
Bild einer Szenenfolge wird sie für alle Konturen verlangt.

Der Superfleck ist ein Grundelement des Modells zur Beschreibung von
Grauwertflächen, die sich aus einer endlichen Zahl von benachbarten
Flecken zusammensetzen. Damit wird die Erfahrung berücksichtigt, daß
die Segmentierung i.a. Bildobjekte in mehrere, benachbarte Flecken
zerlegt.

Der Interpreter delegiert die Aufgabe, aus benachbarten Flecken einen

Superfleck zu bilden, an eine Prozedur, die als Eingabeparameter eine
Liste von Konturstücken erhält, die den Rand des Superflecks bilden
sollen. Die Superfleck-Prozedur benutzt die LF, RF und TV Relationen
und einen Algorithmus, der bestimmen kann, ob ein Punkt außerhalb oder
innerhalb eines geschlossenen Randes liegt.

4. Struktur des Modells

In diesem Teil des Szenenanalyse-Systems sind alle Informationen konzentriert, die das System an die reale Szenenfolge anpassen. Durch Aus-
wechseln nur des Modells läßt sich das System auf verschiedene Mini-Wel-
ten anwenden.

4.1 Aufbau

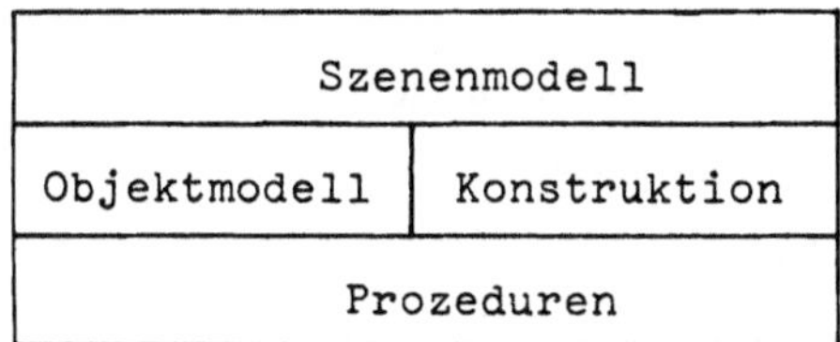

4.2 Definitionen

<u>Relationalstruktur</u>: Eine endliche Menge T zusammen mit einer Zuord-
nung zwischen allen Teilmengen von
$$T^{(n)} = Tx \ \ldots \ xT$$
und den Argumenten von Funktionen
$$f : T^{(n)} \longrightarrow W_f$$
W_f ist der Wertebereich der Funktion f. Die Zuordnungen definieren Relationen über $T^{(n)}$. Wir verwenden nur ein- und zweistellige Relationen.

<u>Objektmodell</u>: Relationalstrukturen MO^k für Objekte k, kurz Modellobjek-
te. Die Trägermenge besteht aus den Elementen
(Ort, Gerade,Kreisbogen und Superfleck).
Die Relationen sind die der Skizze erweitert um ein- und zweistellige
Relationen, die sich aus der Skizze berechnen lassen (Tabelle 2).

<u>Konstruktion</u>:

$$KO^k = (K^k_{k_1}, \ldots, K^k_{k_n})$$

$\quad K^k_{k_i}\quad$ monomorphe Abbildungen: $T^{ki} \longrightarrow T^k$

$\quad T^{k}i\quad$ Trägermenge des Modellobjekts $MO^{k}i$

Die Konstruktion bildet jedes Trägerelement aus der Relationalstruktur der Teilmodelle $MO^{k}i$ in die Trägermenge von MO^k ab.

<u>Stark-Monomorphe Abbildung</u>: Injektive Abbildung

$$A : T^i \longrightarrow T^k$$

mit T^i und T^k Trägermenge der Modellobjekte MO^i und MO^k, so daß für alle Funktionen $f \in F$ mit

$$F = \{f \mid f : T^{(n)} \longrightarrow W_f\}$$

$$f(t^i_1, \ldots, t^i_n) = f(A(t^i_1), \ldots, A(t^i_n)), \quad t^i_l \in T^i \quad l = 1, \ldots, n$$

<u>Substruktur</u>: MO^i ist Substruktur von MO^k, wenn es einen Monomorphismus

$$K^k_i : T^i \longrightarrow T^k \qquad \text{gibt.}$$

<u>Hierarchie</u>: MO^k ist hierarchisch höher als MO^i, wenn es eine Konstruktion KO^k gibt, in der ein Monomorphismus

$$K^k_i : T^i \longrightarrow T^k \qquad \text{vorkommt.}$$

MO^i ist dann Modell-Teilobjekt von MO^k. Die hierarchisch höchsten Objektmodelle kommen in keiner Konstruktion als Urbild vor.

<u>Szenenmodell</u>: Relationalstruktur zur Beschreibung der möglichen Szenen. Die Trägermenge umfaßt die Namen der hierarchisch höchsten Modellobjekte als Verweise auf die entsprechende Relationalstruktur. Aus den Instanzen der Modellobjekte können für diese Namen Eigenschaften und Relationen nach Maßgabe des Szenenmodells berechnet werden.

<u>Prozeduren</u>: Algorithmen, die Relationen berechnen.

4.3 Aufgabe

Das Modell definiert die Grundelemente, d.h. die berechenbaren Abstraktionen über Mengen von Pixeln, die auch in der Skizze verwendet werden, die Modelle für Skizzenobjekte und Skizzen-Teilobjekte, das Szenenmo-

dell und die Konstruktionen. Eine Aufstellung der Grundelemente, Eigenschaften, Relationen und Modellobjekte gibt Tabelle 2. Die Nomenklatur
ist aus Abb. 6 ersichtlich. Nähere Einzelheiten in /32/.

TABELLE 2

Modell:

Grundelemente: Ort

                     Gerade

                     Kreisbogen

                     Superfleck

Eigenschaften: wie in der Skizze

                     zusätzlich:

VX : Objekt $[0,VXmax]$ ⎱

VY : Objekt $[0,VYmax]$ ⎰ Bewegungsvektor

Relationen: wie in der Skizze

                     zusätzlich:

A:	Objekt x Objekt	→ $[0,Amax]$	Abstand
RL:	Objekt x Objekt	→ $[0,7]$	Relative Lage
GLA:	GK x GK	→ $[W,F]$	gleiche Länge
WK:	GK x GK	→ $[0,\pi]$	Winkel
KP:	O x O	→ $[0,KPmax]$	Punktkontakt
RA:	F x GK	→ $[W,F]$	Rand
	F x KRS	→ $[W,F]$	

Modellobjekte: Scheibe, Kasten, Blume, Vase, Hampelmann

5. Interpreter

5.1 Grundsätzliche Arbeitsweise

Der Interpreter besteht im wesentlichen aus einem Algorithmus, der gemeinsame Substrukturen zwischen Relationalstrukturen findet. Der Rechenaufwand ist höher als bei dem Problem der Graphisomorphie oder
Graphinjektion, das als "polynomial-complete" eingeschätzt wird /16,17,
19/. Da wir davon ausgehen, daß die Relationalstruktur der Skizze wegen der Schwierigkeiten der Segmentierung von Grauwertbildern i.a. den
Modellobjekten nicht isomorph ist, muß der Interpreter größte gemeinsa-

me Substrukturen finden, ein Problem, das als "NP-complete" betrachtet
wird /18/. Um eine kombinatorische Explosion zu vermeiden, wird die
Interpretation von Modellobjekten auf die von Modellteilobjekten zurückgeführt. Die Aufteilung in Modellteilobjekte geht bis zur Ebene
der Skizze, in der die Grundelemente von speziellen Operatoren erzeugt
werden. Durch Hierarchisierung der Modellteilobjekte brauchen in dem
Schritt zur nächst höheren Hierarchiestufe nur noch die Kombinationen
der bereits vorliegenden Skizzenteilobjekte untersucht zu werden. In
einer direkten Interpretation eines Modellobjektes müßten sämtliche
Kombinationen von Zuordnungen zwischen Skizze und Modellobjekt gebildet werden. Sorgt man dafür, daß von Stufe zu Stufe nur wenige Eigenschaften und Relationen hinzukommen, wird die Prüfung auf Strukturtreue wesentlich vereinfacht.

Der Interpreter kann sowohl modellgesteuert (top-down) als auch von der
Skizze ausgehend die vorkommenden Skizzenobjekte interpretieren (bottom-up). Die "bottom-up" Interpretation wird bei dem ersten Bild einer Bildfolge angewandt. Der Suchraum erstreckt sich auf die ganze
Skizze, was eine große Kombinatorik vor allen Dingen auf den niedrigen Ebenen der Modellobjekthierarchie zur Folge hat.

Bei Folgebildern wird die Interpretation des Vorgängerbildes benutzt,
um die entsprechenden Modellobjekte mit den Werten der letzten Interpretation zu initialisieren. Der Interpreter verifiziert jetzt die Modellobjekte rekursiv über ihre Modellteilobjekte bis zur untersten
Ebene der Grundelemente in der Skizze. Die Zahl der Kandidaten aus der
Skizze ist wesentlich geringer als beim "bottom up" Prozeß, da bereits
Werte für Eigenschaften und Relationen der Modellteilobjekte spezifi-
ziert sind. Kann ein effektiver Zugriff auf Grundelemente mit vorgegebenen Eigenschaftswerten gefunden werden /23,24,25/, so wird sich auch
der Rechenaufwand bei der Folgebildanalyse stark verringern, was bereits unsere Annahme 2.3.5 nahe legte. Eine Beschreibung der verwendeten Algorithmen findet sich in /32/.

5.2 Formaler Aufbau

Die Aufgabe des Interpreters ist es, die Instanzen der in der Szene
vorkommenden Objekte, d.h. die Zuordnung von Modellobjekten und Skizzenobjekten zu finden.

Als Grundlage der Interpretation dient die Hierarchie der Modellobjekte und das Netzwerk der Konstruktionen, die angeben, aus welchen Modellteilobjekten sich ein Modellobjekt zusammensetzt.

Sei MO^d das Modellobjekt (Nomenklatur Abb. 6), das interpretiert werden soll:

$$MO^d = (T^d, E^d, R^d) \qquad\qquad d, f, g \in [1, D]$$

$$MO^f = (T^f, E^f, R^f)$$

$$MO^g = (T^g, E^g, R^g)$$

$$K^d = \{K^d_f, K^d_g\} \qquad\qquad \text{Konstruktion}$$

$$K^d_f : T^f \longrightarrow T^d$$

$$K^d_f = ((TR^f_1, TR^d_{f_1}), \ldots, (TR^f_{N(f)}, TR^d_{f_{N(f)}})) \qquad \text{Teilkonstruktion}$$

$$K^d_g : T^g \longrightarrow T^d \qquad\qquad f_i, g_i \in [1, N(d)]$$

$$K^d_g = ((TR^g_1, TR^d_{g_1}), \ldots, (TR^g_{N(g)}, TR^d_{g_{N(g)}}))$$

Die Konstruktion K^d gibt an, wie sich das Modellobjekt MO^d aus seinen
Teilen MO^g und MO^f zusammensetzt:

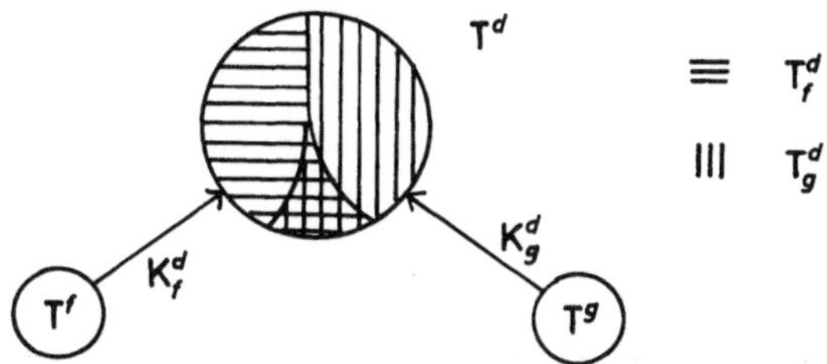

Das Problem, eine Instanz von MO^d, also die größte gemeinsame Substruktur von MO^d und der Skizze, zu finden, bedeutet, aus den Skizzenobjekten, die in den Instanzen von MO^f und MO^g vorkommen, ein Skizzenobjekt
zusammenzusetzen, das unter Erhaltung aller Eigenschaften und Relationen auf das Modellobjekt MO^d abgebildet werden kann.

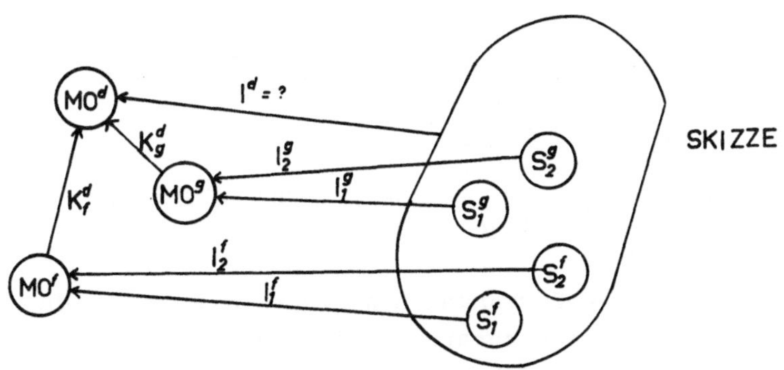

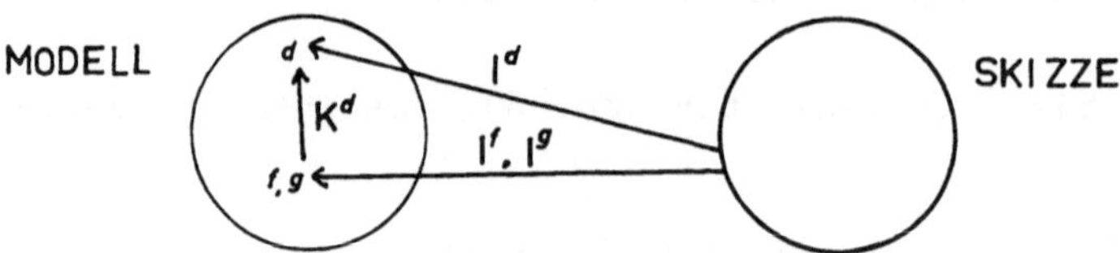

Dieser Prozeß wird in zwei Stufen durchgeführt.

1. Stufe (Binden, d.h. Prüfung auf Erhaltung der Eigenschaften)
Notwendig für die Existenz einer strukturtreuen Abbildung zwischen Skizze und Modellobjekt ist die Übereinstimmung der Eigenschaften der zugeordneten Elemente aus den Trägermengen des Modellobjektes und des vermuteten Skizzenobjektes.

Die Mengen SO^f, SO^g der Skizzenobjekte aus den Instanzen von MO^f und MO^g werden vermöge der Teilkonstruktionen K^d_f und K^d_g auf die entsprechenden Teilmengen T^d_g, T^d_f des Trägers T^d abgebildet und auf Einhaltung der Zusatzeigenschaften geprüft. Dieser Prozeß erzeugt eine Menge von Kandidaten:

$$KAND = \{(T^d_h, S^h_t) \mid t \in [1, T(h)], \quad h \in \{g, f\};$$
$$\bigwedge_{E_a \in \widetilde{E}^d} : E_a(T^d_h) \sim E_a(S^h_t)\}$$

$E_a(T^d_h)$ und $E_a(S^h_t)$ sind Ausdrücke, die gemäß dem Modell ausgewertet werden, da T^d_h und S^h_t Tupel von Trägerelementen bezeichnen. D.h. die Skizzenobjekte werden als Ganzes weitergegeben, da ihre Struktur bereits auf der Ebene der Teilobjekte verifiziert worden ist.

Der Algorithmus sei hier kurz angedeutet:
Sei $(E_a, TR^d_i, W^d_{ai}) \in \widetilde{E}^d$
$$T^d_h = (TR^d_{h_1}, \ldots, TR^d_{h_n}, \ldots, TR^d_{h_{N(h)}}) \qquad h_n \in [1, N(d)]$$
$$S^h_t = (S^h_{t_1}, \ldots, S^h_{t_n}, \ldots, S^h_{t_{N(h)}})$$
$$E_a(T^d_h) \sim E_a(S^h_t) \Longleftrightarrow \bigvee_{n \in [1, N(h)]} : TR^d_{h_n} = TR^d_i \wedge E_a(TR^d_{h_n}) \sim E_a(S^h_{t_n})$$

KAND enthält alle möglichen Zuordnungen zwischen Skizze und den durch die Teilkonstruktionen ausgezeichneten Teilen des Trägers T^d vom Modellobjekt MO^d. Durch die Bezeichnung der Tupel mit Namen wird die Zahl der Kandidaten beträchtlich eingeschränkt (im Vergleich zur elementweisen Zuordnung) und die Tatsache berücksichtigt, daß auf Grund der monomorphen Teilkonstruktionen die Skizzenobjekte aus den Instanzen der Modellteilobjekte als Ganzes übernommen werden können. Die Skizzenobjekte der Modellteilobjekte werden sozusagen hochgereicht. Die Äquivalenzrelation $\sim$ ist im einfachsten Fall Gleichheit der Werte. Wir benutzten Wertebereiche oder Mittelwert und Streuung von Werteverteilungen.

2. Stufe (Verifikation der Strukturtreue, d.h. Prüfung auf Erhaltung der Relationen)

Instanzen von MO^d sind nun solche Teilmengen von KAND, in denen alle Relationen zwischen den Elementen der Trägermenge von MO^d auch zwischen den ihnen zugeordneten Elementen der Skizze gelten. Geprüft werden nur die Zusatzrelationen, da alle anderen bereits bei der Interpretation der entsprechenden Modellteilobjekte verifiziert wurden.

Um diese Teilmengen von KAND zu finden, fassen wir - nach einer Idee von Ambler /15/ - die Elemente der Menge KAND als Knoten eines Graphen auf, in dem eine ungerichtete Relation zwischen den Knoten definiert ist, die angibt, ob die Vereinigung der durch die Knoten bezeichneten Zuordnungen ebenfalls eine strukturtreue Zuordnung ist.

Seien $(S^g_t, T^d_g) = Z_i$ und $(S^f_n, T^d_f) = Z_j$ zwei solche Knoten:

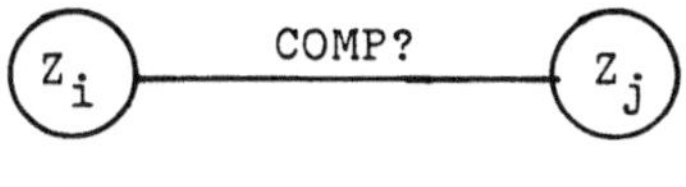

$$Z_i \; \text{——} \; \overset{\text{COMP?}}{} \; \text{——} \; Z_j$$

$$\text{COMP}(Z_i, Z_j)$$
$$= T \text{ falls} \left(\bigwedge_{R_b \in \tilde{R}^d \neq \emptyset} : R_b(T^d_g, T^d_f) \sim R_b(S^g_t, S^f_n) \right) \lor \tilde{R}^d = \emptyset$$
$$= F \text{ sonst}$$

Da T^d_g, T^d_f, S^g_t, S^f_n wie bei der Kandidatenbildung Tupel von Trägerelementen bezeichnen, die Relation aber immer zwischen einzelnen Trägerelementen definiert ist, müssen diese Ausdrücke wie bei der Überprüfung der Eigenschaften ausgewertet werden.

Die größten gemeinsamen Substrukturen zwischen Skizze und Modellobjekt sind nun äquivalent maximalen Cliquen in dem Graphen der Kandidaten bezüglich der Relation COMP.

Ein Beispiel zeigt Abbildung 8.

5.3 Cliquen-Algorithmus

Der Cliquenfinder erzeugt die maximalen Cliquen in einer Baumsuche, in
der Zweige, die nicht zu einer maximalen Clique führen können, durch
eine "Branch and Bound" Methode abgeschnitten werden. Er ist von uns so
modifiziert worden, daß ebenfalls Zweige, die zwar zu einer maximalen
Clique führen, welche aber nicht eine geforderte Mindestanzahl von Knoten enthalten würde, abgeschnitten werden. Der Rechenaufwand pro Clique
ist unabhängig von der Dimension des Graphen. Für spezielle Moon-Moser-
Graphen /31/ mit der Dimension 3k, die 3^k Cliquen enthalten, ist die
Gesamtrechenzeit proportional zu $(3+\epsilon)^k$ mit $\epsilon \approx 0.14$. Der dynamische
Speicherbedarf der Prozedur liegt bei 1/2 M (M+3), wobei M die Größe
des größten total verbundenen Teilgraphen des Graphen ist /20/.

5.4 Übergang auf das Szenenmodell

In der bottom-up Richtung läuft der Interpretationsprozeß des ersten
Bildes einer Szenenfolge von den Instanzen der Grundelemente über die
Konstruktionen bis zu den umfangreichsten Einzelobjekten. Die Instanzen der Einzelobjekte werden in Knoten eines Szenengraphen überführt.
Anhand des Szenenmodells wird nach Bearbeitung der ganzen Szenenfolge
eine Bewertung der gesamten Interpretation vorgenommen. Sie wird sich
zusammensetzen aus

- der Konfidenz für die Interpretation jedes Einzelobjektes in jeder
  Szene, in die der Umfang der gefundenen Substruktur und die Einhaltung der Werte für Eigenschaften und Relationen eingehen,
- aus der Einhaltung des geometrischen Kontextes in jeder Szene und
- aus der Bewertung des zeitlichen Kontextes in der Szenenfolge.

Die Untersuchungen über Formulierung solch einer globalen Bewertung
sind noch nicht abgeschlossen.

In der top-down Richtung läuft der Interpretationsprozeß von der Szenen-
instanz der schon analysierten Bilder über die Modellobjekte mit Hilfe
der inversen Konstruktion bis zum Anstoßen der Elementoperatoren, die
Geraden, Kreise und Superflecke erzeugen. Die Zahl der Kandidaten ist
auf Grund der spezifizierten Eigenschaften wesentlich eingeschränkt,
was den Aufwand des Cliquenfinders reduziert.

6. Zusammenfassung

Realisiert wurden bisher der Skizzengenerator,die Elementoperatoren,
der Cliquenfinder, die Datenstrukturen für das Modell und die Interpretation.

Der Skizzengenerator wurde in PASCAL geschrieben. Bei der weiteren Implementierung, insbesondere beim Interpreter und beim Modell wollen wir
die Programmiersprache SAIL /29/ benutzen, davon ausgiebig die assozia-
tiven Sprachelemente, die LEAP /30/, eine Teilsprache von SAIL, uns
bietet. Sie sind von besonderem Vorteil beim Aufbau der Kandidatenmen-
gen und der Formulierung von Graphen.

Die möglichen Verbesserungen des Systems beziehen sich auf folgende
Probleme:

6.1 Verbesserung des Skizzengenerators

Um die Modellobjekte reichhaltiger formulieren zu können, was eine stär-
kere Differenzierung in der Interpretation bzw. komplexere Bildobjekte
erlaubt, muß die Menge der Grundelemente, Eigenschaften und Relationen
erweitert werden. Vor allen Dingen sind eine bessere Formbeschreibung
nötig und effektivere Verfahren, Mengen von benachbarten Flecken zu
Skizzenobjekten zu gruppieren. Ansätze zu einer reichhaltigeren Beschreibung von Bildern bieten die Arbeiten von Marr /26,27,28/. Voraussetzung dazu ist auch eine bessere Segmentierung des Bildes in Flekken und Konturen. Die Beschränkung auf zwei Richtungen der gefundenen
Kanten führt bei vielen Konturen zu kleinen Lücken, die lokal geschlossen werden müssen. Bei einer top-down Interpretation halten wir auch
direkte Rückgriffe auf das Bild für günstig.

6.2 Erzeugung der Objektmodelle

Die Objektmodelle werden in unserem System intuitiv vorgegeben. Eine
Verbesserung besteht darin, die "Erfahrung" des Systems, also die erfolgten Interpretationen mit ihren Werten in die Objektmodelle rückzu-
koppeln. Das erfordert Formulierung von statistischen Bewertungsmetho-
den zusammen mit Verfahren, die Relationalstrukturen von neuen Objekten automatisch zu generieren.

6.3 Szenenmodell

Eine Erweiterung des Szenenmodells besteht in der Formulierung von Ereignissen, d.h. den Bewegungszuständen von Objekten mit ihren Gesetzen /13,14/. Das würde Aussagen über Wiederholung und Ähnlichkeiten von Ereignissen erlauben. Weiter sind semantische Abstraktionen wie z.B. "Ein Objekt fliegt" aus dem zeitlichen Kontext zu ermitteln.

6.4 Erweiterung auf Stereo-Aufnahmen

Da Stereo-Bilder genau wie Folgebilder einer Szene nach unserer Hypothese ähnlich sind, ließe sich unter Einbeziehung von dreidimensionalen Objektmodellen eine modellgesteuerte Interpretation wie bei Folgebildern anwenden. Das führt dann zu dem Problem, die beste gemeinsame Interpretation von Stereo-Bildern zu finden. Dazu müßte die Struktur des Interpreters und des Skizzengenerators nicht wesentlich verändert werden.

7. Verzeichnis der Abbildungen

Abb. 1: Aufbau des Szenenanalyse-Systems
Abb. 2: Beispiel einer Szene mit den Objekten Hampelmann, Kasten, Vase, Blume und zwei Scheiben
Abb. 3: Segmentierung der Szene: Rekonstruktion der Flecken
Abb. 4: Segmentierung der Szene: Rekonstruktion der Konturen
Abb. 5: Formbeschreibung einer Kontur aus der Skizze in Abb. 7
Abb. 6: Nomenklatur für Modell und Interpreter
Abb. 7: Beispiel für die Relationalstruktur der Skizze
Abb. 8: Schema der Interpretation

8. Literaturverzeichnis

/1/ Roberts, "Machine perception of three-dimensional solids",
   Optical and Electrooptical information processing, S. 154
   -197, MIT Press 1965

/2/ Guzman, "Computer Recognition of three-dimensional objects in a
   visual scene", MIT Report MAC-TR-59

/3/ Winston, "Learning structural descriptions from examples", MIT, AI
   Report TR-76, 1970

/4/ Waltz, "Generating semantic descriptions from drawings of scenes
   with shadows" MIT, AI report TR-271, 1972

/5/ Yakimovsky, "Scene analysis using a semantic base for region growing", STANFORD AIM-209,1973

/6/ Shirai, "Edge finding, segmentation of edges and recognition of
   complex objects", 4 IJCAI, S. 674-681, 1975

/7/ Ohlander, "Analysis of natural scenes", Report Carnegie-Mellon
   University, April 1975

/8/ Barrow et al., "Some techniques for recognizing structures in pictures", in: Frontiers of Pattern Recognition, Watanabe
   (Editor), AP, New York, 1972, S. 1-29

/9/ Aggarwal, Duda, "Computer analysis of moving polygonal images",
   IEEE Transactions on Computers, C-24, 1975, S. 966-976

/10/ Chow, Aggarwal, "Computer Analysis of Planar Curvilinear Moving
   Images", University of Texas at Austin, Report 1976

/11/ Potter, "Scene segmentation by velocity measurements obtained with
   a cross-shaped template", 4 IJCAI, S. 803-810, Tbilisi
   1975

/12/ Nagel, "Formation of an object concept by analysis of systematic
   time variations in the optically perceptible environment"
   Institut für Informatik, Universität Hamburg, Bericht 27,
   1976 und "Computer Graphics and Image Processing"(im Druck)

/13/ Badler, "Temporal scene analysis: Conceptual descriptions of object movements", University of Toronto, Technical Report
   No. 80, 1975

/14/ Tsotsos,"A prototype motion understanding system", University of
   Toronto, Technical Report No. 93, 1976

/15/ Ambler et al., "A versatile system for computer controlled as-
   sembly", Artificial Intelligence 6(1975), S. 129-156

/16/ Vorneil, "An efficient algorithm for graph isomorphism", JACM,
   17(1970), S. 51-64

/17/ Cook, "The complexity of theorem-proving procedures", Proc. 3rd
   Annual ACM Symposium on the Theory of Computing, Ohio
   1971, S. 151-158

/18/ Hayes-Roth, "Patterns of induction and associated knowledge acqui-
        sition algorithms", Carnegie-Mellon University, Mai 1976

/19/ Ullman, "An algorithm for subgraph isomorphism", JACM 23(1976),
        S. 31-42

/20/ Bron, Kerbosch, "Finding all cliques of an undirected graph", CACM
        16(1973), S. 575-577

/21/ Yakimovsky, "Boundary and object detection in real world images",
        4 IJCAI, S. 695-704, Tbilisi 1975

/22/ Pavlidis, Horowitz, "Segmentation of plane curves", IEEE Transac-
        tions on Computers, Vol. C-23, 8(1974), S. 860-870

/23/ Maly, "Compressed tries", CACM, Vol. 19, 7(1976), S. 409-415

/24/ Friedman et al., "An algorithm for finding best matches in loga-
        rithmic time", SLAC-PUB-1549, STAN-CS-75-482, 1975

/25/ Friedman et al., "An algorithm for finding nearest neighbors",
        IEEE Transactions on Computers, Oktober 1975, S. 1000-1006

/26/ Marr, "On the purpose of low-level-vision", MIT AI-Memo, No. 324,
        Dezember 1974

/27/ Marr, "Analyzing natural images", MIT AI-Memo, No. 334, Juni 1975

/28/ Marr, "The low-level symbolic representation of intensity changes
        in an image", MIT AI-Memo, No. 325, Dezember 1974

/29/ Van Lehn, "SAIL User Manual", Stanford AI Laboratory, Memo AIM 204,
        Juli 1973

/30/ Feldman, "An ALGOL-based associative language", CACM 12,(8)1969,
        S. 439-449

/31/ Moon, Moser, "On cliques in graphs", Israel. J. Math.,
        3(1965), S. 23-28

/32/ Bertelsmeier, Dissertation in Vorbereitung

/33/ McKee, Aggarwal, "Computer recognition of partial views of three
        dimensional curved objects", 3 IJCPR, S. 499-503, 1976

Abbildung 1

S E N S O R
Kamera
Analog
Digital
Koverter
B I L D
(Grauwertmatrix)
Skizzengenerator
S K I Z Z E
(symbolische
Beschreibung)
M O D E L L
INTERPRETER
INTERPRETATION
AUSGABE

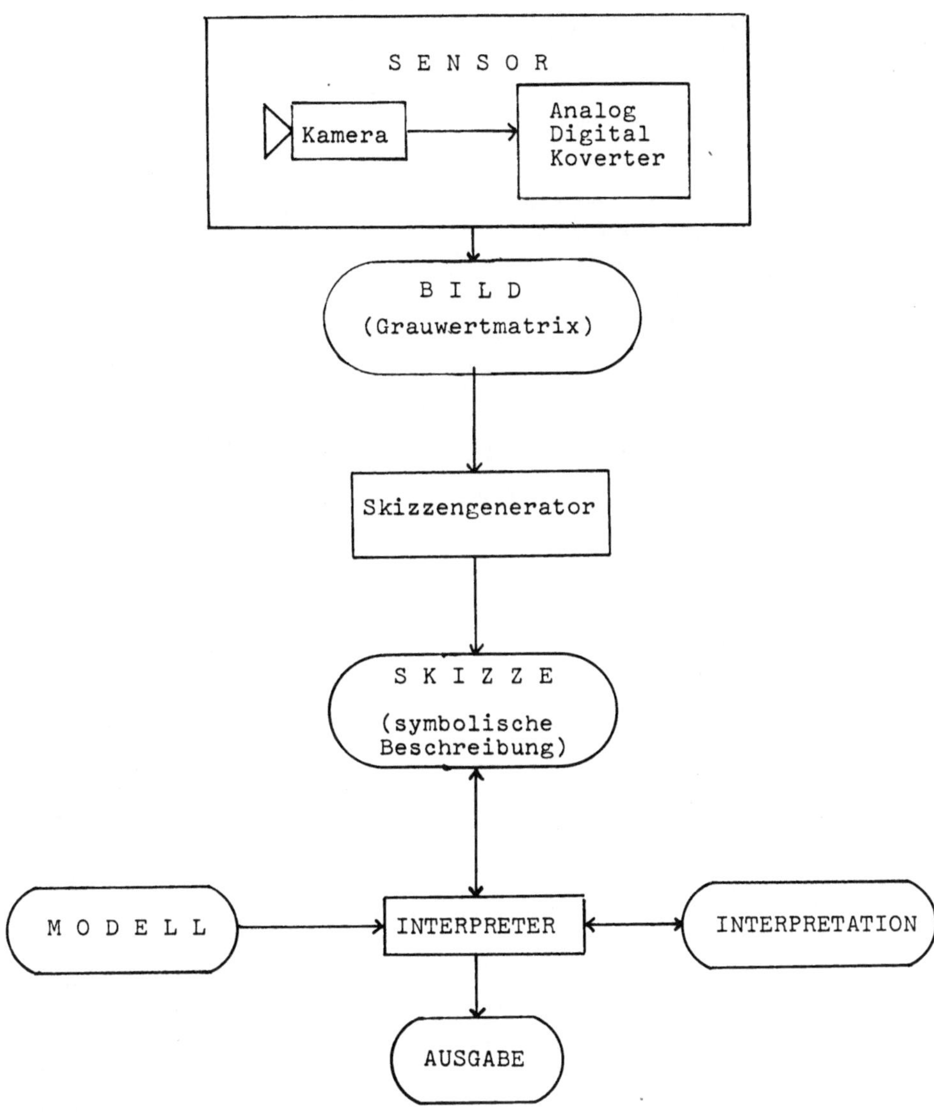

Abbildung 2 und 3

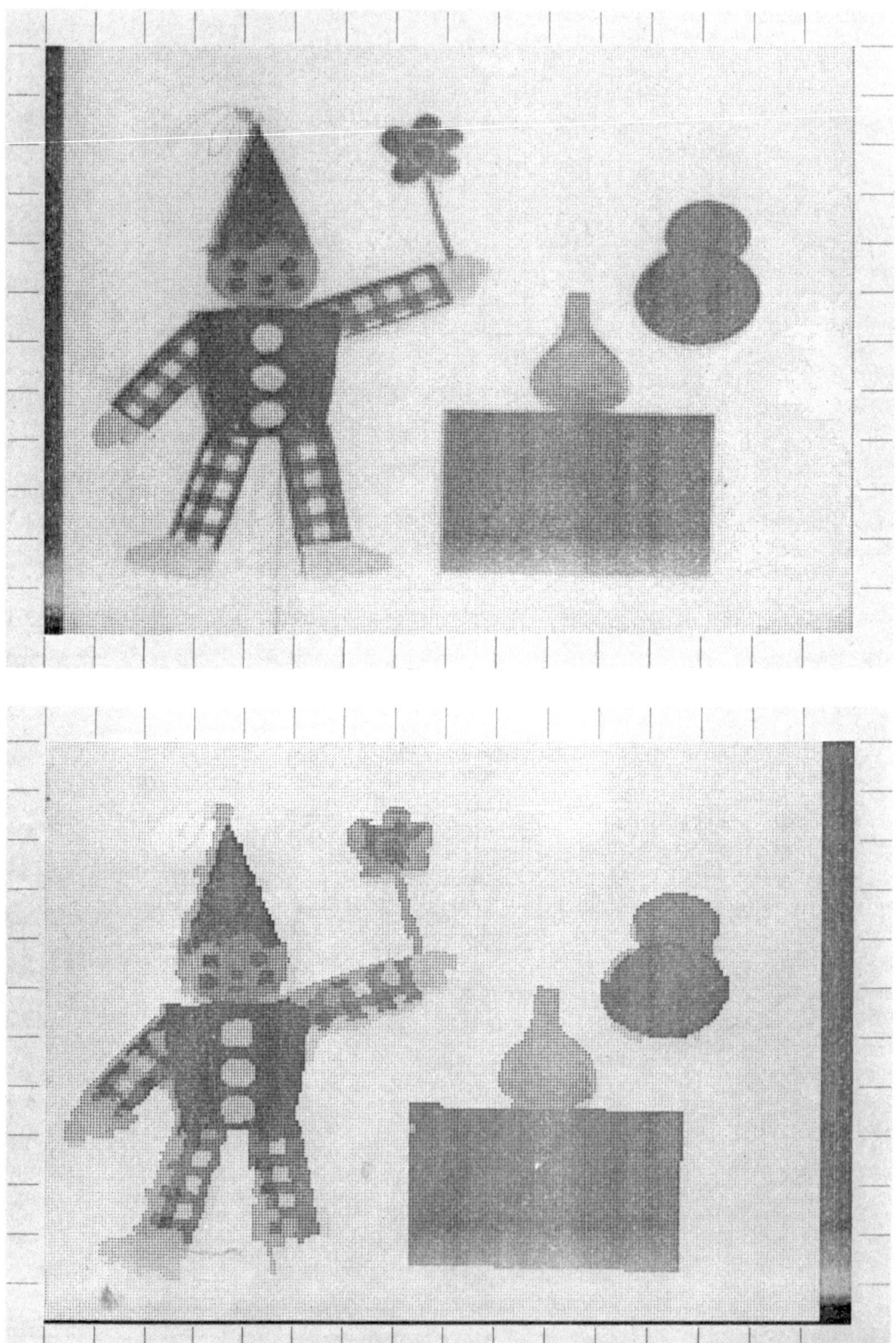

PLOT V=A-6.4   02-JAN-77 19:20:32 PICTURE FROM HERZ .KAB CODE FROM TRANS .COD
WIDTH =C0256   SKIPPED LINES:00000 PLOTTED LINES:00191

ABBILDUNG 4   DARSTELLUNG DER KONTUREN AUS DER SKIZZE

Abb. 4

Abbildung 5

BEGIN AUSSENKONTUR DER VASE

```
          0         1         2         3         4
          01234567890123456789012345678901234567890

40:                      *43
39:                      6 21*9*7
38:                      7         6
37:                     *8         5
36:                      0         4
35:                      1         3
34:                      2         2
33:                      3         1
32:                      4         0
31:                      5         9
30:                      6         8
29:                     87         7
28:                      9         6
27:                      0        *4
26:                   21           3
25:                  *3            21
24:                  5              09
23:                  6            *76
22:                87              54
21:              *09               32
20:             32                  10
19:            54                    98
18:           76                      76
17:           8                       5
16:          09                       43
15:          1                         2
14:          2                         1
13:          3                         09
12:          54                        8
11:          6                         7
10:          7                         6
 9:          8                         5
 8:          *                         4
 7:          01                        *
 6:          2                         2
 5:          34                        01
 4:            5*7                     9
 3:             89                 567*
 2:             1*                 234
 1:             23456789012345678901*1
          0         1         2         3         4
          01234567890123456789012345678901234567890
```

END AUSSENKONTUR DER VASE

ERGEBNIS DES KREISSEGMENT-OPERATORS
FUER KONTURSTUECKE ZWISCHEN '*' UND '*'
STARTPUNKT: RECHTE UNTERE ECKE

```
VON    0 [  30    1]  BIS    8 [  36    3]  RADIUS=-32.0   RASTEREINHEITEN
VON    8 [  36    3]  BIS   13 [  37    7]  RADIUS= 4.40   RASTEREINHEITEN
VON   13 [  37    7]  BIS   38 [  28   23]  RADIUS= 17.4   RASTEREINHEITEN
VON   38 [  28   23]  BIS   45 [  25   27]  RADIUS=-6.45   RASTEREINHEITEN
VON   45 [  25   27]  BIS   58 [  24   39]  RADIUS= 95.3   RASTEREINHEITEN
VON   58 [  24   39]  BIS   60 [  22   39]  RADIUS= 2.24   RASTEREINHEITEN
VON   60 [  22   39]  BIS   65 [  18   40]  RADIUS= 15.8   RASTEREINHEITEN
VON   65 [  18   40]  BIS   69 [  17   37]  RADIUS= 7.09   RASTEREINHEITEN
VON   69 [  17   37]  BIS   84 [  14   25]  RADIUS=-59.3   RASTEREINHEITEN
VON   84 [  14   25]  BIS   91 [  11   21]  RADIUS=-9.32   RASTEREINHEITEN
VON   91 [  11   21]  BIS  109 [   6    0]  RADIUS= 16.0   RASTEREINHEITEN
VON  109 [   6    8]  BIS  116 [   9    4]  RADIUS= 5.62   RASTEREINHEITEN
VON  116 [   9    4]  BIS  120 [  11    2]  RADIUS=-5.52   RASTEREINHEITEN
VON  120 [  11    2]  BIS  142 [  30    1]  RADIUS= 86.2   RASTEREINHEITEN
```

Abbildung 6: Nomenklatur für Modell und Interpretation

a) Träger des Objektmodells

$TM = \{Ort, Gerade, Kreisbogen, Superfleck\}$

b) Eigenschaften (1-stellige Relationen)

$E = \{E_a \mid E_a : TM \rightarrow W_a, a = 1 \ldots A\}$

W_a: Wertebereich der Eigenschaft E_a

c) Relationen (2-stellige Relationen)

$R = \{R_b \mid R_b : TM \times TM \rightarrow W_b, b = 1 \ldots B\}$

W_b: Wertebereich der Relation R_b

d) Objektmodell

$MO = \{MO^d \mid d = 1 \ldots D\}$

e) Modellobjekt

$MO^d = (T^d, E^d, R^d)$

f) Träger eines Modellobjektes

$T^d = \{TR_i^d \mid TR_i^d \in TM, i = 1 \ldots N(d)\}$

g) Eigenschaften eines Modellobjektes

$E^d = \{(E_a, TR_i^d, W_{ai}^d) \; a \in [1, A], \; i \in [1, N(d)]\}$

$E^d = \bar{E}^d \cup \tilde{E}^d \qquad \bar{E}^d \cap \tilde{E}^d = \emptyset$

$\bar{E}^d$: Eigenschaften, die schon im Modellteilobjekt gelten

$\tilde{E}^d$: Zusatzeigenschaften (zu prüfende Eigenschaften)

h) Relationen eines Modellobjektes

$R^d = \{(R_b, TR_i^d, TR_j^d, W_{bij}^d) \mid b \in [1, B]; i,j \in [1, N(d)]\}$

i) Konstruktion eines Modellobjektes

$K^d = \{K_{fc}^d \mid K_{fc}^d : T^f \rightarrow T^d, f \in [1, D], c = 1 \ldots C(f,d)\}$

Teilkonstruktion K_{fc}^d: Monomorphismus: $T^f \rightarrow T^d \quad T^f \in MO^f, T^d \in MO^d$

$C(f,d)$: Häufigkeit, mit der das Modellteilobjekt MO^f in MO^d vorkommt

Bild von T^f: $T_f^d = \bigcup_{c = 1 \ldots C} K_{fc}^d(T^f)$

Teilbild von T^f: $T_{fc}^d = K_{fc}^d(T^f)$

$$T_{fc}^d = \{TR_i^d \mid (TR_i^d \in T^d) \wedge (i \in [1, N(d)]) \wedge (\bigwedge_{j \in [1, N(f)]} \bigvee_{i \in [1, N(d)]} TR_i^d = K_{fc}^d(TR_j^f)\}$$

k) Interpretation eines Modellobjektes

$I^f = \{I_t^f \mid t \in [1, T(f)]\}$

Instanz: $I_t^f = (T^f, S_t^f) := ((TR_1^f, S_{t_1}^f), \ldots, (TR_{N(f)}^f, S_{t_{N(f)}}^f))$

Skizzenobjekt: $S_t^f = (S_{t_1}^f, \ldots, S_{t_{N(f)}}^f) \quad S_{t_i}^f \in$ Trägermenge der Skizze

Abbildung 7a

```
SKIZZE:    4 OERTER   6 KONTUREN    4 FLECKEN
HALDE:   0 K   179 WORTE

ORT NR:  1 XO: 40 YO: 46 K:(  2   6   3   ) ORT NR:  2 XO: 30 YO: 46 K:(  1      4  3) ORT NR:  3 XO: 10 YO: 46 K:(  1      5  4)
ORT NR:  4 XO:  1 YO: 46 K:(  2   6      5)

KONTUR NR:  1 LF:  3 RF:  4 AP:  2 EP:  3 KS:    432.3 KL:124
       KK: ORORRORRROOROOOOOO-OOLOOOLOOLOLOLOLOL-OLLOLOLOOLOOOOOOOO-OOOOLLLLLOLLUUULUU-UUUUUULUUULULUUULU-LLULULULUULUUUULUU-UUURUUR
URULUU
KONTUR NR:  2 LF:  1 RF:  4 AP:  4 EP:  1 KS:    629.4 KL:129
       KK: OOOOOOOOOOOOOOOOOOO-OOOOOOOOOOOOOOOOOO-OOOOOOOOORRRRRRRRR-RRRRRRRRRRRRRRRRRR-RRRRRRRRRRRUUUUUU-UUUUUUUUUUUUUUUUU-UUUUUUU
UUUUUUUU-UUU
KONTUR NR:  3 LF:  4 RF:  2 AP:  2 EP:  1 KS:     59.0 KL: 10 KK: RRRRRRRRR
KONTUR NR:  4 LF:  3 RF:  2 AP:  3 EP:  2 KS:    128.7 KL: 20 KK: RRRRRRRRRRRRRRRRRRR-RR
KONTUR NR:  5 LF:  4 RF:  2 AP:  4 EP:  3 KS:     88.1 KL:  9 KK: RRRRRRRRR
KONTUR NR:  6 LF:  1 RF:  2 AP:  1 EP:  4 KS:    266.2 KL: 57
       KK: UUUUUUUUULLLLLLLLL-LLLLLLLLLLLLLLLLLL-LLLLLLLLLLLL000000-000

FLECK NR:  1 GW:        0 ST:    0.00 FL:      0 XS:  0 YS:  0 RF:() LF:(  2   6)
      NB:(  4   2) TV:(  2   4   3)
FLECK NR:  2 GW:      198 ST:    3.23 FL:    351 XS: 20 YS: 50 RF:(  5   4   3   6) LF:()
      NB:(  3   1   4) TV:()
FLECK NR:  3 GW:      154 ST:   15.99 FL:    752 XS: 21 YS: 31 RF:() LF:(  1   4)
      NB:(  2   4) TV:()
FLECK NR:  4 GW:       40 ST:   22.87 FL:   1003 XS: 19 YS: 17 RF:(  1   2) LF:(  5   3)
      NB:(  3   2   1) TV:()
```

Abbildung 7b

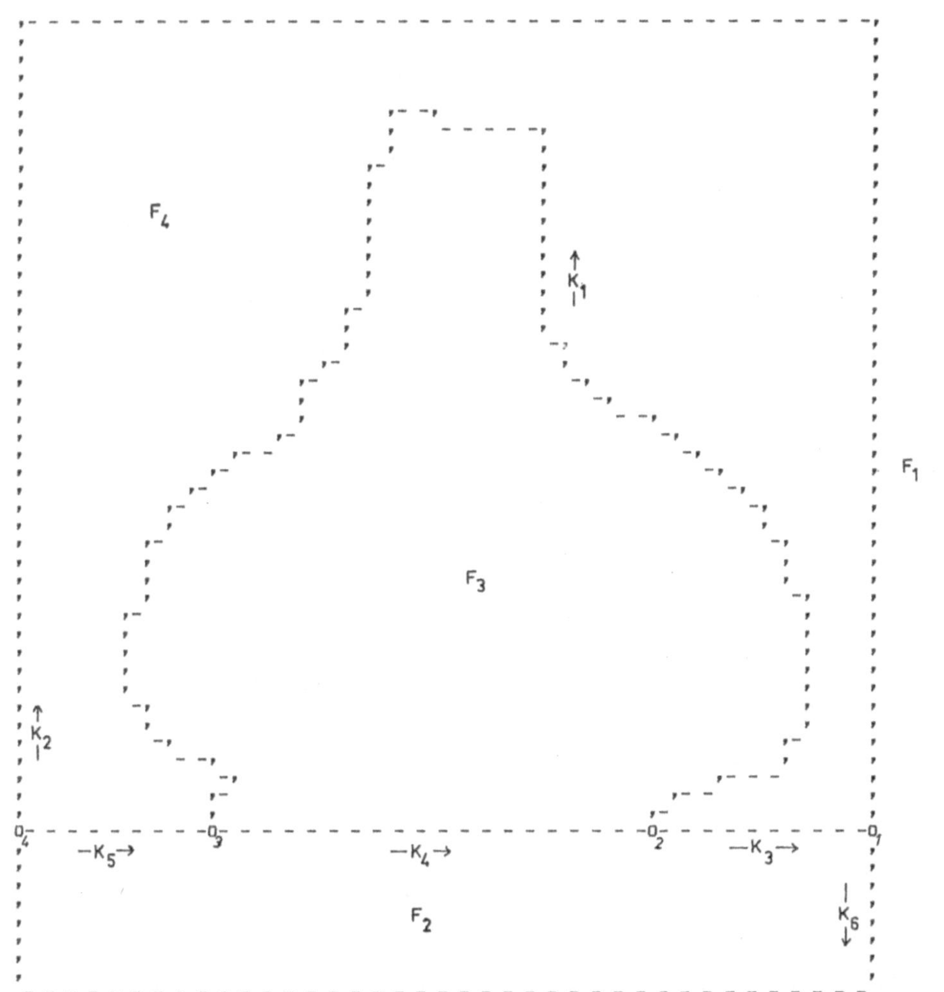

Abbildung 8

SKIZZE

Modellobjekt HAUS

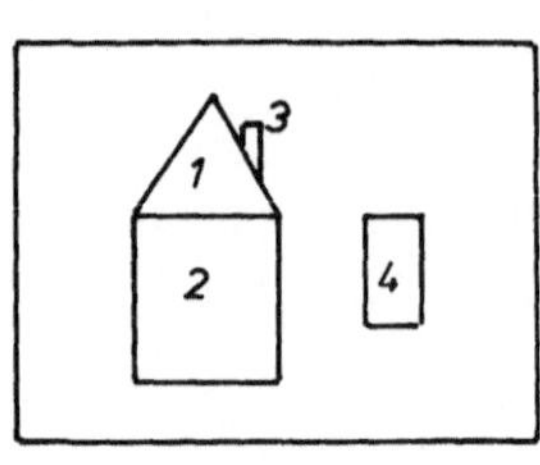

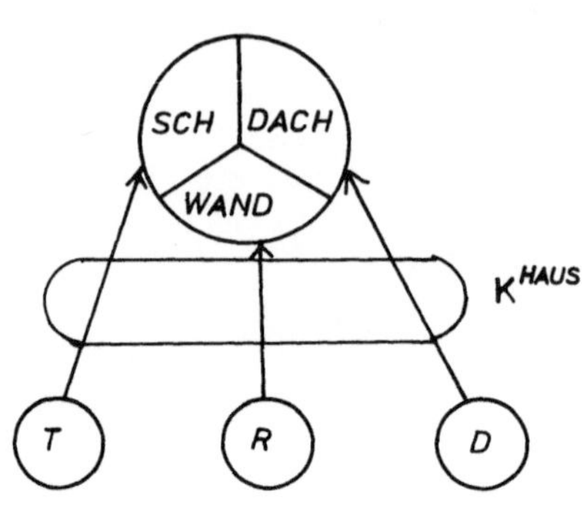

T:=TRAPEZ
R:=RECHTECK
D:=DREIECK

I^{TRAPEZ} = (TRAPEZ,3)

$I^{RECHTECK}$ = ((RECHTECK,2),(RECHTECK,4))

$I^{DREIECK}$ = (DREIECK,1)

$\tilde{R}^{HAUS}$ = ((NACHBAR, SCH, DACH),(NACHBAR, DACH, WAND),(ÜBER,SCH, DACH),(ÜBER,DACH,WAND))

Zuordnungsgraph: (ZG_1, ZG_2, ZG_3, ZG_4)

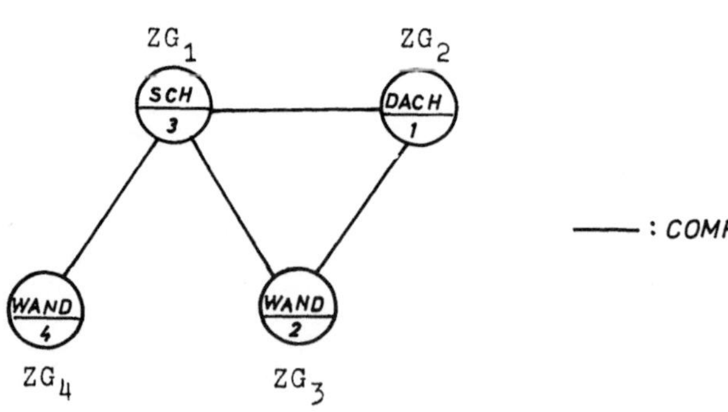

Maximale Clique: (ZG_1, ZG_2, ZG_3)

I^{HAUS} = ((SCH,3), (DACH,1), (WAND,2))

<u>Digitalisation of Pictures and Data Graphs</u>

P. GUICHET

Université de BESANCON (FRANCE)

Introduction

The aim of the model of digitalisation presented in this paper is twofold :

1) The model must allow the representation of topological, and geometrical properties of digitalised pictures on any kind of grid or the description of texture just in terms of strings of characters over a finite set, avoiding us to carry a coordinate system which cauld be heavy.

2) It must helps to implement the picture into the random acces memory of a computer. This is done by remarking that . the model introduced here is a restriction of the concept of data graphs, which are objects, now extensively studied, and whose aim is (among others) to provide tools for the implementation of all classes of data structures.

The paper has three parts, in (1) digitalisation structures are presented, in (2) Data graphs are introduced and the link digitalisation structures is shown ; in (3) two exemples are presented.

1) Digitalisation Structure

Definition 1.1.) Let I be a countable set, and T be a finite set of (possibly partial) Transformations of I. Each member of I being represented by the symbol t_i where i ranges over $1, \ldots,$ card(T)=p. FG(p) denotes the Free Group over $\left\{t_1, \ldots, t_p\right\}$. Given any $w \in FG(p)$, w acts on I by : if $i \in I$, and $w \in FG(p)$, $w = s_1 \cdots s_n$ then $w(i) = (\ldots s_n (s_{n-1}(\ldots s_2(s_1(i))\ldots)$; whenever this composition of functions is defined.

Then if a) for $i = 1,\ldots,p$ the function represented by t_i is without

      fixed point

    b) for $i = 1,\ldots,p$ the restriction of t_i to this domain is one

      to one

    c) FG(p) acts transitively on I

    d) Given $s_1, s_2 \in T$ and $i \in I$, if both expressions $s_1(s_2(i))$ and

      $s_2(s_1(i))$ are defined then they are equal

    Then the pair (I,FG(p)) is a digitalisation structure.

In the sequel, given $w \in FG(p)$ and $i \in I$, $w(i)$ must be interpreted

as the result of the application of s_1 to i, then of s_2 to $s_1(i)$ is

defined and so on ... Of course $w(i)$ may be undefined.

Exemple 1.2.) Let $I = \mathbb{Z} \times \mathbb{Z}$ (where $\mathbb{Z}$ is the set of relative integers), and

$T_2 = \{h, v\}$ h and v are the names of the functions $\begin{cases} (i,j) \xrightarrow{h} (i+1,j) \\ (i,j) \xrightarrow{v} (i,j+1) \end{cases}$

respectively. Then it is easily seen that the properties of digitalisa-

tion structures are verified by the pair (I,T). In practice one must

restrict I to the product of two closed intervals of $\mathbb{Z}$, and then h and

v became undefined on the "border" of I.

Exemple 1.3.) Let $I = \left\{ (i\sqrt{3}, 3j) \mid (i,j) \in \mathbb{Z} \times \mathbb{Z} \right\} \cup \left\{ (2i+1)\, \dfrac{\sqrt{3}}{2}\, , 3(j+\dfrac{1}{2}) \mid (i,j) \in \mathbb{Z} \times \mathbb{Z} \right\}$

and $T_3 = \left\{ h_1, h_2, h_3 \right\}$ where $h_1 : (p,q) \longrightarrow (p + \sqrt{3}\, , q)$

$$h_2 : (p,q) \longrightarrow (p + \dfrac{\sqrt{3}}{2}\, , q + \dfrac{3}{2})$$

$$h_3 : (p,q) \longrightarrow (p - \dfrac{\sqrt{3}}{2}\, , q + \dfrac{3}{2})$$

Then it is easily seen that the pair (I, T_3) is a digitalisation

Structure.

I can be interpreted as the set of tiles of the regular tiling of the plane by hexagons of radius 1.

Remark : In [1] Mylopoulos and Pavlidis present a Model wich is based on
the notion of finitely presented abelian groups, in order to
express topological properties in terms of combinatorial group
theory.

Definition 1.4.) Let $i \in I$, and $w = s_1 s_2 \ldots s_q \in FG(p)$, then the set $\{i, s_1(i),$
$s_2(s_1(i), \ldots, w(i)\}$ is a path from i to w(i). the length of this path
is the length of the word w.

w can be interpreted as a chain code for the set of points
$\{i, s_1(i), \ldots, w(i)\}$

Let (I,T) be digitalisation structure, we define a mapping
$d : I \times I \to R^+ U \{o\}$ by : for all $i, j \in I$ $d(i,j)=Min \{$Length of all paths
from i to j $\}$. the mapping d is well defined for

    1) for every (i,j) there exists a path from i to j because FG(p)
       acts transitively on I

    2) every subset of N (natural integers) has a minimal element.

Lemma 1.5.) the mapping d is a distance on J

  - $d(i,i)=0$ for the length of the word representing the identity
    function on I, is the length of the empty word i:e 0.

  - $d(i,j)=d(j,i)$ for if $w=s_1 s_2 \ldots s_p$ is a path of minimal length from
    i to j then the function represented by $s_p^{-1} s_{p-1}^{-1} \ldots s_1^{-1}$, is defined,
    and can be used to construct a path from j to i. this path will be
    of minimal length.

  - Suppose that there exists $k \in I$ such that $d(i,k)+d(k,j)$ $d(i,j)$,
    then we can construct a "function" ; w ; by composing the functions

used to build the minimal path from i to k, and k to j. the word w

will be of length $<d(i,j)$, wich is impossible since d(i,j) is minimal ;

hence such a k cannot exist.

From Lemma 1.5.) it comes immediatly that if (I,T) is a digitalisation

structure, then (I,d) is a metric space.

Exemple 1.6.) In exemple (1.2.) I = $\mathbb{Z} \times \mathbb{Z}$ is equipped with the "city

block" distance.

Définition 1.7.) Let $i \in I$ and $q \in N$, the set $V: (i,q) = \left\{ j \mid j \in I \text{ and} \right.$

$\left. d(i,j) \leq q \right\}$, is the neighborhood of i, of order q. If $q \leq 1$, and

$(i,j) \in V(i,q)$ then i, and j are said neighbor.

Remark 1.8.) Since the work of Rosenfeld $\begin{bmatrix} 5 , 6 \end{bmatrix}$ it is well known that

when "scanning" the "rectangular (square) grid" of exemple 1.2. one

must use two distances, the distance induced on I by FG(2) and the

distance induced on I by FG(4) where FG(4) is the free   group

over $T_4 = T_2 \cup \left\{ d_1, d_2 \right\}$, d_1 and d_2 being interpreted as $d_1 : (i,j) =$

$(i+1,j+1)$; $d_2 : (i,j) = (i-1,j+1)$,·

Definition 1.9.) A binary pattern on (I,T) is a mapping $P : I \rightarrow \left\{ 0,1 \right\}$ such

that $P^{-1}(1)$ is a finite set. $P^{-1}(1)$ is said to be a binary picture ;

the same P is given to a binary pattern and his associated picture.

Définition 1.10.) Let P be a picture and $i,j \in P$, i dans j are said

connected in P if there exists a path (see 1.4.) from i to j (hence

also a path from j to i) such that every element of the path is in P.

It is easy to verify that connectivity induces an equivalence relation on

the "points" of P. the equivalence classes modulo this relation are

called the connected components of P. The number of connected components of I-P is called the order of connectivity of P.

2) Data Graphs

The concept of data graph was introduced by A. Rosenberg in $[2]$, to study structural uniformity appearing in data structures. We show here that the digitalisation structure introduced in (1) can be naturally imbedded in data graphs ; and even, in fact can be viewed as data graphs of a restricted kind.

Définition 2.1.)   2   A data graph is a pair $G = (C,F)$ where

    a) C is a countable set (the set of data cells)

    b) F is a finite set of partial transformations of C such that for every pair $(c,d) \in C \times C$ there exists a transformation $g \in MF$ such that $g(c) = d$ (MF denotes the monoïd generated over F by functional composition)

  Remark : To the system (C,F), one can associate a labelled oriented graph G, in the following manner : The set of vertices of G will be C, and there is an arc from vertex c to vertex d, with the label $f \in F$ if and only if $f(c) = d$

  Definition 2.2.) An adressing scheme for the data graph G:(C,F) is an application $A:C \longrightarrow MF$ such that

    a) there exists a cell $c_0 \in C$ such that $A(c_0) = 1_c$ (identy element of MF)

    b) for every $f \in F$ and all $c \in Dom(f)$ $A \bullet f(c) = f \bullet A(c)$

  Remark : c_0 is called the base cell of G. The "adress" of the cell f(c) is interpreted as a product in MF. A data graph is adressable if it admits an adressing scheme

Definition 2.3.) A data cell $c_o \in C$ is a root of $G = (C,F)$ if for all g,

$h \in MF$, defined in c_o $g = h$ if $g(c_o) = h(c_o)$

Theorem 2.4.) Rosenberg [2] . A data graph is adressable if and only he is

rooted. Moreover each root of G is the base cell of an addressing scheme

for G, and the base cell of each addressing scheme for G is a root of G.

Exemple 2.5.) Let C be $\{1,...,p\} \times \{1,...,q\}$ and F be $\{h_1,v_1,h_2,v_2\}$ with

$(i,j) \in C$: $h_1 \; (i,j)$ = if $i < p$ then $(i+1,j)$ else undefined ;

$h_2 \; (i,j)$ = if $i > o$ then $(i-1,j)$ else undefined.

$v_1 \; (i,j)$ = if $j < q$ then $(i,j+1)$ else undefined ;

$v_2 \; (i,j)$ = if $j > o$ then $(i,j-1)$ else undefined.

here is the data structure generally used to represent digitalised

pictures.

One can verify that $A:\{1,...,p\} \times \{1,...,q\} \to MF$ defined by (i,j)

$\to h_1^{i-1} \, v_1^{j-1}$ is an addressing scheme for the above data graph.

Exemple 2.6.) Let C be $\{a_o...a_q \mid a_o = o, a_i = 1,2$ for $o < i \leq q$ and

$$a_o...a_q \in C \Rightarrow a_o...a_{q-1} \in C\}$$

Let F be $\{l,r,f\}$ such that

$l(a_o,...a_q)$ = if $a_q = 2$ and $a_o...(a_q-1) \in C$ then $a_o...(a_{q-1})$ else undefined

$r(a_o....a_q)$ = if $a_q = 1$ and $a_o...(a_q+1) \in C$ then $a_o...(a_q+1)$ else undefined

$f(a_o...a_q)$ = if $q > o$ then $a_o...a_{q-1}$ else undefined

(C,F) can be interpreted as a binary tree. A the application of C in

MF recursively defined by $A(a_o) = 1_C$ (identity on C), and $A(a_o...a_q) =$ if

$a_q = 1$ then $l \, A(a_o...a_{q-1})$ else $r \, A(a_o...a_{q-1})$ is an addressing scheme

for (C,F).

Now one can see that any digitalisation structure in the sense of

paragraph (1) is just a data graph. We let C be the set I of "points"
of the structure and F be the set of transforms T over wich generated
FG(p), the group which is used to structure I.

Now the problem is to implement (C,F) in the Random Access Memory of a
Computer.

Definition 2.8.) A realisation of the Data Graph (C,F) is a pair of one
to one applications (m,r) where

a) $m: C \longrightarrow \{1,\ldots,q\}$ m is the "memory map"

b) $r: F \longrightarrow \{\text{partial transforms of } \{1,\ldots,q\}\}$; $\{1,\ldots,q\}$ represents the
storage area.

c) Whenever one of the functions $m \circ g$, or $r(g) \circ m$ are defined , $(g \in F)$
then both are, and they are equal.

the quality of a realisation can be examined through the following criteria.

a) Computational complexity of m : that is difficulty to access any
element.

b) Complexity of traversal : that is given a "path" in FG(p) what is
the computational complexity of the sequence $r(g_1(i))$, $r(g_2 g_1(i))$,....,
$r(g_n - (g_1(i))$. here i is the origin of the path and $g_1 \ldots g_n$
represents the function difining the path

c) Is our utilisation of the memory space efficient ?

In some case we can add an other criterion which is the ease of extension
of (C,F). This concerns the extent to which we must reorganize the storage
space when new elements are added to C. See for exemple Rosenberg $[4]$.

3) Examples

3.1.) It is known that semi regular tesselations can be a useful tool,

in describing texture properties of digital picture ; see Zucker $[8]$.

The Data graph associated with the (4,8,8) tesselation is given here,

togather with a possible realisation.

Let C be $\left\{ (i+\frac{1}{2}, j+\frac{1}{2}) \mid (i,j) \in \mathbb{Z} \times \mathbb{Z} \right\} \cup (Z \times Z)$.

and $F = \left\{ t_1, \ldots, t_4 \right\}$ where for any $(x,y) \in C$

$t_1((x,y)) = $ If $(x,y) \in \mathbb{Z} \times \mathbb{Z}$ then $(x+1,y)$ else undefined.

$t_2((x,y)) = (x+\frac{1}{2}, y+\frac{1}{2})$

$t_3((x,y)) = $ If $(x,y) \in \mathbb{Z} \times \mathbb{Z}$ then $(x,y+1)$ else undefined.

$t_4((x,y)) = (x-\frac{1}{2}, y+\frac{1}{2})$

then one can easily verify that (C,F) is a digitalisation structure, and

thus a Data graph ; the following is a realisation of this data graph.

As a realisation is wanted, C is restricted to a bounded part of the

plane by taking $C' = \left\{ 1, \ldots p \right\} \times \left\{ 1, \ldots, p \right\} \cup \left\{ i+\frac{1}{2}, j+\frac{1}{2} \mid 1 \leqslant i, j \leqslant p \right\}$

let m be defined by : for any $(a,b) \in C'$

$m(a,b) = 2 \left[p(\lfloor a \rfloor - 1) + \lfloor b \rfloor \right] + \left[2(a - \lfloor a \rfloor) - 1 \right]$. As usual $\lfloor x \rfloor$ is the integer part

of x.

then m is a one to one mapping of C' on to $\left\{ 1, \ldots, 2p^2 \right\} \subset N$. m is the

memory map. Let r, a mapping from F into the set of partial transforms

of $\left\{ 1, \ldots, 2p^2 \right\}$, be defined by : for any $x \in \left\{ 1, \ldots, 2p^2 \right\}$

$r(t_1)(x) = $ If $x \equiv o \pmod 2$ then undefined

else if $x \equiv 2p-1 \pmod{2p}$ then undefined   Else $x+2$

$r(t_2)(x) = $ If $(x \equiv o \pmod{2p})$ or $((x > 2p(p-1))$ and $(x \equiv o \pmod 2)))$

then undefined

Else If x ≡ 1 (mod 2) then x+1 Else x+2p+1

$r(t_3)(x)$ = If x ≡ o (mod 2) then undefined

Else if x > 2p(p-1) then undefined Else x+2p

$r(t_4)(x)$ = If (x ≡ 1 (mod 2p)) or ((x > 2p(p-1)) and (x ≡ o(mod 2)))

then undefined

Else If x ≡ 1 (mod 2) then x-1 Else x+2p-1

then r is one to one and (m,r) is a realisation of (C',F) as one can verify.

3.2.) The hexagonal array of center i, and radius R, is defined as the

subset of the hexagonal, regular, tiling of exemple (1.3.) ; consisting

of all the elements of I such that d(i,j) ⩽ R for a given i ∈ I, and

R ∈ N. (In the corresponding digitalisation structure it is the neighbor-

hood of order R of i). Such structures have been studied in terms of

growing Radial L-Systems by Siromoney [7] . A data graph associated

to an hexagonal array and a possible realisation of it are given.

The data graph is defined by mean of **a paging** scheme, together with

a "slice" technique.

C is taken as $\left\{ (s,d,p) \mid 1 \leqslant s \leqslant 6,\ 1 \leqslant d \leqslant R,\ 1 \leqslant p \leqslant d \right\} \cup (o,o,1)$

s is the page number, it is the number of the sextant of the plane,

where the cell is situated ; d is the slice number, a slice being the

set of all elements of a given sextant, situated at the same distance

of the center i ; p is the place number of the cell in its slice, the

cells being numbered in the direct sens.

Defining s_1, s_2, s_3 the elements of F is a tedious job , by lack of

space only s_1 is presented.

$s_1(1,d,p) =$ If $d \leqslant R$ then $(1,d+1,p)$

    else undefined

$s_1(2,d,p) =$ If $p > 1$ then $(2,d,p-1)$

    else if $d < R$ then $(1,d+1,d+1)$ else undefined

$s_1(3,d,p) =$ If $p > 1$ then $(3,d-1,p)$

    else $(2,d,d)$

$s_1(4,d,p) =$ If $p \neq d$ then $(4,d-1,p)$

    else IF $d \neq 1$ then $(5,d-1,1)$ else $(o,o,1)$

$s_1(5,d,p) =$ If $p \neq d$ then $(5,d,p+1)$

    else $(6,d,1)$

$s_1(6,c,p) =$ If $d < R$ then $(6,d+1,p+1)$

    else undefined

$s_1(o,o,1) = (1,1,1)$

    the inverses of s_1, s_2, s_3 are defined in the same way.

Now a realisation of (C,F) can be defined by (m,r) where the memory map m

is : if$(s,d,p) \in C$ then $m((s,d,p)) = 1 + (s-1)\left[\dfrac{R(R+1)}{2}\right] + \dfrac{d(d-1)}{2} + p$

m is a one to one mapping of C onto $\left\{1,2,\ldots,1+3(R(R+1))\right\} = \text{Range}(m)$

For each s_i(or s_i^{-1}) r is defined by

$x \in \text{Range}(m) \qquad r(s_i)(x) = m(s_i(m^{-1}(x)))$.

Note that for some x this can be undefined.

4) Conclusion :

A model for digitalized pictures has been presented ; it has been used to show that digitalised pictures are a special kind of more general object : Data graphs, and that these objects can be used in picture processing for the representation of pictures, or models of Textures in the random access memory of a Computer. They can, also be useful when processing at higher levels, and when using more elaborate Data Structures (e:g Pyramidal Structures).

References

1   Mylopoulos and Paulidis : The Topology of quantized Spaces I and II
                    JACM vol 18, pages 247-254

2   Rosenberg : Data graphs, and addressing schemes. Journal of computer
                    System Science 5, (1971) pages 193-238

3   Rosenberg : Adressable Data graphs
                    JACM vol 19, pages 309-340

4   Rosenberg : Allocating Storage for Extendible Arrays
                    JACM vol 21, pages 652-670

5   Rosenfeld : Connectivity in digital pictures
                    JACM vol 17 pages 146-160

6   Rosenfeld : Arcs and curues in digital pictures
                    JACM vol 20

7   Siromoney : Computer Graphics and image processing - vol 5, pages 353-381

8   Zucker   : Toward a Model of Texture
                    Computer Graphics and image processing vol 5,n°2 pp.190-202

<u>ENHANCING DIGITIZED IMAGES BY CONTROLLED TRANSDUCER TREMOR</u>

Michael J. Magee

Assistant Professor of
Computer Science

University of Wyoming

Laramie, Wyoming
USA

ABSTRACT

A method is proposed for improving the resolution of visual images beyond the limits imposed by stationary transducers. This procedure consists of causing the transducer grid to shift with respect to the visual field, recording the components of the shift, and correlating the transducer element states over many such tremors to achieve a more accurate mapping of the image. The method is investigated in a formal manner by proving three theorems which characterize the refinement capabilities. Simulated mappings are illustrated by employing a computer model which embodies the specified refinement procedure.

INTRODUCTION

Assume that one has the following matrices:

(a) N x N visual field matrix F,

(b) N x N transducer matrix T, and

(c) N x N matrix C.

Now, if the goal is to map F onto C as accurately as possible by projecting F onto T (i.e. $T_{i,j} = F_{i,j}$) and then letting $C_{i,j} = T_{i,j}$, the task is relatively straightforward (if one neglects noise, or varying thresholds of T's elements). However, if the resolution of T is more crude than F and C (i.e. T is M x M and M < N) then the mapping of F onto C in an accurate fashion is not directly achievable since F projects onto T many to one and T maps onto C one to many. To attempt to regain the best resolution of F's mapping onto C through crude transducer T, the following method is proposed.

THE REFINEMENT ALGORITHM

I. The goal will be to map, as accurately as possible, an NxN portion of a visual field matrix F onto an NxN portion of matrix C through an MxM transducer matrix where M < N and N/M is an integer (let R = N/M). For purposes of consistency in later steps let the NxN portions of F and C toward which the mapping is directed be specified by $[F_{i,j}]$, $[C_{i,j}]$ for all i,jϵ S = {R,R+1, ..., R+(N-1)}. This essentially places a border of width (R-1) around the central NxN portions

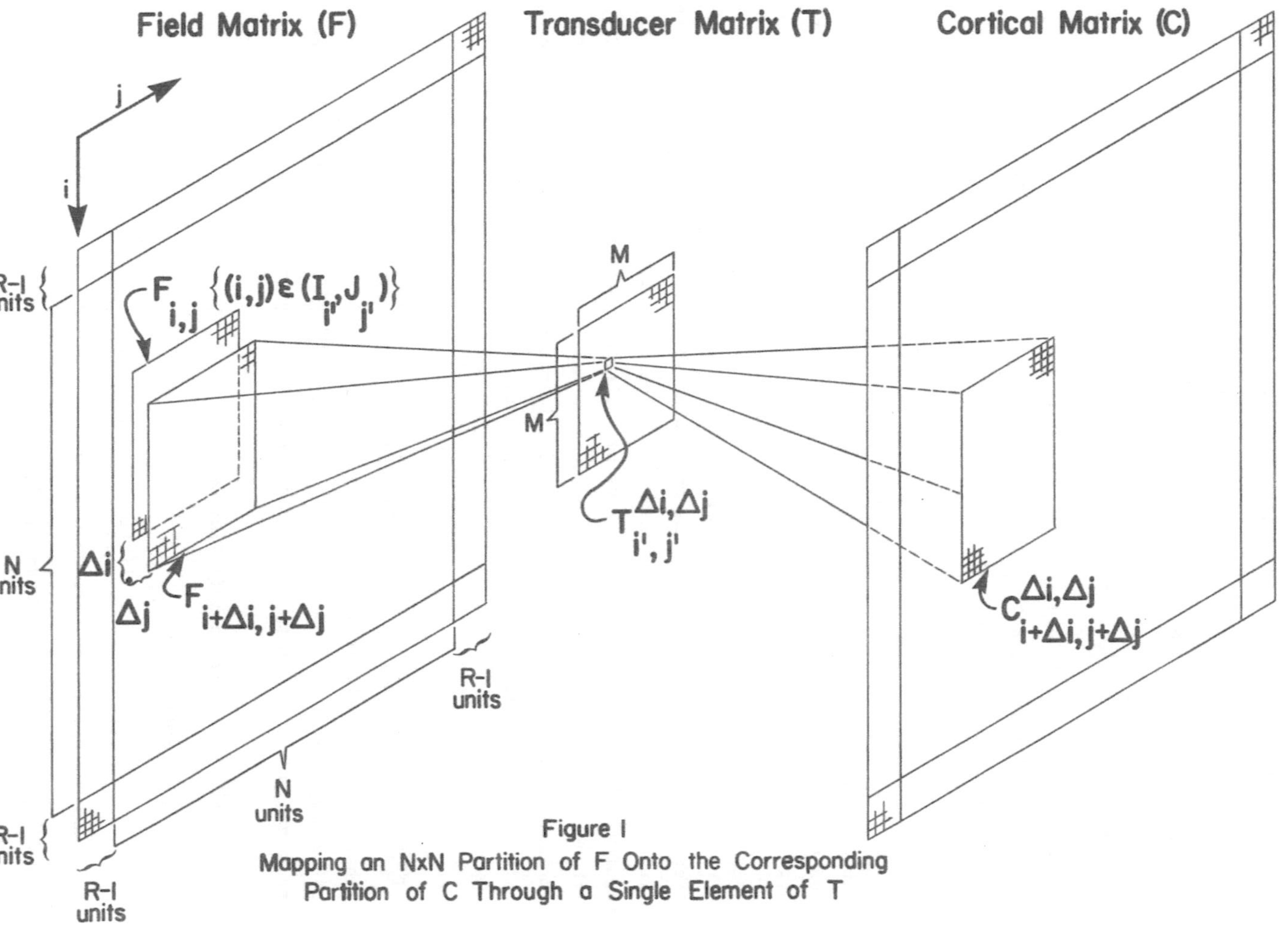

Figure I

Mapping an NxN Partition of F Onto the Corresponding
Partition of C Through a Single Element of T

of F onto which the elements of the transducer can move.

II. Define sets $I_{i'} = \{Ri', Ri'+1, \ldots, R(i'+1) -1\}$,

$$J_{j'} = \{Rj', Rj'+1, \ldots, R(j'+1) -1\}$$

for $1 \leq i', j' \leq M$.

$$\text{Let } I^* = \bigcup_{i'=1}^{M} I_{i'} \, , \; J^* = \bigcup_{j'=1}^{M} J_{j'}.$$

The sets $I_{i'}$, $J_{j'}$ will later be used to define subscript partitions for RxR submatrices of F and C, such that F's partition will map (many to one) onto $T_{i',j'}$ and $T_{i',j'}$ will map (one to many) onto the submatrix of C corresponding to that of F. (Note that $I^* = J^* = S$.)

III. Assume that the initial alignment (before any transducer tremor) of T with respect to F is such that $F_{i,j}$ is projected onto $T_{i',j'}$ for all $i \epsilon I_{i'}$, $j \epsilon J_{j'}$. Thus the NxN central portion of F is projected onto the entire MxM matrix T in an R^2:1 fashion.

IV. Generate (randomly or by other means) integers $\Delta i, \Delta j$ such that $|\Delta i|, |\Delta j| \leq (R-1)$. These will denote the values of the transducer shift (with respect to F) in the directions in which i and j increase. Since neither $\Delta i, \Delta j$ can exceed (R-1) in magnitude, an element of T will always have elements of F projected onto it, although they may not be those in the central NxN portion of F. (Note: For simplicity sake in proofs that follow, consider the initial $\Delta i = \Delta j = 0$ since no shift has taken place after initial alignment.

V. Let

$$T_{i',j'}^{\Delta i, \Delta j} = \Sigma F_{i+\Delta i, j+\Delta j} \text{ for all } (i,j) \epsilon (I_i \, X \, J_j), \; |\Delta i| \leq (R-1), \; |\Delta j| \leq (R-1)$$

where Σ denotes the logical sum (or).

This simply states that after a shift of $\Delta i, \Delta j$, $T_{i',j'}^{\Delta i, \Delta j} = 1$ if there exists at least one <u>on</u> element in the RxR submatrix of F that projects onto it.

VI. (A) Let $C_{i,j}^{\Delta i, \Delta j} = 1$ for all $(i,j) \epsilon (SxS)$

(or equivalently let

$$C_{i+\Delta i, j+\Delta j}^{\Delta i, \Delta j} = 1 \text{ for all } (i+\Delta i, j+\Delta j) \epsilon (SxS)$$

(B) Then for all i', j' such that $1 \leq i', j' \leq M$ let

$$C_{i+\Delta i, j+\Delta j}^{\Delta i, \Delta j} = T_{i',j'}^{\Delta i, \Delta j} \text{ for } (i+\Delta i, j+\Delta j) \epsilon (SxS)$$
$$(i,j) \epsilon (I_i \, x \, J_j)$$

From (A) and (B) it is evident that for any $(i+\Delta i, j+\Delta j) \epsilon (SxS)$

143

$C_{i+\Delta i,j+\Delta j}^{\Delta i,\Delta j}$ can be zero only if the following two conditions are true.

    (1)   There must exist i',j' such that $1 \le i', j' \le M$ and $(i,j)\epsilon(I_{i'} \times J_{j'})$.

    (2) $T_{i',j'}^{\Delta i,\Delta j} = 0$

VII.   Repeat steps IV, V, VI a "sufficient" number of times (e.g. through all allowed $\Delta i, \Delta j$'s).

VIII. Let $C_{i,j}^{*} = \Pi C_{i,j}^{\Delta i,\Delta j}$ for all Δi, Δj generated, $(i,j)\epsilon(S \times S)$.

At this point it is hoped that $C_{i,j}^{*} = F_{i,j}$, though this will in general not be the case. Obviously, if there is no Δi, Δj such that $C_{i,j}^{\Delta i,\Delta j} = 0$ then $C_{i,j}^{*} = 1$ even if $F_{i,j} = 0$.

The following theorems characterize the actual results.

<u>Theorem 1</u>:

$F_{a,b} = 1 \Rightarrow C_{a,b}^{*} = 1$ for all $(a,b)\epsilon(S \times S)$

Proof: Assume $F_{a,b} = 1$ for some $(a,b)\epsilon(S \times S)$. Then for any transducer tremor $\Delta i, \Delta j$ choose $\hat{i}, \hat{j}$ such that $a = \hat{i}+\Delta i$, $b=\hat{j}+\Delta j$.

Now assume that $C_{\hat{i}+\Delta i,\hat{j}+\Delta j}^{\Delta i,\Delta j} = C_{a,b}^{\Delta i,\Delta j} = 0$.

As a result of step VI, it is known that there must exist i', j' such that $1 \le i', j' \le M$, $(\hat{i},\hat{j})\epsilon(I_{i'} \times J_{j'})$, and $T_{i',j'}^{\Delta i,\Delta j} = 0$.

If this is true, however, all

     $F_{i+\Delta i,j+\Delta j}$ must be 0 for $(i,j)\epsilon(I_{i'} \times J_{j'})$

Since (by step IV)

     $T_{i',j'}^{\Delta i,\Delta j} = \Sigma F_{i+\Delta i,j+\Delta j}$ for all $(i,j)\epsilon(I_{i'} \times J_{j'})$.

But $(\hat{i},\hat{j})\epsilon(I_{i'} \times J_{j'})$ and $F_{i+\Delta i,j+\Delta j} = 1$

     (since $F_{a,b} = 1$).

This contradiction implies that if $F_{a,b} = 1$ then

     $C_{a,b}^{\Delta i,\Delta j} = 1$ for any allowed $\Delta i, \Delta j$.

It then follows (from VIII) that $C_{a,b}^{*} = 1$.

     q.e.d.

<u>Theorem 2</u>: If for some $(a,b) \epsilon (S \times S)$

$C^*_{a,b} = 0$ then $F_{a,b} = 0$.

Proof:

Assume that $C^*_{a,b} = 0$ for some $(a,b) \epsilon (S \times S)$. Now if $F_{a,b} = 1$, $C^*_{a,b}$ must also be 1 (by Theorem 1). Hence $F_{a,b} = 0$.

<u>Theorem 3</u>:

Given the following conditions $(C_1, \ldots, C_4)$, $C^*_{a,b} = 1$.

C_1) There exist $(a,b), (a_1,b_1), (a_2,b_2), (a_3,b_3),$

$(a_4,b_4) \epsilon (S \times S)$ such that

C_2) $a_1, a_2, \leq a \leq a_3, a_4$

$b_1, b_4 \leq b \leq b_2, b_3$

C_3) $(a_3 - a_1), (a_3 - a_2), (a_4 - a_1), (a_4 - a_2) \leq R$

$(b_2 - b_1), (b_2 - b_4), (b_3 - b_1), (b_3 - b_4) \leq R$

C_4) $F_{a_1,b_1} = F_{a_2,b_2} = F_{a_3,b_3} = F_{a_4,b_4} = 1$

To prove that $C^*_{a,b} = 1$ under these conditions, the results of the following lemmas are needed.

<u>Lemma 1</u>:

If $a_k = \hat{i}_k + \Delta i \leq \hat{i} + \Delta i = a,$

$\hat{i}_k \notin I_{i^-}$, and $\hat{i} \epsilon I_{i^-}$, then $\hat{i}_k < R \cdot i^-$.

(Similarly if $b_k = \hat{j}_k + \Delta j \leq \hat{j} + \Delta j = b,$

$\hat{j}_k \notin J_{j^-}$, and $\hat{j} \epsilon J_{j^-}$, then $\hat{j}_k < R \cdot j^-$)

Proof:

Let $a_k = \hat{i}_k + \Delta i \leq \hat{i} + \Delta i = a$, $\hat{i}_k \notin I_{i^-}$, $\hat{i} \epsilon I_{i^-}$.

Assume $\hat{i}_k \geq R \cdot i^-$. Since

$\hat{i} \epsilon I_{i^-} = \{R \cdot i^-, R \cdot i^- + 1, \ldots, R(i^- + 1) - 1\},$

there must exist an integer C, $0 \leq C < R$

such that $\hat{i} = R \cdot i^- + C$. Now $a_k \leq a \Rightarrow \hat{i}_k \leq \hat{i}$

which implies $R \cdot i^- \leq \hat{i}_k \leq R \cdot i^- + C = \hat{i}$. But

$\hat{i}_k \notin I_{i'}$ contradicts $R \cdot i' \leq \hat{i}_k \leq R \cdot i' + C$.

Hence $\hat{i}_k < R \cdot i'$.

<u>Lemma 2:</u>

If $a_k = \hat{i}_k + \Delta i \geq \hat{i} + \Delta i = a$, $\hat{i}_k \notin I_{i'}$, $i \varepsilon I_{i'}$,

then $\hat{i}_k \geq R(i'+1)$ (i.e. $\hat{i}_k - R \geq R \cdot i'$).

(Similarly, if $b_k = \hat{j}_k + \Delta j \geq \hat{j} + \Delta j = b$, $\hat{j}_k \notin J_{j'}$,

$\hat{j} \varepsilon J_{j'}$, then $\hat{j}_k - R \geq R \cdot j'$)

Proof: the manner of proof is similar to Lemma 1.

Proof of the main theorem:

Given $C_1 - C_4$ assume that there exist $\Delta i, \Delta j$ such that

$$C_{a,b}^{\Delta i, \Delta j} = 0 \text{ (to be contradicted)}.$$

Then choose $\hat{i}_k, \hat{j}_k$ such that

$\hat{i}_k + \Delta i = a_k, \hat{j}_k + \Delta j = b_k$, for $k = 1, \ldots, 4$ and

$\hat{i}, \hat{j}$ such that $\hat{i} + \Delta i = a$, $\hat{j} + \Delta j = b$.

From VI, there must exist i', j' such that

$1 \leq i', j' \leq M$, $(\hat{i}, \hat{j}) \varepsilon (I_{i'} \times J_{j'})$, and

$T_{i',j'}^{\Delta i, \Delta j} = 0$. This implies that $F_{i+\Delta i, j+\Delta j}^{\Delta i, \Delta j} = 0$ for all

$(i,j) \varepsilon (I_{i'} \times J_{j'})$ (see V). Then

$(\hat{i}_k, \hat{j}_k) \notin (I_{i'} \times J_{j'})$ since $F_{a_k, b_k} = 1$ for $K = 1, \ldots, 4$.

Thus either (or both) $\hat{i}_k \notin I_{i'}$ or $\hat{j}_k \notin J_{j'}$.

This is proved to be impossible by contradicting (denoted by $\#$) given condition C_3 by cases.

<u>Case A:</u> Assume $\hat{i}_1 \notin I_{i'}$.

Lemma 1 $\Rightarrow \hat{i}_1 < R \cdot i'$

<u>Case A.1:</u> Assume $\hat{i}_3 \notin I_{i'}$

Lemma 2 $= \hat{i}_3 - R \geq R \cdot i'$.

Hence $(\hat{i}_3 - \hat{i}_1) > R \Rightarrow (a_3 - a_1) > R$ $(\#)$

since $(\hat{i}_3-\hat{i}_1) = (a_3-a_1)$.

<u>Case A.2</u>: Assume $\hat{i}_3 \ \epsilon \ I_{i'}$. Then $\hat{j}_3 \notin J_{j'}$.

Lemma 2 = $\hat{j}_3 - R \geq R \cdot j'$

<u>Case A.2.a</u>: Assume $\hat{i}_4 \notin I_{i'}$.

Lemma 2 => $\hat{i}_4 - R \geq R \cdot i'$.

Hence $(a_4-a_1) = (\hat{i}_4-\hat{i}_1) > R$ (#)

<u>Case A.2.b</u>: Assume $\hat{i}_4 \ \epsilon \ I_{i'}$. Then $\hat{j}_4 \notin J_{j'}$.

Lemma 1 => $j_4 < R \cdot j'$.

Hence $(b_3-b_4) = (\hat{j}_3-\hat{j}_4) > R$ (#)

<u>Case B</u>: Assume $\hat{i}_1 \epsilon I_{i'}$. Then $j_1 \notin J_{j'}$.

Lemma 1 => $\hat{j}_1 < R \cdot j'$

<u>Case B.1</u>: Assume $\hat{j}_3 \notin J_{j'}$.

Lemma 2 => $\hat{j}_3 - R \geq R \cdot j'$.

Hence $(b_3-b_1) = (\hat{j}_3-\hat{j}_1) > R$ (#)

<u>Case B.2</u>: Assume $\hat{j}_3 \epsilon J_{j'}$. Then $\hat{i}_3 \notin I_{i'}$

Lemma 2 => $\hat{i}_3 - R \geq R \cdot i'$

<u>Case B.2.a</u>: Assume $\hat{i}_2 \notin I_{i'}$.

Lemma 1 => $\hat{i}_2 < R \cdot i'$

Hence $(a_3-a_2) = (\hat{i}_3-\hat{i}_2) > R$ (#)

<u>Case B.2.b</u>: Assume $\hat{i}_2 \epsilon I_{i'}$. Then $\hat{j}_2 \notin J_{j'}$.

Lemma 2 => $\hat{j}_2 - R \geq R \cdot j'$

Hence $(b_2-b_1) = (\hat{j}_2-\hat{j}_1) > R$ (#)

Thus the assumption that $C_{a,b}^{\Delta i,\Delta j} = 0$ is wrong. It then follows that $C_{a,b}^{*}=1$ since all of the $C_{a,b}^{\Delta i,\Delta j}$'s in the product (see VI) are 1's. The essence of this theorem, then, is that is $F_{a,b}$ is surrounded (in the sense defined by C_1 through C_4) by <u>on</u> elements of F, then the resulting $C^*_{a,b}$ will also be on regardless of $F_{a,b}$'s state. (It should be noted here that Theorem 1 is actually a corollary of Theorem 3 for the case that $(a,b) = (a_1,b_1) = (a_2,b_2) = (a_3,b_3) = (a_4,b_4)$.

THE COMPUTER MODEL

The aforementioned procedure (I-VIII) was implemented in an ALGOL 60 program that cycled through all $\Delta i, \Delta j$ combinations randomly. To judge the rate at which refinement proceeded, the following measure was recorded at each tremor.

$$\gamma_m = \frac{(\text{number of extraneous on elements of C that have been eliminated after the mth tremor})}{(\text{number of extraneous on elements of C that can be eliminated after all tremors})} \times 100\%$$

i.e.

$$\gamma_m = \frac{\tau_o - \tau_m}{\tau_o - \tau_n} \times 100\%$$

where n is the total number of tremors allowed,

τ_o is the number of on elements of C before any tremors,

τ_n is the number of on elements of C after all tremors,

τ_m is the number of on elements after M tremors.

DATA

(1) As an initial test the letter A (see Figure 2a) was input with $N = 16$, $M = 4$ ($R = 4$). The rate of refinement (see Figure 2d) was dramatic. After only 7 tremors, γ was almost 80%. This high derivative of γ with respect to m was characteristic (for most samples tested) during the early tremors. Total achievable refinement was considerably later, however, with m usually larger than $(2R-1)^2/2$ (about 25 in this case). The final mapping of F onto C^* (see Figure 2c) shows that "gaps" in F (0's embedded among 1's) are indeed unresolved as Theorem 3 states. Although the accuracy of C^* is hampered by such gaps, in this case it seems to enhance the global structure of the pattern.

(2) The filling of gaps, as demonstrated by the refinement of Figure 2a, causes some rather interesting results when refining Figures 3a, 4a. In the cases of 3a and 4a, if $\delta < R$ units in F, perfect resolution cannot be achieved (see 3b, 4b).

(3) Figure 5a can be resolved into its component line segments as long as $\delta \geq 1$ units on F. However if a dot is added (see Figure 6a) the resolution again suffers as long as $\delta < R$.

(4) The difficulties encountered in resolving concave regions with certain orientations are illustrated by Figures 7a,b,c,d. The net effect is that the middle line

segment's length appears longer if the concavities open away from it.

CONCLUSIONS

It has been shown that an image mapping may be refined beyond the limits of stationary transducers, given that each recorded shift is small with respect to the size of individual transducer elements. The resolution of the mapping increases rapidly in the first few tremors, whereas total achievable resolution is not attained until very late in the procedure. The implications of this theory are that a camera with low resolution sensors could nevertheless be utilized to obtain high quality visual image mappings if its orientation could be accurately controlled and monitored.

```
  1
   1111111111
  111      1111
11           1111
11
111            111
 11            111
111            11
111111111111111
 111 11111  111
11             111
111             1
 11            11
11            111
111            11
111           111
```

The Visual Field Matrix (F)

Figure 2a

```
1111111111111111
1111111111111111
1111111111111111
1111111111111111
1111        1111
1111        1111
1111        1111
1111        1111
1111111111111111
1111111111111111
1111111111111111
1111111111111111
1111        1111
1111        1111
1111        1111
1111        1111
```

The Initial Mapping of F on C^*

$$(\Delta i = \Delta j = 0)$$

Figure 2b

```
  1
   1111111111
  111     1111
111         111
111         111
111         111
111         111
111         111
111111111111111
111111111111111
111         111
111         111
111         111
111         111
111         111
111         111
```

The Final Mapping of F on C^*

(after all allowed Δi, Δj's)

Figure 2c

100.00
90.00
80.00
70.00
60.00
50.00
40.00
30.00
20.00
10.00
0.00
0.00
10.00
20.00
30.00
40.00
50.00
γ_m
m

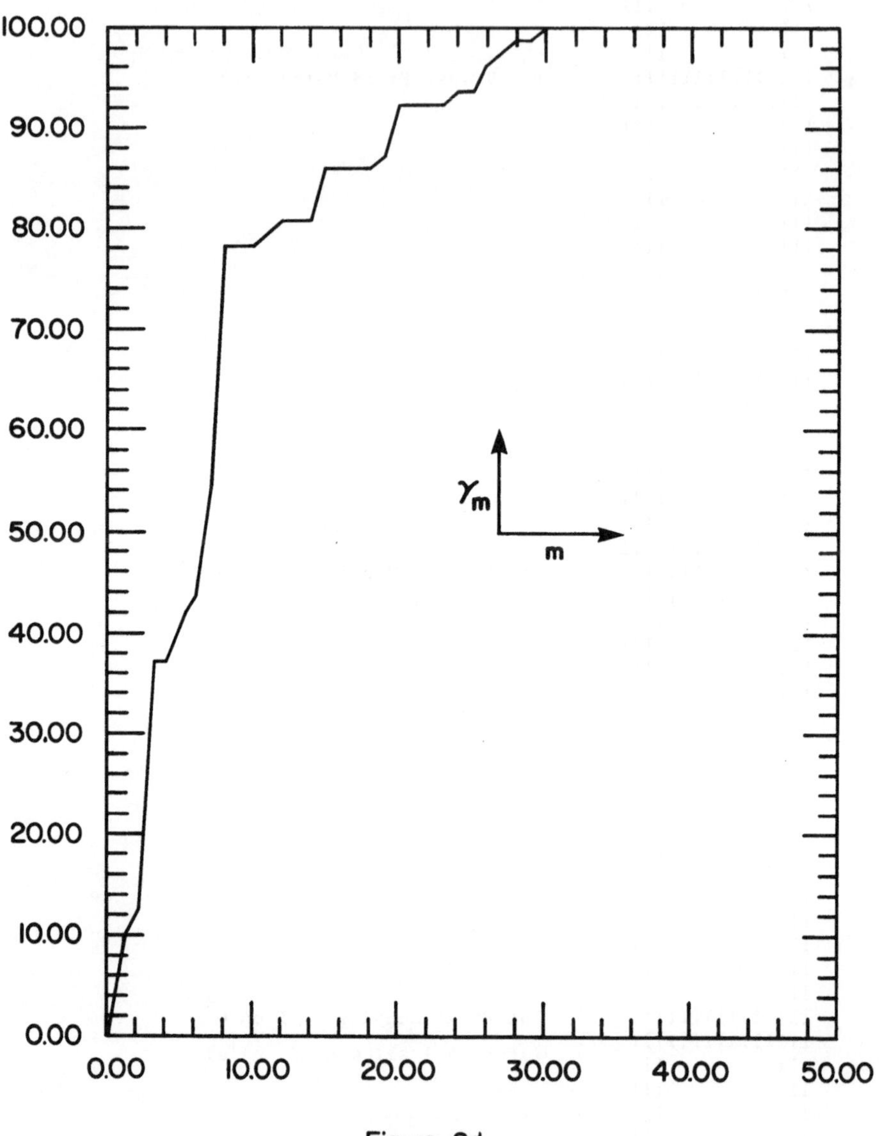

Figure 2d

```
|-δ-|-δ-|-δ-|-δ-|
1   1   1   1   1
1   1   1   1   1                →
1   1   1   1   1              δ<R
1   1   1   1   1                →
1   1   1   1   1
```

Figure 3a

```
11111111111111111
11111111111111111
11111111111111111
11111111111111111
11111111111111111
```

Figure 3b

```
| - δ - |
1
1                    →
1         1        δ<R
1                    →
1
```

Figure 4a

```
1
1
111111111
1
1
```

Figure 4b

```
| - δ - |
1
1
1                    -→
1                  δ≥1
      1              →
      1
      1
      1
```

Figure 5a

```
1
1
1
1
              1
              1
              1
              1
```

Figure 5b

```
| - δ - |
1
1
1                    →
1         1        δ<R
          1          →
          1
          1
          1
```

Figure 6a

```
1
1
1
111111111
              1
              1
              1
              1
```

Figure 6b

Figure 7a

Figure 7b

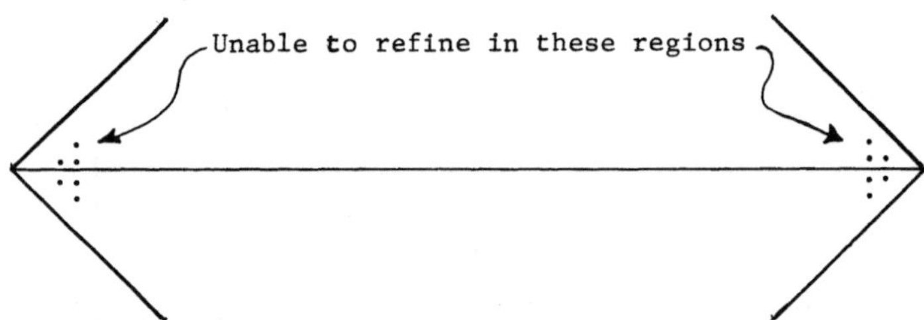

Figure 7c

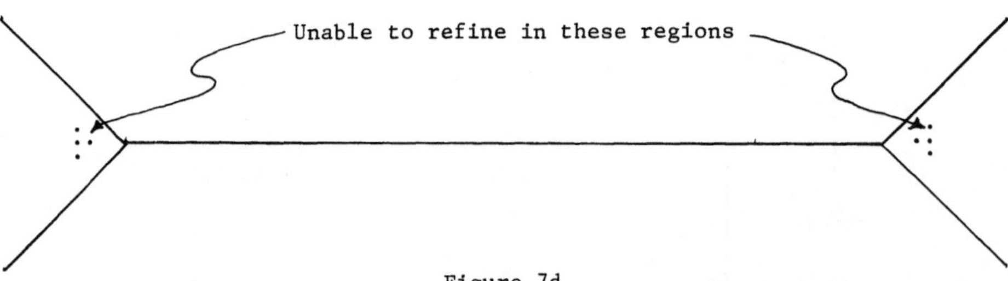

Figure 7d

ADAPTIVE DIGITALE FILTER IN DER SZINTIGRAPHIE

Friedrich M. Wahl
Institut für Nachrichtentechnik
Technische Universität München

Zusammenfassung

Am Beispiel der Optimalfilterung von Szintigrammen soll das Prinzip
und die Realisierung von adaptiven digitalen Filtern erläutert werden. Dabei handelt es sich um 2-D digitale Filter, deren Übertragungscharakteristik an die lokalen statistischen Eigenschaften eines Bild-
signals optimal angepaßt werden können.Insbesondere kann damit die
signalabhängige Störung bei szintigraphischen Bildsignalen im Sinne
des Wienerkriteriums optimal berücksichtigt werden.

Einführung

An Hand von Bild 1 sei kurz das Prinzip der szintigraphischen Abbildung erläutert: Ein 3-dimensionales, Strahlung emittierendes Objekt
(zu untersuchendes Organ) wird von einer Gammakamera als 2-dimensio-
nale Aktivitätsverteilung $o(x,y)$ gesehen. Den szintigraphischen

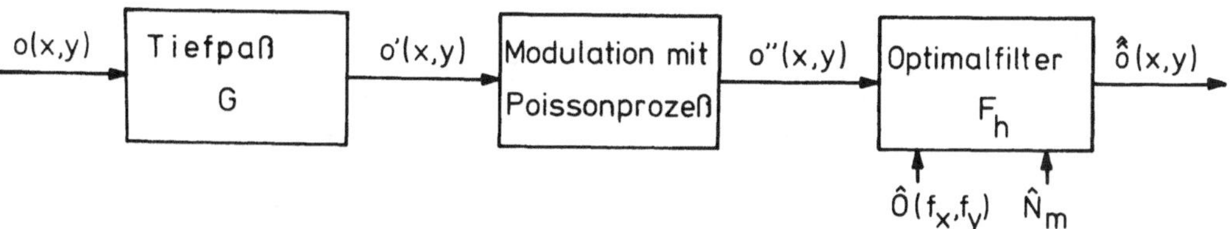

Bild 1: Prinzip der szintigraphischen Abbildung und Optimalfilterung

Bildgewinnungsprozeß kann man mit guter Näherung als Filterung der
Verteilung $o(x,y)$ mit einem Gaußtiefpaß gemäß den Abbildungseigen-
schaften des Kollimators (MTF $G(f_x,f_y)$) und anschließender Überlagerung mit einer signalabhängigen Störung poissonscher Statistik darstellen. Auf das so entstandene Signal $o''(x,y)$ soll nun ein Filter
$F_h(f_x,f_y)$ angewendet werden, das mögliche Tumorstrukturen im Bildsignal besser sichtbar macht und damit die diagnostische Sicherheit bei
der Auswertung von Szintigrammen erhöht.
Viele der aus der Literatur bekannten Verfahren arbeiten nach dem so-
genannten Optimalfilterprinzip(z.B. /1/-/5/), bei dem das Ortsfre-

154

quenzspektrum O"(f_x,f_y) des Szintigramms o"(x,y) mit der Filterfunktion
F_h(f_x,f_y) im Spektralbereich multipliziert wird, wobei nach Wiener gilt:

$$F_h(f_x,f_y) = \frac{1}{G(f_x,f_y)} \cdot \frac{|\hat{O}(f_x,f_y)|^2 \, |G(f_x,f_y)|^2}{|\hat{O}(f_x,f_y)|^2 \, |G(f_x,f_y)|^2 + \hat{N}_m} \tag{1}$$

mit $G(f_x,f_y)$: MTF des Kollimators

$\hat{O}(f_x,f_y)$: Modellspektrum des vermuteten Tumors

$\hat{N}_m$: Schätzwert der mittleren Störleistung

Die zu diesem Zwecke notwendige Schätzung des Leistungspektrums $\hat{O}(f_x,f_y)$
des im gestörten Bildsignal vermuteten Tumors soll nicht Gegenstand
des Vorliegenden sein; es sei hier ein kugelsymmetrischer Defekt oder
Anreicherung angenommen. Vielmehr wird im Folgenden die Möglichkeit gezeigt, die Übertragungscharakteristik eines Optimalfilters bei gegebenem
Modellspektrum $\hat{O}(f_x,f_y)$ der signalabhängigen Störung des Bildes optimal anzupassen.

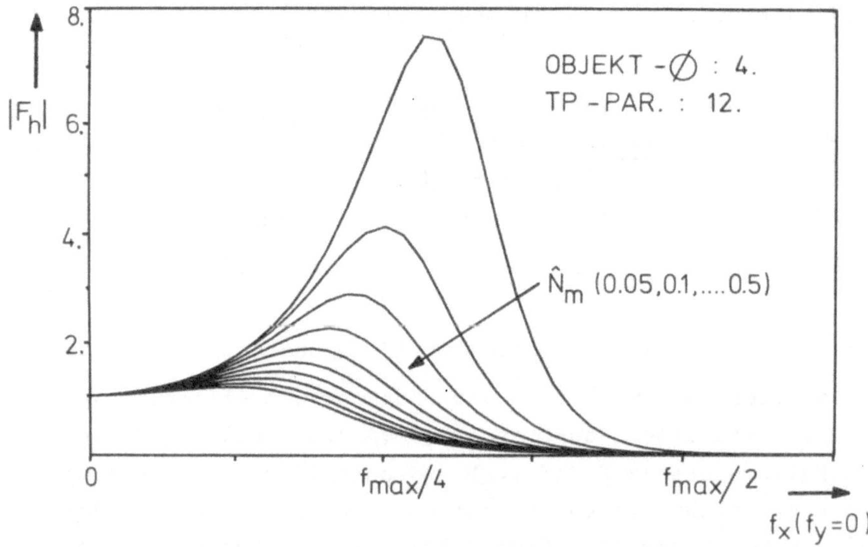

Bild 2: Übertragungscharakteristik des Optimalfilters in Abhängigkeit
von der geschätzten Störleistung

Adaptive Optimalfilterung

Aufgrund der durch den radioaktiven Zerfallsprozeß bedingten Poisson-
statistik der Störung, besteht im Bildsignal zwischen der mittleren lokalen Zählrate und überlagerter Störleistung ein linearer Zusammenhang.
Bei festem Schätzwert $\hat{N}_m$ (in Gl. (1)) ist deswegen das Filter $F_h(f_x,f_y)$
für Bildbereiche mit geringeren mittleren Zählraten zu schmalbandig,
für höhere mittlere Zählraten zu breitbandig. Bild 2 zeigt die jeweils
für eine bestimmte Zählrate (Störleistung) optimale Übertragungscharakteristik.

Die Berücksichtigung der zählratenabhängigen Störung führt zu folgendem signalabhängigen Filter:

$$F_{ad}(f_x,f_y,o''(x,y)) = \frac{1}{G(f_x,f_y)} \cdot \frac{|\hat{O}(f_x,f_y)|^2 |G(f_x,f_y)|^2}{|\hat{O}(f_x,f_y)|^2 |G(f_x,f_y)|^2 + \hat{N}_1(x,y)} \tag{2}$$

$G(f_x,f_y)$, $\hat{O}(f_x,f_y)$ wie in (1)

$\hat{N}_1(x,y)$: zum Signal $o''(x,y)$ proportionale mittlere lokale Störleistung

Das Blockschaltbild des vorgeschlagenen Filterverfahrens ist in Bild 3
dargestellt. Aus dem Bildsignal $o''(x,y)$ wird durch einen Tiefpaß TP
(im einfachsten Fall ein Spalttiefpaß) die mittlere lokale Zählrate
$\hat{i}_1(x,y)$ ermittelt. Die dazu proportionale Rauschleistung $\hat{N}_1(x,y)$ dient
als Steuergröße für das Filter F mit variabler Übertragungscharakteristik.
Um den Aufwand des Filterverfahrens möglichst gering zu halten, wird die
variable Übertragungscharakteristik mit einem Satz fester Filter realisiert.

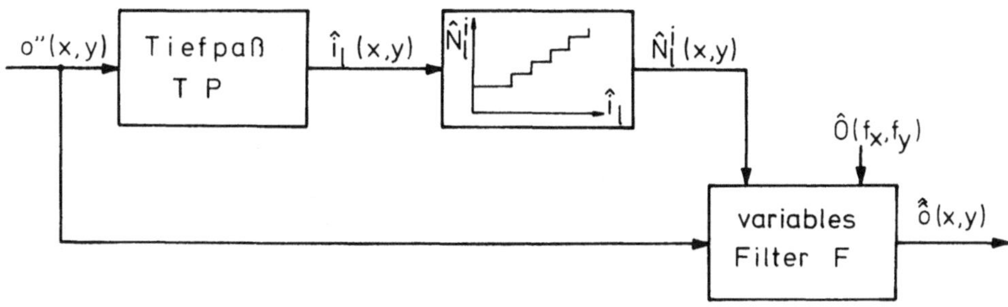

Bild 3: Prinzip des adaptiven Optimalfilters

Dazu wird der mögliche Störleistungswertebereich (von Null bis $\hat{N}_{1max}$) in n Unterbereiche $\hat{N}_1^i$ (i=1......n) unterteilt und nach Gl. (2) für jeden Bereich $\hat{N}_1^i$ das dazugehörige Filter F^i berechnet.

Die Filter F^i werden jeweils durch ein digitales Filter approximiert und die resultierenden Filterkoeffizienten in einer Tabelle abgespeichert. In Bild 4 ist die Verknüpfung von Steuerdaten, Filterkoeffizienten, Eingangs- und Ausgangsbilddaten für ein Filter 2. Ordnung für eine Rekursionsrichtung dargestellt. Für jeden Bildpunkt wird aus der Filtertabelle mit Hilfe der Steuerdaten $c_{m,n}$ das entsprechend der Störleistung $\hat{N}_1^i(x,y)$ optimalste Filter F^i mit den Zählerkoeffizienten a_{jk}^i und den Nennerkoeffizienten b_{jk}^i der korrespondierenden Übertragungsfunktion ausgewählt. Die neuen Bildpunkte berechnen sich aus den Zählraten des unverarbeiteten Szintigramms gemäß folgender Differenzengleichung:

$$r_{m,n} = \sum_{j=1}^{3} \sum_{k=1}^{3} a_{jk}^i \, d_{m-j+1,n-k+1} - \sum_{\substack{j=1 \\ j \cdot k \neq 1}}^{3} \sum_{k=1}^{3} b_{jk}^i \, r_{m-j+1,n-k+1}$$

$d_{m,n}$ Eingangssignal des Filters
    (unverarbeitetes Szintigramm o"(x,y))

$r_{m,n}$ Ausgangssignal des Filters

a_{jk}^i, b_{jk}^i approximierte Filterkoeffizienten des Filters i

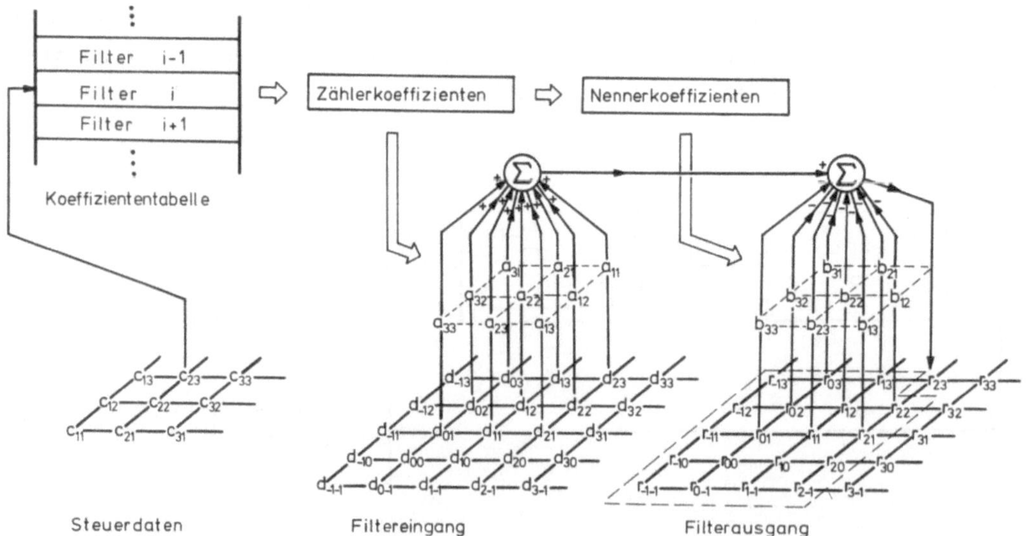

Bild 4: Variables 2-D digitales Filter 2-ten Grades

Realisierung der digitalen Filter

Die Filterkoeffizientensätze der in Bild 4 dargestellten Filtertabelle müssen durch ein geeignetes Entwurfsverfahren z.B. nach /6/ im Ortsbereich oder nach /7/ im $z_1 z_2$-Übertragungsbereich berechnet werden. Im Folgenden sei kurz der Entwurf nach /6/ am Beispiel eines dieser Filter erläutert. Mittels einer 2-D Fouriertransformation läßt sich aus der Übertragungsfunktion (Gl. (2)) die zugehörige Impulsantwort $f_{m,n}$ ermitteln. Da im vorliegenden Fall $f_{m,n}$ rotationssymmetrisch ist (Nullphasensystem), ist eine Dekomposition in 4 Einquadrantenimpulsantworten notwendig:

$$f_{m,n} = f'_{m,n} + f'_{m,-n} + f'_{-m,-n} + f'_{-m,n} \tag{3a}$$

$$\text{mit } f'_{m,n} = \begin{cases} f_{m,n} & \text{für } m,n > 0 \\[2mm] \frac{1}{2} f_{m,n} & \text{für } m=0,\ n>0 \text{ und } m>0,\ n=0 \\[2mm] \frac{1}{4} f_{m,n} & \text{für } m=n=0 \end{cases} \tag{3b}$$

Jede dieser 4 Einquadrantenimpulsantworten läßt sich näherungsweise durch eine rekursive Differenzengleichung darstellen. Für die Impulsantwort des 1. Quadranten gilt:

$$\overline{f'}_{m,n} = \sum_{k=0}^{p} \sum_{l=0}^{p} a_{kl} \delta_{m-k,n-l} - \sum_{\substack{k=0 \\ k+l \neq 0}}^{p} \sum_{l=0}^{p} b_{kl} \overline{f'}_{m-k,n-l} \tag{4a}$$

$$\text{mit } \delta_{i,j} = \begin{cases} 1 & \text{für } i = j = 0 \\[2mm] 0 & \text{sonst} \end{cases} \tag{4b}$$

$$p = \text{Grad der zu realisierenden Übertragungsfunktion}$$

Die Koeffizienten a_{kl} und b_{kl} werden so gewählt, daß die quadratische Abweichung in einem endlichen Intervall $((0,N), (0,N))$

$$J = \sum_{m=0}^{N} \sum_{n=0}^{N} (f'_{m,n} - \overline{f'}_{m,n})^2 \tag{5}$$

minimal wird. Bei den verwendeten Filtern wurde dies nach /6/, ausgehend von einer geeigneten Näherungslösung für a_{kl}, b_{kl}, durch eine Optimierung der Parameter im $2(p+1)^2$-dimensionalen Parameterraum erreicht.

Bild 5 gibt ein Beispiel für ein Filter 2-ten Grades. Dargestellt sind
die gewünschte Einquadrantenimpulsantwort, die Näherungslösung (instabil)
und das Approximationsergebnis.

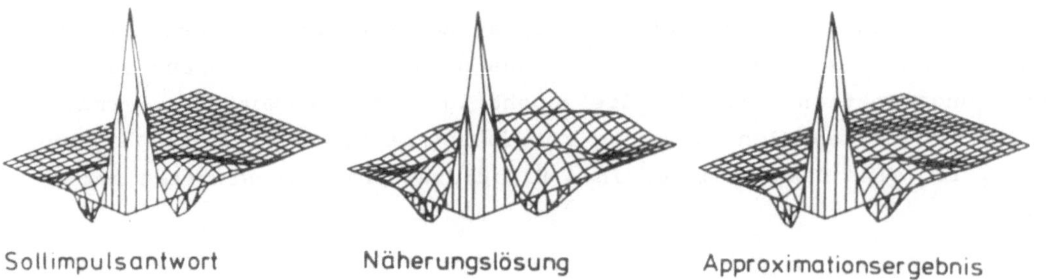

Bild 5: Sollimpulsantwort, Näherungslösung und Approximationsergebnis
eines Optimalfilters, realisiert durch ein 2-D digitales
Filter 2-ten Grades

Durch Rekursion in 4 verschiedenen Richtungen läßt sich nach Gl. (3a)
die gewünschte 4-Quadrantenimpulsantwort $f_{m,n}$ erzeugen. Für ein Filter
2-ten Grades zeigt Bild 6 die Impulsantwort und die korrespondierende
Übertragungsfunktion.

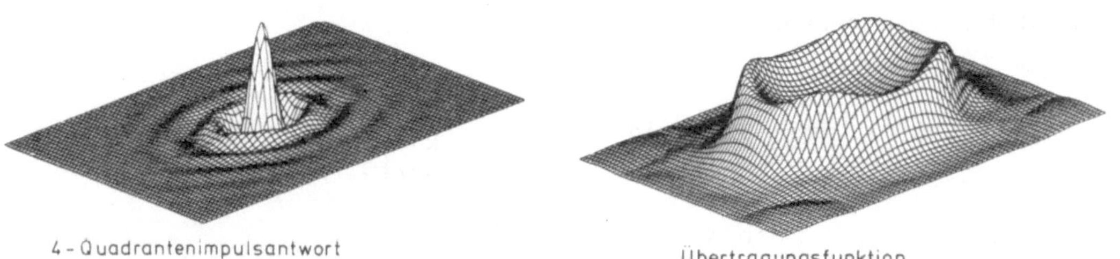

Bild 6: 4-Quadrantenimpulsantwort und zugehörige Übertragungsfunktion
eines Filters 2-ten Grades

Mit der Wahl von Filtern höheren Grades lassen sich die Approximationsfehler reduzieren. In Bild 7 ist der Betrag der Differenz von f' und
$\overline{f}'$ jeweils für ein Filter vom Grad 2, 4 und 6 für die in Bild 5 gezeigte Sollimpulsantwort dargestellt. Die Filter 4-ten und 6-ten Grades sind durch Kaskadierung von Filtern 2-ten Grades realisiert.

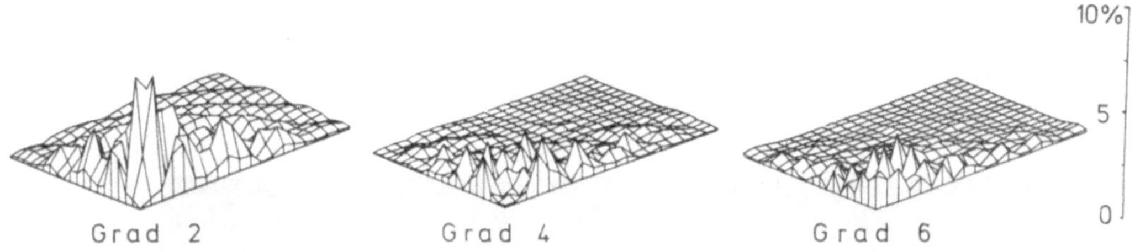

Bild 7: Approximationsfehler der Einquadrantenimpulsantwort

Schlußfolgerung

Mit dem beschriebenen Verfahren wurden Versuche mit verschiedenen Mo-
dellspektren gemacht. Es hat sich gezeigt, daß mit Filtern 2-ter und
4-ter Ordnung bereits beachtliche Bildverbesserungen erreichbar sind.
Bild 8 zeigt am Beispiel einer Phantomaufnahme (a) und zweier Knochen-
szintigramme (c,e) 3 Filterergebnisse (b,d,f) mit einem adaptiven Filter 2-ter Ordnung (128 x 128 Bildpunkte; geschätztes Modellspektrum:
kugelsymmetrisches Objekt mit 6 Bildpunkten Durchmesser). Bei einer
starken Rauschunterdrückung und bei teilweise verbesserter Kanten-
schärfe treten interessierende Bilddetails (sog. "cold spots" und
"hot spots") im verarbeiteten Szintigramm deutlich hervor. Die Möglichkeit der dynamischen Anpassung an die lokale Signalstatistik des
Bildes, die einfache Programmierbarkeit und hohe Rechengeschwindigkeit
digitaler Filter rechtfertigen den relativ hohen Rechenaufwand bei der
Approximation der Filterkoeffizienten. Die klinische Relevanz des
Verfahrens an Hand umfangreichen verarbeiteten szintigraphischen Datenmaterials ist noch zu überprüfen.

Anmerkung

Herrn Dr. I. Bofilias (Institut für Nuklearmedizin, TU München) möchte
ich für die freundliche Überlassung des szintigraphischen Datenmaterials danken.

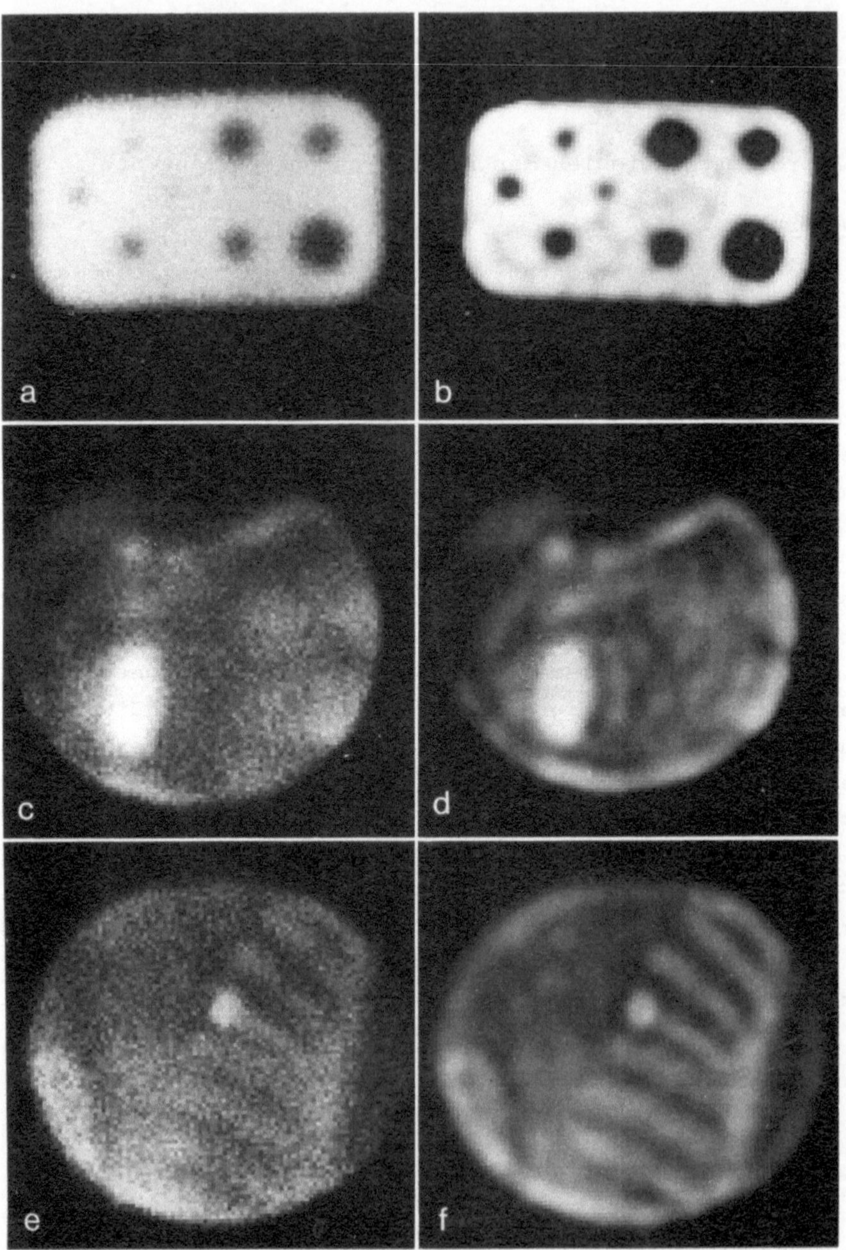

Bild 8: Verarbeitungsbeispiele mit einem Optimalfilter
2-ten Grades

<u>Literatur</u>

/1/ P. Pistor, P. Georgi, G. Walch
The Heidelberg Scintigraphic Image Processing System
Proc. of Second Symp. on Sharing of Computer Programs and
Technology in Nuclear Medicine
Oak Ridge, Tennessee 1972

/2/ W.J. Lorenz, P. Georgi, H.G. Meder, P. Pistor, G. Walch, H. Wiebelt
Interactive Processing and Displaying if Digital Scintigrams
IBM-Publication SM 104/88

/3/ W.A. Hunt, H.G. Meder, P. Pistor, G. Walch, W.J. Lorenz, H. Luig,
P. Schmidlin, H.G. Schmitt
Digital Processing of Scintigraphic Images
IBM-Publication, Heidelberg 1970

/4/ P. Pistor
Digital Processing of Scintigraphic Images by Two-Dimensional
Recursive Wiener Filters
IBM-Publication, Heidelberg 1970

/5/ P. Pistor, G. Walch, W.Ammann, P. Georgi, W.A. Hunt, W.J. Lorenz,
H. Luig, H.G. Meder, P. Schmidlin, H. Wiebelt
Digital Image Processing in Nuclear Medicine
IBM-Publication, Heidelberg 1971

/6/ M.S. Bertran
Approximation of Digital Filters in One and Two Dimensions
IEEE Trans. on ASSP, vol. 23, Oct. 1975

/7/ G.A. Maria, M.M. Fahmy
A lp- Design Technique for Two-Dimensional Digital Recursive Filters
IEEE Trans. on ASSP, vol. 22 No. 1, Feb. 1974

AN IMAGE RESTORATION TECHNIQUE: APPLICATIONS
TO NUCLEAR MEDICINE IMAGES °

V. Cantoni [°°], I. De Lotto [°°°], A. Favino [°°°°], F. Valenziano [°°°]

Abstract

A new procedure for image restoration is presented which involves an estimation of the original image power spectrum to approximate the optimum linear filter. Applications to nuclear medicine images are discussed.

1 - Introduction

Degrading process in imaging systems are generally very complex; in many cases of pratical importance, the ideal image $f(x,y)$ is acted on by a linear system with point-spread function $k(x,y; r,s)$ and a noise $n(x,y)$ is added to the output:

$$g(x,y) = n(x,y) + \iint_{r\,s} f(r,s)\, k(x,y; r,s)\, dr\, ds \qquad (1)$$

where $g(x,y)$ is the intensity of the recorded image in x,y coordinates.

Image-restoration aims to manipulate $g(x,y)$ in order to improve its quality, i.e. to evaluate an estimation $\hat{f}(x,y)$ of $f(x,y)$.

In some simpler cases, $K(.)$ is shift invariant:

$$K(x,y; r,s) = h(x-r, y-s) \qquad (2)$$

°   Work sponsored by G.N.B.C., C.N.R. contract no. 75.00431.02 and HUSPI Project.

°°   L.A.N. - C.N.R. - C.so Carlo Alberto, 5 - Pavia.

°°°   Pavia University and C.I.S.E., cp 3986, Milan - Italy.

°°°°   Pavia University, Clinica del Lavoro, Via Boezio, n° 23, Pavia (Italy).

i.e. the superposition integral in eq. (1) can be written as a convolution:

$$g(x,y) = n(x,y) + f(x,y) * h(x,y) \tag{3}$$

or in the frequency domain:

$$G(u,v) = N(u,v) + F(u,v) \cdot H(u,v) \tag{3'}$$

where $G(u,v)$, $F(u,v)$, $N(u,v)$ and $H(u,v)$ are respectively the two-dimensional Fourier transforms of $g(x,y)$, $f(x,y)$, $n(x,y)$ and $h(x,y)$.
Integral equation (3) can be suitably solved in the unknown $f(x,y)$ when $n(x,y)$, $h(x,y)$ and $g(x,y)$ are given.
Actually $n(x,y)$ is a noise-sample of a process whose mean statistical parameters only are known, for instance the spectral density $\phi_n(u,v)$ for processes independent of the point (x,y). In this case, when $f(x,y)$ and $n(x,y)$ are statistically incorrelated, an optimum linear shift-invariant filter, acting upon $g(x,y)$ computes an estimation $\hat{f}(x,y)$ of the ideal image $f(x,y)$ with the least mean-square error.
Such a filter has the frequency response $L(u,v)$:

$$L(u,v) = \frac{1}{H(u,v)} \cdot \frac{\phi_f(u,v) \, |H(u,v)|^2}{\phi_f(u,v) \, |H(u,v)|^2 + \phi_n(u,v)} = \frac{\alpha(u,v)}{H(u,v)} \tag{4}$$

where ϕ_n and ϕ_f are the power-density spectra of $n(x,y)$ and $f(x,y)$ respectively, and $\alpha(u,v)$ a real number smaller than one [1,2].
In what follows a optimum shift invariant filter is given for scintigraphic images where the noise process is space dependent and a new procedure to estimate $\phi_f(u,v)$ and the optimum linear filter are then presented.

2 - Shift-invariant linear filter for scintigraphic images

The optimum linear filter given in sec. 1 is suitable for space invariant processes. In scintigraphic images on the contrary the noise $n(x,y)$ is Poissonian, as well known, and its correlation function $R(x_1,y_1; x_2,y_2) = \sigma_n^2(x_1,y_1) \cdot \delta(x_2-x_1, y_2-y_1) = < g(x_1,y_1) > \cdot \delta(x_2-x_1, y_2-y_1)$, where $\delta(.)$ is the impulse function and $<.>$ means the ensemble statistical average. That is the noise is a space dependent process, for which the filter of Eq. 4 cannot be evaluated. In this case the optimum filter must be shift-variant[10]. Such a filter is costly and requires long computation times.

In what follows a method to design an optimum linear shift-invariant filter is presented.

The minimum mean square error (MSE) criterion is in general meaningless for this case, because if a particular point (x,y) is selected for the minimization, the corresponding optimum filter can generate unacceptable errors in the other points. A resonable criterion is to minimize the integral over all the space of the weighted mean square error $<E^2>$:

$$< E^2 > = \quad < e^2(x,y) > \quad p(x,y) \, dx \, dy \tag{5}$$

where $< e^2(x,y) > = < (\hat{f}(x,y) - f(x,y)^2 >$ and $p(x,y)$ is a normalized non negative function which weights with a relative penalty the size of $< e^2(x,y) >$ in order to obtain a wanted distribution of the error.

By using two dimensions Fourier transforms (F.T.), the solution which minimises $< E^2 >$ is, in the frequency domain, for the case of an uniform weight $p(x,y) = k$:

$$L'(u,v) = \frac{1}{H(u,v)} \quad \frac{\phi_f(u,v) \cdot |H(u,v)|^2}{M + \phi_f(u;v) \cdot |H(u,v)|^2} \quad = \frac{\alpha'}{H(u,v)} \tag{6}$$

where M is the number of counts of the scintigraphic image (see Appendix 1).

The minimum error $< E^2 >_{min}$ is given by (see Appendix 2):

$$< E^2 >_{min} = \iint_{u \, v} \frac{M \cdot \phi_f(u,v)}{M + \phi_f(u,v) \, |H(u,v)|^2} \, du \, dv \tag{7}$$

Given $\langle E_o^2 \rangle$, the error due to the inverse filter:

$$\langle E_o^2 \rangle = \langle (f(x,v) - g(x,y) * h^{-1}(x,y))^2 \rangle = \iint_{uv} M \cdot |H(u,v)|^{-2} \, du \, dv$$

the ratio $\nu = \langle E^2 \rangle_{min} \Big/ \langle E_o^2 \rangle$ is:

$$\nu = \frac{\iint_{uv} |H(u,v)|^{-2} \cdot \beta(u,v) \, du \, dv}{\iint_{uv} |H(u,v)|^{-2} \, du \, dv} \leqslant 1 \qquad (8)$$

because $\beta(u,v)$ is a real number lower than one:

$$\beta(u,v) = \frac{\phi_f(u,v) \, |H(u,v)|^2}{\phi_f(u,) \cdot |H(u,v)|^2 + M}$$

Moreover notice that in the points where $H(u,v) = 0$ the integrand of Eq. 7 is finite and ν of Eq. 8 is the lower the higher is M. Eq. 6 gives the opportunity of estimating the maximum frequency component which can be restored for a given picture, $H(u,v)$ being known. For simplicity, let us consider a one dimension gaussian image $f = \frac{M}{(2\pi)^{\frac{1}{2}} \sigma_1} \cdot e^{-x^2/2\sigma_1^2}$. The maximum frequency component ω_s which can be restored can be defined as the frequency at which $\alpha' = \frac{1}{2}$ in Eq. 6. At this frequency the squared bias $B(\omega)$ in the estimated F.T. of f :

$$B(\omega) = \left| F(\omega) \cdot \left[1 - H(\omega) \, L'(\omega) \right] \right|^2$$

is equal to the error $A(\omega)$ in the estimated F.T. of f due to the noise:

$$A(\omega) = M \cdot |L'(\omega)|^2$$

It results that:

$$\left| F(\omega) \cdot H(\omega) \right|^2 = M$$

For the given $f(x)$, the ω_s is then given b :

$$\omega_s = \left[\frac{\ln M}{\sigma_1^2 + \sigma^2} \right]^{\frac{1}{2}}$$

which is a well known result [4].

notice that the ω_s grows with M, but very showly. $\omega_s^2(M = 10^4)$ is only twice $\omega_s^2(M = 10^2)$ and 9 times the square of the cut-off frequency of the point spread function.

This means that the limiting factor to the restoration of the scin tigraphic image is obviously the point spread function of the instrument itself. Notice however that the result given by the optimum shift invariant filter presented above are very often far better than those obtainable with a low-pass filter, as can be easily shown compu ting the square errory in the two cases.

3 - The estimation of $\phi_f(u,v)$

Note that Eq. 6 requires the knowledge of ϕ_f. Actually the origi nal-image power spectrum is often unknown: the problem is its estima tion when $g(x,y)$, $h(x,y)$ and M are given.

Evaluation of $\phi_f(x,y)$ by the simple inverse filter $1/H(u,v)$, $\phi_f(u,v) = \frac{|G(u,v)|^2}{|H(u,v)|^2}$, will enormously increase the fluctuation due to the noise component because of zeros or small values of $H(u,v)$ itself. In these points of the frequency domain indeed $F(u,v)$. $H(u,v)$ can be much smaller than $G(u,v)$, owing to noise contribution and the mean-square error of $G(v,u)$ is due only to the noise i.e. $\varepsilon^2_{G^2}(u,v) = 2M^2$ as follows from Eq. 3'.

The mean square error of $\left|F(u,v)\right|^2$ can be evaluated, at these criti cal points, as:

$$\varepsilon^2_{|F|^2}(u,v) = 2\,M^2 / H^4 \tag{9}$$

A better estimate $\hat{\phi}_f$ of $\phi_f(u,v)$ can be obtained by averaging $\{|G|^2 M\}/|H|^2$ with a suitable function which weights data propor tionally to the inverse of the mean-square error $\varepsilon^2_{F^2}(u,v)$:

$$\hat{\phi}_f(u,v) = \frac{1}{K(u,v)} \iint\limits_{u'v'} \frac{\left\{ |G|^2 \; M \right\}}{|H|^2} \cdot \frac{R(u-u',v-v')}{\varepsilon_{F2}^2(u',v')} \cdot du' \; dv'$$

$$= \frac{1}{K(u,v)} \iint\limits_{u'v'} \left[\frac{|G|^2 - M}{2\,M^2} \cdot |H|^2 \right] \cdot R(u-u',v-v') \; du' \; dv' = \frac{1}{K(u,v)} \iint\limits_{u'v'} \psi(u,v) \cdot$$

$$R(u-u',v-v) \; du' \; dv' \tag{10}$$

$$\text{where} \quad K(u,v) = \iint\limits_{u'v'} \frac{R(u-u',v-v')}{\varepsilon_{F2}^2(u'v')} \; du' \; dv' = \iint\limits_{u'v'} \frac{|H(u'v')|^4 \cdot R(u-u',v-v')}{2\;M^2}$$

$$\cdot du \; dv \tag{11}$$

where $R(u-u', v-v')$ is a weighing function which smooths the local
fluctuations of experimental outcomes $|G|^2$:

$$R(u,v) = \frac{1}{2\pi a^2} \; e^{-(u^2+v^2)\big/ 2\,a^2}$$

where $a^2 = D$, the number of points for the x or y coordinate of
the image.

4 – Algorithm description and some results in nuclear medicine image restoration

The implemented algorithm is a sequency of six steps:

1) $g(x,y) \Rightarrow G(u,v)$

   $h(x,y) \Rightarrow H(u,v)$ by a two dimensional F.F. transforms

2) $\left\{ G(u,v) \cdot G^*(u,v) - M \right\} \cdot \dfrac{|H(u,v)|^2}{2 \cdot M^2} = \psi(u,v)$

3) $\psi(u,v) \Rightarrow \hat{\phi}_f(u,v)$ a smoothing of noise fluctuation with a
   weighing function; this operation is performed by F.F. transforms

4) $\hat{\phi}_f(u,v) \Rightarrow L_a(u,v)$ by means of Eq. 6

5) $G(v,u) \cdot L_a(u,v) = \hat{F}(u,v)$

6) $\hat{F}(u,v) \Rightarrow f(x,y)$ by a two dimensional F.F. transform.

Five two-dimensional F.F. transform are than used in this sequence of operations, i.e. two more than in the case in which ϕ_f is known. This algorithm is suitably for implementation on minicomputer [9].

Note that the average performance of the proposed algorithm with respect to the global means-square error is the best after the optimum filter, among those we have utilized.[11]

With respect the C.P.U. time and memory space required, all these tech niques are almost equivalent on a large computer; on small computers on the contrary the proposed algorithm can be implemented in more efficient way.

Three examples of application of the proposed algorithm with nuclear me dicine image are presented in figg. 1 , 2 and 3 , with respect the Philips[5 , 6] and the homomorphic [7,8] restoration.

Fig. 1 represents the scintigraphic image of an head and Fig. 2 repre sents the scintigraphic image of a couple of kidneys. In Fig. 3 the thyroid phantom, standard 3602 of Picker Nuclear, is presented which can be also compared with outputs obtained with low-pass filters avai lable on commercial γ-cameras.

APPENDIX 1. <u>The shift-invariant linear filter with a non-stationary</u>
<u>process</u>

The integral square weighted error is defined as:

$$< E^2 > \; = \iint_{x\,y} < \left[\hat{f}(x,y) - f(x,y) \right]^2 > \cdot p(x,y) \; dy \; dx = \iint_{x\,y} < e^2(x,y) > \cdot$$

$$\cdot \; p(x,y) \; dy \; dx \tag{A1}$$

where e is the difference between the estimate $\hat{f}(x,y)$ and the true
function f and is given by:

$$e(x,y) \; = \iint_{\alpha\,\beta} l(\alpha,\beta) \; g(x-\alpha,\; y-\beta) \, d\alpha \, d\beta \; - \; f(x,y) \tag{A2}$$

and p(x,y) is the weighing function accounting for the position.
It follows that:

$$< E^2 > = \iint_{x\,y} f^2(x,y) \; p(x,y) \; dydx + \iint_{x\,y} < \left[\iint_{\alpha\,\beta} l(\alpha,\beta) \; g(x-\alpha,y-\beta) \, d\alpha \; d\beta \right]^2 > \cdot$$

$$p(x,y) \; dy \; dx - 2 \iint_{x\,y} f(x,y) \left[\iint_{\alpha\,\beta} l(\alpha,\beta) \; g(x-\alpha,y-\beta) \; d\alpha \, d\beta \right] \cdot$$

$$p(x,y) \; dy \; dx \tag{A3}$$

In two-dimensional Fourier trasforms notations we have:

$$
\begin{array}{ccc}
f(x,y) & \Rightarrow & F(u,v) \\
g(x,y) & \Rightarrow & G(u,v) \\
h(x,y) & \Rightarrow & H(u,v) \\
l(x,y) & \Rightarrow & L(u,v) \\
p(x,y) & \Rightarrow & P(u,v)
\end{array}
$$

We may applay Parseval's theorem to the second number of the equation
(A3) and we obtain:

$$< E^2 > = \iint_{u\,v} F^*(u,v) \left[\iint_{\varepsilon\,\zeta} F(\varepsilon,\zeta) \; P(u-\varepsilon,v-\zeta) \; d\varepsilon \; d\zeta \right] dv \; du \; +$$

$$+ \iint_{u\,v} \left\langle \left[L^*(u,v)\; G^*(u,v) \iint_{\varepsilon\,\zeta} L(\varepsilon,\zeta)\; G(\varepsilon,\zeta)\; P(u-\varepsilon,v-\zeta)\; d\varepsilon\; d\zeta \right] \right\rangle \cdot$$

$$\cdot\; dv\; du - 2 \iint_{u\,v} L^*(u,v)\cdot \left\langle G^*(u,v) \right\rangle \left[\iint_{\varepsilon\,\zeta} F(\varepsilon,\zeta)\; P(u-\varepsilon,v-\zeta)\; d\varepsilon\, d\zeta \right] \cdot$$

$$\cdot\; dv\; du \tag{A4}$$

After simple manipulation the integral becomes:

$$\langle E_2^2 \rangle = \iiiint_{u\,v\,\varepsilon\,\zeta} F^*(u,v)\; F(\varepsilon,\zeta)\; P(u-\varepsilon,\, v-\zeta)\; d\zeta\, d\varepsilon\, dv\, du + \iiiint_{u\,v\,\varepsilon\,\zeta} L^*(u,v) L(\varepsilon,\zeta) \cdot$$

$$\left\langle G^*(u,v)G(\varepsilon,\zeta)\right\rangle\cdot P(u-\varepsilon,v-\zeta)\; d\zeta\; d\varepsilon\; dv\, du - 2 \iiiint_{u\,v\,\varepsilon\,\zeta} L^*(u,v)\; \cdot$$

$$\left\langle G^*(u,v)\right\rangle \cdot F(\varepsilon,\zeta)\; P(u-\varepsilon,v-\zeta)\; d\zeta\, d\varepsilon\, dv\, du \tag{A5}$$

Applaying a variational technique we obtain that the filter transfer function must be real, and it is given by the following integral equa tion:

$$\iint_{\varepsilon\,\zeta} L(\varepsilon,\zeta)\; \left\langle G^*(u,v)G(\varepsilon,\zeta)\right\rangle\; P(u-\varepsilon,v-\zeta)d\zeta\; d\varepsilon \;=\; \left\langle G^*(u,v)\right\rangle\cdot$$

$$\cdot \iint_{\varepsilon\,\zeta} F(\varepsilon,\zeta)\; P(u-\varepsilon,v-\zeta)\; d\zeta d\varepsilon \tag{A6}$$

On the basis of the assumption that $n(x,y)$ is non correlated poisso nian process with $\left\langle n(x_1,y_1)\, n(x_2,y_2)\right\rangle = \sigma^2(x_1,y_1)\cdot \delta(x_2-x_1,y_1-y_2)$ and $\sigma^2(x,y) = \left\langle g(x,y)\right\rangle$ we have:

$$\langle G(u,v)\rangle \;=\; F(u,v)\;\; H(u,v) \tag{A7}$$

$$\left\langle G^*(u,v)\; G(u,v)\right\rangle = F^*(u,v)\; F(u,v)\; H^*(u,v)\cdot H(u,v) + \left\langle N^*(u,v)\cdot \right.$$

$$\left.\cdot\; N(u,v)\right\rangle = \Phi_f(u,v)\; \left|H(u,v)\right|^2 + \left\langle N^*(u,v)\; N(u,v)\right\rangle \tag{A8}$$

$$\left\langle N^*(u,v)N(u,v)\right\rangle = \iiiint e^{-u(x_2-x_1)-v(y_2-y_1)}\sigma^2(x_1,y_1)\delta(x_2-x_1,y_2-y_1)dy_2 dx_2\cdot$$

$$\cdot\; dy_1 dx_1 = \iint_{x,y} \langle g(x_1,y_1)\rangle dx_1 dy_1 \;=\; M \tag{A9}$$

For sake of semplicity we suppose that the weighing functions is constant

$$p(x,y) = K \Rightarrow P(u,v) = \delta(u,v) \cdot K \qquad (A10)$$

By substituting A7, A8, A9 into A5 it follons that:

$$L'(u,v) \cdot \left[\phi_f(u,v) \cdot \left| H(u,v) \right|^2 + \langle N^*(u,v)\, N(u,v) \rangle \right] = F^*(u,v) \cdot H^*(u,v) F(u,v)$$

and than

$$L'(u,v) = \frac{\phi_f(u,v) \cdot H^*(u,v)}{\phi_f(u,v) \cdot \left| H(u,v) \right|^2 + M} = \frac{1}{H(u,v)} \cdot \frac{\phi_f(u,v)\, \left| H(u,v) \right|^2}{\phi_f(u,v) \left| H(u,v) \right|^2 + M} \qquad (A11)$$

APPENDIX 2. <u>Minimum integral square error</u>

By substituting A11 into A5 and with some simple manipulations we obtain:

$$\langle E^2 \rangle \min = \iint_{u\,v} \left[\phi_f(u,v) + \frac{\phi_f^2(u,v)\, \left| H(u,v) \right|^2}{\phi_f(u,v)\, \left| H(u,v) \right|^2 + M} \right.$$

$$\left. -\, 2\, \frac{\phi_f(u,v) \cdot H(u,v)}{\phi_f(u,v)\, \left| H(u,v) \right|^2 + M} \cdot F^*(u,v)\, H^*(u,v) \cdot F(u,v) \right] du\, dv$$

$$= \iint_{u\,v} \frac{\phi_f(u,v) \cdot M}{\phi_f(u,v)\, \left| H(u,v) \right|^2 + M}\, dv\, du \qquad (B1)$$

The expected integral square error using the inverse filter can be <u>ob</u>tained by sostituting L(u,v) with $H^{-1}(u,v)$ into A5. It follows that

$$\langle E_H^2 - 1 \rangle = \iint_{u\,v} \left[\phi_f(u,v) + \frac{\phi_f(u,v) \cdot \left| H(u,v) \right|^2 + M}{\left| H(u,v) \right|^2} - 2\, F^*(u,v) \cdot F(u,v) \right] dv\, du$$

$$= \iint_{u\,v} \frac{M}{\left| H(u,v) \right|^2}\, dv\, du \qquad (B2)$$

Thus the ratio betwem $\langle E_{\min}^2 \rangle$ $\langle E_H^2 - 1 \rangle$ is:

$$\frac{\langle E^2_{min}\rangle}{\langle E^2_H - 1\rangle} = \iint\limits_{uv} \frac{\dfrac{\phi_f(u,v)}{\phi_f(u,v)\,|H(u,v)|^2 + M}}{\displaystyle\iint\limits_{uv} |H(u,v)|^{-2}\,du\,dv}\,dv\,du \qquad (B3)$$

BIBLIOGRAFIA

1) C.W. HELSTROM: "Image restoration by the method of least squares" – J. Opt. Soc. Amer. 57 (1967).

2) D. STEPIAN: "Linear least-square filtering of distorted image" J.Opt. Soc. Amer. 57 (1967).

3) A. PAPOULIS: "Probability, Random variables and stockastic processes" Mc Graw-Hill-New York 1965, p. 402

4) W.A. HUNT, M.G. MEDER, P. PISTOR, G. WALCH, W.Y. LORENZ, H. LUIG, P. SCHMIDLIN: "Optimum sample size in digital radioscintingraphy", IBM Publ. 70.09.004 (1970).

5) B.L. PHILLIPS: "A Technique for the numerical solution of certain integral equations of the first kind" J. ACM 9 (1962),pp.84-97.

6) B.R. HUNT:" The application of constrained least squares estimation to image restoration by digital computer" – IEEE Trans. o, Computers C-22, n.9 (1973) pp. 805-812.

7) A.V.OPPENHEIM, R.W. SCHAFER, T.G. STOCKHAM: "Nonlinear Filtering of Multiplied and Convolved Signals" Proc.IEEE, 56 (1968),pp.1264-1291.

8) B.R.HUNT: "Digital Image Processing" Proc. IEEE 63, n° 1 (1975) pp. 693-708.

9) I.DE LOTTO, D. DOTTI: "Two dimensional transforms by municomputers without matrix transposing" Computer Graphics and Image Processing 4 (1975) pp. 271-278.

10) I. DE LOTTO, G. IUCULANO: "Correlation function analysis in non-sta tionary rondom processes" Alta Frequenza 38 (1969) pp. 884-896.

11) V. CANTONI, I. DE LOTTO: "A new algorithm for image restoration" Alta Frequenza, dicembre 1976.

HOMOMORPHIC RESTORATION

ORIGINAL   IMAGE

PHILLIPS RESTORATION

PROPOSED RESTORATION

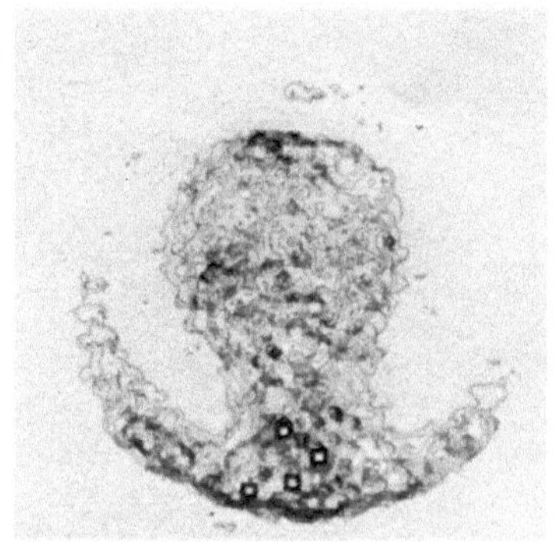

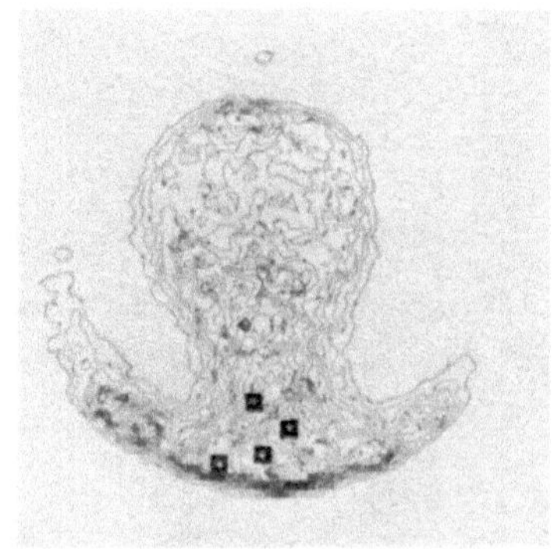

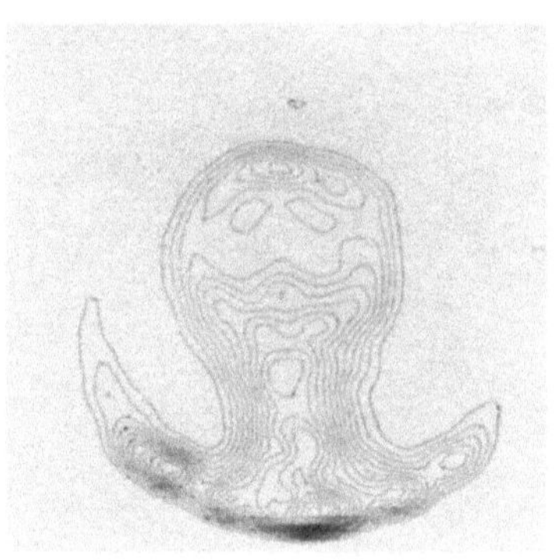

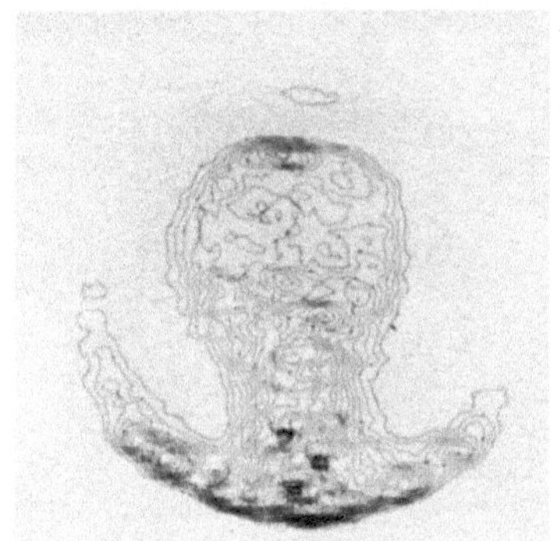

Fig. 1

PROPOSED RESTORATION

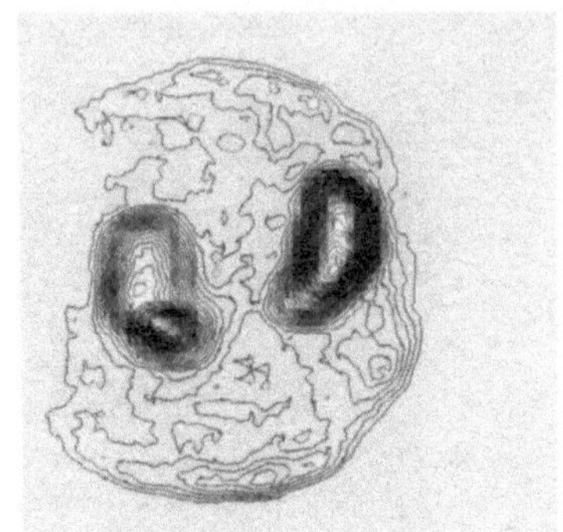

PHILLIPS RESTORATION

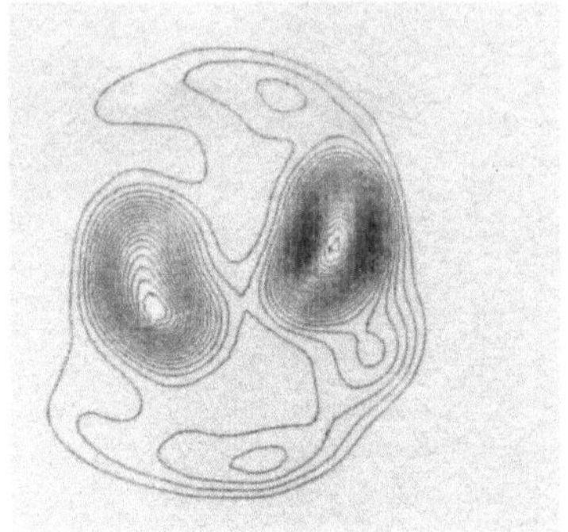

ORIGINAL IMAGE

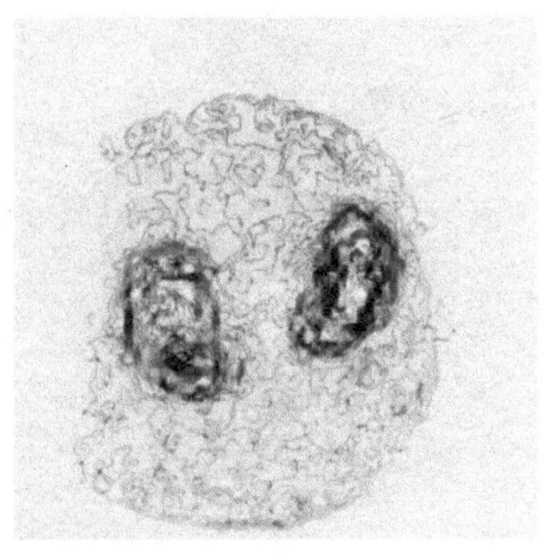

HOMOMORPHIC RESTORATION

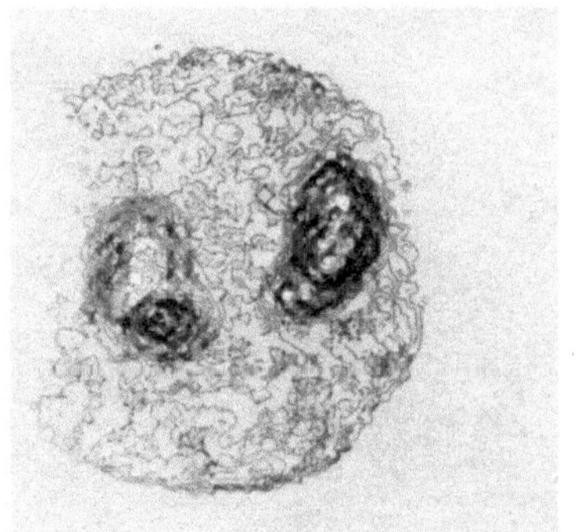

Fig. 2 A

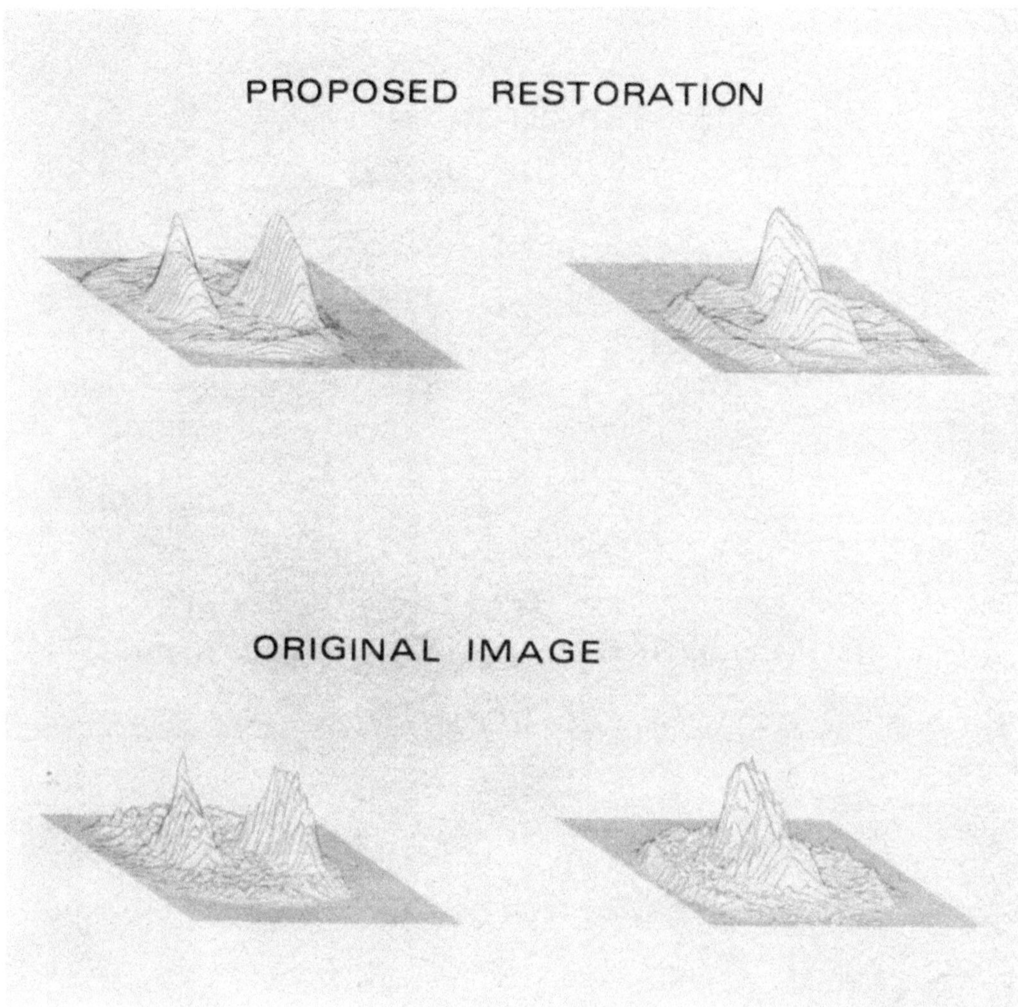

Fig. 2 B

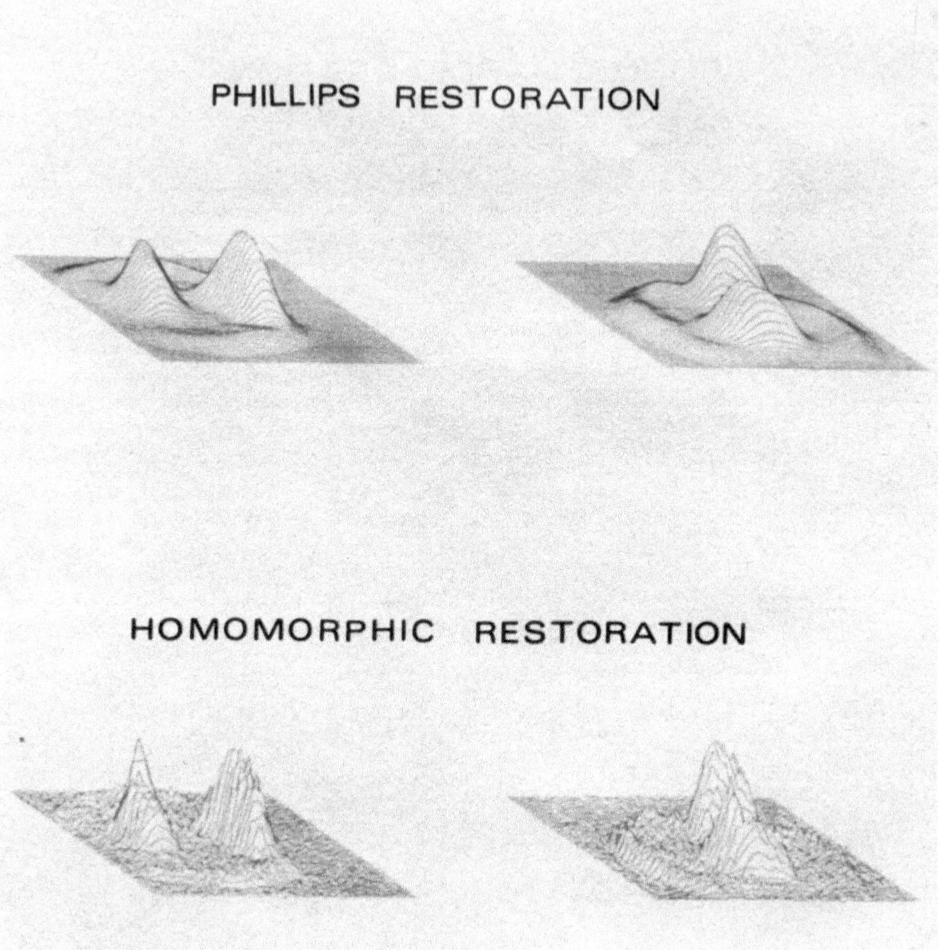

Fig. 2 C

THYROID PHANTOM
peak deep half level
PROPOSED RESTORATION
PHILLIPS RESTORATION
LOW-PASS FILTER
ORIGINAL IMAGE
HOMOMORPHIC RESTORATION

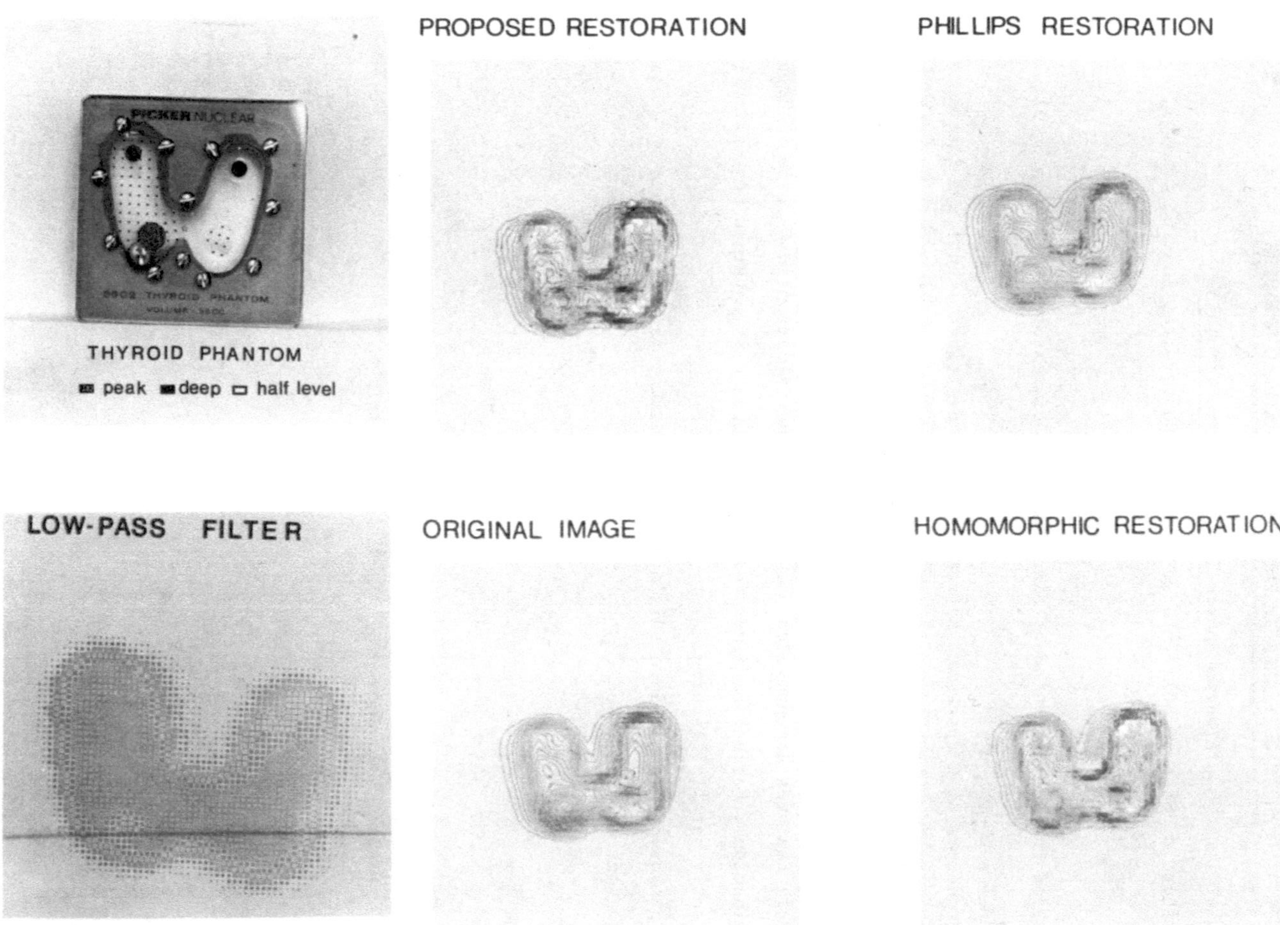

Fig. 3

AN IMAGE TRANSFORM EMPHASIZING TEXTURAL FEATURES

Alberto Apostolico and Sergio Vitulano

Istituto di Scienze dell'Informazione dell'Università, Salerno (Italy)

ABSTRACT

A method for the analysis and discrimination of textures, based on C-calculus, is proposed.

The concepts of C-space and C-transform of a digitized signal are introduced as simple tools, well suited to the visualization of the filtering properties of C-calculus: C-filters are thus introduced and the "natural" role they seem to play in problems concerning textures is investigated in some practical instance. C-transforms of some sample textures are provided and texture classification in C-space is suggested. Discimination of objects against textural background is obtained by C-filtering, in an inherently parallel fashion.

The philosophy involved in this approach is also briefly discussed in a comparison with some extant methods.

AN IMAGE TRANSFORM EMPHASIZING TEXTURAL FEATURES

1.INTRODUCTION

Edge detection and region analysis are widely used as basic tools in the various feature extraction techniques that have been set up over the years in the field of pictorial pattern recognition.

Since texture is a characteristic property of most surfaces, it also conveys in general relevant informations, not only about the nature of materials but also about the displacement of different objects in the visual field (1). The fact that texture has an important discriminating role between surfaces of different nature has stimulated various authors to elaborate measures and algorithms for their analysis and classification (2).

However, even if to a human observer it is quite easy to recognize and describe a texture – perhaps in rough and empirical terms –, this has proved instead to be a much more difficult task to be accomplished by a computer. This is probably so because of the extreme refractoriness to precise definition that textures seem to present.

In order to constitute a texture, an optical pattern must possess a great number of subpatterns of minute dimensions, which can in turn display some internal substructure. These subpatterns must have some rough spatial density and regularity in the entire visual field. It should be emphasized, however, that their characteristic do not have to correspond to those pertaining to the perceptual primitives of the texture being analyzed (3, 4). Various authors (5, 6, 7) try to characterize textures by means of the statistical distribution of values associated with local properties and base the discrimination of diverse textures on the comparison od these statistics. Some easily computable method for the extraction of textural features is found in ref.1 . Although some of these latters relate to standard concepts such as coarseness, contrast, directionality line-likeness, regularity, roughness etc., not all of this meanings is visually clear (8). Besides, for the great part they do not provide easy (and not too time consuming) discriminant algorithms.

More in general, it has been rightly pointed out (5) that the procedures set up for texture characterization are seldom amenable to direct use in the separation of different regions in a same scene.

In this paper, we shall introduce an image transform that seems to emphasize textural properties as far as the naïvest possible definition of a texture is agreed upon. According to this definition, a texture i) is constituted by pieces that are roughly uniform with respect both to their dimensions and variations of tones of grey within the textural region and ii) the number of such pieces is extremely large compared with that of other object that could be extracted from the picture.

A filtering process based on C-Calculus (9) - a formalism used by us in previous works (10, 11) to approach some standard problems of pattern analysis - is presented next. We shall try to show on some simple concrete instance how this filtering takes place in the transformed space in a natural and inherently parallel fashion.

2. C-TRANSFORMS

To the aim of simplicity, we shall assume throughout in the present discussion that the features involved in texture perception (primitive patterns along with their 'regularities') are displayed row-wise in the array representing the picture. Our definitions and results, however, shall be seen to be easily extensible to the most general case.

As mentioned in the preceding section, our method is essentially based on the assumption that at the perceptual level the textural effect is ultimately due to the concurrent action of somewhat prevalent elementary stimuli, which are in turn rather homogeneous as for their shape and dimension. Therefore, it seems reasonable to trascure the many features that can characterize the details of their shape, and just privilege, in a first approximation, the grey level differences of elementary patterns and their dimensions. These two parameters are easily relatable to familiar concepts of vision physiology, namely contrast (12) and resolving power of the eye.

The *(row) C-transform* can be then introduced quite naturally as a statistic of the absolute number of joint occurrence of fixed values of these parameters along the rows of the picture array.

More precisely, we introduce the (row) C-transform as follows: in a row by row (directionality preserving) scanning all differences in tones of greyness that are found at the extrema of regions wherein the "signal" is monotonic are computed. These differences are reported on the first axis "u" of a space that is called *C-space*. On the second axis "v" of the C-space half the width of the monotonic region plus one is reported. The reason why to take this apparently cumbersome measure will become clearer in the following sections. Each point (u,v) will occur

in the picture with a multiplicity t which is either reported on a last,
perpendicular axis (completing thus the definition of C-space and its points) or
attached to a (u,v) point as a numerical value (or a tone of grey in a convenient
scale). This latter representation of the picture we define as its (row) C-transform,
although we will mostly resort to the former for the illustrations contained in
this work.

Fig.1a,b below shows the C-transform of a triangular pulse train. Notice that
the signal has to be spatially limited in order for its transform to be kept within
finite values. A stretching of the abscissa axis results in a shift of the transform
parallel to the v axis (dashed lines in the figure). Instead, if the amplitude of
the pulse is amplified , a shift along the u axis occurs.(dotted lines). Finally, if
both parameters are evenly increased shift is obtained in the (u,v) plane along a
straight line segment from the origin .

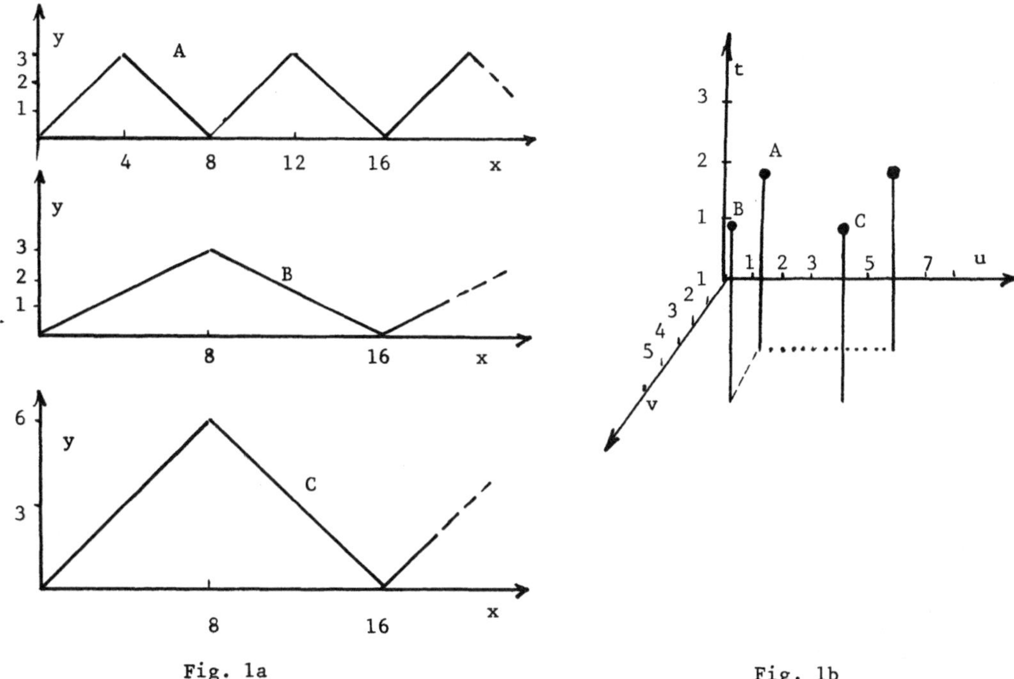

Fig. 1aFig. 1b

It is seen that some frame of a sine, or an (even) Walsh function, map into a
single point of the (u,v)-plane. More generally, all signals that have the same
spatial frequency and amplitudes yield exactly the same transform regardless of the

details of their shape. Therefore, C-transforms do not admit of a unique inverse
transformation.

Fig.2(a,b) shows a digitized newspaper page and the corresponding C-transform.
It was found that the two clusters found in the C-space were due to the headings
and text, respectively. A discrimination procedure acting in the C-space could
therefore fruitfully filter out one of these components while not blurring the other
in any way.

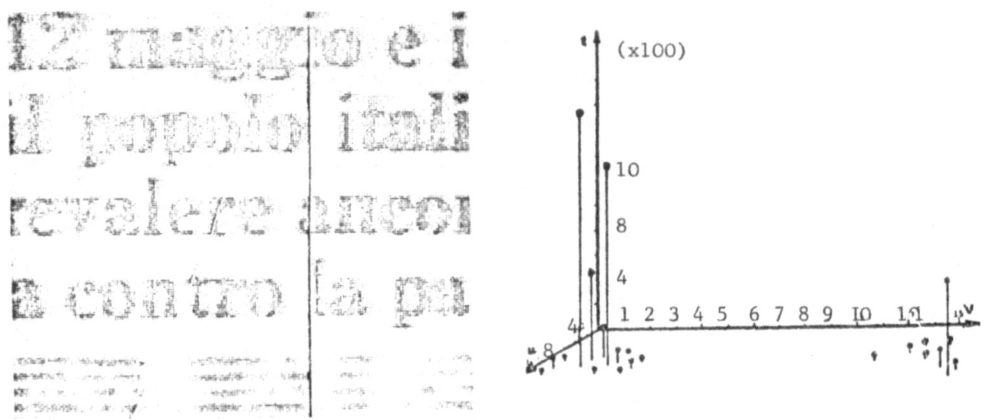

Fig. 2a   Fig. 2b

3. C-TRANSFORMS AS POWER SPECTRA

In this section, some semiquantitative arguments are listed in an effort to
relate C-transforms to familiar concepts of signal processing and vision psychophysio-
logy.

To start with, we notice that focusing our attention on max-min differences
and relative distances is tantamount to decompose the spatial signal in to a train
of pulses of suitable shape, resting each on a rectangular pedestal that accounts for
the displacement of the significant grey tone variation about the abscissa axis. The
"duration" v of each such pulse, i.e., the distance between the minimum and maximum
grey tones, could be then interpreted as the "rise time" of the pulse: as is well

known, this relates to the bandwidth B required to transmit the pulse by means of
the simple inverse relationship :

$$B = \frac{k}{v}$$

where k is usually assumed in practice to be an integer between 1 and 5 (13).
Therefore, one could say that the v-values reported in the C-transform yield
information about the spectral properties that are "locally" prevalent in the
spatial signal.

Grey tones, in their turn, as the output of some light sensitive transducer
are intrinsically analog to the energy of the incident radiation. As a consequence
the product p=u·v for each pulse is then in fact homogeneous with a power,namely, the
power locally conveyed by the signal fragment as far as luminance gradients are
concerned.

Trascuring pulse pedestals seems to be reasonably defendable on a physiological basis: indeed, it seems to be a rather established point of vision physiology
that the human eye can compare luminances whereas it is unable to appreciate their
absolute value (14).

The preceding discussion seems to support the view that C-transforms could
be interpreted as being peculiar power spectra.

The fact that the two factors in p have been split and plotted along two
different axes is due to the circumstance that local knowledge of both factors can
be required in some cases. Thus, for instance, it is known that the resolving power
of the eye is limited (15), so that even a high luminance gradient is not perceived
if it is concentrated in a too narrow interval. We shall recall this fact when
discussing the peculiarities of C-filters.

To conclude these few comments, we would like to add that an analytic
expression of C-transforms is rather cumbersome, due their inherent non-linearity.
A formal treatment of these aspects does not appear out of question, though. Perhaps,
it will call for the introduction of ad-hoc mathematical concepts and shall be the
object of further work.

4.APPLICATIONS TO TEXTURE ANALYSIS

The preceding discussion leads to expect textures to yield rather sharp
C-transforms. Tests made by us with several types of textures confirm fully this
prediction.

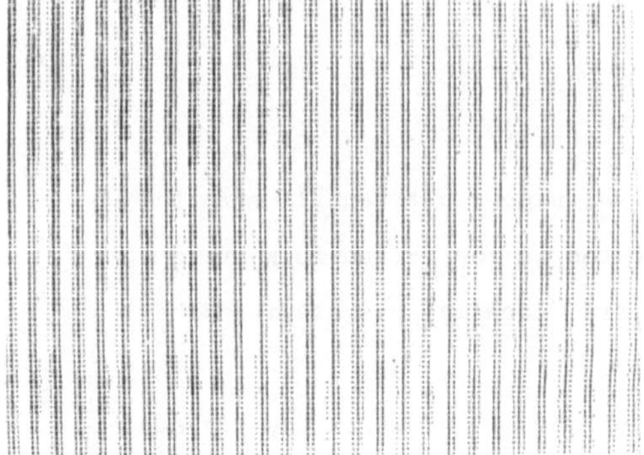

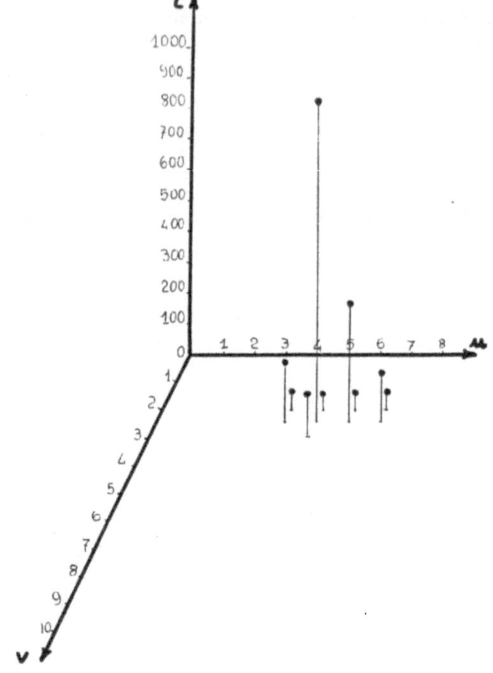

Fig. 3: a) Texture A and
b) its C-Transform

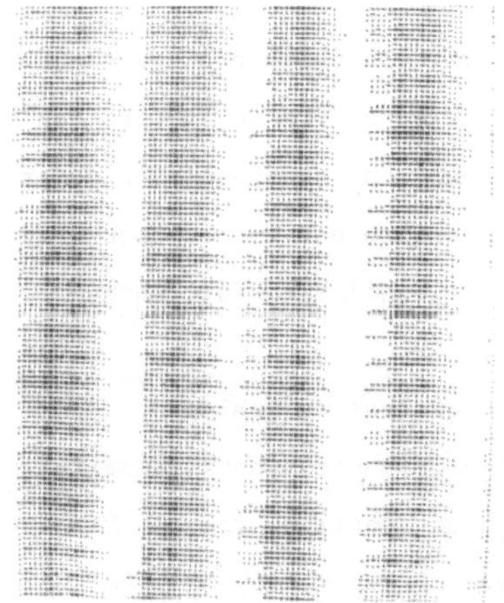

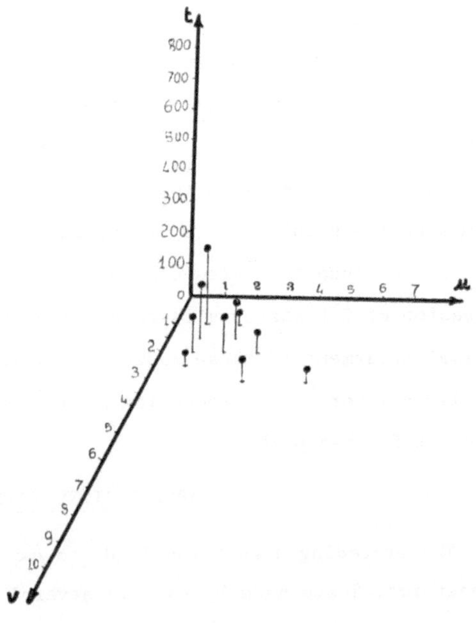

Fig. 4: a) Texture B and
b) its C-Transform

Fig. 5   Fig. 6

Fig. 7

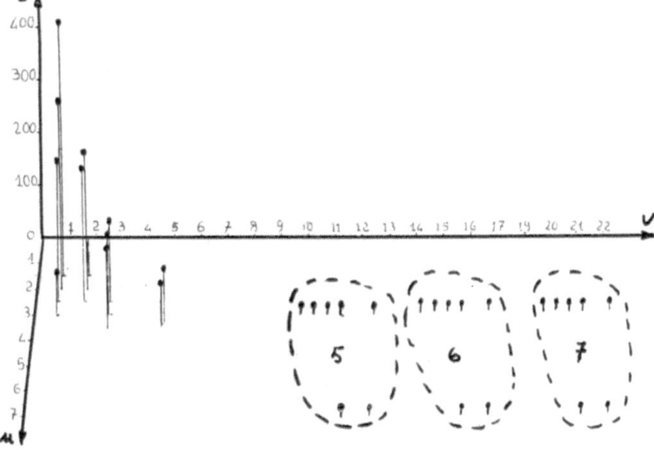

Fig. 8

Fig. 9a

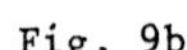

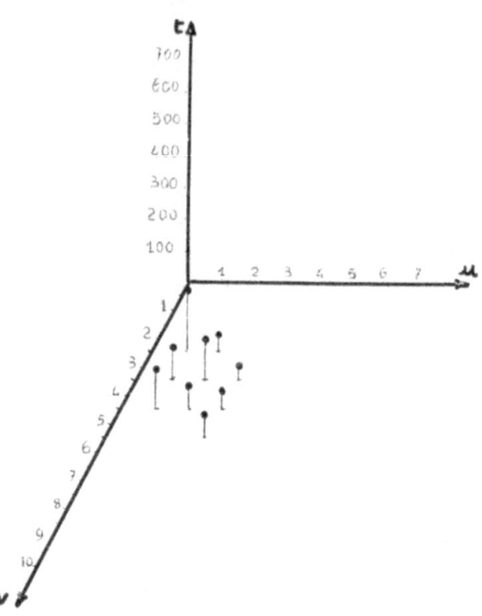

Fig. 9b

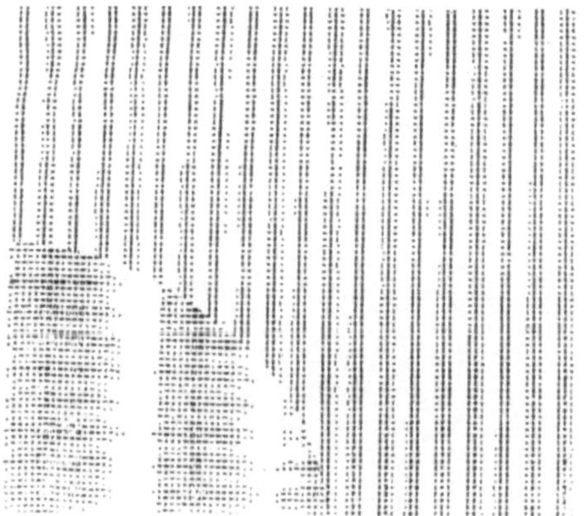

Fig. 10a

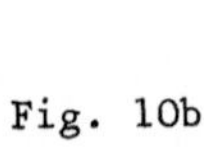

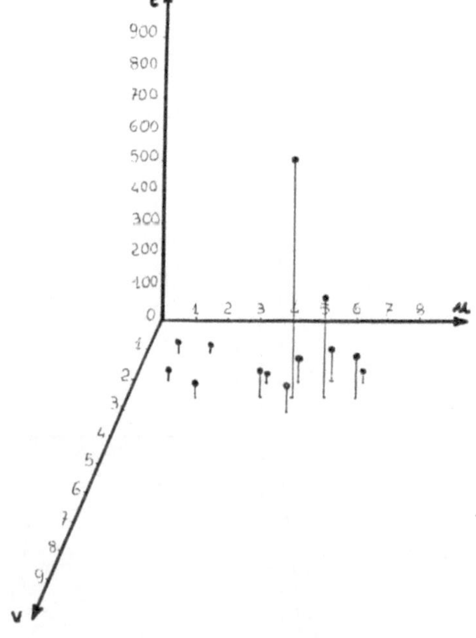

Fig. 10b

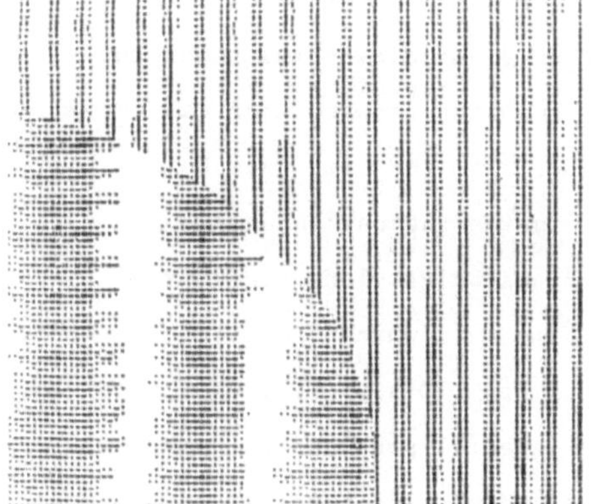

Fig. 11a

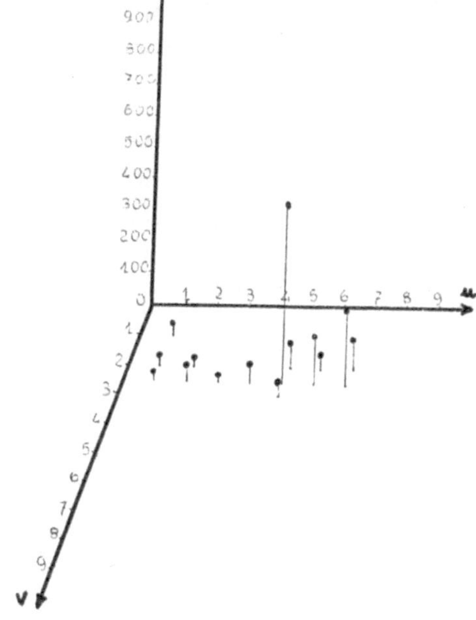

Fig. 11b

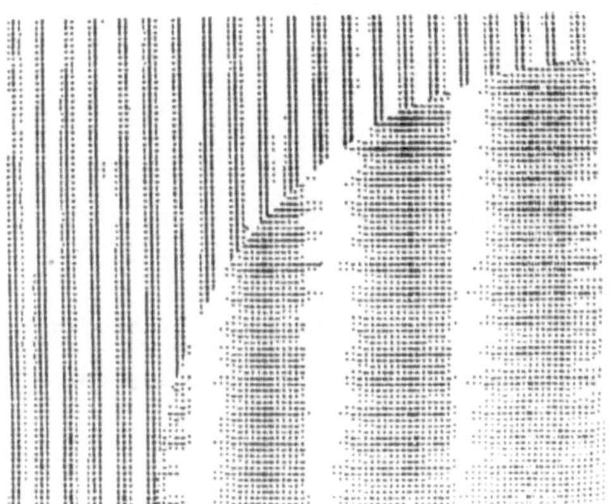

Fig. 12a

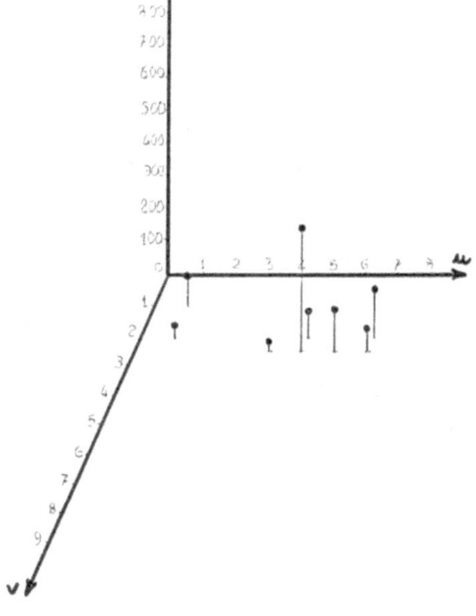

Fig. 12b

Fig.3,4 a,b show typical transforms of characteristic row-directed textures from 120 x 120 sample pictures.They both show rather tight clustering about the values (5,2) and (1,1)respectively.Figs. 5,6,7,8 show the transform of the second texture after it has undergone nonlinear stretchings of the time axis.Notice that while contribution from the fundamental variation inside the dark area almost remains unaffected,the components due to the white bands shift along the v axis.

Fig. 9(a,b) show a linear stretching of the time axis,which results in a shift along a segment of straight line in the (u,v) plane. Fig. 10(a,b),11(a,b),12(a,b) show one of the textures contamined with increasing spatial portion of the other. As is seen in the figure the resultant C-transforms and up in a combination of the two prvious ones; in particular the dominant peak of textures A decreases the more and the more as the other cluster,contributed from texture B appears.It has also been found experimentally that any contribution from texture B in the transform becomes vanishing and confused with noise,as should be expected,as soon as the related spatial portion gets so limited as to prevent recognition of any textural feature to the human eye. It is easily seen that the separation of two region characterized with different textures could be fruitfully achieved by mean of suitable discriminant function in the C-space. In next paragraph,we shall try show how this can in fact be obtained by C-filters.

5. PICTURES AND C-SETS

In this section, we recall from ref.10 those basic features of *C-calculus* that are needed in order to introduce our filtering procedure. The reader is referred to this work for detailed mathematical proofs.

The main idea of C-calculus is to take over from the ordinary number system the two distinct roles of figures, value and position, so to define, with appropriate interpretation, strings of sets and operations on them. Its core definitions and rules can be listed in a very compact form:

a) if α_n, α_{n-1},..., α_o represents some covering of a given set U, the correspon-ding C-set is described by the string α_n, α_{n-1},...,α_o.

b) Sum $\oplus$ and product $\otimes$ among describing strings are dealt with like the corresponding operations of arithmetic, with the only provision that the sum (product) of digits be substituted with the union (intersection) of sets (or other operations having the same formal properties).

Assuming that a digitized picture be presented as usual as an n x n matrix

$A = \left[g_{ij}\right]$, a C-set is then readily associated with A in the following way.

Suppose that an instrument (reader, window) is provided, which can tell the *maximum* M and *minimum* m values attained by g over some finite area w, when A is looked at through a window matching w.

Further, arrange a scanning of the picture that leads the reader successively onto contiguous non overlapping positions within the same row and then on the other rows so as to "cover" completely the matrix. This is tantamount to looking at A through a *grid* that partitions A into a set of rectangles, each bearing information about the maximum and minimum value assumed by g within its area.

For computing purposes, each rectangle may be individuated by associating to it a set of numbers that account for its position as well as for its "value". Thus, for instance, a "quadruple" can be assigned to the generic rectangle: its first two elements represent coordinates (x,y) of its lowest left corner, while the second two stand for the corresponding minimum and maximum values.

If positions in the grid are ordered now in some way (for instance, following the scanning sequence of the picture which is yielded by the reader) and the numbers within each quadruple are regarded as closed intervals in the continuum, then the alignment of all quadruples in a string represents (the description) of a C-set; this is referred to in the sequel as C_o. Thus, C_o clearly is a sampling of A by means of quadruples, as rough as the window is wide.

Have now the grid undergo a rigid translation (giving the scanner some non-zero initial phase) and let C_1 be the second C-set thus obtained. Upon multiplication of C_o and C_1, not only a finer partition is achieved of the supporting euclidean space (first two elements of the quadruple), but also a more detailed description of the picture itself (more shades of grey, from the second two elements.

If several such products are carried out among appropriately chosen C-sets, one would intuitively expect to get, eventually, a complete resolution of the picture under conditions that we are going to analyze.

It is simpler to restrict our attention to the corresponding onedimensional problem induced on a single row; this means referring to a histogram represented, e.g., by the equation:

$$y_n = g(t_n)$$

where (see fig. 13) t_n stands for the interval (x_n, x_{n+1}) and

$$x_n = n \cdot u$$

in terms of the unit measure u. In the sequel, it shall be assumed that u=1.

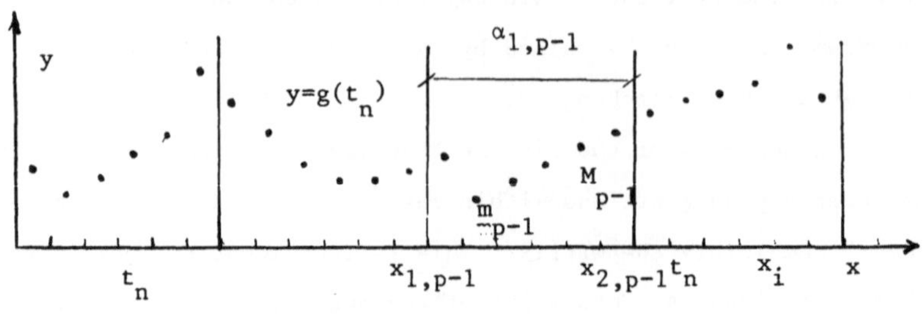

Fig. 13

Let the family of C-sets superimposed to the system be denoted by

$$\{C_i\} = \{\alpha_{ip} \ldots \alpha_{i1}\} .$$

As before we assume that, for each i and k, the element α_{ik} is represented
by a quadruple, whose first two elements determine an interval on the x-axis,
while the second two are the minimum and maximum for g in this interval, respectively; thus, we write this as:

$$\alpha_{ik} \equiv (x_{1k}, x_{2k}; m_k, M_k)_i .$$

Next, we need to show how quadruples are operated upon.

If digits are treated as cardinalities of sets, one can apply to them the operators $\oplus$ and $\otimes$ so as to express operations among quadruples in terms of these
operators. Thus, if

$$\alpha_{jm} \equiv (x_{1m}, x_{2m}; m_m, M_m)_j$$

is some element from C_j we define the product

$$\beta = \alpha_{ik} \otimes \alpha_{jm}$$

as:

1) $\beta \equiv (x_1, x_2, m, M) = (x_{1k} \oplus x_{1m}, x_{2k} \otimes x_{2m}; m_k \oplus m_m, M_k \otimes M_m)$

Let $X(\beta)$, $Y(\beta)$ stand for the closed intervals $[x_1, x_2]$ and $[m, M]$, respecti-
vely, and let in general $|t|$ indicate the length of the interval t. Then
$|X(\alpha_{ik})|$ is the *window* through which the "dynamic" – absolute value of maximal
variation within $X(\alpha_{ik})$, which we call $Y(\alpha_{ik})$ – of g within $X(\alpha_{ik})$ is
determined. In the following, both $X(\alpha_{ik})$ and $|X(\alpha_{ik})|$ will occasionally be
indicated by w, for short, if no confusion can arise and w is taken to be a
constant.

We say that the pair (m,M) in (1) *refines (blurs)* g in $X(\beta)$ $(= X(\alpha_{ik}) \times X(\alpha_{jm}))$ iff the values m,M are (are not) both attained by g somewhere within $X(\beta)$, i.e., if m and M are (are not) the minimum and maximum of g in $X(\beta)$. Furthermore, (m,M) will be called an *upper (lower) refinement* of g in $X(\beta)$ iff M (m) is attained by g somewhere within $X(\beta)$.

The following propositions obviously hold:

<u>Proposition 1</u>. For any given g and for any pair α_{ik}, α_{jm} such that $X(\beta) \neq \Phi$, the dynamic of g in $X(\beta)$, here indicated by $g|X(\beta)|$, is contained in $Y(\beta)$. Formally: $g|X(\beta)| \subseteq Y(\beta)$.

<u>Proposition 2</u>. The above relation reduces to identity $(X(\beta) = Y(\beta))$ if g is monotonic in X (γ) (when $|X(\beta)| = 1$, iff g is monotonic in $X(\gamma)$ $(= X(\alpha_{ik}) + X(\alpha_{jm}))$.

We are now in the position to study the problem of reconstructing the signal from a suitable family of C-sets. In order to do so, let us assume that:

$$C_o = \alpha_{op} \cdots \alpha_{o1}$$

is the C-set obtained by scanning the x-axis from left to right into contiguous non-overlapping intervals with a window of fixed width w, and let further:

$$C_i = \alpha_{ip} \cdots \alpha_{i1} \qquad (i=1,\ldots,w-1)$$

represent for each i the C-set obtained when the initial position of the reader is shifted i units to the right.

Call $P_o = C_o$ and consider the products:

$$2) \qquad P_{i+1} = P_i \times C_{i+1} \qquad (i=0,1,\ldots,w-1).$$

Clearly, at each iteration, a finer partition is achieved of the x-axis. Let:

$$3) \qquad X(P_i) = \bigcup_{1}^{(i+1)p} {}_k X(\beta_{ik})$$

stand for the partition corresponding to the $(i-1)$-th step. Along the same lines, the related intervals between pairs of minima and maxima determine a covering of the y-axis. Let this latter be denoted as:

$$Y(P_i) = \bigcup_{1}^{(i+1)p} {}_k Y(\beta_{ik}) .$$

Obviously, by the w-th iteration one will get from (3):

$$4) \qquad X(P_{w-1}) = \bigcup_{1}^{pw} {}_k t_k$$

that is, $X(P_{w-1})$ partitions the x-axis into contiguous non-overlapping unit intervals. Following Propositions 1 and 2, one cannot expect in general that the corresponding $Y(P_{w-1})$ refines the values of g within each such unit interval, unless,
quite trivially, g is monotonic all along the x-axis. However, the behavior of g
can be always retrieved at each "point" from $(X(P_{w-1}),Y(P_{w-1}))$ if the elements in
$Y(P_{w-1})$ are either refinements, or upper of lower refinements of g for the
corresponding intervals.

For the onedimensional case, it has been shown (10) that *a sufficient condition for the procedure to "converge" at each point of g is that:*

$$w \leq \frac{D}{2} + 1$$

*where D is the length of the smallest interval within which g displays a monoto-
nic behavior.*

6. FILTERING IN C-SPACE

Some light upon the significance of blurred points is shed by a second theoretical result in ref. 10. According to this theorem, the final values associated
with each point are just *the highest minimum and the lowest maximum which are seen
by the window when it scans the interval of width 2w-1 centered at that point,*
regardless of the scanning order. This circumstance enables to consider a very
peculiar mapping of the variation of g in a neighborhood of some point onto the
point itself and is at the basis of our filtering procedure. Thus, for instance,
considering a signal that shows some periodicity in a certain region and a non-periodic behavior outside that region, we can isolate these two different behaviors and
screen out one of the two without blurring the other in any way. The underlying
principle is that, for a window width larger than the period, all C-sets in the
family will display constant (m,M) values. Reconstruction with such window
width leads therefore to non convergence in all points in the region of periodicity,
while in the non-periodic region some convergence necessarily arises, thus enabling
to select automatically a window width and a scanning pattern that extract the region
that displays the wanted characteristics or features from it alone.

More precisely, it is easy to see, from the theorem just quoted above, that
if within some interval a signal is periodic then also the *reconstructed* signal
is periodic, regardless of the window width. If the latter is greater than the
period, then the reconstructed signal is a constant. As the window width decreases,
the frequency of the transformed signal increases and eventually, for $w < D/2 + 1$,

it reaches the value of that truly possessed by the signal.

In the general case, the theoretical results just quoted show that the window width plays a relevant role in the analysis of a picture. Indeed, convergence occurs only for those regions of the picture where the distances involved among contiguous grey level extrema are constrained by the inequality. Therefore, the application of the procedure with arbitrary window width leads to the definition of two classes of regions within the picture, those where the procedure converges and those where it does not. Each class can be easily discriminated against the other, so that the procedure acts as a filter; we call it *C-filter*.

The action of C-filters is best visualized in C-space. Indeed, it is easily seen that the plane v=w divides this space into two regions: reconstruction with a window of width w will not converge for all points whose neigborhoods "fall" between this plane and the plane v=0, whereas it converges for all other points. We just call *C-filtering* the operation that discriminates two such regions in C-space by working with a window width w. In general, it is possible to conceive of "low-pass", "high-pass" and "band-pass" C-filters along the same lines as is done with classical frequency filters.

It is easily seen that such concepts seem to play a "natural" role in problems concerning both texture-texture and object-textural background discrimination. In fig. 14 a,b one such example is reported: in a "binary" picture, two regions characterized with different textures have been easily discriminated against each other, upon reconstruction with a suitable window width.

7. CONCLUDING REMARKS

Filtering in C-space seems to be a computationally simple and inherently parallel operation. Perhaps at the present stage it would not mark an high score in many classification problems, compared with those of other extant methods. Yet the formalism introduced here seems flexible enough to be amenable to significant improvement through the adoption of finer specifications. Thus, for instance, the concept of C-transform could be extended so as to include features other than luminance gradients and related distances. Then C-filtering would be still accomplished by the same means, or nearly so.

Loci of equal "pulse power" are hyperbola in the (u,v) plane. In section 2, it was mentioned that contrast sensitivity is limited by the resolving power of the eye. By recalling the way a fixed window width acts as a discriminant function in

Fig. 14a

Fig. 14b

the C-space, we would feel encouraged to conclude that a C-filter performs just as well.

ACKNOWLEDGEMENTS

We are deeply indebted to Professor E.R. Caianiello for illuminating discussions and to Doctor E. Fischetti for his generous help in the preparation and running of programs and for his constructive criticism.

REFERENCES

1. Haralick,R.M., Shanmugam, K. and Dinstein, I., "Textural features for image classification", IEEE Transactions of Systems, Man and Cybernetics, Vol. SMC-3, No.6, Nov. 1973.

2. Rosenfeld, A., "Visual texture analysis: an overview", Tech. Rep. TR 406, Computer Science Center, University of Maryland, College Park, Aug. 1975.

3. Pickett, R.M., "Visual analyses of texture in the detection and recognition of of objects", Picture Processing and Psychopictorics (B.S. Lipkin and A. Rosenfeld, eds.). Academic Press, New York, 1970, 289.

4. Rosenfeld, A. and Lipkin, B.S., "Texture Synthesis", ibidem, 309.

5. Rosenfeld, A., Lee, Y.H. and Thomas, R.B., "Edge and curve detection for texture discrimination", ibidem, 381.

6. Muerle, J.L., "Some thoughts on texture discrimination by computer", ibidem,371.

7. Julesz, B., Foundations of Cyclopean Perception , The University of Chicago Press, 1971.

8. Tamura, H., Shunji, M. and Yamawaki, T., "Psychological and computational measurements of basic textural features and their comparison", Proc. of the Third International Joint Conference of Pattern Recognition, Coronado, Ca., Oct. 1976.

9. Caianiello, E.R., "A calculus for hierarchical systems", Proc. of the First International Joint Conference on Pattern Recognition, Washington, D.C., 1973.

10. Apostolico, A., Caianiello, E.R., Fischetti, E. and Vitulano, S., "C-calculus: an elementary approach to some problems in Pattern Recognition", submitted for publication to Pattern Recognition, Aug. 1976.

11. Apostolico, A., Caianiello, E.R. and Vitulano, S., "A new approach to some problems of pattern analysis", Proc. Informatica 76, Bled, Oct. 1976.

12. Michelson, A.A., Studies in Optics, The University of Chicago Press, 1927.

13. Schwartz, M., Information, Transmission, Modulation and Noise, McGraw Hill, New York, 1970.

14. Vernon, M., <u>Experiments in Visual Perception</u>, Penguin Books, Harmondsworth
     Middlesex, 1966.

15. Campbell, F.W., "The human eye as an optical filter", Proceedings IEEE, Vol. 56,
     No. 6, 1968.

<u>AN INSTALLATION FOR INTERACTIVE TRANSFER OF INFORMATION FROM OBLIQUE</u>
<u>AERIAL PHOTOS TO MAPS</u>

I. Scollar, T.S. Huang, B. Weidner, Laboratory for Field Archaeology
Rheinisches Landesmuseum, Bonn
G. Tang, School of Electrical Engineering, Purdue University, West
Lafayette, Indiana, USA

The ancient monument protection service of the Rhineland has installed
a system for transforming archaeological information in oblique aerial
photos to 1:5000 base maps. A comprehensive software-hardware plan
was implemented. Windowing, enhancement, pseudo-color density slicing
and merging are employed. A simple map compression scheme which offers
a reasonable compromise between bit rate and computing time has been
developed.

The major river valleys in the temperate parts of Europe have been
occupied by man for many thousands of years. During this time he has
constructed dwellings, settlements, fortifications, roads and cemeter-
ies, and has completely transformed the appearance of the landscape
with agriculture. It is one of the major tasks of modern archaeology
to trace this development, and it is the function of an archaeological
monument protection service to conserve as much of the fragmentary evidence as possible. Unfortunately, the qualities of the land which
made an area attractive for settlement in the past often continue to do
so in the present. Hence the rate of destruction of these vestiges
through modern construction is high. The best way to preserve the
cultural heritage of material remains lying in the ground is to leave
them there untouched as long as possible for future planned scientific
exploration and study. This presupposes foreknowledge of what is there
and where it is. Accurate data must be provided for planning authorities so that modern works may by-pass important archaeological concentrations whenever possible. At the least, the field archaeologists
must be given advance warning of impending destruction of an ancient
buried monument so that they will not have to excavate in haste.
Up to now, long lists of endangered sites, found by walking through
the fields and looking for traces of remains on the surface, have
been used. This is of limited use for few planning authorities have
enough personnel to deal with them. What is needed is a set of over-
lays for the largest scale map available, preferably the same scale

as used in planning. These can be placed over the planning maps and
one may see at a glance what is there.

How do archaeological sites come to be buried? Most structures either
collapse after a time due to natural decay processes or they are pull-
ed down on purpose and leveled.   Subsequent agriculture and natural
soil movement due to weather and earthworms buries the remains. Little
or nothing is visible on the surface. However, just below the surface
there is an anomalous zone which has different physical and chemical
properties from that of the surrounding undisturbed earth. A buried
wall, for example, is more poorly drained than the surrounding soil
and retains less moisture. A buried ditch, filled with fine surface
loam is more water retentive. Under appropriate dry conditions, crops
grow poorly over buried walling and better over better ditches as
shown below.

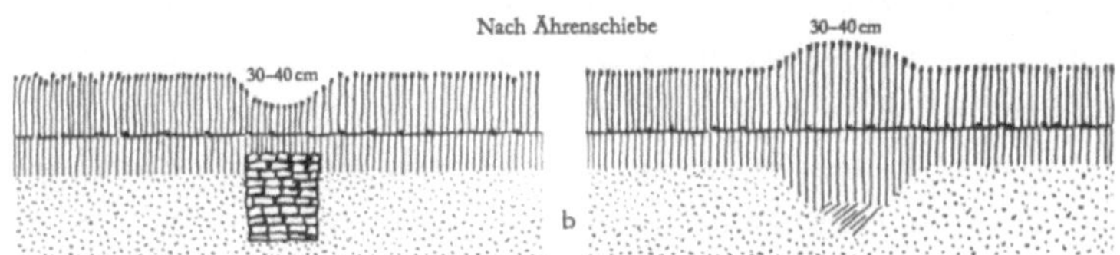

Figure 1

From the air, these markings can be clearly seen and photographed with
normal panchromatic film when flying at low altitude. Maximum contrast
is in the yellow-green region reflecting differences in the chlorophyll
xanthophyll and carotene concentrations in growing plants. This technique has been used for the last fifty years or so, starting in south-
ern England in 1924 and since 1960 in France and Germany to explore
systematically for buried archaeological sites (Scollar, 1970). At the
Laboratory for Field Archaeology where the technique was introduced by
the first author, many thousands of black and white photographs made
from a low flying light aircraft with a hand held camera have been
produced. Typical examples are shown in Plates 1 and 2. In the left
lower center of Plate 1, the dark gray outline of a square enclosure
with rounded corners can be seen along with a number of irregular markings. This is due to the buried defensive ditch of a small late Roman
fort. Plate 2 shows the outline of the foundation walls of a Roman
farmhouse. Both photos are exceptionally clear and they require no

enhancement. Precise mapping of the sites means using analytic photo-
grammetric techniques (Scollar, 1975). With coordinate information
derived from points visible in the photographs also visible on the base
maps, the position of the aircraft and the angles of view can be computed by an interative technique. From this knowledge, the projective
transform matrix can be obtained. With a pair of pictures, height information can be obtained. The photos are usually taken in a sequence
of five or more when flying around the site in a tight circle. Using
the set as pseudo-stereo pairs, points of archaeological interest can
be converted to map coordinates. Vertical air cover obtained by mapping cameras do not show as much detail. The archaeologist-photographer
unconciously snaps the picture when he observes maximum contrast in the
viewfinder. This contrast only appears at certain angles relative to
the sun's illumination, and the likelihood that a vertical picture will
produce this by chance is small.

Formerly, our technique was to measure contact transparencies in a
stereo comparator and type film coordinates and map coordinates for
ground control points along with points of archaeological interest
into a terminal connected to a time-sharing remote machine. The interactive analytic photogrammetry program returns ground coordinates for
the archaeological features, and these are plotted by hand on the base
maps. The technique allows for no enhancement of the image, is very
slow and subject to human error through fatigue. Of the thousands of
photographs in the Landesmuseum's collection, only a tiny fraction have
been treated in this way.

In the Rhineland, we are fortunate in having a nearly complete base
map survey. It was decided that all aerial archaeological finds must
be recorded at this scale, or in some instances at 1:1000 where the
detail required it. In other parts of the world like England, where
aerial archaeology has been going on for nearly two generations, there
are at least a million photos in the files of various services awaiting
evaluation and mapping. Before the backlog in Germany becomes quite
so great, it was decided to automate the method by introduction of
image processing techniques. We obtained financial support for the
purchase of a dedicated system. This made it possible to think in
terms of a problem-oriented "top down" design, starting with the anti-
cipated application software, chosing the appropriate type of operating
system, and only then selecting the hardware to implement the concept.

The principal operations envisaged are enhancement, windowing, inter-

Plate 1- Roman Fort in the Rhineland, Freig. Reg. Präs. D'dorf.
16/28/5515

Plate 2-Roman Farmhouse in the Rhineland, Breig. Reg. Präs. D'dorf.
16/22/1387

actively controlled feature extraction, photogrammetry and merge with
scanned base maps. Automatic recognition of archaeological features
appears to be beyond the state of the art. Hence the system was
designed as an interactive one, with archaeologists unskilled in computer matters making the appropriate pattern recognition decisions.
At the same time, a number of terminals for program development by
skilled users was also needed. This dictated the choice of a real-time
or time sharing operating system. Financial considerations of overhead, core store requirements and the need for a swapping disk eliminated the time sharing choice and a real-time multitasking operating
system was decided upon. Later versions of this system must have time
slicing which allots a finite time segment to each task according to
a priority scheme so that compute bound tasks cannot monopolize the
CPU.

Unskilled users are not expected to interact with the operating system
directly. An executive monitor is interposed between them and the
system and controls all resources. A table driven parser is to be
adapted to analyse user requests. As much of the software as possible
had to be made from standard operating system components and written
in a high-level language for future system compatibility. Since peri-
pherals of various manufacturers had to be connected together, software interfacing had to be as easy as possible, and where practical
nearly device independent. Thus standard manufacturer's hardware
interfaces of only one type were to be used. Other considerations,
such as total cost, hardware maintenance support, number of systems
produced and length of time for which operating system software has
been offered lead to the choice of a Digital Equipment PDP 11 as
the basic machine with a version of the RSX11 operating system.
Picture processing is extremely I/O intensive when large areas of the
image cannot be stored in core memory. Therefore the PDP 11/70 which
has a separate I/O bus 32 bits wide as well as the usual Unibus was
chosen. The configuration built around this machine is shown in Figure
2.

High requirements for geometric accuracy and long term stability were
imposed on the hard copy output device. In addition gray scale capability for future plans to create photo mosaics was also specified.
A large format film was needed. The Optronics P 1500 drum writer
met most of these requirements. The input pictures are mostly on 5
inch aerial film with a square image area of 11x11cm. Contact trans-

ORTRONICS P1000 SCANNER
DR 11Bequiv
DMA Interface
DEC PDP 11/10 32 KB
DR 11Bequiv
DMA Interface
OPTRONICS P1500 FILMWRITER
25/50/100 micron resolution, 20x20 cm. scan, 256 gray level
200 KB/Sec DMA core-core link
resolution as per scanner
DA 11B
LA36 matrix writer
DMA Interface
DR 11B
DEC PDP 11/70 2KB Cache 256KB Core
Serial Interfaces
5 x DL11A
VT50 A/N term.
32 Bit I/O Bus
RP 04
RWP 04
TWU 16
TU 16
VT50 A/N term.
176 Megabyte Disks & Controller
1600/800 BPI Mag. Tapes
VT50 A/N term.
Joystick
RAMTEK GX-100 B 640/512*512 pixels
Keyboard
VT50 A/N term.
256 level gray b/w
16 level full color
Operating System RSX11D/6B
Fortran Plus Ver. 2
(Real time event driven multi-tasking)
BARCO MMD 1
BARCO CDCT 2/51
SONY PVM 90 (2)
SONY AV 3620
b/w   color   b/w   b/w video
TV Raster Displays   Recorder
PICTURE PROCESSING SYSTEM
RHEINISCHES LANDESMUSEUM
BONN, GERMANY   Figure 2

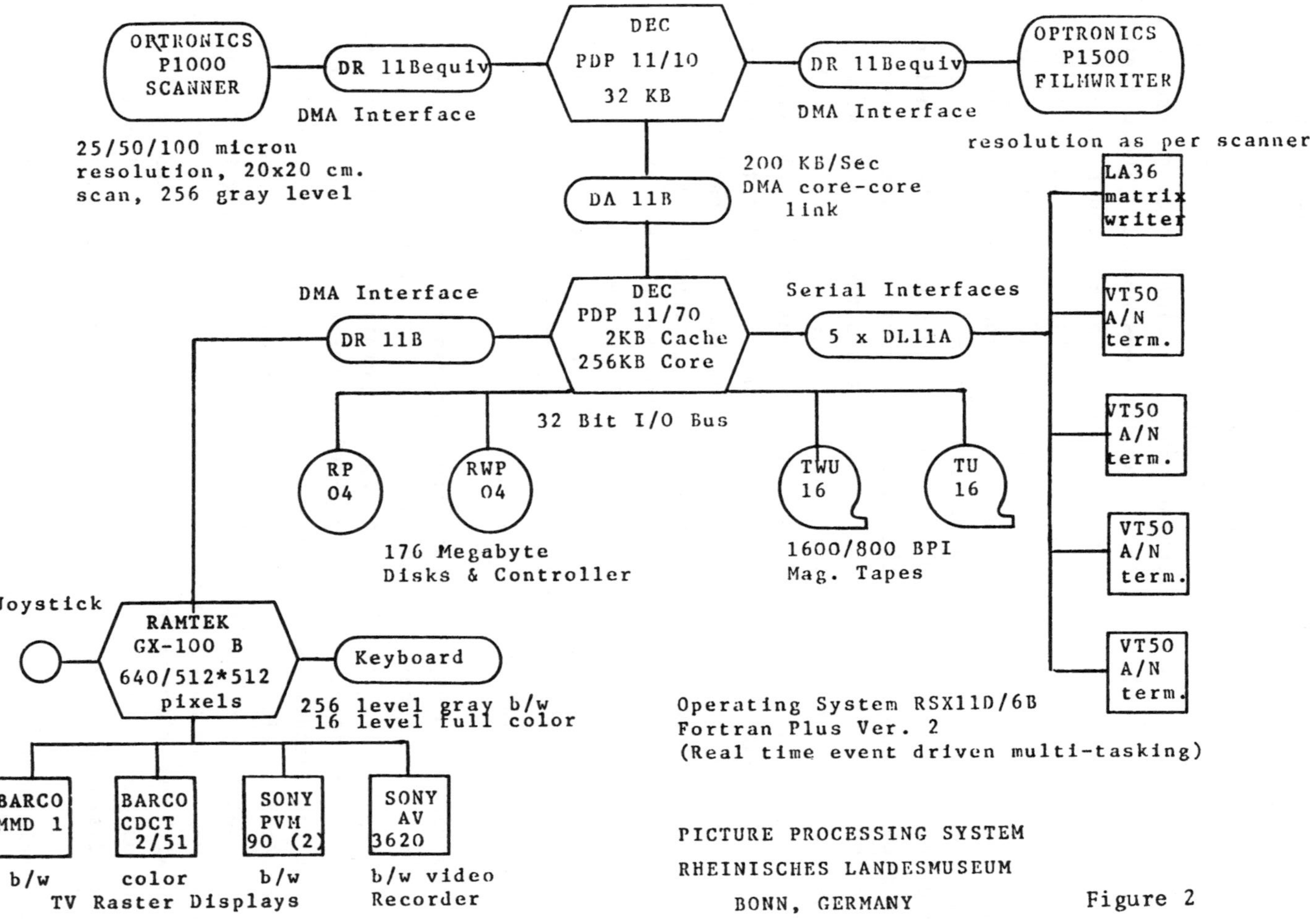

Figure 2

parencies are to be scanned, four at a time, to minimize handling of
precious unrepeatable original negatives and to reduce mechanical
operations in the scanner. A very wide range of gray level resolution
with good accuracy was needed since films vary considerably in density
and gamma. High geometric accuracy for determination of control point
information along with long term stability was needed. These features
were also of great importance when scanning the reduced base maps.
The Optronics P 1000 with 25-100 micron resolution met the requirements.
It does not, however, provide convenient rapid random access to any
area of the image. An image point is digitized or written every
33 microseconds and two pixels are buffered before going as double bytes
to the interface. Every 16 microseconds a word has to be transferred
to or from the computer. Although the transfers are direct memory
access (DMA), to avoid Unibus conflicts it was thought advisable to
buffer a complete scan or write line before transfer to PDP11/70 memory by interposing a PDP11/10 as a data concentrator. This small
machine runs under a stripped down version of the multi-tasking system.
The link to the PDP11/70 is essentially two DMA units back-to-back
with synchronization of the Unibusses during transfer of a line of
data. The transfer rate of the link is 50% faster than that of the
combined data rate from the scanner and the writer, so that no bottle-
necks occur. A separate task in the 11/70 writes the scanned lines
immediately to disk, or takes a line from disk into core and sends
it out over the link when ready.

Pictures reside on big disks as direct access files. This allows some
degree of random access to any data point. A circular buffer scheme
is used in the 11/10 so that overlapped operation of the writer, scanner
and link is feasable. A picture pipeline cesign was decided upon
for best throughput. While one set of up to four pictures is being
scanned, the previously scanned set is being worked on, and the results
from the set before that combined with map data is going to the writer.
In this way it is hoped to achieve throughput times which are commen-
surate with the time needed to change films in scanner and writer and
develop output images, after fine tuning of the system. The use of
the big disks for main picture sotrage required two units, so that
input and output operations reside on separate machines. This allows
some overlapping of input/output operations. The system is capable
of a resolution which would result in 64 megabytes for four images
of the size stated. The amount of I/O required at this resolution
would clog the pipeline. In practice it has been found unnecessary
to digitize the input images to better than 50 microns, and the output

maps, if done one at a time can also be written at this resolution, for
a 20x20 cm area. Thus considerable reserve storage on the disks is
available for program and system files. Back-up for the disks, both
for short term storage of images and for long term storage of maps is
given by two 1600BPI tape units. For programming purposes there are
four alphanumeric terminals and a matrix printer terminal for paper
copy.

A very critical point in a system designed around man-machine interaction is the picture display. This item was not available in a proved
model on the international market until the middle 70's. When the
hardware configuration was made final in May 1975 there were only two
systems which fulfilled the quality requirements, but only one, the
Ramtek GX100B, which used an all solid state picture refresh memory.
It was chosen for ease of maintenance. The display system memory of
327 Kilobytes stores a picture with either 640 or 512 elements per
line and 512 lines, interlaced. Each element is 8 bits fed into a
programmable look-up table which maps into either 8 bit black and
white or to three 4 bit color digital-analog converters. To avoid
flicker, the display refresh runs at 30 pictures per second. In order
to avoid interference with the 50 cycle power line, Barco CDCT 2/51
and MMD 1 studio color television monitors were chosen. Additionally,
a Sony AV3620 black and white video recorder was modified to accept
the 577 line 30 frame interlaced Ramtek signal. The recorder is used
for documenting programs under test so that they can be examined off-
line without rerunning them over and over again. The recorder is
displayed on the modified Sony PVM90 monitor. The sound track is
used to record additional comments. A second Sony monitor is mounted
permanently near the display controller for repair purposes. It is
used together with the recorder when static screen photographs are
inadequate to record errors in the display memory. The user of the
system interacts with the Ramtek via a joystick and a keyboard.
It is planned to install a graphic tablet in the near future to allow
finer control of the software cursors than the joystick affords.

The success of this mixed hardware design was proven during system
integration. As components from various manufacturers arrived they
were hooked up to the standard DMA interfaces in a matter of a few
days. Software integration using a single type of primitive synchron-
ous handler required about two man-weeks to write. The more sophistica-
ted asynchronous handlers now in use needed about three man-months

work.   Initial component deliveries began in December 1975 and final
deliveries and connection in May of 1976.   All system software ran
correctly in early September of that year.   A few application programs
and picture utilities were ready for an official opening at the end
of that month.   At the time of writing, application programs for
histogram equalization, convolution filtering, pseudo-color density
slicing and contrast enhancement, and polygon coarse feature extraction
are in operation.

A few preliminary results, photographed from the display monitor, are
shown in Plates 3-6.   In plate 3, a windowed area of the Roman fort
(Plate 1) is shown without treatment.   The original was contact print-
ed with low contrast.   This was scanned at 50 microns giving a 2048
by 2048 pixel image.   A 512x512 window was extracted and displayed.
The density histogram in the small window was extracted and the
histogram streched (Hummel, 1975).   The result was applied to the look
up table in the display memory and the result is shown in Plate 4.
A similar procedure was followed with the farmhouse in Plate 5 and 6.

After enhancement, a line following schem being developed will be used
interactively, with the archaeologist indicating critical points
with the joystick or tablet.   The coordinates corresponding to these
features will be transferred to the analytical photogrammetry task.
The process will be repeated for multiple images in the sequence
and the photogrammetry task will return map coordinates to the
writer task.   This will be followed on a display which has been
simulated in Plate 7.

For the Rhineland there are about 4000 base maps at 1:5000.   Digitized
byte for byte and recorded on tape, these would exceed our physical
storage capacity.   With a simple table look-up algorithm and a threshold, the byte images are transformed to bit images of the map in black
and white.   This effects a data compression of 8 times.   To obtain
further compression, a simple run-length coding scheme has been devised.
In this scheme, two 8 bit bytes making one word are used.   If the
first bit in the first byte is off, then the run length to next black
or white is given by the next 7 bits.   If the first bit is on,
then the run length is given by the 7 bits as before, plus the 8 bits
in the next byte.   This code, christened 8-16 is particularly rapid
to compute for compression and decompression.   A test was made on the
Deutsche Grundkarte 1:5000, Sheet Ri11, 2536 R/5718H, as representative
of partly built-up areas in the Rhineland.   The map was scanned from

Plate 3- Display Monitor, Unenhanced windowed image

Plate 4- Enhanced image, histogram equalizing from window

Plate 5-Display Monitor, Unenhanced windowed image

Plate 6-Enhanced image, histogram equalizing from window

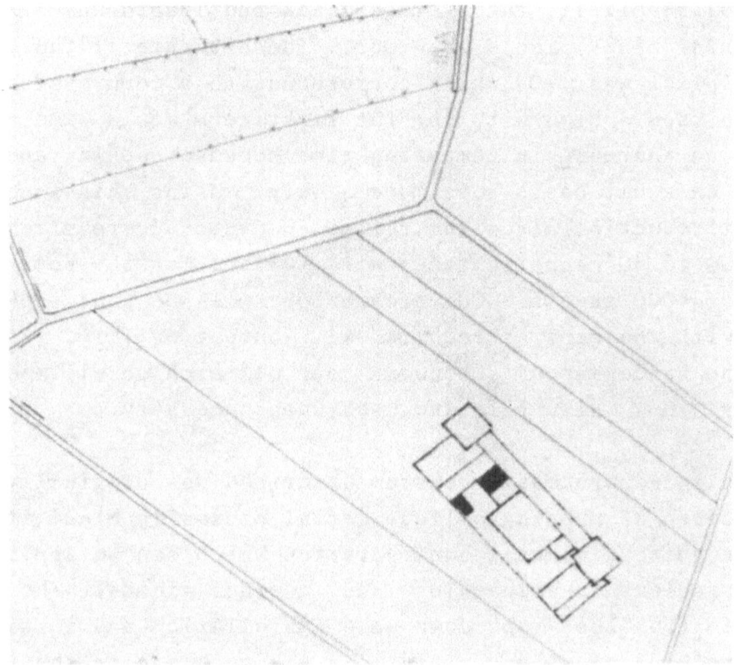

Plate 7-Display Monitor, simulated extracted feature and insertion in scanned map with reference gray scale. The actual scanned and reproduced map with the photomgrammetrically corrected data cannot be reproduced for copyright reasons.

a 20 x 20 cm. negative made from the original plate by the Landesver-
messungsamt, Bad Godesberg for us. This is a 2:1 reduction. 50
micron resolution was used giving 16 megabytes. The average white run
length was 51.98 pixels, the average black run length was 3.52 pixels.
The fraction of black pixels was .063. The bit rate of the 8-16 code
in bits per pixel was .304 which corresponds to a compression of 3.3.
A code which used 5 or 6 bits for the first term would give more compression at an increase in computing time because packing and unpacking
of the data on a bit basis goes more slowly. Using this code plus
the byte bit reduction algorithm reduces map storage requirements so
that about 50 to 60 magnetic tapes will suffice for the entire
collection of 4000 sheets. The archaeology will be kept separately
and merged with the maps as required with output on film. Additional
data from the Landesmuseum's hundred year old archive will be recorded
symbolically in a third file and used when necessary.

Although the image processing system described was originally planned
with the problem of mapping oblique aerial photos in mind, it has
proven to be quite a general configuration which can be applied to
many other problems in archaeology and in other fields. The design
of the system from the "top" down made installation and initial operation relatively painless and rapid. It was much easier than comparable
systems which were made up of hardware accumulated over a period of
time, for which software was composed ad hoc. The approach is highly
recommended when planning a new system. The concept of standard
hardware interfaces with similar handlers is the key to system integration.

Responsibility:
The first author was responsible for the overall system design and
for the hardware configuration. He also designed the 8-16 map compression code. The second author was responsible for the map compression statistics. The third author planned and produced the system
software and the windowing and density slicing application software,
as well as many utilities. The fourth author programmed the histogram equalization and digitial filtering sshemes.

Acknowledgements:
We sincerely wish to express our deepest appreciation to the Stiftung
Volkswagenwerk whose generosity made it possible to obtain most of
the hardware and to the Landschaftsverband Rheinland who agreed to

carry all construction and future costs. The second author is very
grateful to the Humboldt Stiftung for presenting a Senior U.S. Scientist
Award which made possible his stay at the Labor für Feldarchäologie
of the Rheinisches Landesmuseum while on sabbatical from Purdue University. The fourth author whishes to thank the School of Electrical
Engineering, Purdue University for underwriting his stay in Germany.
Finally the first author wishes to thank the many people at a large
number of image processing laboratories in the United States and
in Germany who, over the years told him which mistakes to avoid,
and to the Deutsche Forschungsgemeinschaft who provided the travel
expenses for these consultations.

Bibliography

R.A. Hummel, Histogram Modification Techniques, Computer Graphics and
          Image Processing, 4, Nr. 3, 1975, 209-224
I. Scollar, Einführung in neue Methoden der archäologischen Prospektion.
          Rheinland Verlag, Düsseldorf, 1970
I. Scollar, Transformation of extreme oblique aerial photographs to
          maps or plans by conventional means or by computer. in
          Aerial Reconnaissance for Archaeology, Research Report
          12, The Council for British Archaeology, London, 1975,
          52-58

<u>EINIGE EXPERIMENTE ZUR DATENREDUZIERTEN DARSTELLUNG VON</u>

<u>DIGITISIERTEN MUSTERN DURCH DIE MITTELACHSEN-TRANSFORMATION</u>

V. Märgner, P. Zamperoni
Institut für Nachrichtentechnik der
Technischen Universität Braunschweig
Schleinitzstraße 23, 3300 Braunschweig

1. Einleitung

In der vorliegenden Arbeit wird gezeigt, daß die Mittelachsen-Transfor-
mation (MAT) für digitisierte Zweipegelbilder einige Eigenschaften besitzt, die zur Datenreduktion günstig ausgenützt werden können. Es ist
im allgemeinen möglich, die Datenmenge eines mittelachsentransformier-
ten Bildes ohne Informationsverlust durch Redundanzreduktion zu kompri-
mieren. Bei vielen Bildern läßt sich zusätzlich eine wirksame Irrelevanzreduktion durchführen. Für Grautonbilder wurde die MAT im Hinblick
auf eine Datenreduktion bereits untersucht /1/ und für diese Anwendung
als schlecht geeignet gefunden.

Die MAT ist ein bekanntes Verfahren, um zweidimensionale Muster zu Ske-
lettlinien zu reduzieren /2/. Jeder Bildpunkt der Skelettlinie erhält
einen Wert, der seinen minimalen Abstand vom äußeren Objektrand kenn-
zeichnet. Algorithmen zur Berechnung der MAT sind aus der Literatur bekannt /3/.

Die MAT führt zu einer reversiblen Bilddarstellung, die den Vorteil hat,
visuell besonders relevante Bildpunkte hervorzuheben. Dieser morphoLogische Aspekt der MAT wurde in /5/ untersucht. Das <u>Bild 1</u> zeigt einen
Ausschnitt aus einer Textvorlage, in dem auf jedem schwarzen Bildpunkt
die entsprechende (minimale) Entfernung zum Hintergrund eingetragen ist.
Das <u>Bild 2</u> zeigt den entsprechenden Ausschnitt aus dem Skelettbild. Ein
dargestelltes Objekt kann bekanntlich als die Vereinigungsmenge aller
"Kreise" aufgefaßt werden, deren Zentren auf der Skelettlinie liegen
und deren Radien von den errechneten Abstandswerten angegeben werden /4/.
Das Wort "Kreis" mit Radius R (R = positive ganze Zahl) bezeichnet hier
die Menge aller Bildpunkte, deren Abstand vom Zentrum, nach der festgelegten Rastermetrik, kleiner als R ist. Legt man für die MAT eine 8-
Nachbarschaft zugrunde, so ergeben sich "Kreise" quadratischer Form /3/.

2. Einige Eigenschaften der MAT

Die MAT-transformierten Bilder weisen einige Formeigenschaften auf, die
im Hinblick auf eine kompakte Bilddarstellung und auf eine Bildsynthese
mit einem reduzierten Grundmustervorrat von Interesse sind:
a) Die Entfernung d_{AB} zwischen zwei Skelettpunkten mit den Abstandswerten A und B ist:

$$d_{AB} > |A - B|$$

b) In einer senkrechten oder waagerechten Folge von 2n Skelettpunkten
mit dem gleichen Wert n sind die $2(n-1)$ mittleren Punkte redundant.
Auch wenn diese Punkte gelöscht werden, erhält man durch die Rücktransformation das Originalbild wieder.
c) "1"-er der Skelettlinie sind nie redundant, da keine teilweise Über-
lappung eines "Kreises" mit Radius 1 (Einzelpunkt) mit einem größeren "Kreis" möglich ist.

Diese Eigenschaften folgen unmittelbar aus der verwendeten Transforma-
tionsregel /3/ unter Voraussetzung einer 8-Nachbarn-Metrik und können
ohne weiteren Beweis leicht überprüft werden.

Irrelevante "1"-er, die 1-Bildpunkt-Zacken der Konturen darstellen, können aus dem Bild getilgt werden, ohne daß diese Operation die topologischen Zusammenhänge der dargestellten Objekte verändert (z.B. bestehende
Linien oder Flächen werden weder unterbrochen noch verbunden). Die Abstände d zwischen "1"-ern, die in diesem Sinne irrelevant sind, und beliebigen Skelettpunkten x, y aus ihrer Umgebung erfüllen die folgende
Bedingung:

$$d_{1x} + d_{1y} > d_{xy}$$

In Abhängigkeit vom verarbeiteten Bild führt die Anwendung der MAT zu
qualitativ unterschiedlichen Ergebnissen, die in die folgenden zwei
Fälle grob eingeteilt werden können:
I. Bei Linienbildern:
   - Die meisten visuell relevanten Bildpunkte bleiben in der Skelett-
     linie erhalten; diese weist nur wenige Unterbrechungen auf.
   - Die MAT-Darstellung ist stark redundant, da sich häufig "Kreise"
     ergeben, die sich gegenseitig teilweise überlappen.
   - Infolge der Redundanz besitzt die MAT-Darstellung eine große Stör-
     festigkeit.
II. Bei Flächenbildern:
   - Die Skelettlinie enthält sehr wenig visuelle Information über das
     Originalobjekt.
   - Die MAT-Darstellung ist wenig redundant.
   - Die Störfestigkeit des transformierten Bildes ist gering.

Störfestigkeit und Redundanz von MAT-transformierten Bildern wurden an
Hand von gerasterten Bildvorlagen (Schrift, Zeichnungen, geometrische
Muster) untersucht. Zur Beurteilung von eventuell auftretenden Verzerrungen wurde anschließend die Rücktransformation durchgeführt. Als ty-
pisches Bildmaterial wurden Schrift und Zeichnungen in A4-Format untersucht, die mit einer Auflösung von 4 Bildelementen/mm abgetastet wurden. Große Ausschnitte aus den Originalvorlagen A und B nach der Digitisierung sind in den **Bildern 3 und 4** gezeigt. Auf Grund der begrenz-
ten Speicherkapazität der vorhandenen Rechenanlage konnte die MAT nur
für Bildvorlagen mit einer Strichbreite $\leq$ 13 Bildpunkte gerechnet werden. Somit umfaßt das untersuchte Bildmaterial überwiegend Linienbilder
und ist von vornherein für eine Datenreduktion mit Hilfe der MAT besonders gut geeignet.

3. Störfestigkeit der MAT

Um die Störfestigkeit der MAT zu untersuchen, wurde in das transformierte Skelettbild (wie z.B. Bild 2) eine Zufallsstörung eingeführt
und das so gestörte Bild anschließend rücktransformiert. Nach der Wiedergabe der rücktransformierten Bilder in Originalformat kann man die
Auswirkung der Störung visuell beurteilen. Die Abstandswerte (1 bis 7)
wurden mit $\pm$ 1 gestört, wobei die mittlere Störrate zwischen 12,5% und
100% der Skelettpunkte lag. Das **Bild 5** zeigt als Beispiel einen gestörten Bildausschnitt (Störrate 25%) und **Bild 6** das entsprechende rück-
transformierte Bild. Um die Auswirkung der Störung zu verdeutlichen,
wird im **Bild 7** ein großer Ausschnitt aus der rücktransformierten Vorlage A mit einer Störrate von 25% - entsprechend dem Bild 5 - gezeigt.
Die **Bilder 8 und 9** zeigen die entsprechenden Rücktransformationsergeb-
nisse für die Vorlage B mit einer Störrate von 12,5% bzw. 100% der Skelettpunkte.

Es zeigt sich, daß selbst bei starken Störraten die wesentliche Form
der dargestellten Objekte nach der Rücktransformation erhalten bleibt.
Erst dann, wenn jeder Skelettpunkt gestört wird, sind Buchstaben und
Zeichnungseinzelheiten kaum mehr erkennbar.

4. Redundanzreduzierte MAT-Bilddarstellung

Mit dem Ziel, eine möglichst stark datenreduzierte Darstellung eines
MAT-transformierten Bildes zu erreichen, wurden aus der Skelettlinie
redundante Bildpunkte getilgt. Die Eigenschaft b) der MAT wird dazu
ausgenutzt, um "Kreise" zu eliminieren, die von benachbarten "Kreisen"

ganz überdeckt werden. **Bild 10** zeigt die Anwendung dieser Reduktion an Bild 5.

Läßt man auch geringe Verfälschungen eines rekonstruierten Bildes (Zakkenentfernung) zu, dann ist es möglich, an Hand der Eigenschaft c) die somit als irrelevant betrachteten "1"-er aus der Skelettlinie zu entfernen. Dadurch kann man eine weitere - meistens jedoch nicht beträchtliche - Reduktion der Datenmenge erzielen. Die so verarbeiteten Bilder zeigen, daß die Verfälschungen im Vergleich mit dem Original geringfügig sind.

Zur Beurteilung der Datenreduktion, die durch Eliminierung redundanter "Kreise" und irrelevanter "1"-er erreicht werden kann, müssen zwei Aspekte betrachtet werden. Einerseits kann man die zur MAT-Darstellung mit und ohne Datenreduktion erforderlichen Datenmengen miteinander vergleichen. Andererseits kann man die MAT als Bildcodierungsverfahren im Hinblick auf Datenreduktion und auf sonstige Eigenschaften der codierten Daten mit anderen bekannten Codierverfahren (z.B. statistische Codierung, Konturcodierung) vergleichen. Dieser Aspekt der MAT wird im Abschnitt 6 näher betrachtet. Der erste Aspekt ist das Hauptziel der vorliegenden Arbeit, und die entsprechenden Ergebnisse werden nun an Hand der Tabelle I erläutert.

	Vorlage A		Vorlage B	
	S	$\frac{S_u}{S}$	S	$\frac{S_u}{S}$
a) MAT unreduziert $\quad S = S_u$	45877	1	12198	1
b) MAT mit Redundanz- reduktion	30657	1,50	9910	1,23
c) MAT mit Redundanzreduktion und Tilgung irre- levanter "1"-er	28466	1,61	9580	1,27
P = Bildelemente/Bild	931000		739000	

pel = picture element (Bildelement)

S = Skelettpunkte/Bild

$\frac{S_u}{S}$ = Reduktionsfaktor

Tabelle I: Anzahl der Skelettpunkte bei der MAT mit Datenreduktion
(N = 3 bit/pel)

Die Tabelle I zeigt, daß durch Eliminierung der redundanten "Kreise"

und der irrelevanten "1"-er eine spürbar kompaktere MAT-Darstellung
(ohne nennenswerte Bildverzerrungen) erreichbar ist. Die Reduktions-
faktoren liegen in der Größenordnung von 1,25 bis 1,6, d.h. die Zahl
der notwendigen Skelettpunkte sinkt auf etwa 80% bis 60% des ursprünglichen Wertes. Dabei ist jedem Skelettpunkt ein Abstandswert zugeordnet, der mit $N = 3$ bit/pel dargestellt wird.

5. MAT-Darstellung mit konstanten "Kreisen"

Die festgestellte Störfestigkeit der MAT (siehe Abschnitt 3) legt die
Frage nahe, ob und für welches Bildmaterial die Abstandswerte der Ske-
lettpunkte sich auf einen einheitlichen Wert reduzieren lassen, ohne
daß im rücktransformierten Bild wesentliche Verfälschungen auftreten.
Es ist in anderen Worten zu untersuchen, ob sich ein Bild ohne große
Qualitätsverluste in "Kreise" mit konstantem Radius zerlegen läßt. Der
Vorteil einer solchen Manipulation ist, daß dadurch nur die Lage der
Skelettpunkte, aber keine Abstandswerte angegeben werden müssen ($N = 0$).
Damit kann das Bild mit einer wesentlich kleineren Datenmenge darge-
stellt werden.

Die **Bilder 11 und 12** zeigen das Ergebnis der Rücktransformation, wenn
man in der MAT alle Abstandswerte gleich einem konstanten Wert (3 in
Bild 11 und 2 in Bild 12) setzt. Es zeigt sich, daß eine datenreduzierte MAT-Darstellung mit konstanten "Kreisen" für typische Linienbilder
durchaus geeignet ist, da die Qualitätsverluste - insbesondere für die
Vorlage A - klein sind.

6. Datenreduktionsfaktor der MAT im Vergleich mit anderen Codierungs-verfahren

Zur Beurteilung der MAT als Datenreduktionsverfahren sind in der **Tabelle II** einige Ergebnisse zusammengestellt:

	Datenreduktionsfaktoren	
Codierverfahren	Vorlage A	Vorlage B
MAT-Darstellung, unreduziert	2,02	3,65
MAT mit Redundanzreduktion	2,63	3,99
MAT mit konstanten "Kreisen"	2,93	4,43
MAT mit konstanten "Kreisen" u.Redundanzreduk-tion	3,52	4,91
Statistische Codierung:		
Run-Länge-Codierung/1 pel - Prädiktor	3,39	4,75
Run-Länge-Cod./2 pel-Prädiktor, 2-dimensional	3,79	7,84

Um einen Vergleich zwischen der MAT-Darstellung und der statistischen
Codierung zu ermöglichen, wurde in beiden Fällen die gleiche Adresscodierung (Run-Länge-Codierung mit konstanter Codewortlänge und Über-
lauf) der anfallenden Bilddaten durchgeführt. Der Datenreduktionsfak-
tor C ist das Verhältnis zwischen der Datenmenge des Originalbildes
(1 bit/Bildpunkt, P bits/Bild) und der des codierten Bildes. In der
MAT-Darstellung (ohne konstante "Kreise") besteht die zweite Datenmenge
nicht nur aus Bits für die Adresscodierung der Skelettpunkte, sondern
auch aus Bits, die die Abstandswerte angeben (N = 3 bit/Skelettpunkt).
Es gilt:

$$C = \frac{P}{D + N \cdot S} \quad \text{mit } N = \begin{cases} 3 & \text{für die MAT ohne konstante "Kreise"} \\ 0 & \text{sonst} \end{cases} \tag{1}$$

und D = Datenmenge für die Adresscodierung allein.

Ein Vergleich der MAT mit anderen bekannten Bildcodierungsverfahren für
Zweipegelbilder im Hinblick auf die Datenreduktion zeigt, daß trotz Re-
dundanz- und Irrelevanzreduktion die MAT die Wirksamkeit einer einfachen statistischen Codierung nicht erreicht. Diese aus der Literatur
bekannte Aussage (/1/, /4/) wird für die hier untersuchten typischen
Linienbilder bestätigt. Nur dort, wo sie ohne wesentliche Bildverschlech-
terung angewandt werden kann, erreicht die MAT-Codierung mit konstanten
"Kreisen" eine mit der statistischen Codierung vergleichbar wirksame
Datenreduktion.
Die Vorteile der MAT liegen hauptsächlich in der großen Störfestigkeit
und im besonderen Format der codierten Bilddaten. Dieses bietet die
Möglichkeit, ein Bild durch unterschiedliche, zunehmend detailreichere
Teilbilder (z.B. durch Verwendung von "Kreisen mit abnehmendem Radius)
aufzubauen. Außerdem bildet die MAT-Darstellung einen günstigen Ausgangspunkt zur Bildanalyse, da aus ausgesuchten "Kreisen" visuell be-
deutsame Teilbilder erzeugt oder Merkmale erkannt werden können. Es ist
noch zu klären, inwieweit die oben ausgeführten Betrachtungen auch für
ausgeprägte Flächenbilder (z.B. Mikroskopbilder von Zellen) gelten.

Die Verfasser sprechen Herrn Prof. Dr.-Ing. E. Paulus ihren Dank aus
für die nützlichen Anregungen und Diskussionen über das Thema dieser
Arbeit.

Schrifttum

/1/ J.C. Mott-Smith, T. Baer: "Area and volume coding of pictures" in:
    "Picture Bandwidth Compression" (edited by T.S.Huang and O.H.Tre-
    tiak, Gordon and Breach, New York 1972

/2/ H. Blum: "A transformation for extracting new descriptors of shape"
     in: "Models for the perception of speech and visual form",
     edited by W. Wathen-Dunn, MIT Press, Cambridge, Mass. 1967,
     S. 362 - 380.

/3/ A. Rosenfeld: "Picture processing by computer", Academic Press,
     New York - London 1969, S. 141 - 148.

/4/ I.L. Pfaltz, A. Rosenfeld: "Computer representation of planar re-
                gions by their skeletons"
                Communications of the ACM, Vol. 10, N.2
                (Feb. 1967) S. 119 - 125.

/5/ C. Arcelli, L. Cordella, S. Levialdi: "A grassfire transformation
                for binary digital pictures"
                Proc. of 2nd. Intern. Conf. on Pattern
                Recognition, Aug. 1974, S. 152 - 154.

Bild 1:

Kleiner Ausschnitt aus dem Originalbild A. Schwarze Bildpunkte durch ihre Abstandswerte dargestellt.

Bild 2:

MAT-Darstellung des Bildes 1.

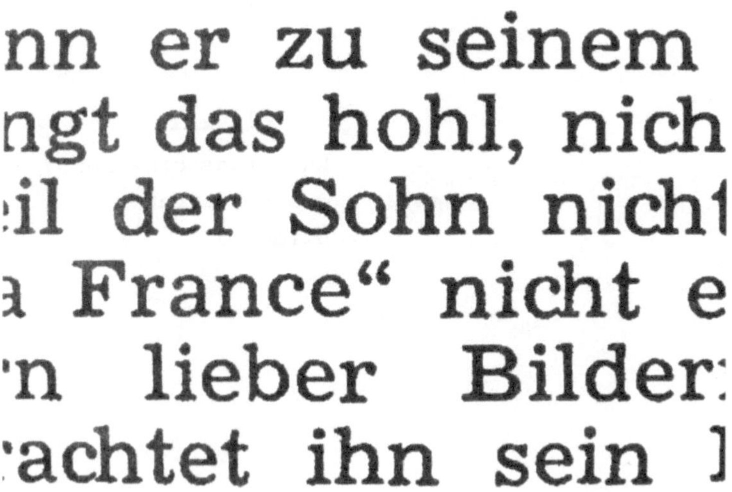
nn er zu seinem
ngt das hohl, nich
il der Sohn nicht
a France“ nicht e
n lieber Bilder
achtet ihn sein

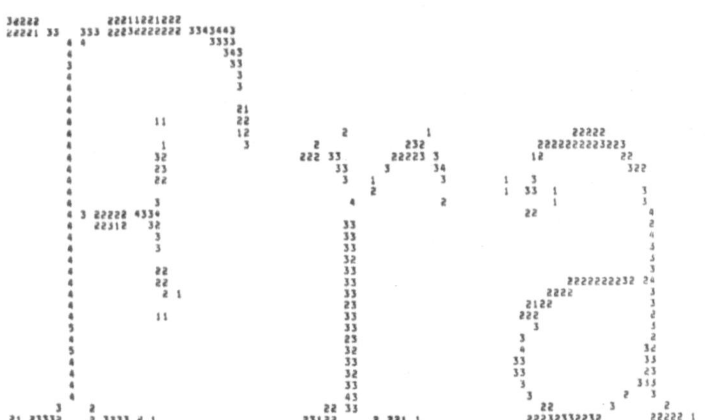

<u>Bild 3</u>:
Großer Ausschnitt aus dem diskretisierten Originalbild A.

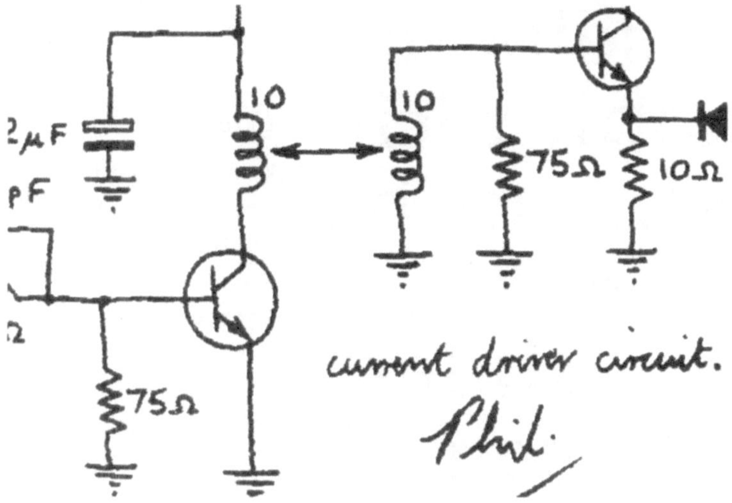
10
10
75Ω
10Ω
75Ω
current driver circuit.

<u>Bild 4</u>:
Großer Ausschnitt aus dem diskretisierten Originalbild B.

<u>Bild 5</u>:
Skelettbild mit Störung der Abstandswerte um ± 1 und Störrate =25% der Skelettpunkte (Ausschnitt aus Vorlage A).

Bild 6:

Rücktransformation des gestörten Bildes 5.

Bild 7:

Rücktransformation des gestörtes Skelettbildes A (Störrate = 25% der Skelettpunkte).

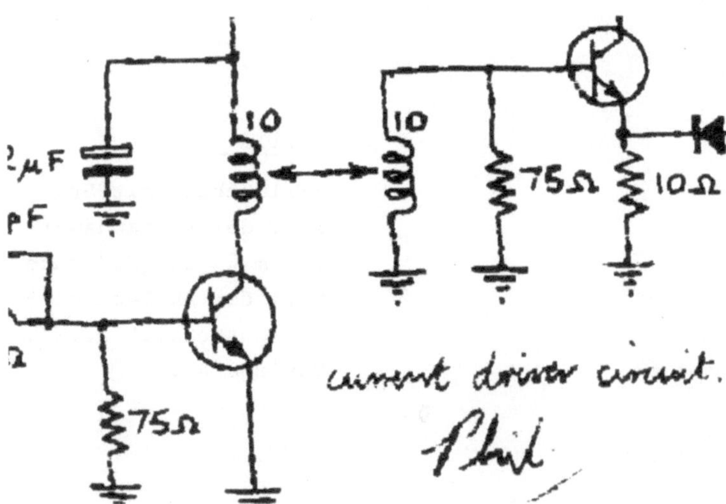

Bild 8:

Rücktransformation des gestörten Skelettbildes B (Störrate =12,5% der Skelettpunkte).

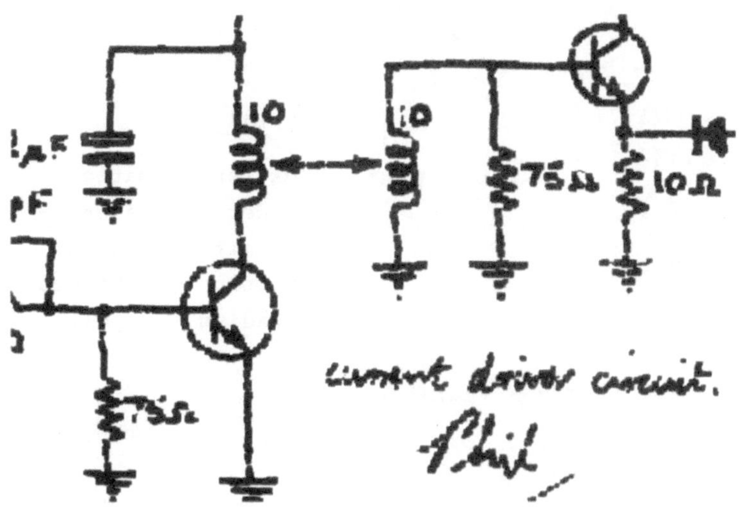

Bild 9:

Rücktransformation des gestörten Skelettbildes B (Störrate = 100% der Skelettpunkte).

Bild 10:

MAT-Darstellung mit Redundanzreduktion (vgl. Bild 2).

nn er zu seinem

ngt das hohl, nich

il der Sohn nicht

a France" nicht e

n lieber Bilder:

achtet ihn sein I

Bild 11:

Rücktransformation aus der MAT-Darstellung mit konstanten "Kreisen" des Bildes A (Radius = 3 pel).

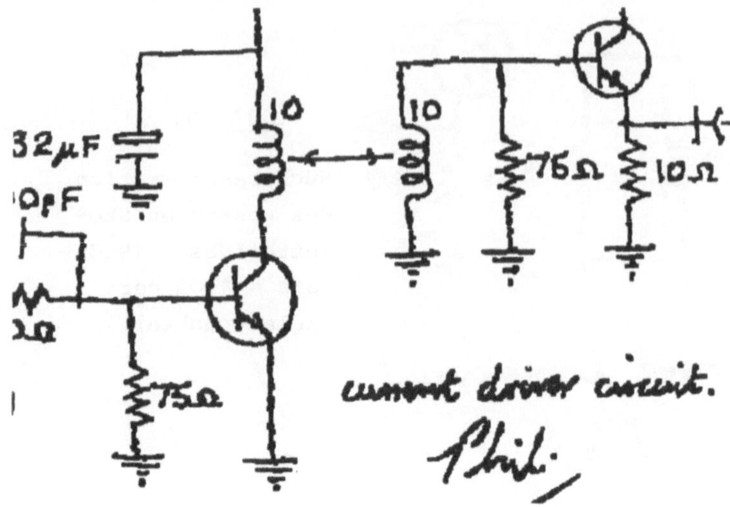

Bild 12:

Rücktransformation
aus der MAT-Darstel-
lung mit konstanten
"Kreisen" des Bildes
B (Radius = 2 pel).

<u>SKELETTIERUNG UND LINIENVERFOLGUNG IN RASTER-</u>
<u>DIGITALISIERTEN LINIENSTRUKTUREN</u>

Thomas Kreifelts

Gesellschaft für Mathematik und
Datenverarbeitung Bonn mbH
5205 St. Augustin

Problemstellung

Der Aufbau von computerorientierten Analyse- und Planungssystemen sowie
von Systemen zur DV-gestützten Automation in der Kartografie erfordert
die Digitalisierung umfangreichen Datenmaterials, das in grafischer Form
als Karte, Plan o.ä. vorliegt. Dazu müssen die in der grafischen Vorlage
enthaltenen Linien als Koordinatenfolgen verschlüsselt werden. Beispiele
für zu digitalisierendes Datenmaterial sind Höhenlinienkarten, Gewässer-
karten, Pläne von Verkehrsnetzen und Flächennutzungen.

Gegenwärtig wird die Erfassung grafischer Daten überwiegend mit handge-
führten Digitalisiergeräten vorgenommen. Dies geschieht durch manuelles
Nachfahren von Linien. Vor allem bei dichtbesetzten Karten mit unregel-
mäßigen Linien ist dieses Verfahren zu arbeitsaufwendig. Hier sollen automatische Digitalisierverfahren, an deren Entwicklung bei vielen Insti-
tutionen gearbeitet wurde und wird (vgl. /1/), Abhilfe schaffen. Man beschränkt sich dabei in der Regel auf Karten, deren Linien dieselbe Bedeutung haben, wie dies bei Höhenlinien-, Gewässer- oder Flächennutzungs-
karten der Fall ist.

Automatische Digitalisierverfahren

Der am weitesten verbreitete Ansatz für eine automatische Digitalisierung von Linienstrukturen ist das Abtasten der gesamten zu erfassenden
Vorlage durch einen Raster-Scanner mit anschließender softwaremäßiger
Linienverfolgung. Dabei wird die Vorlage zeilenweise in diskreten Sprün-
gen abgefahren, und die jeweils gemessenen Helligkeitswerte werden in
digitale Form umgewandelt. Es entsteht eine Matrix aus 0-1- oder Grauwerten, je nach Arbeitsweise des Scanners. Das Linienverfolgungsprogramm
muß dann die Extraktion der in der Bildmatrix enthaltenen Linien in Form
von Koordinatenfolgen leisten.

Die automatischen Digitalisierverfahren, die mit rastermäßiger Erfassung

arbeiten, unterscheiden sich im wesentlichen durch die Prinzipien, die
bei der softwaremäßigen Linienverfolgung zur Anwendung kommen. Die hier
angewandten Methoden sind teilweise (meist wegen geplanter kommerzieller
Verwertung) nicht oder nicht sehr ausführlich dokumentiert. Die verwendeten Scanner sind in der Regel Trommelscanner, eine neuere Entwicklung
sind die Flatbedscanner mit Sensorenarray (Calspan Corp., Buffalo, USA
/2/; Messerschmitt-Bölkow-Blohm GmbH, München). Während die rastermäßige
Erfassung heute in der Regel keine Schwierigkeiten bereitet, ist die Linienverfolgung noch nicht befriedigend gelöst. Die Hauptprobleme sind
Linienverfolgungsfehler, die manuell korrigiert werden müssen, und die
Verarbeitungszeiten für die großen Datenmengen, die ein Scanner liefert
(neuerdings wird aus diesem Grund die Möglichkeit untersucht, einen Feld-
rechner für die Linienverfolgung einzusetzen /3/).

Ein weiterer Ansatz zur automatischen Digitalisierung ist die direkte
Linienverfolgung mit einem steuerbaren Laserstrahl. Ein nach diesem Verfahren arbeitendes Gerät ist von I/Ometrics in San Francisco, USA, entwickelt worden. Es stellt eine Weiterentwicklung des für die automatische Auswertung von Blasenkammerfotografien gebauten "Sweepnik" der Firma LaserScan Ltd. in Cambridge, England, dar. Beim heutigen Stand dieses Verfahrens sind noch häufige manuelle Eingriffe erforderlich.

Nach /1/ wird bis auf die Ausnahme des Canada Geographic Information
System (IBM-Trommelscanner, IBM-Linienverfolgungssoftware /8/) kein automatisches Digitalisierverfahren zu routinemäßiger Produktion eingesetzt, und auch das CGIS-Verfahren kann wegen der Notwendigkeit der sorg-
fältigen manuellen Vorbereitung der zu erfassenden Vorlagen noch nicht
als in jeder Hinsicht vorbildlich bezeichnet werden.

<u>Vorgehen im IGS</u>

Im Institut für grafische Datenverarbeitung und Strukturerkennung (IGS)
der Gesellschaft für Mathematik und Datenverarbeitung Bonn mbH (GMD) arbeitet eine Forschungsgruppe an einem automatischen Digitalisierverfahren, das auf dem rastermäßigen Erfassungsprinzip basiert und bei der Linienverfolgung mit einem Skelettierungsverfahren arbeitet. Ziel der Arbeiten ist neben der anwendungsgerechten Aufbereitung und Strukturierung
der erfaßten Linien die Entwicklung eines Linienverfolgungsprogramms,
das möglichst keine zusätzlichen Fehler bei den Linien verursacht und
mit für praktische Zwecke vertretbaren Laufzeiten auf einem üblichen
Großcomputer auskommt. Zur Extraktion der Linien aus dem Rasterbild werden die Linien zunächst auf ein Bildelement Breite abgemagert (skelettiert), um so eine einfache und eindeutige Linienverfolgung zu ermögli-

chen. Die Skelettierungsverfahren wurden ursprünglich für Mustererken-
nungsprobleme beim automatischen Lesen von handgeschriebenen oder maschi-
nell erstellten Zeichen sowie im biologischen Bereich entwickelt (s. etwa /4/,/6/,/7/).

Seit April 1975 werden die Aktivitäten des IGS auf dem Gebiet der automatischen Digitalisierung durch das Bundesministerium für Forschung und
Technologie aus Mitteln des DV-Programms unter dem Projektnamen ARLIP
(Aufbereitung rastermäßig erfaßter Linienstrukturen zu Planungszwecken)
gefördert. Das im Rahmen dieses Projekts realisierte Linienverfolgungs-
verfahren soll im folgenden genauer erläutert werden (s. auch /5/,/9/).

Rastermäßige Erfassung

Die rastermäßige Erfassung von Linienstrukturen wird zur Zeit mit Trom-
melscannern durchgeführt. Benutzt werden der Concord-Control-Scanner des
Instituts für Angewandte Geodäsie in Frankfurt a.M. sowie der in der GMD
befindliche P 1000-Scanner der Firma Optronics International Inc.. Diese
Scanner können Vorlagen von einer Größe bis zu 60x60 cm (Concord Control)
bzw. 50x50 cm (Optronics) verarbeiten. Die Rasterweite beträgt 63.5μ
(Concord Control) bzw. wahlweise 25μ, 50μ oder 100μ (Optronics). Der
Concord-Control-Scanner liefert 0-1-Werte, der Optronics-Scanner Grau-
werte in 256 Stufen.

Für die in ARLIP zu bearbeitenden Linienstrukturen ist in der Regel eine Erfassung mit etwa 100μ Rasterweite ausreichend. Ausgangspunkt für
die Linienextraktion ist also das Binärbild einer Linienstruktur mit
ungefähr 5000x5000 Bildelementen. Die Umwandlung eines vom Optronics-
Scanner gelieferten Grauwertbildes in ein Binärbild erfolgt durch einfache Schwellensetzung. Die bei Abtastung größerer Vorlagen durch den
Concord-Control-Scanner entstehenden Binärbilder werden durch Zusammenfassung von vier benachbarten Bildelementen zu einem Bildelement auf die
oben angegebene Größe gebracht.

Linienextraktionsverfahren

Die nach der rastermäßigen Erfassung erhaltene digitale Form der Linienstruktur, ein Binärbild von ca. 25 Millionen Bildelementen, ist für die
Weiterverwendung in computergestützten Systemen für planerische oder kar-
tografische Zwecke nicht geeignet. Aus diesem Grund müssen die im Binärbild dargestellten Linien in Folgen von Koordinatenpaaren umgewandelt
werden. Im Idealfall sollten diese Polygonzüge etwa in der Mitte der Bi-
närbild-Linien verlaufen. Außer den Linien müssen auch Knoten, d.h. Punk-

te, in denen mehr als zwei Linien zusammentreffen, erkannt und extrahiert werden. Solche Knoten sind nämlich bei netzartigen Linienstrukturen eine wesentliche Komponente der Struktur, bei Isolinienkarten deuten sie in der Regel auf Erfassungsfehler hin.

In ARLIP vollzieht sich die Linienextraktion in drei Phasen:

- Skelettierung,
- Linienverfolgung,
- Nachbearbeitung.

In der Skelettierungsphase werden die Linien im Binärbild auf ein Bildelement Breite abgemagert. Die anschließende Linienverfolgung, die eigentliche Linienextraktion, wird dadurch einfach und eindeutig. Skelettierung und Linienverfolgung geschehen wegen des beschränkten Kernspeicherplatzes nacheinander für Teilstreifen des Binärbildes, bis das ganze Binärbild bearbeitet ist. In der Nachbearbeitungsphase werden Linien, die wegen der streifenweisen Bearbeitung des Binärbildes gestückelt erfaßt werden, zu durchgehenden Koordinatenfolgen zusammengesetzt.

Skelettierung

Unter Skelettierung wird hier eine Transformation des Original-Binärbildes in ein anderes Binärbild, in dem die ursprünglichen Linien auf ein Bildelement Breite reduziert sind, verstanden. Im skelettierten Binärbild hat also ein Punkt einer Linie genau zwei benachbarte Linienpunkte, es sei denn, es handelt sich um einen End- oder Knotenpunkt. Bei der Skelettierung dürfen keine "Löcher" in den Linien entstehen, und der ursprüngliche Zusammenhang muß erhalten bleiben. Zweck dieser Operation ist die Ermöglichung einer einfachen Linienverfolgung.

Die Skelettierung eines Binärbildes wird iterativ realisiert, indem man eine bestimmte abmagernde Transformation, einen Skelettierungsschritt, so oft auf das Binärbild anwendet, bis sie keine Verbesserung mehr bringt. Bei einem solchen Skelettierungsschritt entscheidet man nacheinander für jeden Bildpunkt (1-Bildelement) des Binärbildes, ob er für die Linienstruktur von Bedeutung ist, und löscht ihn widrigenfalls, indem man ihn auf 0 setzt. Diese Entscheidung kann man für jeden Bildpunkt treffen, wenn man lediglich seine Nachbarschaft kennt. Deshalb wird ein Skelettierungsschritt durch sequentielle Anwendung lokaler Nachbarschaftsoperationen realisiert, wobei man jeden Bildpunkt in Abhängigkeit von seinen Nachbarn löscht oder stehenläßt.

Ein Bildpunkt hat 8 Nachbarn, infolgedessen gibt es $2^8 = 256$ verschie-

dene Nachbarschaften. Berücksichtigt man Symmetrien, d.h. die Tatsache,
daß einige dieser Nachbarschaften durch Rotation oder Spiegelung in andere übergehen, so bleiben noch 51 verschiedene Nachbarschaftstypen übrig:

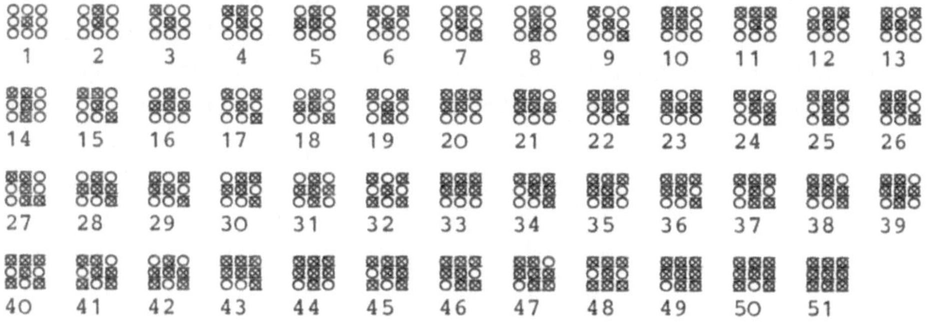

1 2 3 4 5 6 7 8 9 10 11 12 13
14 15 16 17 18 19 20 21 22 23 24 25 26
27 28 29 30 31 32 33 34 35 36 37 38 39
40 41 42 43 44 45 46 47 48 49 50 51

Ein Skelettierungsschritt ist vollständig beschrieben, wenn man die Reihenfolge angibt, in der man die Bildelemente eines Binärbildes abarbei-
tet, und wenn man die Teilmenge von Nachbarschaftstypen angibt, bei deren Vorliegen ein Bildpunkt gelöscht werden soll.

Die Auswahl der Nachbarschaftstypen für die Skelettierung muß garantie-
ren, daß die Anzahl der Linien erhalten bleibt (kein Auseinanderreißen
von Linien) und daß keine Löcher in den Linien entstehen. Die maximale
Teilmenge von Nachbarschaftstypen, die dies leistet, besteht aus 20 Elementen, nämlich den Typen 2, 3, 4, 5, 10, 11, 12, 16, 20, 21, 24, 28,
33, 34, 35, 38, 42, 46 und 50 (nach der obigen Numerierung). Die Nachbarschaftstypen 2 und 3 bewirken bei der Skelettierung eine unerwünsch-
te Verkürzung von freien Linienenden und werden deshalb nicht verwendet.
Die dadurch entstehenden "Stoppeln" an den Linien werden während der Linienverfolgung behandelt. Nachbarschaftstyp 1, der bei der Skelettierung
die Anzahl der Objekte verringert, wird bei der Skelettierung von Linienstrukturen vorteilhaft zur Unterdrückung bedeutungsloser Punkte (Verun-
reinigungen) eingesetzt. Die maximale Menge von Nachbarschaftstypen für
die Skelettierung von Linienstrukturen besteht dann also aus 19 Elementen, indem man in der obigen Menge die Typen 2 und 3 durch Typ 1 ersetzt.

Bei der Behandlung von Linienstrukturen erweist es sich darüberhinaus
als günstig, sich bei den ersten Skelettierungsschritten auf gewisse
Skelettierungsnachbarschaften zu beschränken, um möglichst glatte Li-
nienskelette mit möglichst wenig Stoppeln zu erhalten. Anschließend muß
mit der oben beschriebenen maximalen Menge skelettiert werden, um ein
echtes Skelett zu bekommen. Die bei dem ARLIP-Algorithmus gewählten Nachbarschaftstypen für die ersten Skelettierungsschritte sind 1, 4, 5, 10,
11, 12, 20, 21, 24, 33, 34:

Die Reihenfolge, in der man die einzelnen Punkte des Binärbildes abar-
beitet, hat einen Einfluß auf das entstehende Skelett. Einfaches zeilen-
oder spaltenweises Vorgehen verschiebt das Skelett auf den Rand der ursprünglichen Linien. Um dies zu vermeiden, zerlegt man das Binärbild in
vier disjunkte Teilmengen, die wie folgt mit 1, 2, 3 und 4 gekennzeichnet sind:

1	3	1	3	1	3	1	3
4	2	4	2	4	2	4	2
1	3	1	3	1	3	1	3
4	2	4	2	4	2	4	2
1	3	1	3	1	3	1	3
4	2	4	2	4	2	4	2

Die vier Teile des Binärbildes werden beim Skelettieren nacheinander
spaltenweise bearbeitet. Die Skelettierung wird abgebrochen, wenn ein
Skelettierungsschritt, der mit der maximalen Menge von Nachbarschaftstypen arbeitet, das Binärbild unverändert läßt.

Die folgenden beiden Abbildungen zeigen den Ausschnitt eines Binärbildes, das durch Abscannen einer Höhenlinienkarte entsteht, sowie das mit
dem hier beschriebenen Algorithmus erhaltene Skelett.

Da die Skelettierung des Binärbildes in Streifen geschieht, sind an den
Nahtstellen der Streifen besondere Vorkehrungen erforderlich, um ein Auseinanderreißen von Linien zu vermeiden. Deshalb fungiert bei der Skelettierung eines Streifens die letzte Zeile des vorigen und die erste Zeile des nächsten Streifens als nicht zu bearbeitender Rand. So ist gewährleistet, daß durchgehende Linien zusammenhängend bleiben.

<u>Linienverfolgung</u>

Ausgangspunkt der Linienverfolgung ist das skelettierte Binärbild der
Linienstruktur. Zunächst werden im Skelett Linienenden (Bildpunkte mit
genau einem Nachbarn) und Knoten (Bildpunkte mit mehr als zwei Nachbarn)
markiert. Dann werden die Knoten zusammen mit ihren Nachbarn in der Aus-
gabedatei abgespeichert und die Knoten werden im Binärbild gelöscht. Die
Knotennachbarn werden als Linienenden markiert. In der Nachbearbeitungs-

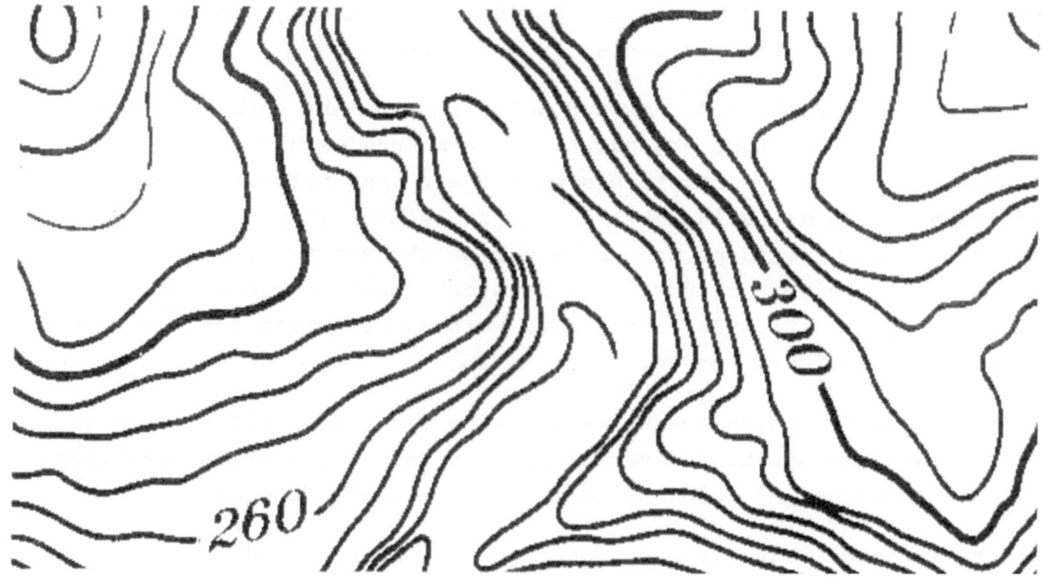

Rasterdigitalisierter Ausschnitt einer Höhenlinienkarte.

Derselbe Ausschnitt nach der Skelettierung.

phase erfolgt die Verlängerung der Linien in die Knoten hinein sowie
die Zuordnung der einzelnen Linien zu den Knoten.

Das skelettierte Binärbild, das nun keine Knoten mehr enthält, wird zeilenweise nach Linienenden abgesucht. Ist ein Ende gefunden, wird die
entsprechende Linie verfolgt, bis wieder ein Ende auftritt. Bei der
Verfolgung werden die Bildpunkte der Linie gelöscht, um eine zweimali-
ge Erfassung zu vermeiden. Es werden nur solche Punkte der Linie ausgegeben, in denen eine Richtungsänderung stattfindet. Darüberhinaus kann
durch ein Approximationsverfahren eine weitere Reduktion der auszugeben-
den Daten durchgeführt werden.

Sind so alle Linienenden bearbeitet, werden die bisher nicht erfaßten
einfach geschlossenen Linien verfolgt, wobei ein willkürlich gewählter
Punkt als Anfangs- und Endpunkt einer solchen Linie fungiert.

Bei der Linienverfolgung können außerdem noch Stoppeln, d.h. Linien,
die eine gewisse, durch Parameter zu definierende Länge nicht überschreiten, unterdrückt und eng benachbarte Knoten zu einem einzigen Knoten zusammengefaßt werden.

Nachbearbeitung

Die Datenmenge, die bei der Rasterdigitalisierung einer Karte entsteht,
ist in der Regel so groß, daß die Skelettierung und Linienverfolgung des
entsprechenden Binärbildes im Kernspeicher eines Computers nur stück-
weise nacheinander erfolgen kann. Bei dem hier beschriebenen Verfahren
geschieht dies streifenweise. Das Nachbearbeitungsprogramm hat die Aufgabe, Linien über Streifengrenzen hinweg zusammenzusetzen. Außerdem werden Linien gegebenenfalls denjenigen Knoten zugeordnet, in denen sie an-
fangen oder enden, was vor allem bei der Erfassung netzartiger Strukturen wesentlich ist.

Implementierung und Laufzeit

Das Programm zur Skelettierung und Linienverfolgung ist in Assembler
geschrieben und umfaßt etwa 2700 Statements. Da die Binärbildverarbeitung im Kernspeicher geschieht, ist die Anwendung dieses Programms nur
auf Großrechenanlagen sinnvoll. Das Programm läuft zur Zeit auf den DV-
Anlagen Siemens 4004/151 und IBM/370-158 der GMD.

Das Programm zur Nachbearbeitung ist in Fortran geschrieben (etwa 600
Statements) und zur Zeit nur auf der Siemens 4004/151 lauffähig, da die
indizierte Zugriffsmethode mit variabler Satzlänge des Betriebssystems

BS 2000 ausgenutzt wird. Dieses Programm kann durch Einsparung von Ein/
Ausgabeoperationen in seiner Effizienz noch gesteigert werden.

Für die Laufzeiten der Programme auf der Siemens 4004/151 nun drei Beispiele aus dem Bereich der topografischen Kartografie.

Art der Vorlage	Größe des Binärbildes	Laufzeit (in Min)	
		Skelettierung & Linienverf.	Nachbearb.
50m-Höhenlinien einer topograf. Karte 1:50000	4000x4130	18:22	3:50
Alle Höhenlinien einer topograf. Karte 1:50000	4500x4800	29:22	28:43
Gewässer 2. Ordnung einer top. Karte 1:50000	4000x4015	18:20	2:05

Literatur

/1/ Boyle, A.R., The present status of automated cartography, Computer
Graphics (ACM-Siggraph) 9(1975),260-266.

/2/ Boyle, A.R., Results of a comprehensive series of tests of automatic
line digitization using the Calspan line following system, C.I.S.
Conference, Winnipeg, Kanada, Mai 1976.

/3/ Goodyear Aerospace Corp., Associative array processing of raster
scanned data for automated cartography, Tech. Rep. ETL-0046, Akron,
Ohio, USA, 1976.

/4/ Gray, S.B., Local properties of binary images in two dimensions,
IEEE Transactions on Comp. C-20(1971), 551-561.

/5/ Kreifelts, Th., Pick, K., Wißkirchen, P., Woetzel, G., Erfahrungen
mit der Digitalisierung von rastermäßig erfaßten Linienstrukturen I,
GMD-Mitteilungen Nr. 30, St. Augustin 1974.

/6/ Rosenfeld, A., Pfaltz, J.L., Sequential operations in digital picture
processing, J. ACM 13(1966), 471-494.

/7/ Stefanelli, R., Rosenfeld, A., Some parallel thinning algorithms for
digital pictures, J. ACM 18(1971), 255-264).

/8/ Tomlinson, R.F., A technical description of the Canada Geographic
Information System, Ottawa, Kanada, 1973.

/9/ Woetzel, G., Linien- und Knotenextraktion aus Rasterbildern, erscheint in GMD-Mitteilungen.

<u>AN INTERACTIVE SYSTEM FOR CLINICAL APPLICATION OF ANGIODENSITOMETRY[+]</u>

K.H. Höhne, G. Nicolae, G. Pfeiffer, W.-R. Dix, W. Ebenritter
Deutsches Elektronen-Synchrotron DESY, Hamburg

D. Novak[++], M. Böhm, B. Sonne, E. Bücheler
Radiologische Klinik des Universitätskrankenhauses Hamburg Eppendorf

INTRODUCTION

In conventional x-ray diagnostics the physician's diagnosis is mainly based on form, size and structure of organs shown on an x-ray projection. This point of view called *morphological* diagnostics has been essentially improved by the computed tomography[1], which allows a threedimensional reconstruction of the density of the tissue. In a growing number of cases, however, the physician is interested in the time course of processes in organs, which may contain information on the *function* of the organ examined. For this purpose a series of x-ray pictures of the organ is recorded on film or video tape (angiogram) after the injection of a contrast medium. Conventionally this series is examined by the physician in a qualitative manner. Heintzen et al.[2] and Vanselow, Heuck et al.[3] have shown that the diagnostic value can be essentially improved by quantitative measurements. However, with the technology available up to now these methods require complicated procedures. Thus a large scale clinical application was not possible.

[+] This project is supported by the BMFT (DVM 130).

[++] Now Städtische Krankenanstalten Ludwigshafen.

OBJECTIVES OF THE SYSTEM

We have designed and partly implemented a system to overcome these difficulties.
From many possible applications we chose the measurement of the regional blood flow
in the kidney.

The kidney vessels are made visible by injecting a contrast medium. Its propagation
is detected by the image converter-video system of the x-ray device. The system
under development digitizes and stores the picture series and enables the physician
to get information on velocity and amount of contrast medium in selected vessels or
regions. Besides that the system produces functional images, e.g. maps in which each
picture element represents a functional parameter such as the slope of a local washout curve. The requirements to the system are:

- It should be usable in *clinical work* by physicians untrained in computer
  science.
- The results of the picture analysis should be *quantitative*.
- Data management for *large numbers of patients* should be possible.
- The expenditures for a *transfer* to other hospitals should be limited.

These requirements lead to the following porperties of the system:

To enable the *clinical application*

- the picture series are digitized in real time
- and may be analyzed with an interactive graphic display system
  immediately after acquisition.

For this purpose a special dialog language has been developed[4].

Quantitative analysis requires rather complicated algorithms applied to large
amounts of data:

- therefore a computer system with sufficient computing and storage capacity
  is necessary.

For the analysis of *large numbers of patients* we need a

- picture data base with
- a higher level query language for the medical user.

The *transfer* of the hardware components is simplified by

- connection to the standard TV-system, which is part of the x-ray equipment.

HARDWARE CONFIGURATION

The above described properties lead to the configuration shown in fig. 3. A computer
PDP/11-45 controls digitisation, analysis and display of the data. It is connected
to the DESY computer center which runs the data base and the more complicated analysis programs. Essential components in our application are the digitizing and the
display units which are described in more detail.

Digitisation Unit

The digitisation unit provides a digital image of the x-ray picture in real time
(50 frames/s). Since there is no system of justifiable size and cost, which could
store and process these data in real time, data reduction during acquisition is necessary. It is helpful in our case that the physician looks at regions of interest
of limited size. Only these regions of interest have to be digitized. The resolution
required may vary depending on the case. Consequently the data acquisition parameters are programmable in order to reduce the flow of data (table 1). The requirements
concerning speed and flexibility are met by a pipe-line structure for the digitizing
unit. It consists of three major components:

- The digitizer, which digitizes the TV-signal according to the programmed
  parameters.
- The line buffer with a first-in - first-out structure, which smoothes
  the difference in speed between digitizer (temporarily 10 MHz) and
  picture storage (5 MHz).
- The transfer logic, which controls the data flow to the picture
  storage.

The digitisation unit, which is realized as a microprogrammed processor, has been
in operation since 6 months ago.

Display Unit

The display unit presents the analog and/or the digitized picture on a color TV-Monitor. In contrast to the available commercial display controllers the transformation
of data to chrominance and luminance are freely programmable. Two sequential RAM-
look-up tables filled by the host computer are read by the microprogrammed control
unit to generate density slicing and/or color tracking in real time. Especially we
want to add to the morphological structure represented by the gray levels additional
information represented by color without destroying the morphological information.
The display unit is near to completion. The pictures shown in this paper (fig. 1)
are produced by a display unit used in our nuclear medicine project[5].

SOFTWARE

Physician - Computer Communication

Since the system is to be used by physicians with no training in computer programming we have paid special attention to the problem of physician - computer communication. Experience shows that interactive systems which have been programmed "ad hoc" do not offer sufficient flexibility to meet the physicians requirements. In order to generalize the dialog between physician and computer we have designed a dialog language, the structure of which is adapted to

- the problem of image processing and
- the interactive mode of operation by the physician.

A detailed description is given in reference 4.

Picture Analysis

The picture-analysis programs have two main objectives:

1. Extraction of quantitative data from the regions of the picture selected by the physician (see fig. 2) such as
   - velocity V,
   - volume/unit time Q of blood,
   - concentration C of contrast medium.

2. Generation of functional images of an organ
   (e.g. images in which the color of each picture element represents a functional parameter such as the slope of the corresponding local washout curve).

In parallel to the development of the system we investigated algorithms to extract the above mentioned quantities. A major problem in the data analysis is the elimination of effects like
   - inhomogeneity of the primary radiation in space and time,
   - nonlinearities of the imaging system,
   - digitisation inaccuracy,
   - movement of the organ or vessels within the organ.

In a digital system as the one described above these effects can be eliminated. Fig. 4 demonstrates the imperfections of the primary image. It shows a cut through the intensity distribution of a picture with equidistant objects. The slope of the background is generated by the inhomogeneity of the radiation source, the decrease of the relative maxima is due to the nonlinearity of the imaging system.

We are presently determining the correction matrices and functions to eliminate
the above errors.

The blood velocity is computed from the time difference of the arrival of the contrast medium at two different points of a vessel (fig. 5). The time resolution of
20 ms given by the TV-system may be improved essentially by the repetition of the
measurement at various points.

Much more difficult is the measurement of the volume of contrast medium from the radiation absorption. The absorption law says

$$I = I_o\, e^{-kcd}$$

where I   = measured intensity,
      I_o = primary intensity (intensity in the environment of the object),
      k   = absorption coefficient,
      c   = concentration of the contrast medium,
      d   = thickness of the object.

The intensity distribution caused by a circular vessel is described by

$$\ln I_o/I(x) = 2\,k\,c\,\sqrt{r^2 - (x-a)^2}$$

where a is the coordinate of the center of the vessel and r its radius. If this
function is fitted to the measured intensity distributions, c, r and a may be
computed (see fig. 6). The blood flow through the vessel may then be calculated as

$$Q = v \cdot \pi \cdot r^2.$$

Our investigations are not yet completed. Especially it has to be examined, whether
the method is accurate enough to give significant medical results, since in the present state we analyse only one projection of the organ. If so, the algorithms have
to be optimized for their utilisation in our interactive mode.

The Data Base

In our project the special problems of the data base arise from the untrained users,
the large amount of image data and the particular requirements concerning the secu-
rity and privacy of the data. Furthermore, a high degree of flexibility is required,
since the users intentions vary with time.

None of the commercially available data-base systems meet our requirements. Thus we
are now developing a system based on the relational model. It consists of four levels which are implemented successively. These are

- physical access level (1),
- access path level   (2),
- basic logical level   (3),
- complex logical level (4).

Virtual storage techniques on level 1 make physical reorganization on secondary storage media simple and inexpensive. Access paths on level 2 may be created or dropped without effect to user programs or commands. Some redundancy on data storing allows quick recovery from the most frequent failures (system crash, I/O-error). The basic logical level 3 offers mainly the facilities of relational algebra and is used to implement a SEQUEL-like query and manipulation language on level 4.

In a future state of the project the language requirements of special user groups will be met by problem-oriented terminology and syntax.

A detailed design of the data base system does already exist. Restrictions may be necessary due to constraints on available manpower and implementation time.

PROSPECTS

The development of the system was started in 1976. It is scheduled to be completed at the end of 1978. The described special hardware components are in operation. The dialog language has been tested in a preliminary implementation. Concerning the algorithms of picture analysis the majority of problems has still to be solved. As a first application we have started an investigation on the dependency hypertonus on regional blood flow.

REFERENCES

1 G.N. Hounsfield, Computerized Transverse Axial Tomography, 2nd Congress of European Association of Radiology, Amsterdam 1971.
2 J.H. Bürsch, P.H. Heintzen, R. Simon, Videodensitometric Studies by a New Method of Quantitating the Amount of Contrast Medium, European Journal of Cardiology, 1/4 (1974) 437.
3 K. Vanselow, F. Heuck, Neue Grundlagen und Theorien zur Verbesserung der Angio-Cine-Densitometrie, Fortschr. Röntgenstr. 123, 5 (1975) 468.
4 G. Pfeiffer, K.H. Höhne, A Dialog Language for Interactive Processing of Scintigraphic Data, IVth International Conference on Information Processing in Scintigraphy, Orsay 1975.
5 W. Ebenritter, K.H. Höhne, A Display Controller for the Interactive Analysis of Scintigrams with a PDP-8 Computer, Kerntechnik 15 (1973) 499.
6 E.F. Codd, Relational Algebra, Courant Computer Science Symposia 6, "Data Base Systems", New York, May 1971, Prentice Hall, New York, 1971.
7 D.D. Chamberlin, R.F. Boyce, SEQUEL: A Structured English Query Language, Proc. ACM-SIGMOD Workshop on Data Description, Access and Control, May 1974, ACM, New York (1974) 249 - 264.

Table 1   Properties of the digitisation unit

Sample rate

   horizontal . . . . . 512 elements/line (10 MHz)

                or   256 elements/line (5 MHz)

   vertical . . . . . . 256 lines/frame

Frequency . . . . . . up to 50 frames/s

Digitized region . . . rectangular with

                $\leq$ 64 K picture elements

Gray scale . . . . . . 256 levels

a)

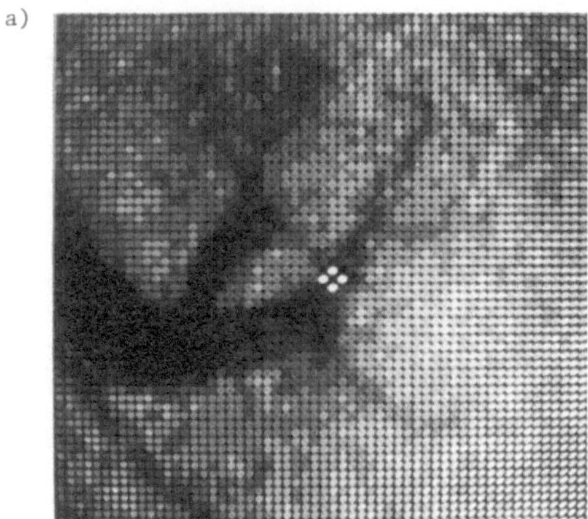

b)

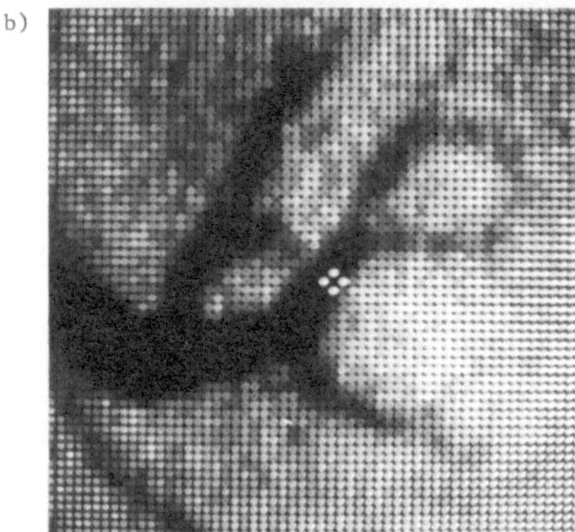

Fig. 1   Three phases of a
          kidney angiogram
          digitized in real time,
          displayed with
          16 gray levels

c)

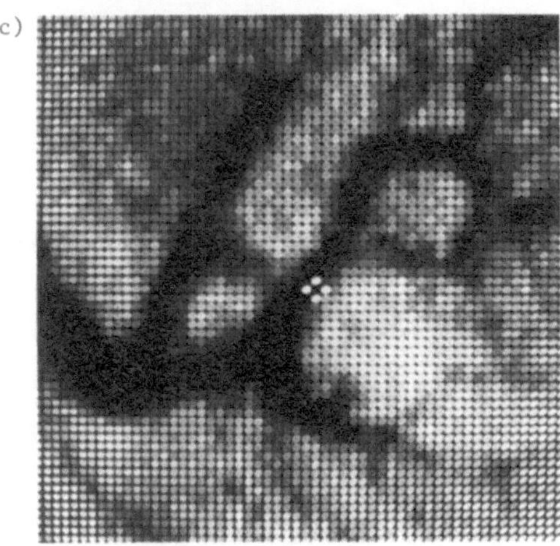

Fig. 2   Labelling of a region of interest via light pen

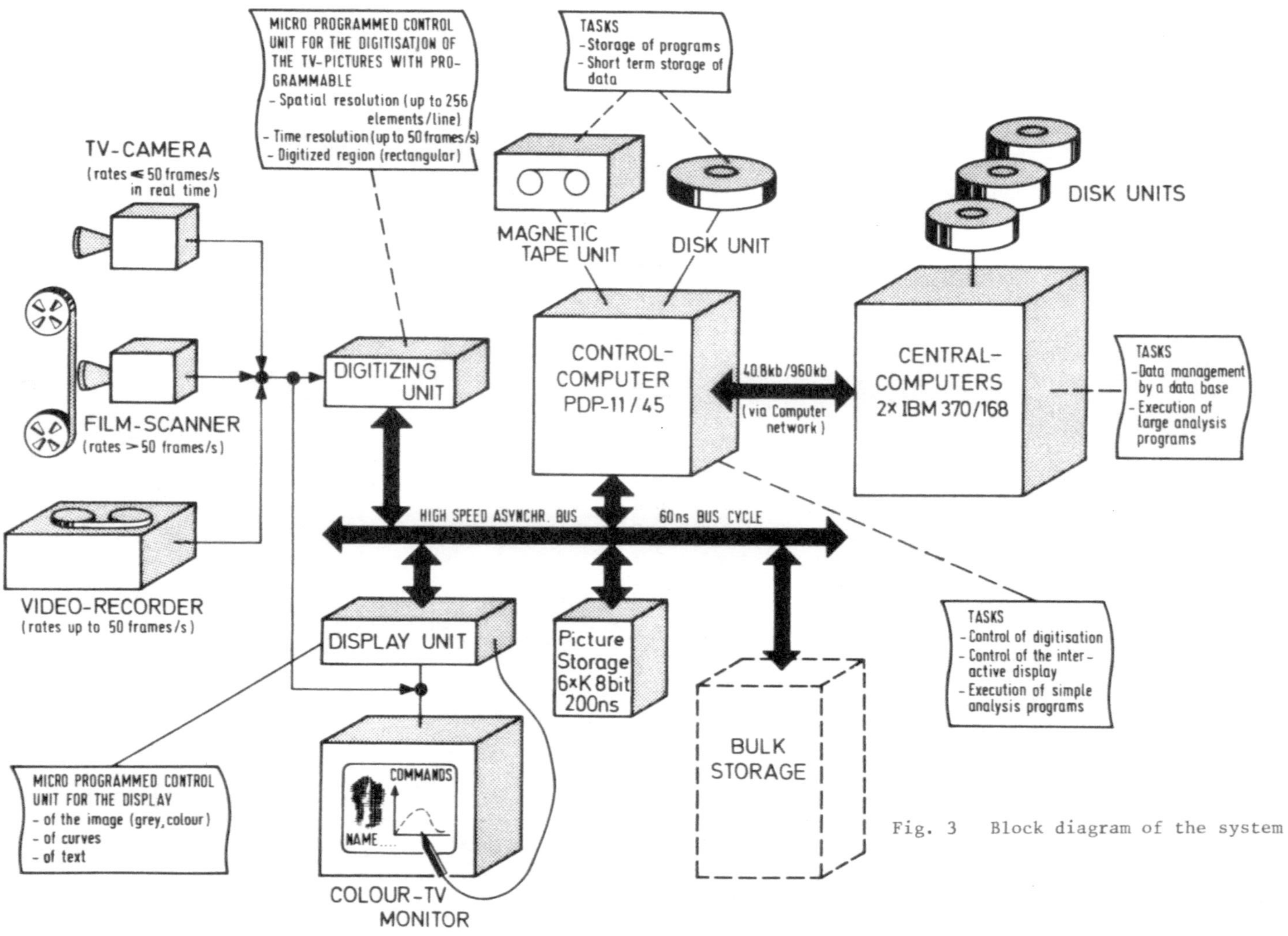

Fig. 3 Block diagram of the system

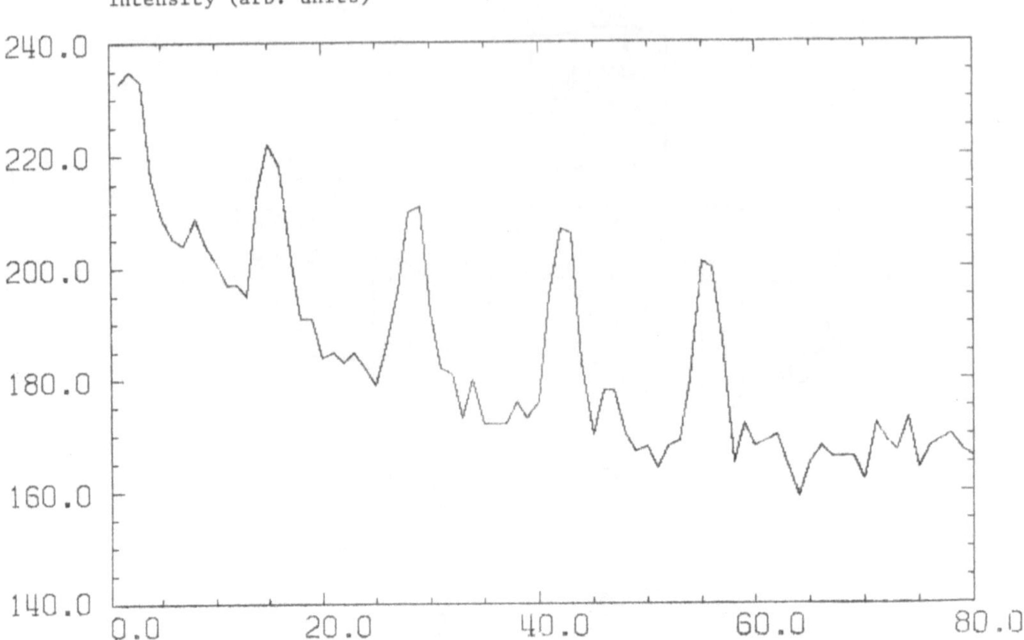

Fig. 4   Intensity distribution of equidistant objects
(copperwires of 1 mm diameter and 10 mm distance),
unit 0.75 mm/div.

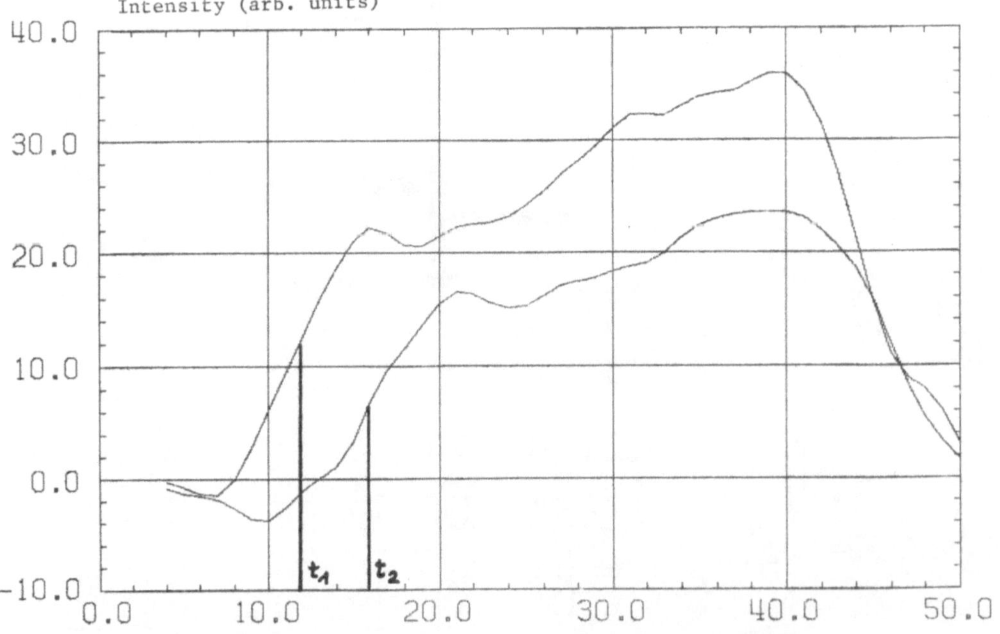

Fig. 5   Intensity as a function of time at two subsequent vessel
locations, unit 0.02 s/div.

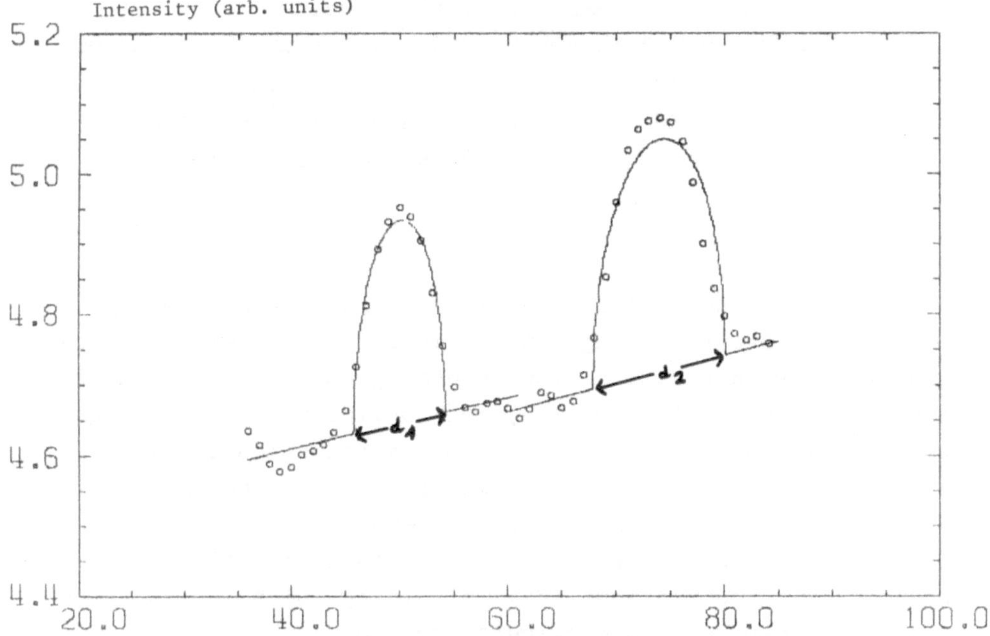

Fig. 6   Intensity distribution of two vessels (circles)
and in addition the fitted function (smooth curve),
unit 0.5 mm/div.

COMPUTERIZED VIDEO-IMAGE PREPROCESSING
WITH APPLICATIONS TO CARDIO-ANGIOGRAPHIC ROENTGEN-IMAGE SERIES.

R.Brennecke, T.K. Brown, J.Bürsch, P.H. Heintzen [*]
Department of pediatric cardiology and bioengineering,
Christian-Albrechts-University, Kiel, West-Germany

1. ABSTRACT

We report on the enhancement of video-angiocardiographic image-
series by digital preprocessing methods including a newly developed
technique of interframe subtraction recording as well as computerized image subtraction, integration, and nonlinear representation
techniques. Background suppression and noise reduction obtained
through these processes applied to roentgen images from animal experiments are demonstrated. Image-series handling and storage are
simplified by combining a new method of digitally formatted video-
tape recording with conventional digital storage of selected image
data in the periphery of a minicomputer system.

2. INTRODUCTION

Angiocardiography is considered an important component of diagnostic
procedures in patients with heart disease. This roentgenologic examination requires the injection of roentgen-opaque material into
the circulation and provides structural and functional information
of the heart and the vessels by film or television viewing. Video-
angiocardiograms are defined as recordings of chest x-ray images
taken shortly before and during the flow of contrast medium through
the various heart chambers and vessels. Accurate visualization of
anatomic abnormalities is optimum when large amounts or high concentrations of material are contrasting the circulatory system. The use
of such large amounts of dye for angiocardiography, however, is dis-
advantageous for quantitative analysis of the cardiograms because
cardiac function and blood flow are significantly altered by injections of large volumes (1,2).
Relatively low contrast in addition must be expected during the
late phase of the angiocardiograms because a bolus of contrast

* Supported by Deutsche Forschungsgemeinschaft.

medium is continuously diluted during flow through the heart chambers, vessels and the lung.

Our primary goal, therefore, was to evaluate image enhancement methods which would significantly increase angiocardiographic contrast and thereby improve the visualization of heart chambers and vessels in images produced with small contrast medium injections or after the dye was significantly diluted in transversing parts of the cardio-vascular system, e.g. intravenous injection to opacify the left ven-tricle. Among the preprocessing techniques used are low-noise video-image recording, digitized image subtraction, temporal averaging,and nonlinear rescaling of the processed image data.

3. SYSTEM DESIGN

3.1.) <u>Some problems of digital storage of videoangiograms.</u>

Computerized processing of video image series has the advantages of the high signal-to-error ratio inherent in digital devices and of the flexibility in processing the image data. However, video image series require high data rates and a large storage capacity. A typical closed-circuit x-ray TV-signal with a bandwidth of 5 MHz must be sam-pled at a minimum sampling rate of 10 MHz. Even large, advanced com-puter systems (3) can only store data at this rate for some 100 ms. However, several seconds of an angiocardiogram must be acquired for a typical analysis involving dynamic changes in heart volume or shape. To store 10 sec of an angiogram with a grey level resolution of 8 bits (256 grey levels) requires 30 M Words (16 bits) of digital memory. Thus, a small data bank of some 50 angiograms seems not practical in digitized form.

Consequently, several methods have been developed to store angio-cardiograms primarily on large capacity analog media such as video tape and to subsequently digitize them using stroboscopic techniques of digitization to reduce the mean data rate (4,5,6).
Since the signal-to-noise ratio of angiograms obtained using cinepuls-operation of the x-ray generator is significantly reduced by recording on magnetic tape or disk and the time base jitter inherent in the replay of images from mechanical image storage devices further deterio-rates the signal to noise ratio of the data, we devised other methods to help offset the signal degradations due to the limitations of analog storage.

3.2.) <u>Storage of video-angiocardiograms and physiological data.</u>

In our system, video images are primarily recorded on video tape to
fullfill the requirement of large storage capacity. 200 to 300 angiocardiograms can be stored on one inexpensive video tape. During subsequent digitization the mean digitized data rate is reduced by a
modified stroboscopic technique described in section 3.3. By a new
method of interframe subtraction the signal to noise ratio of video
information recorded on video tape is improved.

Fig. 1 shows the scheme implemented for subtraction recording. One
TV-field obtained before dye-injection is digitized and stored in a
fast digital memory unit (field store) capable of storing and recir-
culating 64 K pixels (8 bit) at a data rate of 6 Megasamples/sec.

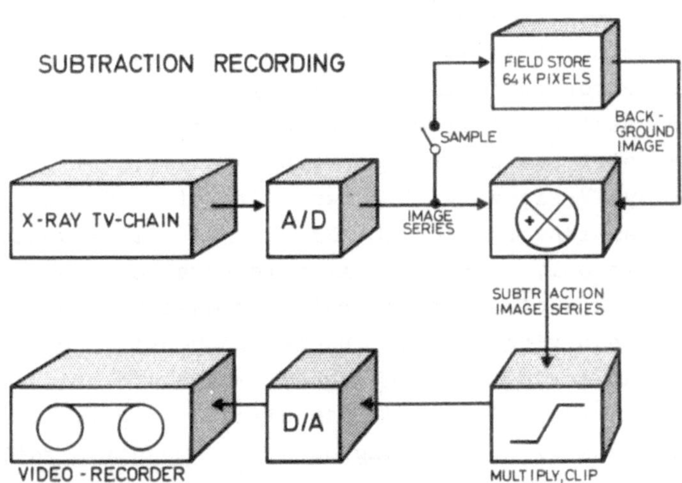

Fig.1: Real-time video image subtraction for recording small temporal
signal changes on video tape with an improved signal-to-noise
ratio.

This digitized reference field is digitally subtracted in real-time
from all succeeding digitized images of the angiogram by an arithmetic
unit. Thus, the output of this unit is proportional to temporal brightness changes in the video image. Since these changes are usually much
smaller than the total dynamic range of the video signal, they can be
multiplied by factors between 2 and 8 before D/A-conversion and video
tape recording. Thus, the relevant information in a video-angiogram,
namely the voltage change caused by temporal changes in image brightness, is amplified before recording and the ratio of this signal to
the noise generated in tape recording is decreased accordingly. In

addition to this effect on tape recording noise, the problem of digitization errors due to time-base jitter of the replayed video signal is also decreased. Stationary background structures such as the sharp brightness steps at the edge of the blanking circle of the TV-camera, which are critical in digitizing tape recorded angiograms, are removed in the process of subtraction recording because a precise lock between the strobe signal of the video A/D-converter (Fig.1) and the central synchronization of the x-ray TV-system can be maintained.

Especially in medical imaging, subtraction recording has the additional advantage of delivering improved image contrast before computer processing. This helps assure the quality of an angiogram, even of low primary contrast, is sufficient before the patient has left the catheterization laboratory. The comparison of Fig.8 with Fig.9 exemplifies this advantage. To retain the background information, which is removed from the recording in the subtraction process, the background picture subtracted from the image series is also recorded on video tape together with the subtraction recorded angiogram.

Another feature of the image processing system implemented is the storage of digitally coded physiological data (ECG, pressure, etc.) and parameters (TV-field number etc.) in a bit pattern recorded on

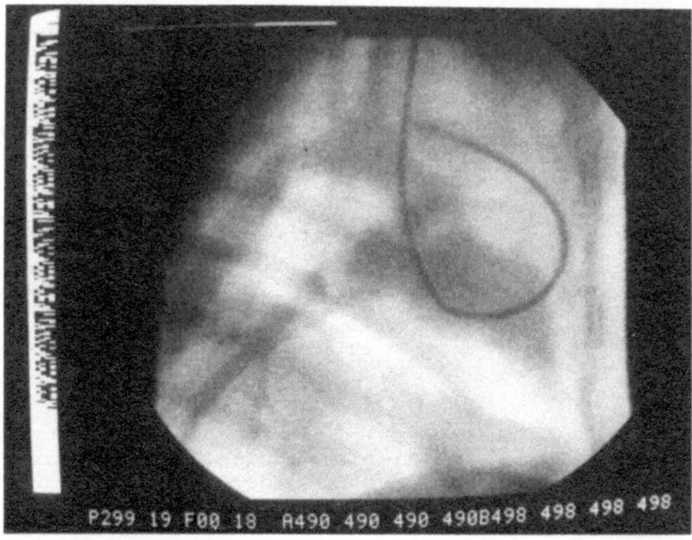

Fig.2: Digitized data encoding used for combined video and physiological data storage on video tape. The bit pattern shown at the left edge of the monitor carries six digitized analog channels and three digital channels.

tape together with the video image series. This system is described
in more detail elsewhere (7). Fig. 2 shows a TV-field from an angiogram carrying the described bit pattern at its left edge. These additional data allow computer-controlled retrieval of selected TV-fields
and facilitate the generation of computer files containing both images
and the simultaneously gathered physiological informations.

3.3.) <u>Video-computer interface.</u>

The video-computer interface adapts the high data rate of the video
signal to the much slower rate of regular computer channels. While
a video disk recorder is usually required for the repetitive replay
of each TV-field while it is being sampled stroboscopically (4,5,6),
the system shown in Fig.3 digitizes complete TV-fields in real-time
during normal replay from video tape. The trigger generator shown

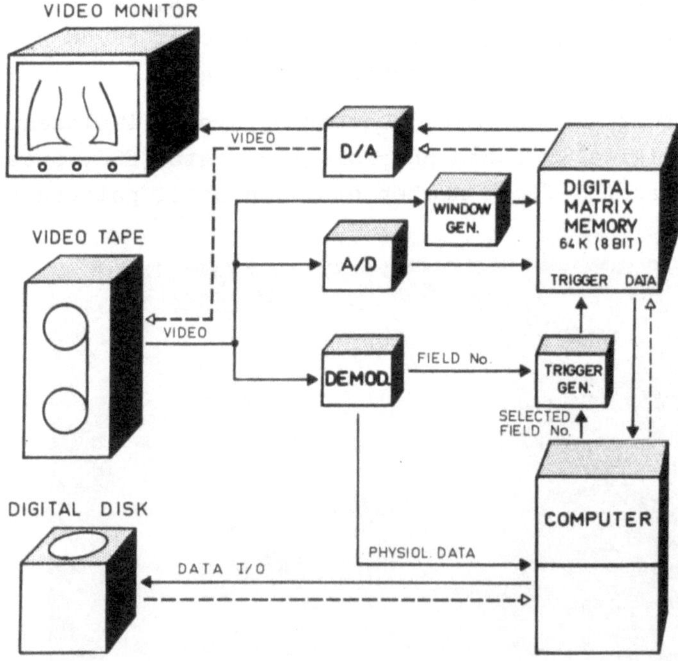

Fig.3: Video-computer interface. In on-line applications avoiding
storage of the video image series on video tape, the input
to the A/D-converter is directly from the x-ray TV-chain.

compares the TV-field number encoded into the video image (Fig.2)
with the number selected manually or by computer program and triggers
the read-in of this TV-field into the fast semiconductor memory
(matrix, compare also Fig.1). From this buffer, data are read to the
computer at a much slower rate. To digitize each TV-field in an image

series, the tape must be replayed about 15 times. The matrix memory
also allows the transfer of video information from the computer to the
closed-circuit TV-system (CRT-monitor, video-recorder).

The window generator also shown in Fig.3 enables one to set a mask
over selected areas of an image. With this option, only the area of
the window, between 16 pixels and 64 K pixels, in each TV-field is
digitized and transferred through the fast buffer to the computer
system. A more complete description of the windowing implemented is
given elsewhere (8). Working in conjunction with the temporal windowing
provided by the trigger generator (Fig.3),these masking techniques
help confine digitization to relevant data. This is especially important in a minicomputer system during involved quantitative studies on
time series of image data where digitization, computation, and evaluation time are significant. Moreover, in some applications this feature
makes feasible real-time acquisition of the relevant parts of many
digitized video images avoiding the noise and time-base jitter introduced by primary recording on a video tape-recorder. Examples of the
analysis of windowed data are given in section 5.1.

4. SOFTWARE FOR IMAGE-DATA ACQUISITION, ANALYSIS, ENHANCEMENT, AND DISPLAY.

Versatility was a prime consideration in our image processing software.
We have experienced in our work that the variables of each image modification technique have to be closely matched to the class of images
processed in order to obtain optimal results. Alphanumeric and graphic
terminals are used in combination with the video-computer interface,
which provides image display, for the interactive control of video-
data retrieval, processing, analysis and storage. Fig.4 shows in
schematic form the capabilities implemented.

Another goal was to make use of the computer not only for data storage,
filtering, and enhancement but also to provide statistical data and
descriptors of the input and processed images.

4.1.)   Image input/output, file creation.

Programs were written to read and write the high-speed TV-field buffer
memory (Fig.3) and to read and write magnetic disk (for active storage
of unprocessed and processed pictures) and magnetic tape (for back-up
and documentation).

Each digitized TV-field is assigned a block of 32 K words (16 bits).
The first and the last 128 words in each block corresponding to the
first and last TV-line are, however, blanked and used for the storage

of the following reference data:
a) Experiment number
b) TV-field number
c) ECG and pressure values.

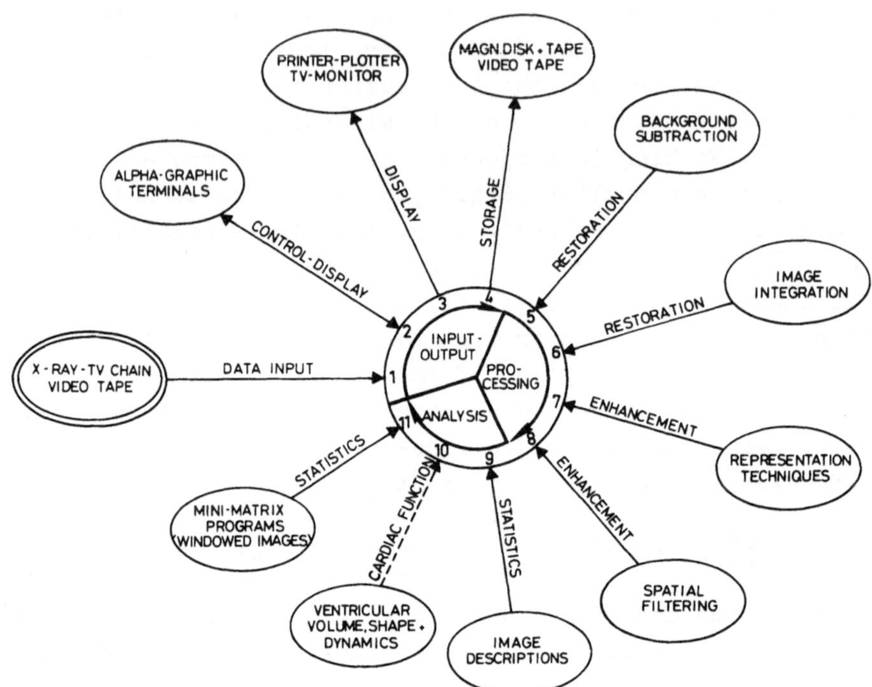

Fig.4: Software available for data retrieval, processing, analysis,
and storage of image series.

While these data are entered into the image file when digitizing
images and decoding physiological data from the video-tape recorder
(Fig.3)and used to facilitate image data handling and analysis, other
data are written into the spaces defined above during image processing
to avoid overhead by repeated calculation of often used parameters,
such as mean value, standard deviation, maximum and minimum values of
processed image data (density data, see section 4.2).
All image processing programs can then access these reference data.

Hardcopies of processed images can be obtained by photographing an
output image from the TV-monitor driven by the video-computer interface (Fig.3) or, with reduced grey-level resolution, from an electrostatic printer-plotter. For reproducible development of negatives and
production of the photo prints and slides, the picture number, the
date and a reference grey-scale can optionally be added to the monitor

picture. Another routine allows the combination of regions of interest from up to four images into one TV-field for combined output (collage) on TV-monitor or plotter (Fig.5,6). Finally, text can be entered into any portion of an image through an alphanumerical computer terminal (Fig. 5).

Image-data output to the electrostatic printer-plotter include:
a) Sixteen grey-level, dot-density modulated output. Optically weighted characters or randomized dot-arrays may be used (9).
b) Continuous tone representation computed from a novel combination of a 16 x 16 dither-matrix and the minimized average error method (10). In contrast to option a) this method is also capable of producing variable output image sizes.

4.2.) <u>Logarithmic background subtraction, subtraction-image integration.</u>

Angiography is a method of evaluating regional changes in roentgen-density, which result from injecting contrast material into the circulation. If a sufficient amount of contrast material is used, the experienced operator can outline the selectively opacified region by simply inspecting the images. Detection of small amounts of dye and the quantitative analysis of angiographic images, however, require the suppression of interfering background structures of bones and tissue.

Let the total thickness of material transradiated by x-rays with incident intensity I_o be equal to L. Then the output intensity I_1 will be:

$$I_1 = I_o \exp\, (-\mu_1 L) \tag{1}$$

where μ_1 is the absorption coefficient. If a region in this material with original absorption coefficient μ_1 and of thickness 1 is replaced by a dye solution with absorption coefficient μ_2, the output intensity is changed to:

$$I_2 = I_o \exp(-\mu_1(L-1))\exp(-\mu_2 1) \tag{2}$$

Subtracting the natural logarithm of (2) from that of (1) results in the roentgen-density D of the dye-filled region:

$$D = \ln(I_1/I_2) = (\mu_2 - \mu_1)\, 1 \tag{3}$$

which is independent of the magnitude of the background absorption contained in the directly measured intensity value I_2 (Eq.2). The computation of density values D given in (3) is performed for each pixel of a roentgen image. The result of logarithmically subtracting

a video line in an opacified image from the equivalent video line in
a background image is called a density profile (see section 5.1).
Similar computational steps can be applied to subtraction-recorded
angiocardiograms.

The application of this subtraction principle (11,12) to cardiovascu-
lar images is complicated by the periodic background image intensity
changes occurring even without dye injection due to heart motion.
Therefore, the background and the opacified pictures have to be taken
at the same phase of heart action. The required heart-phase synchroneous image selection is simplified in our system by the integrated recording of video images and physiological data on video tape (see 3.2)
and the creation of digital data files combining images with reference
data (see 4.1). Another prerequisite to image subtraction, good spatial
registration of subtracted images, is provided by the video techniques
of image storage and A/D-conversion used in the previously described
system.

Averaging a number of adequately opacified subtraction images (13)
taken at the same heart phase during successive heart cycles may enhance image quality mainly due to an increase in the signal-to-noise
ratio. If noise is additive and its value is normally distributed
with mean zero, RMS noise decreases proportional to the inverse
square-root of the number of images averaged (14). In model experiments, we found that the noise in subtraction images which were calculated from tape recorded x-ray pictures follows this statistical law
very accurately (15). Another effect of image integration is the reduction of the errors due to inhomogeneous mixing of dye and blood.

4.3.) Representation techniques.

The result of the processing of image data by integration and loga-
rithmic subtraction are density data. The regular method of linearly
rescaling these data by normalizing them to the dynamic range of the
output device, e.g., to the 256 grey levels obtainable from an 8 bit
video D/A-converter, does not usually provide adequate pictures. A
few large subtraction artifacts produced, e.g., by catheter movement,
time-base jitter of the video-tape recorder, or by video-tape dropouts,
can limit the true density data to a small part of the usuable grey
scale. Therefore, we evaluated a number of rescaling methods in order
to test their applicability to subtraction images obtained from angiocardiograms (15).

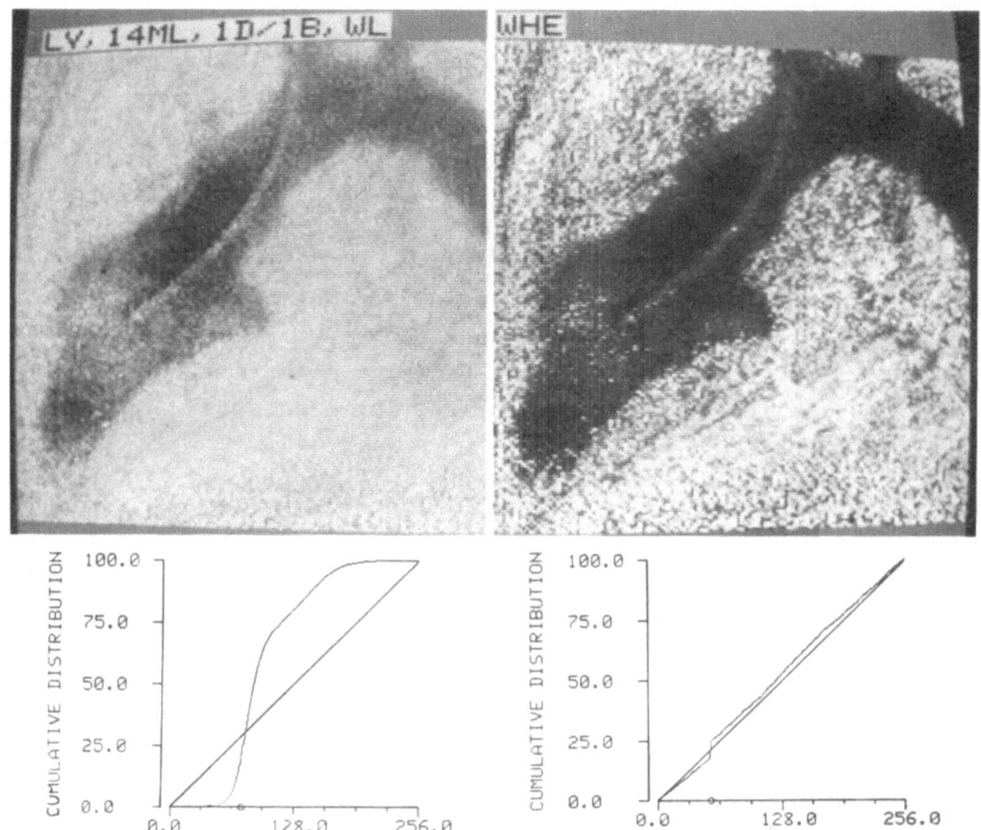

Fig.5: Results of different rescaling techniques. Left part: linear rescaling after windowing. Right part: histogram equalization after windowing.Diagrams: cumulative grey-level distributions.

For the rescaling of the computer processed images shown in the section on applications of computerized image processing, we used the method of histogram equalization. This technique (16) attempts to assign an equal number of pixels to each grey level of the output image. This procedure was developed to optimize the use of the grey levels of the image output device. In our application, the effect of histogram equalization is often very large due to the reassignment of the desired density data to a larger and more optimally located grey level range than occurs in regular linear rescaling. Even when using a window to mask out the critical sharp brightness step at the blan- king circle of the video camera, a marked gain in contrast is pro- vided by applying histogram equalization (right part of Fig.5)instead of linear rescaling (left part of Fig.5).

The cumulative distribution of grey levels is given below each part
of this picture. A very large number of pixels at the grey level which
corresponds to zero density (marked by a small zero on the x-axis)
could not be removed by the rescaling technique.A density value of zero
is equivalent to the absence of temporal brightness changes at the position of the respective pixels.

4.4.) Spatial filters.

Image integration as described above reduces noise by averaging
images of a time series. The next paragraphs discuss some spatial
smoothing filters as well as a simple new edge-detection algorithm
especially suited for operation on subtraction-images.

4.4.1) Smoothing filters.

A linear two-dimensional convolutional filter was implemented which
replaces the grey-level of each pixel by a weighted average of itself
and its neighbors. The neighborhood can be chosen to include 3 x 3 or
5 x 5 pixels. Gaussian weighting factors are normally used (bell-
shaped filter). While this filter smoothes the grainy structure of
subtraction-image noise, it also blurs the edges between opacified
and non-opacified regions. Sofar, we have not obtained significant im-
provements in human pattern recognition capabilities by applying these
smoothing filters.

A nonlinear filter suggested by Rosenfeld (14) can be used for
smoothing a picture with reduced blurring. The neighborhood of a
pixel E is described by the matrix:

$$A \quad B \quad C$$
$$D \quad E \quad F$$
$$G \quad H \quad I$$

If the absolute value of the difference between the grey-level of E
and the arithmetic mean value of its eight neighbors is smaller than
a preselected value X, E is left unchanged. If this difference is
larger than X, E is replaced by its neighbors' mean value. An application of this filter is given below.

4.4.2) Sharpening filter.

Automatic edge detection is important for the analysis of cardioangio-
grams since the outlining of ventricular borders is the basis for the
determination of ventricular volumes and wall motion. Following again
a proposal by Rosenfeld (14), we implemented a two-dimensional digital
gradient filter defined by:

$$E = \text{const.} \ |(A+B+C)-(G+H+I)|+|(A+D+G)-(C+F+1)|$$

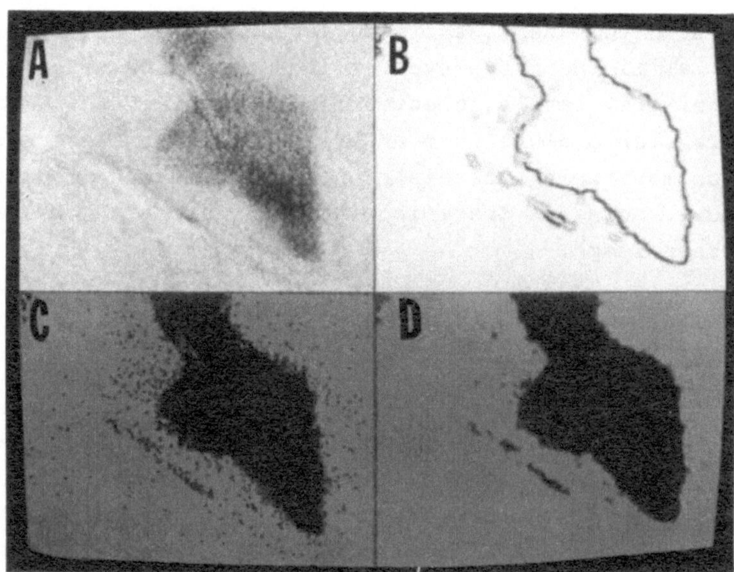

Fig.6: Edge-detection by a sequence of thresholding (C), nonlinear
       filtering (D), and digital-gradient (B) techniques.

A simple edge-detection scheme was developed using this filter. An
averaged subtraction-image of a left ventricle (Fig.6 A)was transformed into a bilevel picture (Fig.6 C) by slicing it at a grey-level
equal to 4 standard deviations of background-image noise. By applying
the nonlinear smoothing filter described above four times, isolated
noise spikes were eliminated or reduced in amplitude and size (Fig.6 D).
This smoothed version was then differentiated by the sharpening filter
described above (Fig.6 B). The result was not fully sufficient as an
automatic border outlining technique in this case where extremely low
amounts of dye (8 ml Urografin 15g%) were used for the visualization
of the left ventricle.

4.5) <u>Image statistics and descriptors.</u>

The following data are available to the operator to facilitate interactive control of image processing steps:
a) Data included in the image file (see 4.1) such as mean values and
   standard deviations of grey-levels in subtraction images and the
   numbers of images averaged.
b) Plot of grey-levels along a selected TV-line.
c) Signatures of subtraction-images (17). These help to identify the
   center of the opacified region (region of interest) in a subtraction-
   image.
d) Collage of bilevel pictures. Each picture of the collage represents

a slice between two user-specified grey-levels. A dot in this
picture is set if the grey-level of the respective pixel is within
the limits of grey-levels selected for this slice. This method of
mapping a regular picture into a series of bilevel pictures is
valuable for monitoring the distribution of features contained in
an image (e.g. noise vs opacified vessels) across the grey-scale
of a processed image.

5. APPLICATIONS

5.1.) <u>Densitometric dimension measurements.</u>

The result of image subtraction and image integration described in
section 4.2 is an array of density data. These data can, in principle,
be used to calculate dimensions of transradiated, transiently opacified structures. However, the complicity of the measurement system
comprised of an x-ray generator, the transradiated inhomogeneous body,
the blood mixed with contrast material, the video camera, the video-
tape recorder, and the A/D-converter is so great that we consider it
important to analyze, at first, the capability of the system to measure
dimensions of simple, well-defined phantoms.

The phantoms used in these experiments are water-filled rectangular
cuvettes into which cylinders are immersed. The lower parts of these
cylinders are also filled by water, while the upper parts contain dye.
The axis of these tubes are parallel to the input screen of the image
intensifier (horizontal direction of radiation). A slit in a lead
plate perpendicular to the axis of the cylinder confines radiation
to a narrow region across the cylinder. From each TV-field, one video
line across this aperture was digitized and transfered in real-time
through the matrix memory to the computer (see section 3.3.). By
moving the cuvette in the direction of the axis of the cylinder, the
water-filled and the dye-filled parts sequentially enter the transradiated region. Pulsed radiation (80 kV, 300 mA, 2msec) was filtered
by a copper sheet (1 mm thickness).

Image subtraction and integration are performed on these data as
described in section 4.2. The averaged density profile obtained is
displayed on the screen of a graphic computer-terminal (Tektronix
4010). Using the cursor, a section of the density profile (region of
interest) comprising the profile of the tube is defined by two limiting
markers. The program than cross-correlates the density profile within
these limits with a series of computer-generated density profiles

calculated assuming circular cross sections with variable diameters and locations. The cross section and alignment delivering a maximum of the cross correlation coefficient defines the diameter and the center (expressed in pixels) of the density profile of the cylinder.

In the next step, the density values of the pixels outside the region of interest, but inside an overlapping larger marked region, are averaged to determine the mean deviation of the baseline of the density profile from the ideal zero density value. The complete density profile is corrected for this baseline offset. Now, the corrected density data are approximated by a least mean squared error fit.This is performed by generating a series of density profiles of circular cross sections possessing the center and the diameter computed by cross correlation but variable density values.

Fig.7 shows density data obtained from phantom measurements and the fits generated by the computer. These plots are obtained by symmetrically mirroring the profiles about the computer-determined baseline. All data are from measurements using a cylinder (diameter 36 mm) filled with Urografin with a concentration c = 2.77 g% (equivalent to 10 g% cm). From left to right, the number of background (B) and opacified (D) video-lines integrated increases as indicated. The data shown at the right correspond to an averaging time of about 2.5 sec. The gain in signal-to-noise ratio provided by subtraction-image integration is demonstrated.

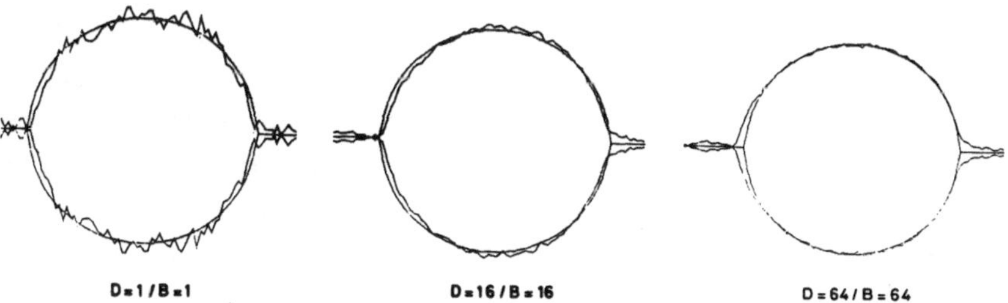

Fig.7: Symmetrical plots of density profiles from a transradiated dye filled tube. Computer-generated fits are superimposed. The number of TV-fields averaged increases from left to right as indicated.

To calibrate these measurements a cylinder of known diameter and dye
concentration is analyzed as described above. The known dimension
and concentration are entered and enable the program to evaluate diameters and dye concentrations for other tubes or vessels with circular
diameters and axis perpendicular to the directions of the radiation
and of the video lines if brought to the same position of the x-ray/
image-intensifier system. One of the applications of similar measurements could be the determination of volume of the left ventricle from
density data (18).

5.2.) <u>Image restoration and enhancement.</u>

In previous experiments (15) we applied the methods of heart phase
synchroneous image integration and subtraction (section 4.2) to video
tape recordings of angiograms performed by injecting low amounts of
dye into the left ventricle or the pulmonary artery of pigs. In the
experiments reported here, the left ventricle of a pig was visualized
after dye injection into the neck vein (vena jugularis), a point even
more peripheral than the pulmonary site. Under these conditions,the
injected bolus of dye is diluted before entering the left ventricle
by passing through the right heart and the lungs. The resulting low-
contrast images of the left ventricle were stored by the new method
of subtraction recording and, for a comparison, also by regular video
tape recording. As a reference for the assessment of image quality obtained under these unusual experimental and technical conditions, we
additionally performed a selective injection into the left ventricle
of the same animal resulting in images with much higher primary contrast.

Fig. 8 combines three pictures derived from the intravenous dye injection (20 ml of 76 g% Urografin). R e g u l a r video tape recording was used. The image in the middle part shows the best opacification of the left ventricle obtained. The picture at the right
results from image subtraction of the picture recorded before dye injection, shown at the left, and after histogram equalization of the
resulting density data.

To demonstrate the effect of tape recording noise, the same sequence
of images as demonstrated in Fig.8, but from a s u b t r a c t i o n
recorded angiogram (intravenous injection, 18 ml of 76 g% Urografin)
is shown in Fig.9. Even before computer processing, a much higher
contrast of the opacified left ventricle in the subtraction recorded
image of the left ventricle (Fig.9, middle part) is realized. The

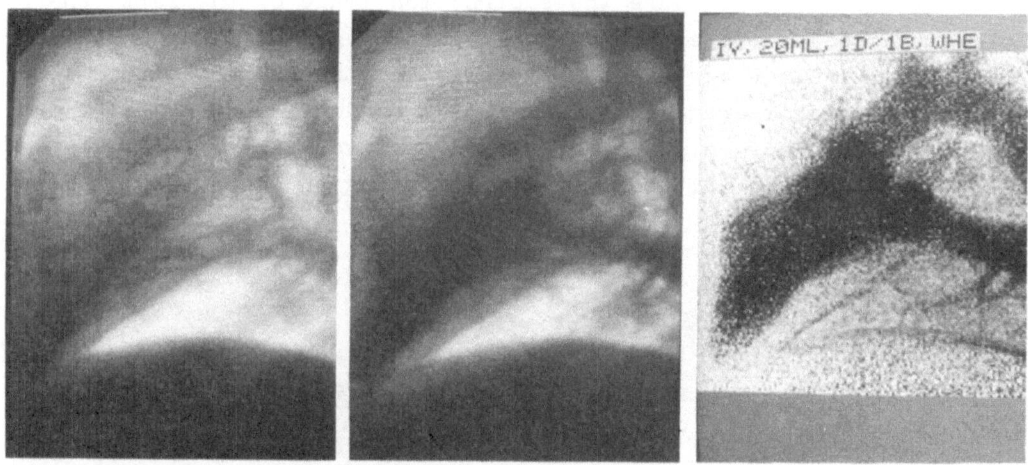

Fig.8: Collage of pictures from video-angiogram performed by intravenous injection of dye. The subtraction picture shown at the
right was obtained by computerized subtraction of the left
(background) image from the central (opacified) image.

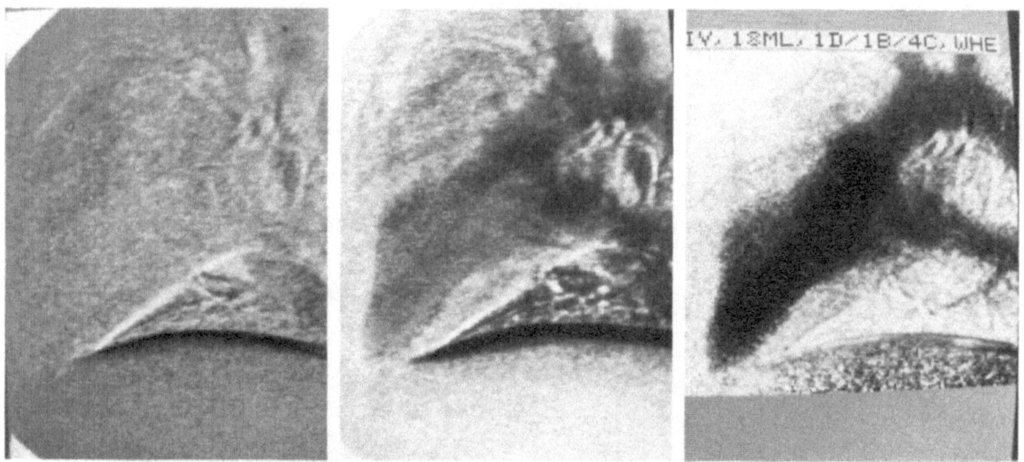

Fig.9: Collage of pictures from a subtraction-recorded angiogram
performed by intravenous injection of dye. Sequence of
images shown is equivalent to that in Fig.8.

comparison of pictures obtained by image subtraction and histogram
equalization from the regular and from the subtraction-recorded angiogram, shown at the right in Fig.8 and Fig.9, respectively,demonstrates
the improved signal-to-noise ratio of subtraction-recorded angiograms
(Fig.9). However, a general evaluation of the advantages provided by
subtraction recording has obviously to be performed under conditions
which are completely comparable.

The last two pictures compare the subtraction image of the left ventricle extracted from the subtraction-recorded angiogram which was performed by i n t r a v e n o u s injection to the subtraction images obtained from (regular) video-tape recordings of the s e l e c t i v e l y o p a c i f i e d left ventricle (14 ml of 76 g% Urografin). The left part of Fig.10 was again generated by

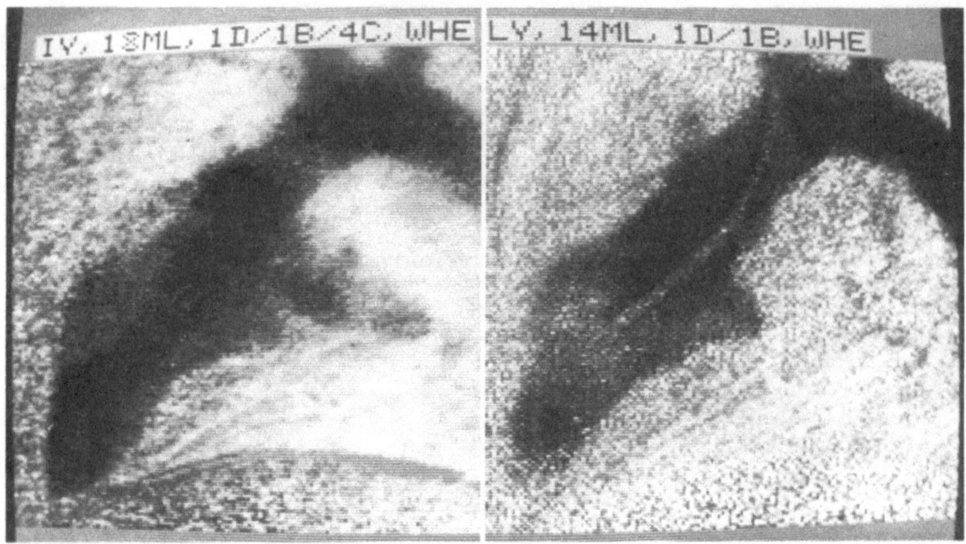

Fig.10: Subtraction-images of the left ventricle. Opacification by intravenous dye injection (left) is compared to opacification of the same ventricle by selective dye injection (right).

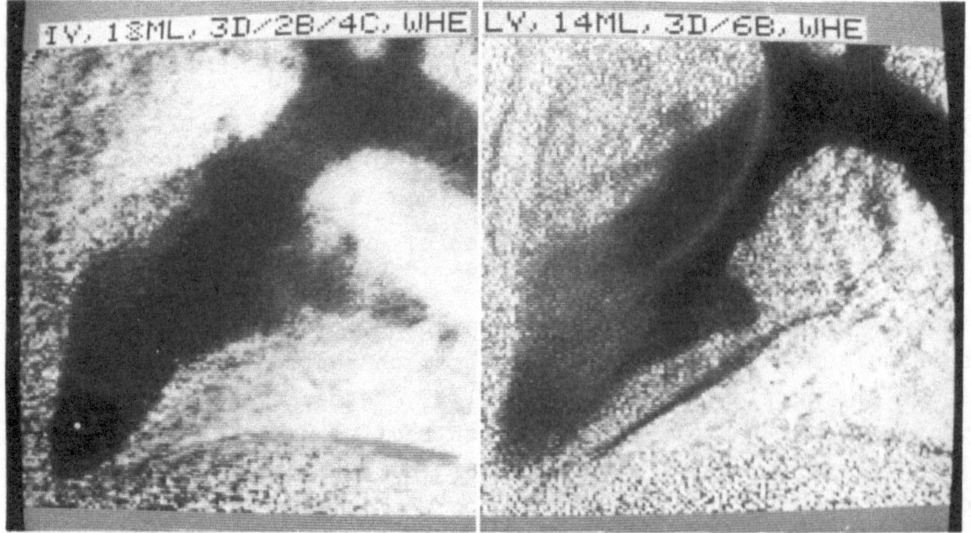

Fig.11: Effect of image integration. Regular subtraction: see Fig.10.

subtracting one subtraction-recorded, opacified image from one background image (compare Fig.9). In this case, however, the background
image was chosen from a heart cycle shortly before opacification of
the left ventricle so that the pulmonary circulation was already opacified. This removes a large part of the structures interfering with
the visualization of the left ventricle in Fig.8 and Fig.9. At the
same time, the shorter time delay between the subtracted images reduces the influence of motion and respiration artifacts. The right
side of Fig.10 shows as a reference the image obtained from the selective left ventricular injection. Note that distribution of dye in
the left ventricle after intravenous injection (left part in Fig.10)
is better than after selective left ventricle injection (right part
in Fig.10).

Image integration allows a further increase in image quality. The
left part of Fig.11 shows the result of averaging three opacified and
two background images of the left ventricle after i n t r a v e n o u s
dye injection (compare Fig.10, left) and the result of the same processing steps (integration of three opacified, six background images)
performed on pictures obtained by s e l e c t i v e left-ventricular
injection (compare Fig.10, right). In spite of the dilution of the
dye bolus after intravenous injection, large parts of the left-
ventricular silhouette opacified by intravenous injection can be out-
lined with a precision comparable to the case of the selective injection. The distribution of dye seems to be better in the case of
intravenous injection.

Finally, the comparison of the middle part of Fig.8 (left ventricle
after intravenous injection without computer processing) and of the
left part of Fig.11 (the best result of the combined methods of subtraction recording and computerized image subtraction, integration,
and histogram equalization) indicates the total gain in image quality
thus far obtained. An immediate application of the reported image-
series acquisition, preprocessing, and display options will be to
interface them to our existing computerized ventricular-volume
determination and contraction-pattern analysis procedures (9) in
order to increase their ease of data handling, speed of operation,
and, hopefully, accuracy of results.

REFERENCES

(1) S.H.Rahimtoola, J.P.Duffy, H.J.C.Swan: Circulation, 35, 70 (1967).

(2) N.Gootman, A.M. Rudolph, N.M.Buckley: Amer.J.Cardiol.25,59 (1970).

(3) B.K. Gilbert, M.T. Storma, C.E.James, L.W.Hobrock, E.S.Yang,
     K.C.Ballard, E.H.Wood: IEEE Trans.Comp. C 25, 1089 (1976).

(4) R.W.Mc Caughern, D.M.Caughey, H.Rombeek, W.S.Davidson:
     IEEE Trans.Comput. C 21, 738 (1972).

(5) R.A.Robb, S.A.Johnson, J.F.Greenleaf, M.A.Wondrow,E.H.Wood:
     Proc.Soc.Photo-Optical Instrumen., 40, 27 (1973).

(6) P.D.Clayton, L.D.Harris, S.R.Rumel, H.R.Warner:
     Comput.Biomed.Res.7, 369 (1974).

(7) R.Brennecke, P.H.Heintzen: Biomed.Technik 21 (Suppl.),33 (1976).

(8) R.Brennecke, T.K.Brown, J.H.Bürsch, P.H.Heintzen:
     2nd International Workshop Conference on Roentgen-Video-
     Techniques, Kiel 1976. In press.

(9) P.H.Heintzen, R.Brennecke, J.H.Bürsch, P.Lange, V.Malerczyk,
     K.Moldenhauer, D.Onnasch: Computer, 55, July 1975.

(10) J.F.Jarvis, C.N. Judice, W.H.Ninke: Computer Graphics
      Image Processing, 5 , 13 (1976).

(11) B.G.Ziedses des Plantes: "Subtraktion", Thieme Verlag,
      Stuttgart 1971.

(12) C.K.Chow, T.Kaneko: Comput.Biomed.Res. 5 , 388 (1972).

(13) C.A.Mistretta, M.G.Ort, F.Kelcz, J.R.Cameron, M.P.Siedband,
      A.B.Crummy: Invest.Radiol. 8 , 402 (1973).

(14) A.Rosenfeld: "Picture Processing by Computer", Academic Press,
      New York 1969.

(15) R.Brennecke, T.K.Brown, J.Bürsch, P.H.Heintzen:
      Proc.of Computers in Cardiology, 1976, in press.

(16) E.L.Hall, R.P.Kruger, S.J.Dwyer, D.L.Hall, R.W.Larsen,
      G.S.Lodwick: IEEE Trans.Comput. C 20, 1032 (1971).

(17) R.H.Selzer, Proc.Rochester Conf.on Data Acquisition in Biology
      and Medicine, 5, 309 (1966).

(18) B.G.Trenholm, D.A.Winter, D.Mymin, E.L.Landsdown:
      Med.Biol.Engn.10, 163 (1972).

COMPUTERVERARBEITUNG VON RÖNTGENFILM-MAMMOGRAMMEN ZUR KENNZEICHNUNG UND HERVORHEBUNG KRANKHAFTER VERÄNDERUNGEN

W. Spiesberger, A. Hoyer
Philips GmbH Forschungslaboratorium Hamburg,
2000 Hamburg 54, FRG

I ZUSAMMENFASSUNG

Die Diagnose von Karzinomen im Bereich der Brustkrebserkrankungen
stützt sich im allgemeinen auf Anamnese, Palpation und Röntgenbild
der Brust. Mit Methoden der digitalen Bildverarbeitungen soll ein ob-
jektiver und reproduzierbarer Befund erreicht werden. Insbesondere
zur Durchführung von Reihenuntersuchungen ist man auf automatische
Auswerteverfahren angewiesen, da nicht genügend speziell ausgebildete
Ärzte zur Befundung zur Verfügung stehen. Über die Detektion von
Mikroverkalkungen mit Hilfe lokaler Operationen und der Hervorhebung
von großflächigen Veränderungen wird berichtet. Die aufgezeigten Ergebnisse sind vielversprechend und motivieren die Fortsetzung der
Arbeiten.

II EINLEITUNG

Die digitale Verarbeitung medizinischer Bilder wird seit einigen Jahren besonders in den Gebieten der Nuklearmedizin [12], Blutzellen-
untersuchung (Zytologie) [23], der Chromosomenanalyse [23] und Rönt-
gendiagnostik [11,17]   (Knochenerkrankungen [18,19], Blutdurchfluß-
messung [13], Herzfehler [4,5,22,25], Lungentumore [2,3] und Cine-
angiogramme [27,28]) angewendet.

Eine Ausdehnung auf Mammogramme (Röntgen-Xerogramme [1,29,30],
Thermogramme [31,34], Ultraschall CT und Röntgenfilme) ist nur ver-
einzelt in der Literatur bekannt geworden.

Ziel unserer Untersuchungen ist deshalb, die Anwendbarkeit digitaler
Bildverarbeitungsmethoden auf Film-Mammogramme zu studieren und ihre
medizinische Relevanz zu testen.

Schon seit langem wird die Mammographie für die Untersuchung
[6,7,9,14,15,32,33] der weiblichen Brust eingesetzt. Als Reihenunter-
suchungsmethode ist sie jedoch noch nicht voll akzeptiert, da einerseits nicht genügend qualifiziertes Arztpersonal für die Befundung

zur Verfügung steht, andererseits das Risiko einen Tumor zu induzie-
ren, statistisch nicht ausgeschlossen werden kann. Gleichwohl ist bekannt, daß die Mammographie [8,10,14] zur Früherkennung von Brustkrebs beiträgt, wenn sie auf genügend viele Patientinnen angewendet
wird.

Übereinstimmend mit der Literatur reicht es nicht aus, einen rechts-
links-Vergleich durchzuführen, vielmehr müssen auch solche Strukturen
wie Mikroverkalkungen detektiert werden, da sie eine wichtige Indika-
tion für "okkulte" (klinisch nicht nachweisbare) Tumore darstellen
[15,16]. Gruppierte oder linear angeordnete Mikroverkalkungen sind
40 bis 60% signifikant [20,21] und manchmal der einzige Hinweis für
ein sehr frühes Stadium wachsenden Krebses.

Im folgenden wird berichtet über die Erkennung von Mikroverkalkungen
sowie die Hervorhebung großflächiger schwachkontrastiger Muster, die
auf krankhafte Veränderungen des Brustgewebes schließen lassen.

III LOKALISIERUNG VON MIKROVERKALKUNGEN

Bei der Diagnostik der Brusterkrankungen ist die Erkennung von Mikroverkalkungen in Röntgen-Mammogrammen (Bild 1) von größter Bedeutung,
da bereits 5 Verkalkungen pro cm^2 eine 30%-ige Wahrscheinlichkeit für
Brustkrebs darstellen, 10 pro cm^2 entsprechen 59% [21]. Für den Arzt
ist die Erkennung der Verkalkungen meist nur unter Zuhilfenahme einer
Lupe und sorgfältigem Lesen des Bildes möglich - eine sehr anstren-
gende und ermüdende Aufgabe. Da die Größe der Verkalkungen zwischen
50 µm - 1000 µm schwankt, muß das Bild für die maschinelle Verarbeitung mit einer sehr hohen "Sampling"-Rate abgetastet werden (∼ 25 µm).
Der anfallende Betrag an Bilddaten - ca. 68 Mio bei 18 cm × 24 cm -
läßt sich nicht in Speichern der heutigen Technologie ablegen, so daß
nur das Bild selbst als Speicher angesehen werden kann. Ein lokaler
Operator [24] (Bild 2) wird deshalb zeilenweise über das Bild geführt
und daraus werden Merkmale abgeleitet, die die Mikroverkalkungen
kennzeichnen. Gemäß der in einem Entscheidungsbaum [26] festgelegten
Konditionen wird eine genauere Analyse des Operator-Bereichs nur dann
durchgeführt, wenn die ersten Beurteilungskriterien bereits erfüllt
waren. Bild 3 zeigt das Flußdiagramm für die Rechenvorschrift. Da die
Mikroverkalkungen sich als helle Punkte im Bild abzeichnen, ist das
erste Kriterium, daß die Zentralzelle des Operators ein lokales Maximum darstellt. Die Verarbeitungsgeschwindigkeit kann durch geeigneten
Zeilenvorschub erhöht werden (Bild 4). Wurde ein lokales Maximum de-

tektiert, so kann der Operator gleich um n Bildelemente verschoben
werden. Als zusätzliche Kriterien haben wir noch die Helligkeitsdif-
ferenz zwischen Zentralzelle und Mittelwert der Randelemente sowie
die Standardabweichung der Randelemente herangezogen. Die Bilder 5a,
5b zeigen vergrößert entsprechende Ergebnisse von detektierten Verkalkungen und das zugehörige Mammogramm in Originalgröße.

Durch Fehler in der Filmemulsion oder durch Kratzer können im Bild
Objekte vorgetäuscht werden, die Verkalkungen sehr ähnlich sehen.
Durch Auswerten der beiden Projektionen (Bild 6), die normalerweise
angefertigt werden, kann zwischen Mikroverkalkungen und Fehlern unterschieden werden. Verkalkungen sind nämlich lagemäßig korreliert und
in beiden Ebenen vorhanden, Fehler unkorreliert und nur in einer
Ebene.

IV HERVORHEBUNG GROSSFLÄCHIGER VERÄNDERUNGEN

Neben den Mikroverkalkungen treten großflächige "Muster" als Zeichen
krankhafter, schlimmstenfalls krebsiger Veränderungen auf. Szirrhöses
(Krebs-)Gewebe stellt sich im Mammogramm als unscharf begrenzte,
sternförmig auslaufende Verdichtung dar, solide Karzinome bilden unscharf begrenzte runde Gebilde, im Unterschied zu Zysten, die scharf
begrenzt im Röntgenbild erscheinen.

Da bislang noch keine Versuche bekannt geworden sind, mit dem Computer zwischen krankhaften und normalen Strukturen im Mammogramm zu
unterscheiden - es ist dies oft auch für den erfahrenen Arzt proble-
matisch - beschränken sich unsere Ansätze auf eine Bild-zu-Bild-Ver-
änderung, um schwer erkennbare Strukturen oder Konturen leichter erkennen zu können.

Eine Möglichkeit der Kontrastanhebung besteht in der Modifikation der
Grauwertverteilung. Bild 7 zeigt ein Histogramm eines logarithmisch
abgetasteten Mammogramms. Die niedrigen Graustufen (dunkle Bildpunkte)
überwiegen im allgemeinen. Da das Auge Kontrastunterschiede im Dunk-
len nur sehr schlecht wahrnehmen kann, wurde das Histogramm linearisiert, also gleiche Wahrscheinlichkeit für alle Schwärzungswerte angenommen, Bild 8a, 8b. Bei der Umverteilung der Bildinformation werden insbesondere dunkle Bereiche komprimiert und helle Anteile stark
hervorgehoben.

Es zeigte sich, daß dieses Verfahren geeignet ist, in kontrastschwachen Bildern suspekte Regionen überhaupt aufzudecken (Bild 9a, 9b).

Bei kontrastreichen Bildern ist das Verarbeitungsergebnis eher unbefriedigend und führt oft zur Verschleierung wichtiger Bildinformation (Bild 10a, 10b).

Im Bild vorhandene Konturen können durch Berechnung des Gradientenfeldes extrahiert werden. Mit verschiedenen lokalen Operationen wurde versucht, den Betrag des Gradienten als neue Information bildhaft darzustellen.

Wenn $f(i,k)$ der Grauwert des Bildpunktes am Ort (i,k) ist, so errechnet sich der Betrag des Gradienten am Ort (i,k) nach [3] zu:

$$g(i,k) = [(f(i,k-n) - f(i,k+n))^2 + (f(i-n,k) - f(i+n,k))^2]^{1/2}$$

Hierbei ist n der Abstand der zur Konturberechnung verwendeten Bildpunkte von (i,k). Die Gleichung wurde als Operator G1 in das in unserem Labor bestehende Bildverarbeitungssystem implementiert und daraus

$$\text{G2: } g(i,k)=[(f(i-n,k-n)-f(i+n,k+n))^2+(f(i-n,k+n)-f(i+n,k-n))^2]^{1/2}$$

$$\text{G3: } g(i,k)=[(f(i,k-n)-f(i,k+n))^2+(f(i-n,k)-f(i+n,k))^2 +$$
$$+(f(i-n,k-n)-f(i+n,k+n))^2+(f(i-n,k+n)-f(i+n,k-n))^2]^{1/2}$$

und

$$\text{G5: } g(i,k)=[(f(i,k)-f(i+n,k+n))^2+(f(i,k+n)-f(i+n,k))^2]^{1/2}$$

abgeleitet.

Außerdem wurde mit maximalen Grauwertdifferenzen gearbeitet:

$$\text{G4: } g(i,k)=\max(|[f(i-n,k-n)+f(i-n,k)+f(i-n,k+n)$$
$$-f(i+n,k-n)-f(i+n,k)-f(i+n,k+n)]|,$$
$$|[f(i-n,k-n)+f(i,k-n)+f(i+n,k-n)-f(i-n,k+n)$$
$$-f(i,k+n)-f(i+n,k+n)]|) \quad .$$

Es zeigt sich, daß die Verfahren G4 und G5 stärker auf lokale Kontrastsprünge reagieren und dadurch der Anteil aus Rauschpunkten höher als in den Verfahren G1-G3 ist (Bild 11a-f).

Die Rauschempfindlichkeit wirkt sich besonders stark bei kontrastschwachen Mammogrammen aus, obwohl andererseits gerade G4 etwas höhere Gradientenwerte liefert. Zur besseren Darstellung der Gradientenbilder wurde eine Helligkeitsschwelle aus einem Histogramm abgeleitet und anschließend ein Verdünnungsoperator angewendet (Bild 12a-d).

V AUSBLICK

Für die Durchführung von Reihenuntersuchungen zur Brustkrebsfrühdiagnose erscheint es notwendig, durch maschinelle Verarbeitung der Mammogramme besondere Informationen anzuheben und besser darzustellen. In erster Linie wurden die sehr kleinen Mikroverkalkungen herausgearbeitet, die sonst nur unter Zuhilfenahme einer Lupe erkannt werden können. Großflächige Schwachkontraste können durch Histogrammodifikation oder Konturverstärkung oftmals besser erkannt werden. Allgemeine weiterführende Untersuchungen sind notwendig, um Verfahren zu erarbeiten, die unabhängig vom jeweiligen Kontrastumfang zu besseren Ergebnissen führen. Ebenso müßten auch noch die technologischen Probleme schneller, hochauflösender Abtastung, der Bildspeicherung und Verarbeitung gelöst werden. Möglichkeiten ergeben sich z.B. durch den Einsatz von Parallelprozessoren oder von spezieller Verarbeitungs-Hardware.

Die diesem Bericht zugrundeliegenden Arbeiten wurden mit Mitteln des Bundesministeriums für Forschung und Technologie (Förderungskennzeichen DVM 135) gefördert. Die Verantwortung für den Inhalt liegt jedoch allein beim Autor.

LITERATUR

[1] ACKERMAN, L.V., GOSE, E.E.: "Breast Lesion Classification by
     Computer and Xeroradiography", Cancer, Vol. 30, Oct. 1972,
     S. 1025-1035.
[2] BALLARD, D.H., SKLANSKY, J.: 2nd Int. Joint Conf. on Pattern
     Recognition, 13-15. Aug. 1974, Kopenhagen. Hirarchic recognition
     of tumors in chest radiography.
[3] BALLARD, D.H., SKLANSKY, J.: Comp. and biomed. research 6 (1973),
     S. 299-321. Tumor detection in radiographs.
[4] MEYER, P.H., SWEENEY, J.W., and NICE, C.M.: "Digital computer
     determination of a medical diagnostic index directly from chest
     X-ray images, IEEE Trans. BME-11, S. 67-72, (1974).
[5] DWYER, S.J., LODWICK, G.S.: "Automated radiographic diagnosis
     via feature extraction and classification of cardiac size and
     shape descriptors, IEEE Trans. BME-19, (1972), S. 174-186.
[6] EGAN, R.L.: "Mammography and breast deseases". Baltimore:
     William Wilkins Co. 1970.
[7] EGAN, R.L., et al.: "Team approach to the study of deseases of
     the breast". Cancer 23, S. 847-854 (1969).
[8] GERSHON, J. Cohen et al.: "Mammographic screening for breast
     cancer". Radiology 88, S. 663-667 (1967).
[9] GERSHON-Cohen: "Atlas of Mammography", Berlin (1970).
[10] GRIESBACH, W.A., EADS, W.S.: "Experience with screening for
     breast carcinoma". Cancer 19, S. 1548 (1966).
[11] HARLOW, C.A., EISENBEIS, S.A.: "The Analysis of Radiographic
     Images, Conf. on Two-Dimensional Signal Processing, University
     of Missouri-Columbia, Columbia, Missouri (1971); and IEEE Trans.
     C-22, S. 678 (1973).
[12] HARLOW, C.A., LEHR, J., PARKEY, R., GARROTTO, L., LODWICK, G.S.:
     Radiology 97, S. 269 (1970).
[13] HEINTZEN, P.H.: "Röntgen-, cine- and videodensitometry", Thieme
     Verlag, Stuttgart, 1971.
[14] HOEFFKEN, W., LANYI, M.: "Röntgenuntersuchung der Brust", Stutt-
     gart 1973.
[15] HÜPPE, J.R.: "Der Weg zur Auffindung des okkulten Mammakarzi-
     noms - ein Appell an Radiologen, Chirurgen und Pathologen zur
     Teamarbeit". Radiologe 13 (1973), S. 477-481.
[16] HOLLENDER, L.F., GORS, Ch.: "Röntgenuntersuchung der klinisch
     nicht tastbaren Mammakarzinome". Langenb. Arch. Klin. Chir. 313,
     S. 380-384 (1965).
[17] KRUGER, R.P., DWYER, S.J., HALL, D.L., LODWICK, G.S.: "IAL Tech-
     nical Report: "Computer Processing of Radiographic Images",
     Image Analysis Laboratory, Departments of Electrical Engineering
     and Radiology, University of Missouri-Columbia, Columbia, Mis-
     souri (1971).
[18] LEVINE, M.D., LEEMET, J.: Pattern Recognition 7 (1975), S. 177-
     185, Computer Recognition of human spinal outline using radio-
     graphic image processing.
[19] LODWICK, G.S.: "The Bones and Joints" (Year Book Medical Publish-
     ers, Chicago 1971).
[20] MENGES, V., FRANK, P., PRAGER, P.: "Zahlenmäßige Zunahme von
     Mikroverkalkungen, ein wichtiges röntgendiagnostisches Krite-
     rium für das okkulte Mammakarzinom". Fortschr. Röntgenstr. 124,
     4 (1976), S. 372-378.
[21] MENGES, V., WELLAUER, J., ENGELER, V., STADELMANN, R.: "Korrela-
     tion zahlenmäßig erfaßter Mikroverkalkungen auf dem Mammogramm
     und dadurch diagnostizierter Karzinome und Mastopathietypen".

[22] ROELLINGER, F.X., KAHVECI, A.E., CHANG, J.K., HARLOW, C.A.,
DWYER, S.J., LODWICK, G.S.: Computer Analysis of Chest Radio-
graphs, U.S.-Japan Seminar on Picture and Scene Analysis, Kyoto,
Japan (1973).
[23] PRESTON, K.: "Digital Picture Analysis in Cytology", aus
"Digital Picture Analysis", ed. A. Rosenfeld 1976.
[24] ROSENFELD, A.: "Picture Processing by Computer". New York, Academic Press, 1969.
[25] SPIESBERGER, W.: "Klassifizierung von Herzfehlern durch digitale
Röntgenbildverarbeitung, Biomed. Technik 20, Ergänzungsband Kon-
greß Medizin-Technik 1975, Stuttgart.
[26] TASTO, M.: "Automatische Mammographie-Auswertung: Erkennung von
Mikroverkalkungen". Biomedizinische Technik Bd. 20. Ergänzungsband, Mai 1975, S. 273-274.
[27] TASTO, M.: "Motion extraction for left-ventricular volume measurement, IEEE Trans. BME-21, (1974), S. 207-213.
[28] TASTO, M., BLOCK, U.: "Locating objects in complex scenes using
a spatial distance measure, Proc. 2nd Int. Joint Conf. on Pattern Recognition, Kopenhagen 1974   S. 336-340.
[29] WEE, W.G., MOSKOWITZ, M., NAI-CHING CHANG, YEOUNG-CHING TING:
"Evaluation of Mammographic Calcifications Using a Computer Program". Radiology 116, Sept. 1975, S. 717-720.
[30] WINSBERG, F., ELKIN, M., MACY, J., BORDUG, V. jr., WEYMOUTH, W.:
"Detection of radiographic abnormalities in mammogramms by means
of optical scanning and computer analysis". Radiology 89,
S. 211-215, (1967).
[31] WINTER, J., STEIN, M.: "Computer image processing techniques for
automated breast thermogram interpretation". Comput. Biomed.
Res. 6, S. 522-529, (1973).
[32] WITTEN, D.M., THURBER, D.L.: "Mammography as a routine screening examination for detecting breast cancer". Americ. J. of
Roentgenology 92 (1964), S. 14-20.
[33] WOLFE, J.N.: "Mammography as a Screening Examination in Breast
Cancer". Radiology 84 (1965), S. 703-708.
[34] ZISKIN, M.C., NEGIN, M., PINER, Ch., LAPAYOWKER, M.S.: "Computer
Diagnosis of Breast Thermograms". Radiology 115, S. 341-347,
Mai 1975.

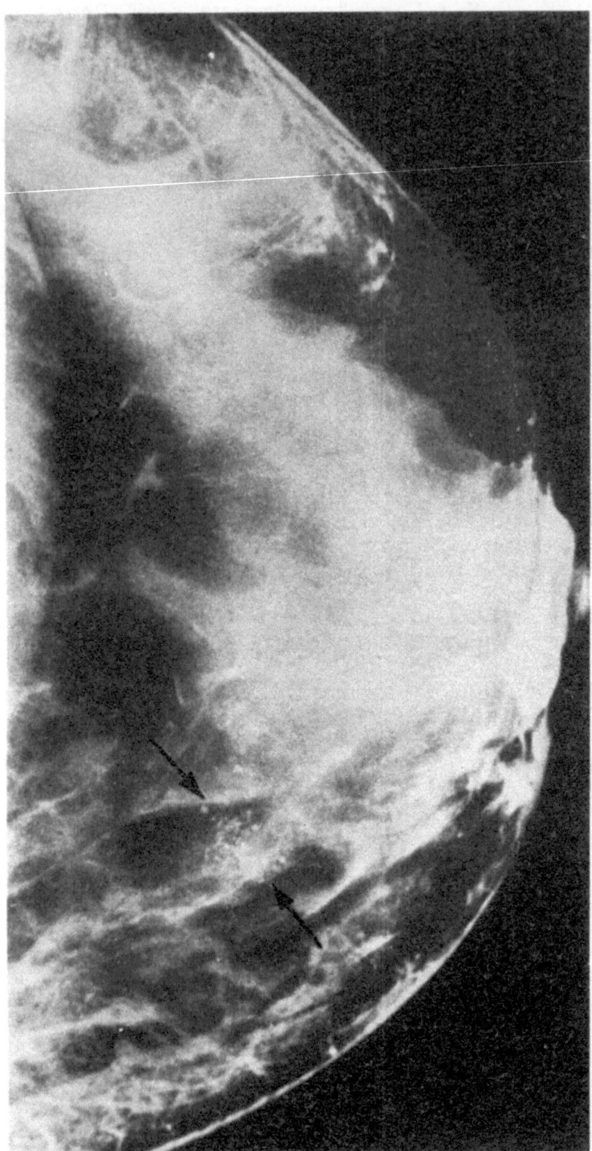

Bild 1: Filmmammogramm mit Mikrokalzifizierungen
(zwischen den Pfeilen)

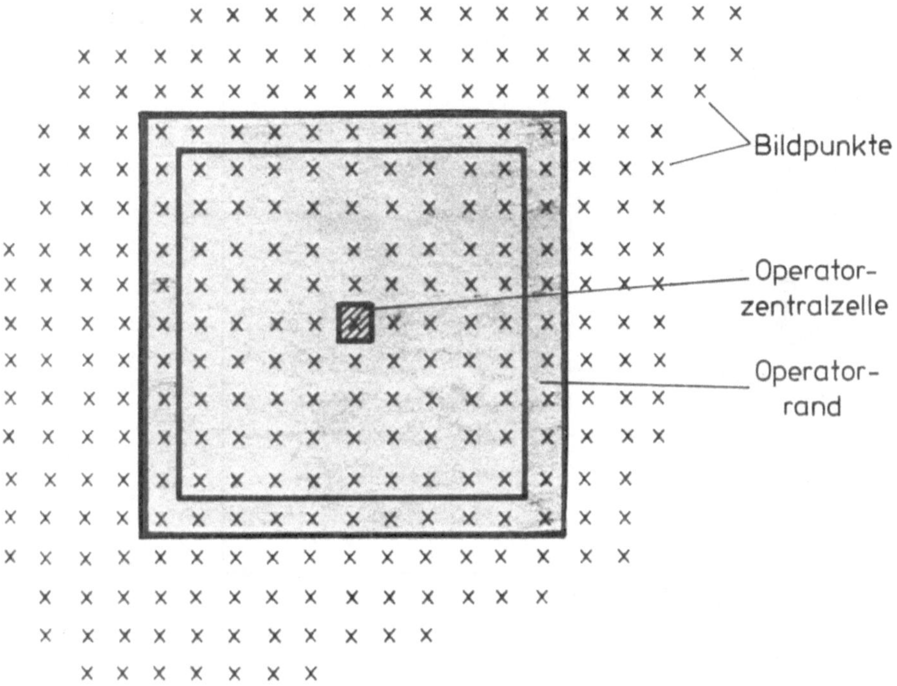

Bild 2: Lokaler Operator zur Merkmalsgewinnung
(Beispiel 11x11 Bildpunkte)

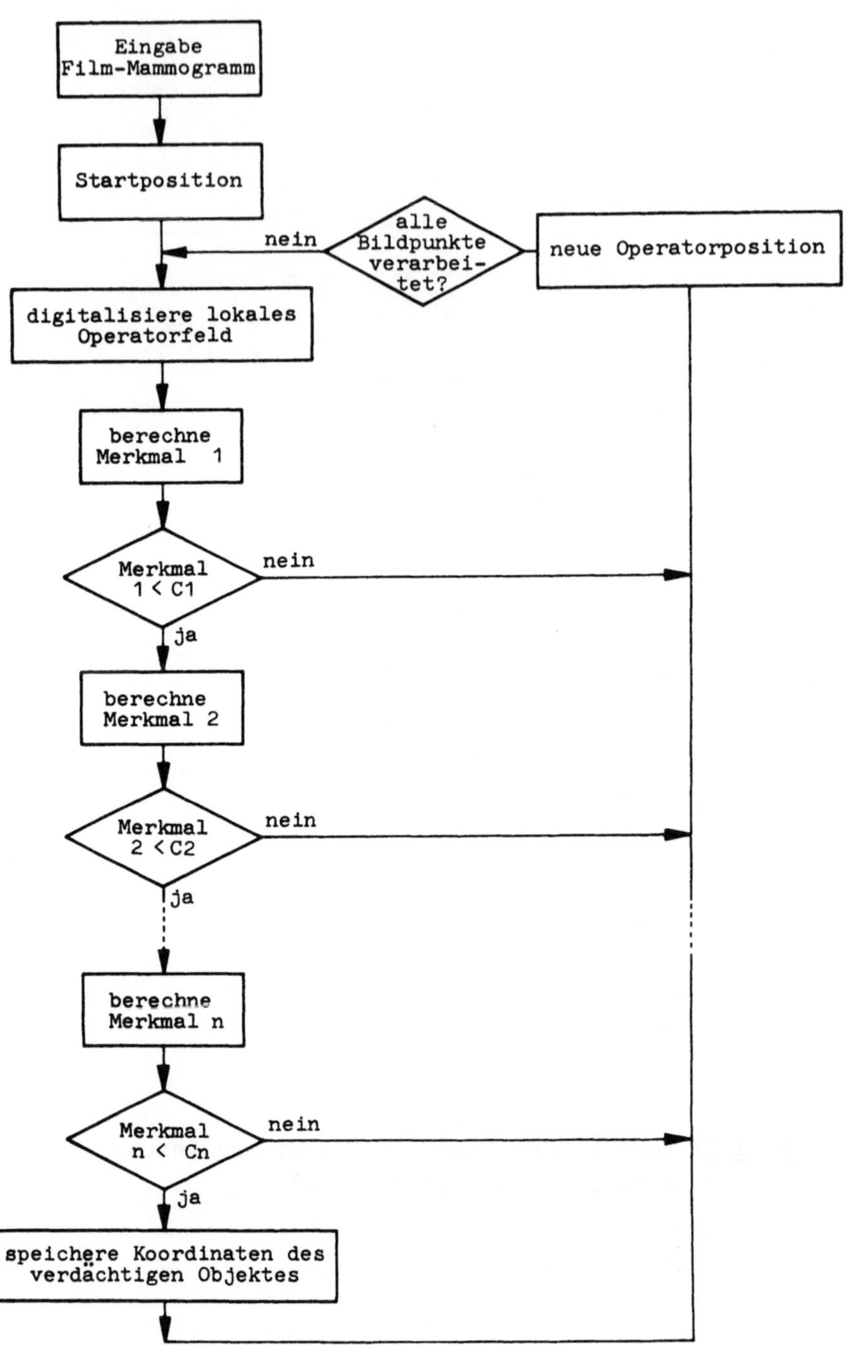

<u>Bild 3:</u> Blockdiagramm zur Mikrokalkerkennung

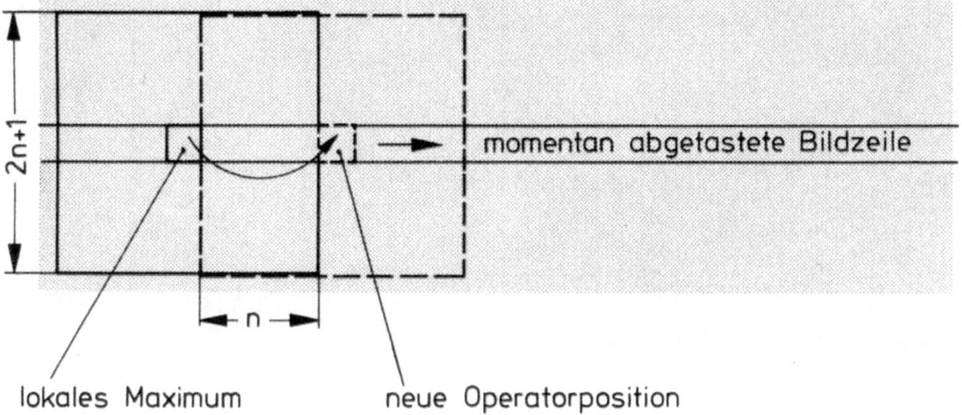

Bild 4: Berechnung der nächsten Operatorposition

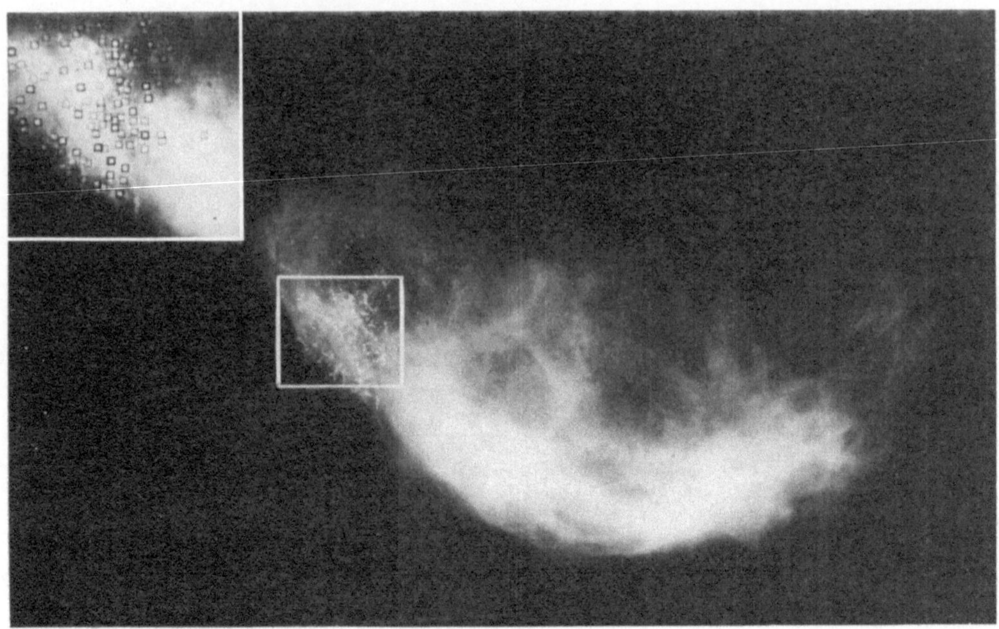

Bild 5a: Entdeckte Mikrokalzifizierungen cranio-candal

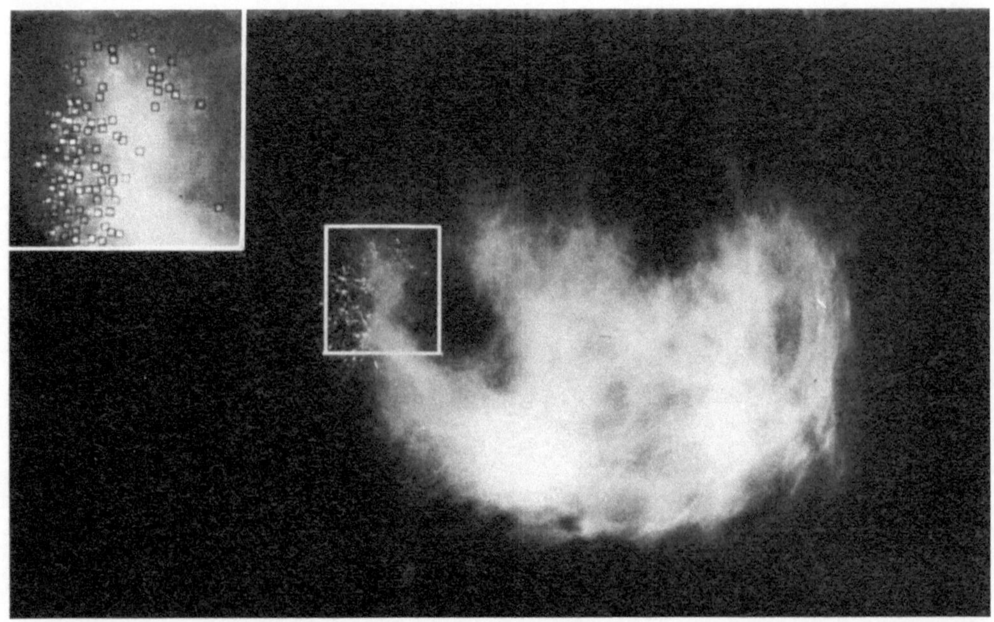

Bild 5b: Entdeckte Mikrokalzifizierungen latero-medial

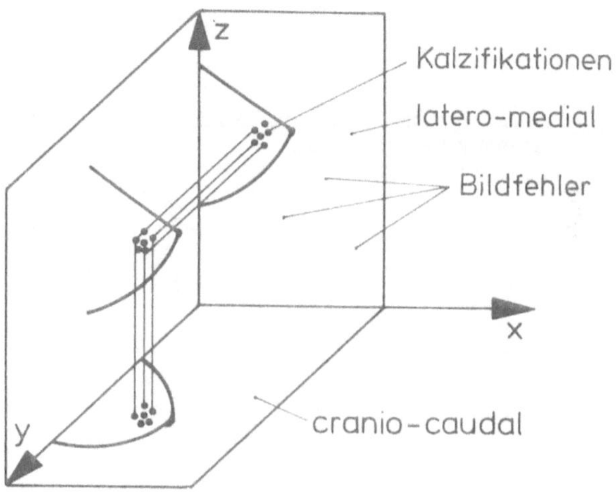

Bild 6: Erkennung von gruppierten Mikroverkalkungen
durch Korrelation der Dichtefunktionen

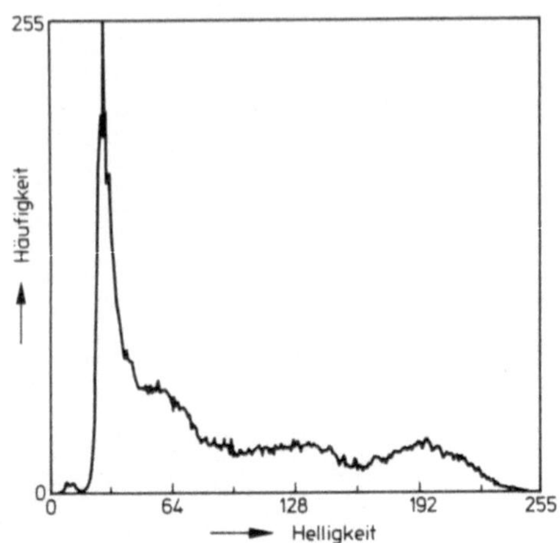

Bild 7: Histogramm des in Bild 11a gezeigten Mammo-
grammausschnitts

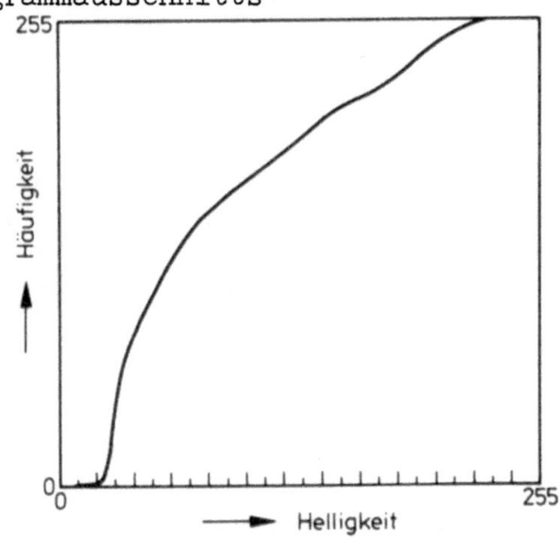

Bild 8a: Kumulative Verteilung von Bild 11a

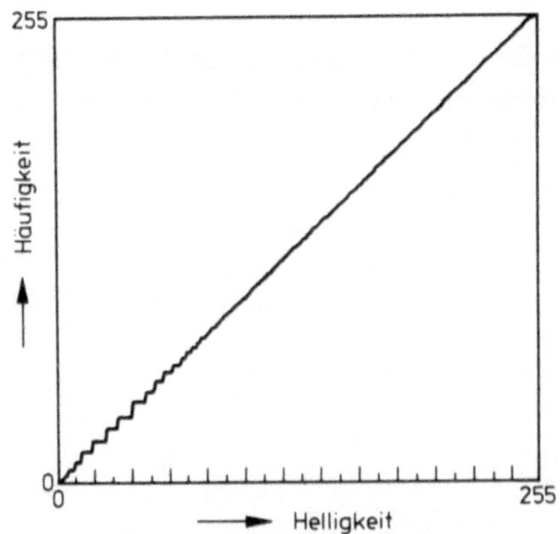

Bild 8b: Linearisierte Verteilung von Bild 11a

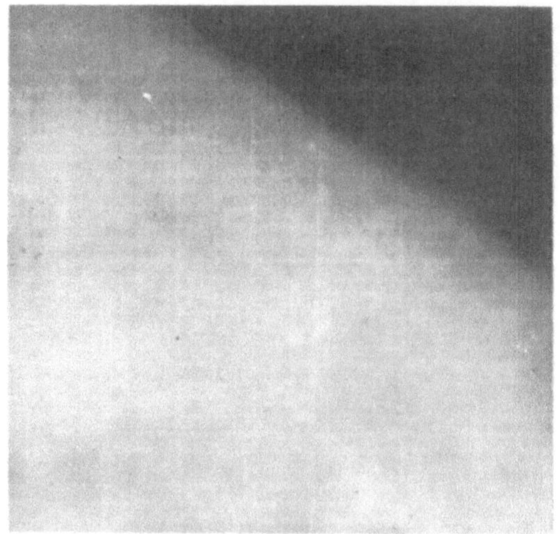

Bild 9a: Ausschnitt eines kontrastschwachen Mammogramms logarithmisch abgetastet und digitalisiert

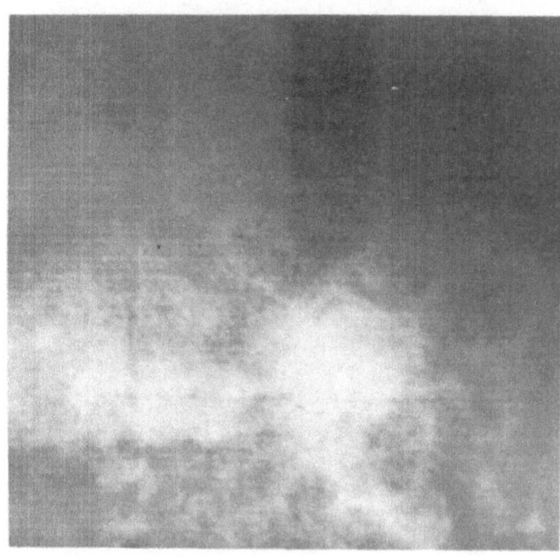

Bild 9b: Nach Histogramm-linearisierung. (Ein im Bild enthaltenes Karzinom ist als Verdichtung erkennbar.)

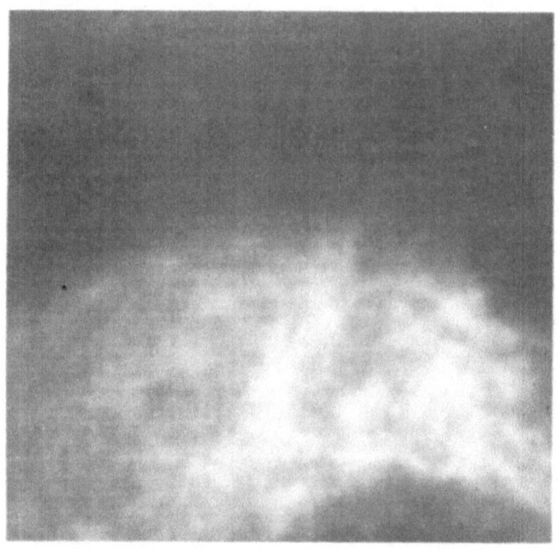

Bild 10a: Ausschnitt eines kontrastreichen Mammogramms logarithmisch abgetastet (gesundes Brustgewebe)

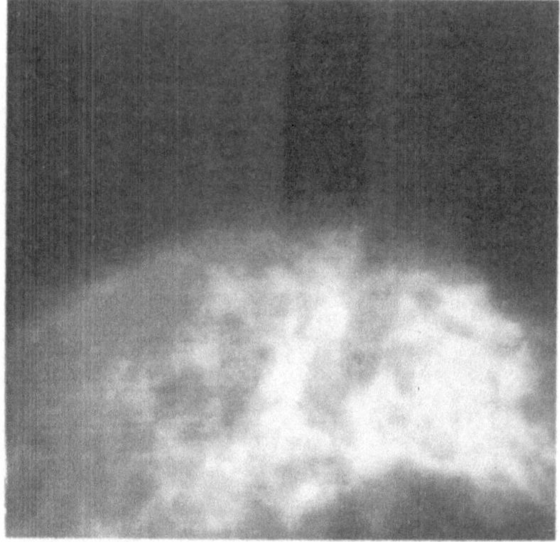

Bild 10b: Nach Histogrammmodifikation (eine Verdichtung wird vorgetäuscht)

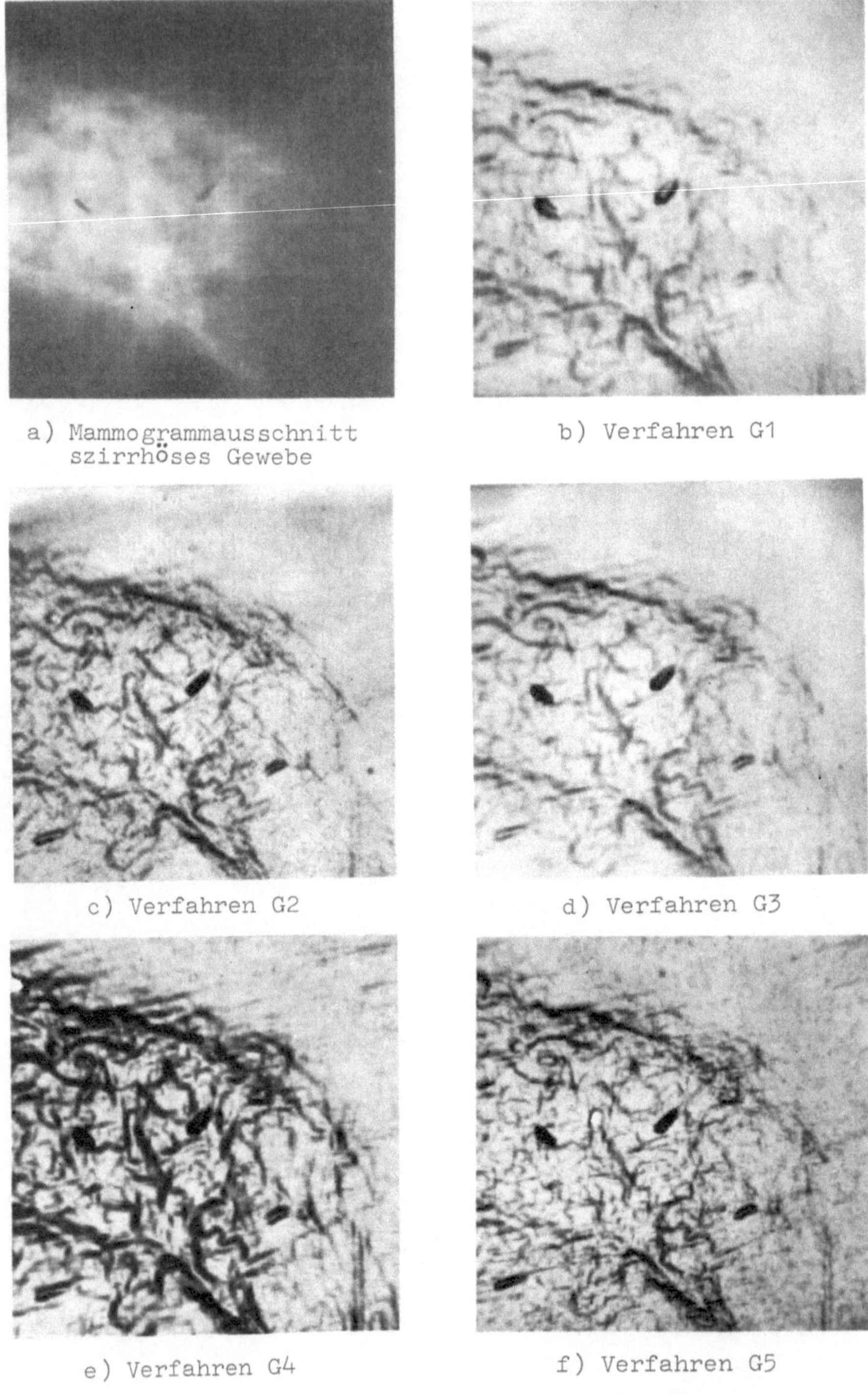

<u>Bild 11</u>: Anwendung verschiedener Gradientenverfahren
sternförmige Struktur wird sichtbar

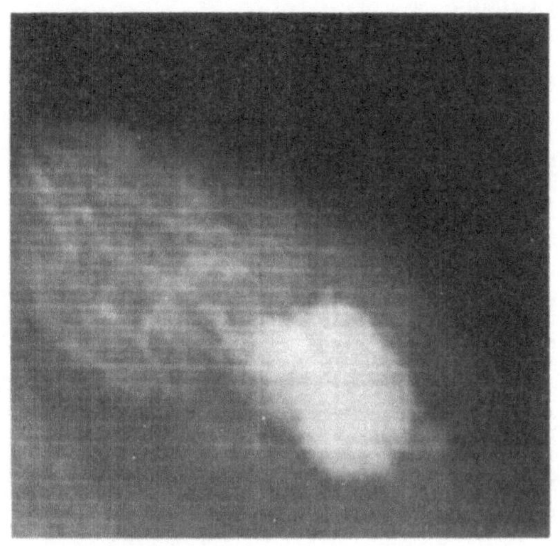

a) Mammogrammausschnitt
   (solides Karzinom)

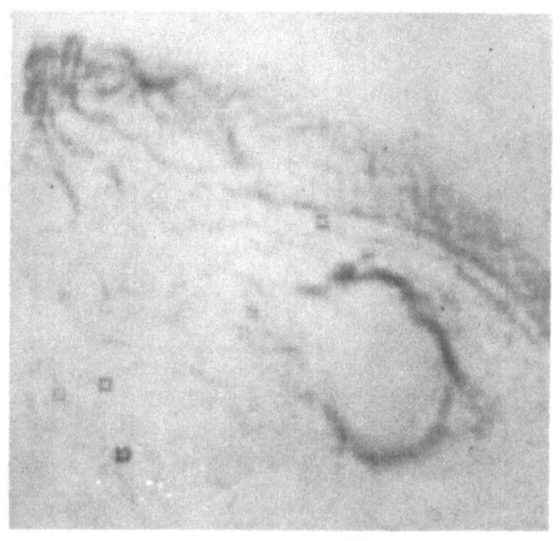

b) Anwendung von G3

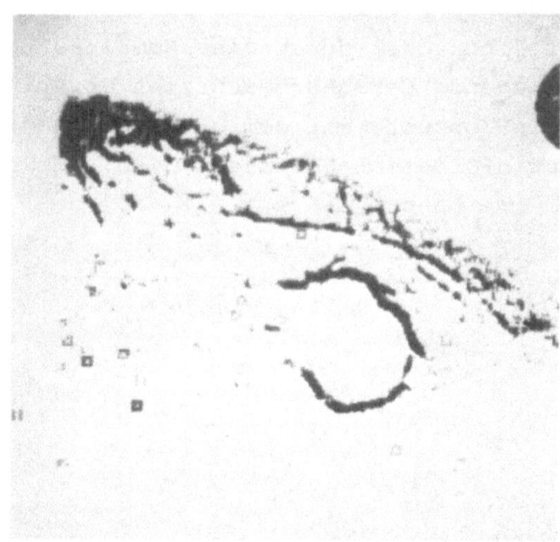

c) binäres Bild nach Schwellwertoperation auf Bild b

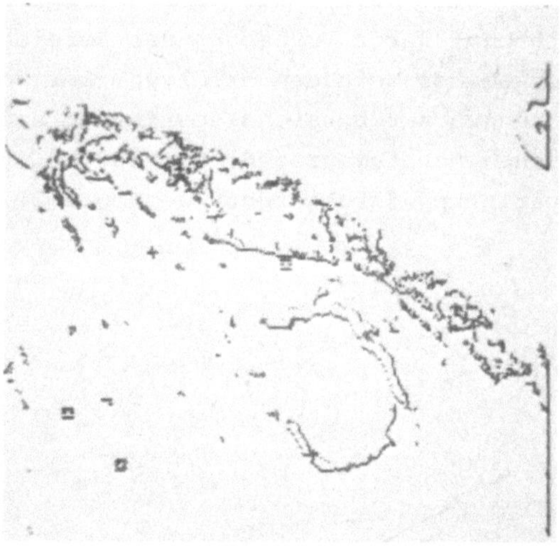

d) Verdünnungsoperator
   angewendet auf Bild c

Bild 12: Konturextraktionsverfahren

Untersuchungen zur mehrkanaligen Bildverarbeitung
und Objektseparierung

R. Schärf

Institut für Informationsverarbeitung und Mustererkennung (FIM),
Breslauerstr. 48, 75 Karlsruhe

Zusammenfassung

Für die Auswertung multispektraler Bilddaten aus umfangreichen Flugzeug-
oder Satellitenemissionen (Fernerkundung) sind Bildverarbeitungsopera-
tionen notwendig, die zu einer automatischen Bildbereichsseparierung
und -beschreibung führen. Bildbereiche sind Gebiete homogener oder durch
statistische Merkmale beschreibbarer Intensitätsverteilung in den spektralen Kanälen. Sie sind Teil eines Objekts (z.B. Dachfläche), identisch
mit einem Objekt (z.B. Straße) oder enthalten mehrere gleichartige Objekte (z.B. Wald). Die Bereichsseparierung kann durch Konturlinienermittlung, durch Erfassung der Bereichsflächen oder durch eine Kombination beider Methoden erfolgen. Der vorliegende Bericht beschreibt Untersuchungen zur Bereichsseparierung und ein Konzept, mit dem durch einen
Flächenwachstumsprozeß, der durch Konturinformation gesteuert wird, die
Separierung durchgeführt werden soll.

Einleitung, Strahlungseigenschaften der Objekte

Die Verarbeitung mehrkanaliger Bildinformationen ist vor allem in der
Fernerkundung durch umfangreiche Flugzeug- und Satellitenemissionen
in den Vordergrund getreten. Für Untersuchungen stehen hier die verschiedensten Systeme wie z.B. Farbfotos, Farbauszüge (Hasselblad),
4-kanalige I^2S-Aufnahmen, 11-kanalige Line-Scanner-Daten des Flugzeug-
meßprogramms usw. zur Verfügung. Der erfaßte Frequenzbereich erstreckt
sich vom Ultraviolett (ca. 250 nm) über den sichtbaren Bereich bis zum
thermischen Infrarot (ca. 1200 nm). Eine Analyse der spektralen Strah-
lungsverteilung der Bilddaten führt zu einer Unterscheidung einzelner
Objekte, weil das Strahlungsverhalten der Objekte (emittierte und reflektierte Strahlung) sehr stark von den Eigenschaften der Objektflächen und des Materials abhängt. Andere Einflüsse, wie z.B. die spektrale Intensitätsverteilung von Lichtquellen (Sonnenlicht, Radar, usw.),
absorbierende Eigenschaften der Atmosphäre, diffus reflektierte Strahlung der Objektumwelt usw. überlagern sich zum Teil störend.

Eine direkte Auswertung der Strahlungseigenschaften führt zu einer
'pixel-by-pixel' Klassifikation, wobei die Intensitätswerte der Kanäle eines multispektralen Bildes als Komponenten eines Merkmalraumes
definiert werden und eine Clusterbildung der Bildpunkte einer Objekt-
klasse erwartet wird /1, 2/. Eine Klassifikation nach einem der bekannten Verfahren ist dann möglich.

Der Vorteil dieses Vorgehens ist die Einfachheit. Die Nachteile liegen darin begründet, daß außer den Strahlungseigenschaften der Objekte keine weiteren objektspezifischen Merkmale für die Klassifikation
berücksichtigt werden. Die Unterscheidung der einzelnen Objektklassen
wird durch die oben angegebenen Störungseinflüsse erschwert. Unterschiedliche Objekte können gleiches oder ähnliches Spektralverhalten
haben. Mit der Objektklassifikation ist keine Objektlokalisierung
verbunden. Dies erfordert eine umfangreiche Nachverarbeitung, die nur
dann entfallen kann, wenn aufgrund der Aufgabenstellung als Antwort
genügt: 'Ein Objekt einer speziellen Klasse ist im Bild enthalten oder
nicht enthalten'. Außerdem beeinflußt eine zunehmende Zahl der in einem Muster zu unterscheidenden Objektklassen ebenfalls nachteilig die
Unterscheidungsfähigkeit und das Klassifikationsergebnis und macht
die Erweiterung des Merkmalraumes durch weitere Kriterien notwendig.

Ansätze zur Bereichsseparierung

Zur Vermeidung der oben genannten Schwierigkeiten bei der Auswertung
multispektraler Daten kann auf wesentliche Merkmale wie Kontur, Formkri-
terien, Texturkriterien und topologische Eigenschaften nicht verzichtet werden. Um diese Merkmale extrahieren zu können, ist es notwendig,
eine Separierung des Bildes in einzelne Bildbereiche und später in Objektflächen durchzuführen. Ansätze hierzu sind z.B. die Extraktion von
Flächenkonturen /3, 4, 5/ und ein Verfahren zum Flächenwachstum /6, 7/.
Beide Verfahren sollen hier diskutiert werden.

Konturlinienermittlung

Die Ermittlung von Flächenkonturen aus der Intensitätsinformation wird
in zwei Schritten durchgeführt: 1. Die Hochpaßfilterung der Intensitätsinformation. 2. Die Verfolgung der Kontrastinformation. Ziel ist die
möglichst vollständige und genaue Erfassung der im Intensitätsbild enthaltenen Objektkonturen als Konturlinien.

Für die Hochpaßfilterung sind eine Reihe von Verfahren bekannt, die Informationen über Bereiche hoher Ortsfrequenzen extrahieren. Eine allgemeine Hochpaßfilterung mit einem Filter nach Abb. 1 erfordert eine
Fouriertransformation der Bild- und der Filterinformation, eine Multiplikation beider im Ortsfrequenzbereich und eine Rücktransformation des
Ergebnisses in den Bildbereich. Den Nachteil des großen Rechenaufwands

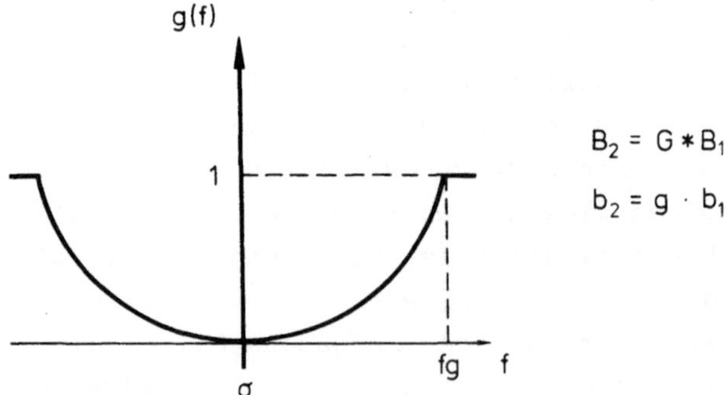

Abb. 1: Allgemeines Hochpaßfilter

vermeiden Verfahren, die im Bildbereich mit lokalen Operationen durchgeführt werden. Hierzu gehören die Punkt- und Balkendifferenzmethode
/3/, die Ebenenapproximation /3/ und das phasendiskriminierende Verfahren /5/. Die beiden zuletzt genannten Verfahren markieren nicht

nur die Lage von Bildpunkten mit hohem Frequenzanteil, sondern liefern zusätzlich Information über Richtung und Betrag der Kontrastgradienten.

Im zweiten Schritt erfolgt die Erzeugung von Konturlinien durch Auswertung der Informationen über die Kontrastgradienten mit Hilfe von Verfolgungsalgorithmen. Dies kann systematisch durch Verfolgung aller Bänder mit Gradienteninformation im Bild geschehen /5/ oder objektspezifisch durch Auswahl von Kontrastinformation mit speziellen Eigenschaften /4/ z.B. lange, paarweise parallel verlaufende Konturstücke (Straßen) oder Polygonzüge gerader Konturstücke, die Flächen einschließen (Hausdächer, usw.). Abb. 2 zeigt das Prinzip der systematischen Erfassung der Gradienteninformation, Abb. 3 das Prinzip der Verfolgung der Gradientenbänder durch Definition trichterförmiger Erwartungsbereiche.

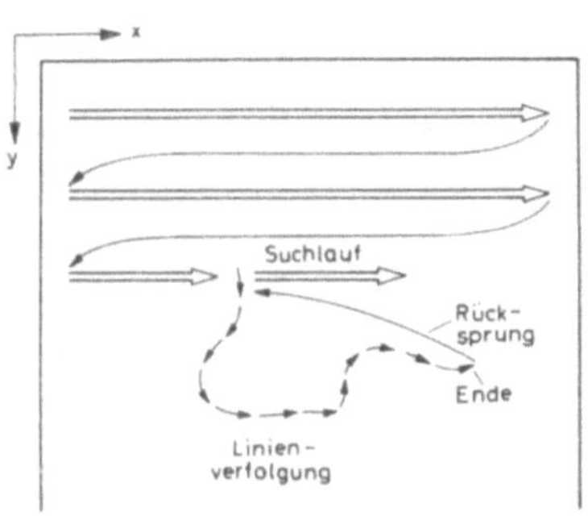

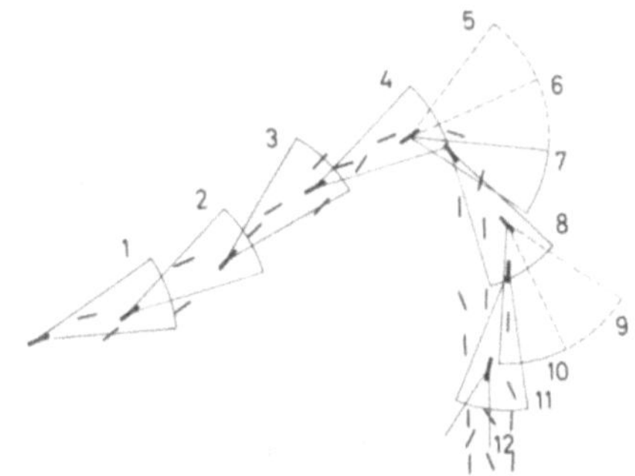

Abb. 2: Systematischer Suchlauf   **Abb. 3:** Konturverfolgung

Ergebnisse der Hochpaßfilterung nach dem phasendiskriminierenden Verfahren und der systematischen Konturlinienermittlung sind weiter unten in den Abb. 15 bis 17 dargestellt.

Beeinflussende Faktoren der Konturlinienerzeugung sind die Qualität der Intensitätsinformation z.B. Nutz-Störsignalverhältnis, Stärke der Kontraste, das Auflösungsvermögen der Verfahren und prinzipielle Verfahrenseigenschaften. Das führt dazu, daß die Konturlinienbilder unvollständig sind, daß die Konturen Lücken aufweisen, daß Ecken abgerundet und Verzweigungen aufgerissen sind. Für eine Objektseparierung und Merkmalextraktion sind die Verfahren ungeeignet.

Flächenwachstum

Ausgehend von einem kleinen Bildbereich (Keimzelle K) wird versucht, Nachbarbereiche N anzulagern, die aufgrund von Merkmalen zur gleichen Fläche gehören. Abb. 4 zeigt das Arbeitsprinzip /8/. Ein anzulagernder Bereich wird mit der Keimzelle verschmolzen (Abb. 4c) und die Anlagerung einer neuen Nachbarzelle versucht (Abb. 4d). Anlagerungskriterium ist ein Vergleich zwischen den Merkmalen der Keimzelle K und denen der Nachbarzelle N (Mittelwert, Varianz). Zu Beginn des Prozesses besteht die Keimzelle entweder aus einem Bildpunkt oder aus einer Menge von Bildpunkten. Entsprechendes gilt für die Nachbarzelle. Das Wachstum kann für jede der im Bild definierten Keimzellen zeitlich sequentiell, oder für alle Keimzellen gleichzeitig wachsen. Abb. 5a zeigt den Nachteil des sequentiellen Wachstums, die Gefahr des Auswucherns in Nachbargebiete, Abb. 5b die gegenseitige Abgrenzung der Keimzellen bei "gleichzeitigem"

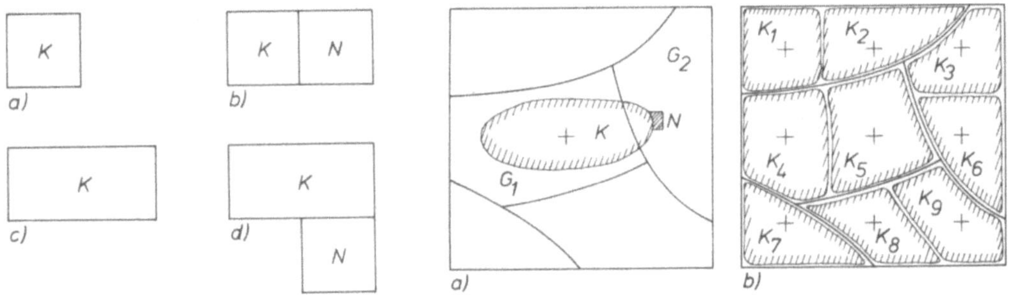

Abb. 4: Flächenwachs-   Abb. 5: a) Wachstum   b) Wachstum "gleich-
        tumsprinzip   sequentiell   zeitig"

Wachstum. Untersuchungen /6/ haben gezeigt, daß bei "gleichzeitigem" Wachstum die Abgrenzungen häufig nicht den Kontrastgrenzen entsprechen sondern zufällig entstehen. Ein weiterer Nachteil besteht in der Definition der Keimzellen, die entweder interaktiv festgelegt werden müssen oder automatisch durch systematische Verteilung nach Abb. 6 generiert werden. Der Nachteil der zweiten Vorgehensweise wird in Abb. 6 deutlich: Es werden Flächen entweder garnicht oder mehrfach erfaßt, oder es werden Kontrastzonen getroffen, die für eine Merkmalgenerierung ungeeignet sind. Abb. 7a zeigt ein Zwischenstadium, Abb. 7b das Ergebnis des Flächenwachstums in einem Intensitätsbild. Die Glättung der Flächenrandzonen erfordert eine umfangreiche Nachverarbeitung. Aufgrund der

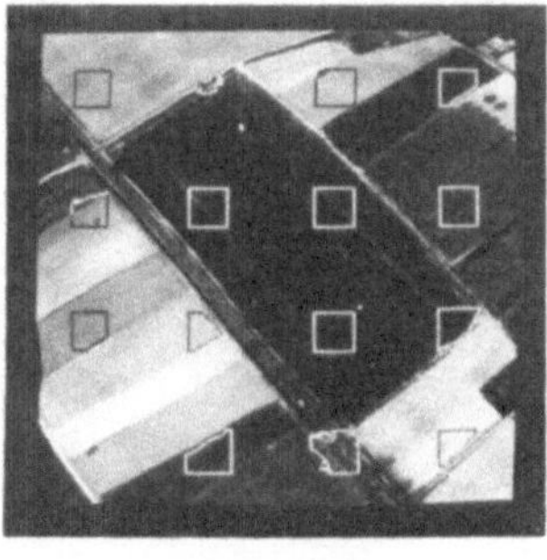  

Abb. 6: Keimzellen system. verteilt   **Abb. 7:** Keimzellen interaktiv verteilt
a) Zwischenwachstum b) Endstadium des Wachstumsprozesses

Speicherstruktur bei dem realisierten Verfahren entstehen Einschnürungen. Eine Bereichsseparierung wird mit diesem Verfahren nicht befriedigend gelöst.

Konzept zur Separierung von Bildbereichen

Systemstruktur

Ein zu konzipierendes neues System zur Separierung von Bildbereichen, basierend auf dem oben beschriebenen Flächenwachstum, muß folgenden Anforderungen genügen:

- automatische Generierung der für ein Flächenwachstum geeigneten Keimzellen;
- verbesserte Wachstumskriterien;
- verbesserte Speicherstruktur;
- konturgesteuerte Gebietsbegrenzung;
- Merkmalerzeugung durch gebietsbezogene iterative Verarbeitungsstruktur.

Abb. 8 zeigt die konzipierte Struktur des Verarbeitungssystems. Die Separierung der Bildbereiche wird mit einem Flächenwachstumsprozeß durchgeführt, der durch die vorher gewonnenen Konturinformationen gesteuert wird. Eine zusätzliche Steuerung erfolgt durch statistische Flächenmerkmale, die in den Keimzellen generiert werden und während des Wachstums verbessert werden können. Aus dem Konturbild werden nach der sog. Abstandstransformation Grundflächenbereiche generiert, die als Keimzellen dem Flächenwachstum zugeführt werden. Dieser Prozeß wiederholt sich iterativ für verschiedene Flächengrößentypen. Wenn der Separierungs-

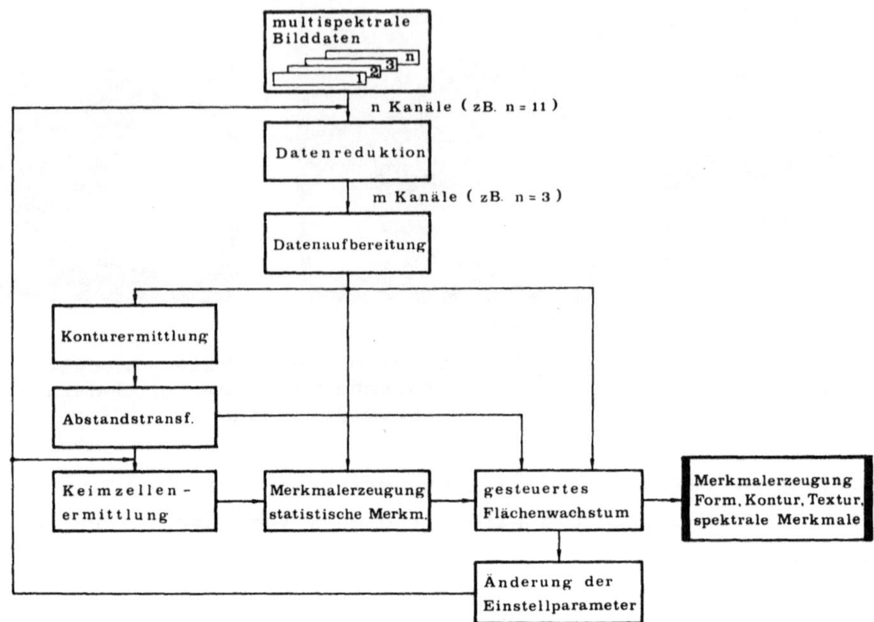

Abb. 8: Struktur der Bereichsseparierung (Blockdiagramm)

prozeß abgeschlossen ist, können die Verarbeitungsschritte nun mehrfach gebietsbezogen wiederholt werden. Dadurch besteht die Möglichkeit, Feinstrukturen und Merkmale höherer Ordnung zu extrahieren. Die einzelnen Verarbeitungsblöcke werden nachfolgend beschrieben.

Datenreduktion mit Hilfe der Hauptkomponentenanalyse

Geht man von multispektralem Bildmaterial mit z.B. 11 Kanälen aus, so ist für viele Objektflächen eine lineare Abhängigkeit zwischen den spektralen Kanälen festzustellen. Dies wird in Abb. 9 am zweidimensionalen Beispiel verdeutlicht. Es zeigt die Umhüllende einer Datenpopulation mit einer ausgeprägten Vorzugsrichtung. Die Projektion der Bildpunkte auf die Koordinatenachsen bringt für beide Kanäle etwa den gleichen Informationsgehalt.

Durch eine Lineartransformation des Koordinatensystems z.B. Drehung, so daß eine Koordinatenachse parallel zur Achse der Datenpopulation mit der größten Varianz verläuft (gestrichelte Koordinaten in Abb. 9), wird diese Abhängigkeit weitgehend beseitigt. Das bekannte Verfahren der Hauptkomponentenanalyse /9/ ermöglicht die Berechnung der Transforma-

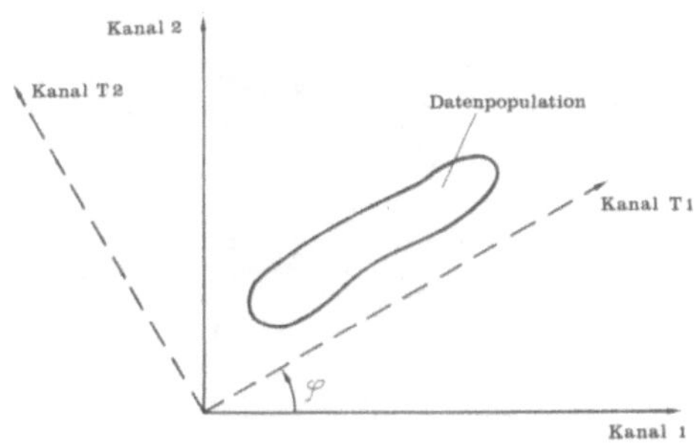

Abb. 9: Zur Hauptkomponentenanalyse

tionsvorschrift für die gegebenen n-kanaligen Bildvektoren. Auf eine
mathematische Formulierung wird hier verzichtet. Eine wichtige Eigenschaft der Transformation ist die, daß die Bildinformation auf die
ersten Kanäle komprimiert wird. Bei Abbruch der Transformation nach
den ersten m Komponenten wird der mittlere quadratische Fehler im Vergleich zu allen anderen möglichen Lineartransformationen ein Minimum.

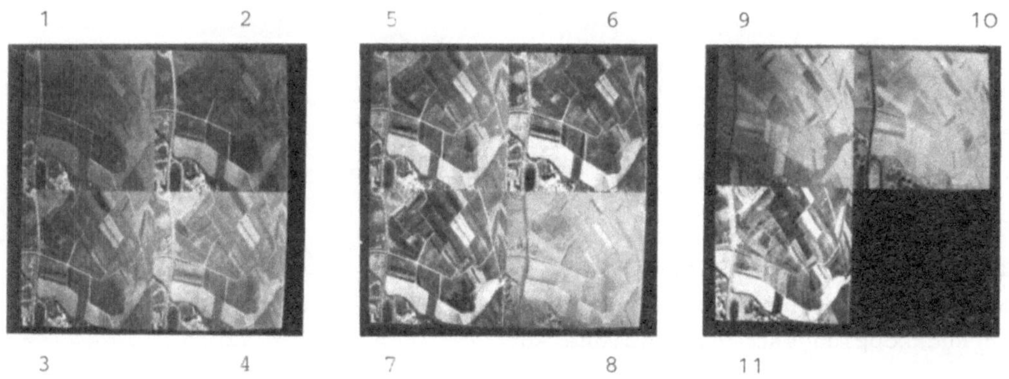

Abb. 10: Intensitätsbilder Luftbildausschnitt; 11 Kanäle

Abb. 10 zeigt die Intensitätsbilder eines 11-kanaligen Luftbildaus-
schnitts vor der Transformation, Abb. 11 die 11 Ergebniskanäle. Die
relative Größe der Eigenwerte λ_i (i = 1 ... 11), die ein Maß für die
Varianz der Informationen in den einzelnen Ergebniskanälen darstellen,
sind grafisch in Abb. 12 angegeben. Der mittlere quadratische Fehler
bei Weiterverarbeitung von m = 3 Kanälen beträgt $\bar{e}_{K3}^2$ = 0,022 = 2,2%.

Ein Problem ist die Schaffung neuer linearer Abhängigkeiten durch die
Transformation für einzelne vorher linear unabhängige Objekte, da die
Transformation die statistische Informationsverteilung des gesamten

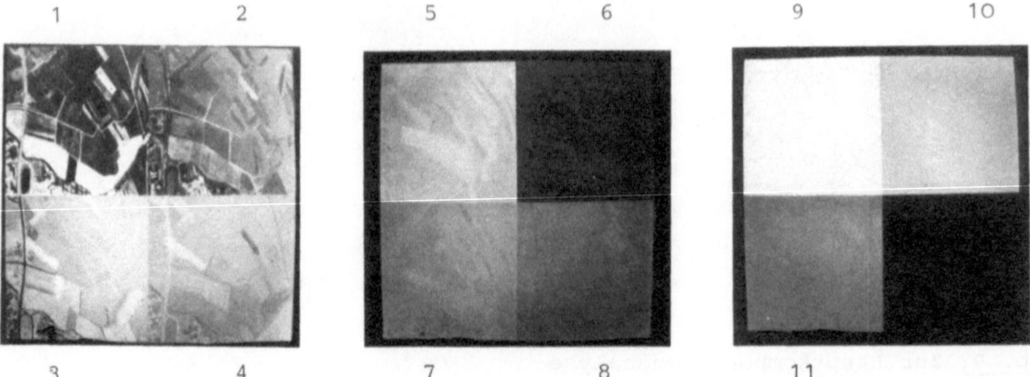

Abb. 11: Ergebnis der Transformation von Abb. 10; 11 Kanäle

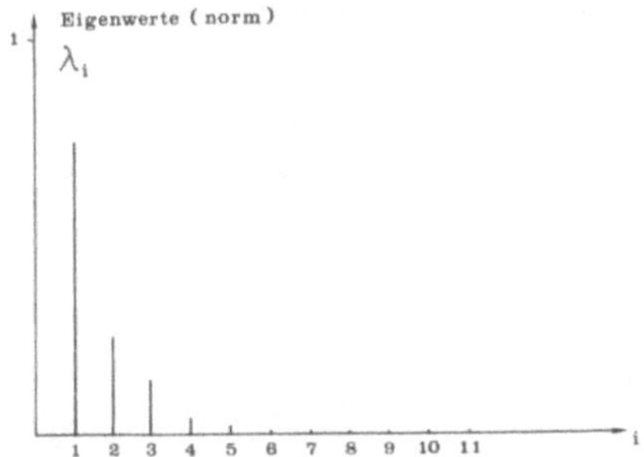

Abb. 12: Eigenwerte λ_i (i = 1 ... 11), normiert auf $\sum\limits_i \lambda_i$

Bildes berücksichtigt. Dies läßt sich korrigieren durch gebietsbezogene Hauptkomponentenanalyse zu einem späteren Verarbeitungszeitpunkt in einer Rückkopplungsschleife (siehe Abb. 8).

Datenaufbereitung

Oft ist es sinnvoll, eine Aufbereitung der Bilddaten zur Erzeugung möglichst guter Kontraste durchzuführen. Hierzu eignen sich Verfahren wie das lineare Spreizen des Varianzbereichs in jedem Kanal auf die zur Verfügung stehende Grauwertskala oder die Linearisierung der kumulativen Häufigkeitsverteilung nach Abb. 13. Hier wird die kumulative Häufigkeitsverteilung linearisiert. Abb. 14 zeigt die drei ersten Kanäle der Abb. 11 mit Histogrammeinblendung nach der Aufbereitung.

Konturermittlung in multispektralen Bilddaten

Eine Konturermittlung hat hier die Funktion

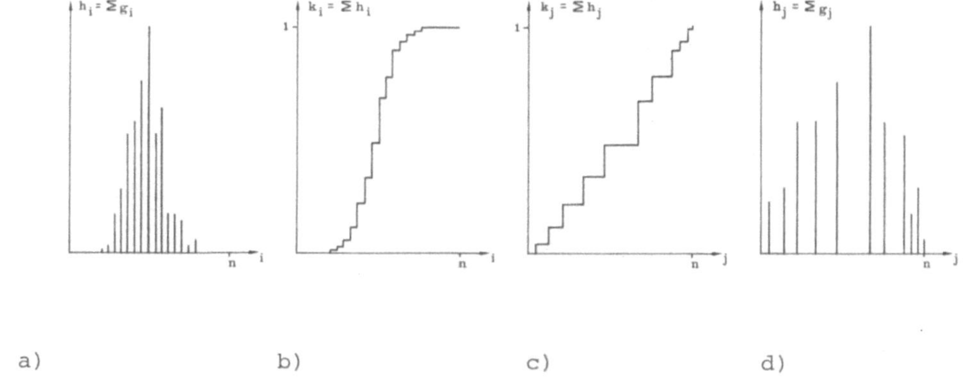

Abb. 13: Histogrammlinearisierung a) Histogramm, b) kumulative Häufigkeit,c) Häufigkeitsverteilung aus b) linarisiert,d) Ergebnishistogramm

Abb. 14: Ergebniskanäle 1, 2 und 3 aus Abb. 11 nach Anpassung, Histogramme eingeblendet

- einer vorläufigen Gebietsbegrenzung
- einer Steuerung des Wachstumsprozesses
- einer Stütze zur automatischen Generierung von Keimzellen

Verwendet werden können die bereits genannten Verfahren zur Hochpaßfilterung und zur Konturlinienermittlung. Zur Verarbeitung multispektraler Daten wurden drei Vorgehensweisen untersucht:

1. Die Hochpaßfilterung eines durch Überlagerung der Bildkanäle entstandenen Intensitätsbildes mit anschließender Konturlinienermittlung.

   Dies entspricht einer Projektion der Punktpopulation auf die Diago-

nale des m-dimensionalen Spektralraumes, die eine z.T. erhebliche Ver-
ringerung der Kontraste mit sich bringt und deshalb zu einem sehr
unvollständigen Konturbild führt.

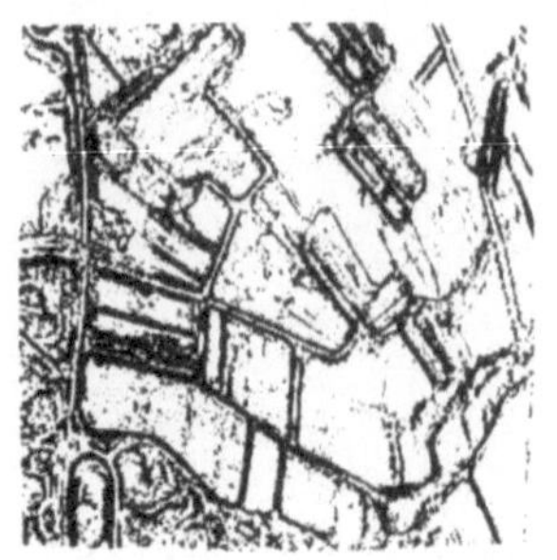

Kanal 1　　　　　　　　　　Kanal 2　　　　　　　　　　Kanal 3

<u>Abb. 15:</u> Hochpaßfilterung der Kanäle 1, 2 und 3

2. Die Hochpaßfilterung nach Kanälen getrennt (Abb. 15) mit anschließender Überlagerung der Kontrastgradienten und Konturlinienermittlung.
   Die Überlagerung ist in Abb. 17b, die resultierende Konturermittlung
   in Abb. 17c dargestellt.

Kanal 1　　　　　　　　　　Kanal 2　　　　　　　　　　Kanal 3

<u>Abb. 16:</u> Konturlinienfilterung der Kanäle 1, 2 und 3

3. Hochpaßfilterung und Konturlinienermittlung nach Kanälen getrennt mit
   anschließender Überlagerung der Ergebnisse. Die Konturlinienbilder
   sind in Abb. 16a, b und c, die Überlagerung in Abb. 17a dargestellt.

Ein Vergleich der Ergebnisse von 2. und 3. zeigt, daß beide Verfahren
weitgehend gleichwertig sind.

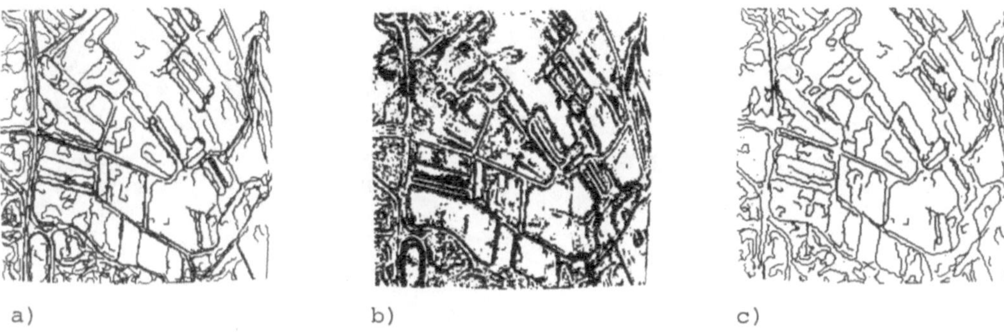

Abb. 17: a) Überlagerung der Kanäle Abb. 16, b) Überlagerung der Kanäle Abb. 15, c) Konturlinienfilterung von 17b

Abstandstransformation, Keimzellenermittlung

Durch eine sog. Abstandstransformation gelingt es, die Information über die Konturlinien in die konturfreien Flächenbereiche zu transformieren. Dies erfolgt durch Erzeugung sog. "Wellenfronten", d.h. Linien gleichen Abstandes, die sich von den Konturlinien ausgehend in die freie Fläche ausbreiten und in den Matrixpunkten abgespeichert werden. Diese Abstands- matrix dient der Keimzellenerfassung durch eine Schwellwertoperation. Damit werden die Bereiche der Abstandsmaxima erfaßt, die als Keimzellen für das Flächenwachstum benutzt werden. Es ist im Wechsel mit dem Wachs- tumsprozeß erforderlich, mehrere im Zahlenwert abnehmende Schwellen anzu- wenden, um sequentiell Flächen verschiedener Größenklassen zu erfassen. Abb. 18 zeigt erfaßte Flächen bei den Schwellen s = 12, 8, 6 und 4. Im Gegensatz zu der Darstellung in Abb. 18 werden die Bereiche, die durch den Wachstumsprozeß einmal bearbeitet worden sind, in der Abstandsmatrix gelöscht, so daß eine mehrmalige Erfassung durch die Keimzellengenerie- rung mit niedrigeren Schwellen vermieden wird.

Die Steuerfunktion der Abstandsmatrix wird z.B. folgenden Forderungen gerecht:

- kein Wachstum über eine Konturlinie, oder
- kein Wachstum über ein Abstandsminimum
- Veränderung statistischer Parameter bis zum Abstand k
- Neuberechnung statistischer Parameter bei Abstand l
- Änderung der Wachstumsstrategie bei Abstand m

Gesteuertes Flächenwachstum, Merkmalerzeugung

Das Prinzip des Flächenwachstums wurde bereits erläutert. Der wesentli-

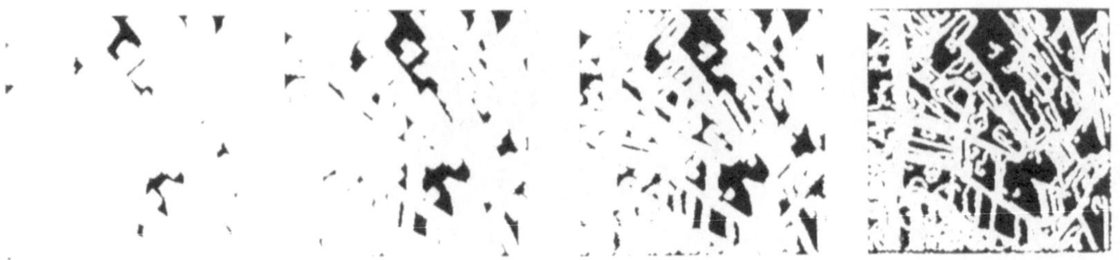

Abb. 18: Zur Keimzellenerfassung

che Unterschied besteht in der Steuerung durch die Abstandsmatrix, die
für jeden Bildpunkt dessen Abstand zur nächstliegenden Kontur angibt.
Ein Wachstum über eine bereits gefundene Konturlinie hinaus wird dadurch
vermieden, eine Änderung der Verarbeitungsstrategie in den kritischen
Konturzonen ermöglicht.

Merkmale werden zunächst in der Keimzelle der Mindestgröße n (z.B.
n = 100 Elemente) ermittelt, z.B. statistische Merkmale wie:

- Mittelwert: $MIT = \sum_g g \cdot h(g)$

- Varianz: $VAR = \sum_g (g-MIT)^2 \cdot h(g)$

- Schiefe: $SCH = \sum_g (g-MIT)^3 \cdot h(g)$

     mit $h(g)$ = relative Häufigkeit des Grauwertes g (g = 1 ... G)

- Mehrgipfligkeit des Histogramms.

Diese Merkmale werden für alle zu verarbeitenden Kanäle ermittelt. Sie
charakterisieren einige Flächenklassen, z.B. sehr kleine Varianz in
allen Kanälen $\triangleq$ homogener Farbton, oder Histogramm mit zwei ausgeprägten Gipfeln, oder charakteristische Schiefe eines Histogramms usw.,
nach denen die Wachstumsstrategie ausgewählt wird. Abb. 19 zeigt zwei
verschiedene Vorgehensweisen bei der Anlagerung von Punkten p_N. Nach
Abb. 19a werden die Intensitätskomponenten von Punkt p_N geprüft, ob sie
innerhalb entsprechender Vertrauensintervalle liegen, die aus den Mittel-
werten und Varianzen der Kanäle von K berechnet wurden. Diese Prüfung
ist nur sinnvoll bei sehr kleinen Varianzen in K, d.h. homogenem Farbton
des Gebiets.

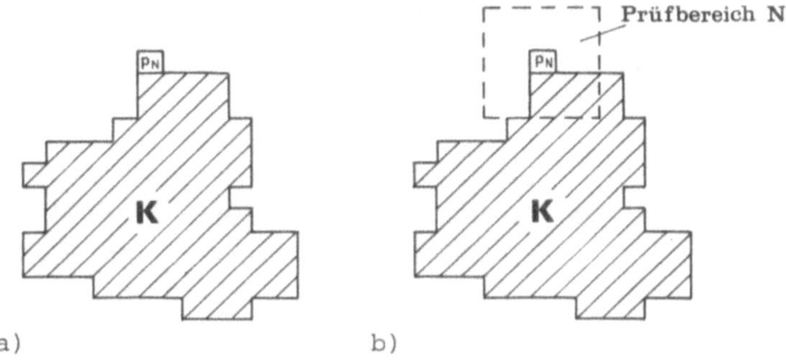

Abb. 19: Flächenwachstum a) punktuelle Auswertung, b) Gebietsauswertung

In anderen Fällen erfolgt die Auswertung eines Prüfbereichs von m x m Elementen in der Umgebung von p_N, z.B. mit m = 5 (Abb. 19b), in dem die statistischen Merkmale errechnet und mit denen der Keimzelle verglichen werden. Zur Bestimmung des Vertrauensbereichs kann die χ^2-Funktion oder der Kolmogoroff-Smirnow-Test, wenn die kumulative Häufigkeitsverteilung von K bekannt ist, angewendet werden. In Abb. 20 ist die kumulative Häufigkeit der Grauwerte g der Kanäle zweier Bereiche aufgetragen. Ein Ähnlichkeitskriterium besteht z.B. in der Größe der von

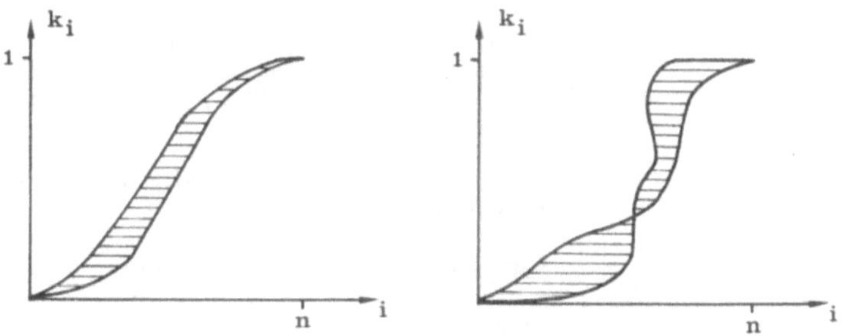

Abb. 20: Vergleich kumulativer Häufigkeiten

beiden Kurven eingeschlossenen Fläche (schraffiert), oder im maximalen Abstand der beiden Kurven. Nach den dargestellten Verfahren werden nicht alle Bereiche eines Mehrkanalbildes erfaßt werden können, insbesondere solche Bereiche, für die eine Beschreibung mit den bisher ermittelten Merkmalen nicht ausreicht. Für diese restlichen Bereiche besteht die Möglichkeit, eine nochmalige gebietsbezogene Hauptkomponentenanalyse, Differentiation und Konturermittlung durchzuführen, damit weitere Texturmerkmale erzeugt werden können. Diese Merkmale beziehen sich z.B. auf eine Kontrast-, Gradienten- und Linienlängenanalyse

Stand der Arbeiten

Bisher wurden umfangreiche Untersuchungen zu den einzelnen Verarbeitungsschritten Datenreduktion, Datenaufbereitung, Bilddifferentiation, Konturermittlung und Flächenwachstum durchgeführt. Der Aufbau der Programmstruktur nach Abb. 8 und Untersuchungen zur geeigneten Merkmalerzeugung werden zur Zeit durchgeführt. Eine Implementierung der notwendigen lokalen Bildoperationen mit einem Parallelprozessor, der zur Zeit aufgebaut wird, ist vorgesehen.

Literaturhinweise

/1/   Dittel, R.H.   "Digitale Auswertung multispektraler Bilddaten"
Lehrgang Nr. 3015/46.12, Techn. Akademie Esslingen 1976

/2/   Nagao, M.   "Agricultural Land Use Classification of Aerial Photographs by Histogram Similarity Method"

/3/   Holdermann, F.
Kazmierczak, H.   "Preprocessing of Grey-Scale Pictures"
Computer Graphics and Image Processing Vol. 1, No. 1. pp. 60-88, 1972

/4/   Enderle, G.   "Ermittlung von parallelen Konturen in einem vorverarbeiteten Grautonbild"
Diplomarbeit am NTI, Universität Karlsruhe 1970

/5/   Schärf, R.   "Erzeugung linienhafter Bildmuster aus Grautonbildern mit Hilfe der Kontrastgradienten"
BMVg-FBWT 73-10, Karlsruhe 1973

/6/   Ernst, D.   "Zweidimensionale Ermittlung der Gebietszugehörigkeit in Luftbildern"
FIM-Bericht Nr. 32, Karlsruhe 1976

/7/   Ernst, D.
Bargel, B.
Holdermann, F.   "Processing of Remote Sensing Data by a Region Growing Algorithm"
III. International Joint Conference on Pattern Recognition, Colorado, California 1976

/8/   Bargel, B.   "Nutzeranalyse zur Fernerkundung in der BRD mit Bewertung der digitalen Bildverarbeitung"
FIM-Bericht Nr. 28, Karlsruhe 1975

/9/   Niemann, H.   "Methoden der Mustererkennung"
Akademische Verlagsgesellschaft, Frankfurt a.M. 1974

BESCHREIBUNG EINES SYSTEMS ZUR VORVERARBEITUNG
MULTISPEKTRALER SCANNERDATEN

H. Engel, J. Gredel, W. Rattei

DFVLR - GSOC, 8031 Oberpfaffenhofen

Zusammenfassung. Mit der ständig wachsenden Anzahl von Fernerkundungsdaten, die mit multispektralen Scannersystemen gewonnen werden, ergibt sich nach der Datenakquisition die Notwendigkeit einer routinemäßigen Vorverarbeitung, um den wissenschaftlichen Nutzern das für die Auswertungen notwendige Datenmaterial zur Verfügung zu stellen. Für diese Vorverarbeitungsaufgaben im Rahmen des erdwissenschaftlichen Flugzeugmeßprogrammes (FMP) der Bundesrepublik Deutschland wurde in der Hauptabteilung Raumflugbetrieb der DFVLR die Bildkonvertierungsanlage aufgebaut, ein Softwaresystem (ARGUS) für Bilddatenvorverarbeitung am Großrechner entwickelt, ein Fotolabor eingerichtet und ein Datenmanagementsystem bereitgestellt.

Diese Systeme bieten im Routinebetrieb die folgenden Möglichkeiten:

- Quick-Look für Scannerdaten
- Datenumsetzung von Analog- auf Digital-Magnetband
- Bilderzeugung
- fotografische Entwicklung
- Datenvorverarbeitung - Kontrastverbesserung, radiometrische und geometrische Korrekturen - für ausgewählte Daten auf Anforderung
- Datenmanagement (Archivierung, Datenverteilung).

1. Einleitung. Seit März 1976 wird in der Bundesrepublik Deutschland das erdwissenschaftliche Flugzeugmeßprogramm (FMP) durchgeführt. Im Rahmen dieses Projekts wird ein wesentlicher Teil der Fernerkundungsdaten mit einem Multispektral-Scanner (M^2S) der Firma Bendix akquiriert und auf Analogmagnetband aufgezeichnet. In Ergänzung dieses Systems stehen ein Präzisions-Strahlungs-Thermometer (PRT5), ein LANDSAT-kompatibles Radiometer (EXOTECH), ein umfassendes Avionik-System und fotografische Aufnahme-Systeme, bestehend aus 6 Hasselblad-Kameras und einer Zeiss-Reihenmeßkamera, zur Verfügung. Alle nicht fotografischen Daten werden mit hoher Schreibdichte auf 12 Spuren eines 14-Spur-Analogmagnetbandes (HDDT) aufgezeichnet. Zur routinemäßigen Aufbereitung und Bilderzeugung von Scannerdaten wurde in der Hauptabteilung Raumflugbetrieb der DFVLR die Bildkonvertierungsanlage (BKA) geplant und aufgebaut. Zur Ergänzung dieser Anlage für Vorverarbeitungsschritte, die den Prozeßrechner-Rahmen überschreiten, wurde ein Softwaresystem am Großrechner unter der Bezeichnung ARGUS entwickelt. Im folgenden wird ein Überblick über Hardware, Software und Datenformate der BKA gegeben und es wird das Programmsystem ARGUS dargestellt.

2. **Bildkonvertierungsanlage BKA.** Für die routinemäßige Datenaufbereitung und Bilderzeugung der Scannerdaten des Flugzeugmeßprogramms wurde im GSOC (German Space Operations Center) die Bildkonvertierungsanlage aufgebaut. An dieser Anlage können auch auf Anforderung Methoden der Vorverarbeitung durchgeführt werden. Seit Anfang 1976 wird dieses System operationell für die Aufgaben im Rahmen des FMP eingesetzt. Außerdem bietet die BKA Möglichkeiten zur Datenverarbeitung und Bildausgabe anderer multispektraler Scanner-Systeme (LANDSAT, SMS).

2.1 **Hardware.** Bild 2.1 zeigt die Hardware-Konfiguration der Bildkonvertierungsanlage. Das System besteht aus einem Prozeßrechner mit Standardperipherie sowie Prozeßperipherie zur Durchführung von Quick-Look, Aufbereitung und Bilderzeugung. Der Prozeßrechner ist ein schneller, byte-orientierter Minirechner mit 64 KByte Kernspeicher, 10 MByte Plattenspeicher, 4 Magnetbandgeräten (9 Spuren, 800 / 1600 BPI), einem Kartenleser, einem Schnelldrucker und DMA-Kanälen zum Anschluß von Prozeßperipherie. Die Herstellersoftware besteht aus einem Echtzeit-Plattenbetriebssystem, Assembler, FORTRAN-IV-Compiler und Testhilfen.
Folgende Geräte gehören zur Prozeßperipherie der BKA:

- Ein Analogmagnetbandgerät, Typ Ampex FR 2000, zur Wiedergabe der auf 14/28-Spur-Bändern aufgezeichneten Scannerdaten.
- Ein FMP-Scansynchronisierer als Interface zwischen Bandgerät und Rechner für Synchronisation, Deskewing und parallelem Datentransfer für 12 Kanäle.
- Ein oszillographisches Aufzeichnungsgerät, Typ Honeywell Modell 1856, das eine Grauwertaufzeichnung zur Durchführung eines Quick-Look ermöglicht. Dieses System kann am Rechner oder off-line betrieben werden.
- Ein Trommel-Bildein/ausgabesystem mit Rechnerinterface zur hochauflösenden Bildabtastung/belichtung. Das Gerät, Typ LINOSCAN der Firma Linotype-Paul Ltd. (England), hat ein Lesesystem zum Abtasten von Farbvorlagen und vier Schreibsysteme zur gleichzeitigen Belichtung von 4 Schwarz/weiss-Bildern mit 7 Bit radiometrischer Auflösung. Zwei Planfilme im Format 50 x 32 cm^2 können auf der Trommel aufgespannt werden. Bei der FMP-Bilderzeugung arbeiten zwei der vier Schreibsysteme bei einer Trommelgeschwindigkeit von 5 U/sec und einer Schreibdichte von 16 Linien/mm.

2.2 **Software.** Die zur Bearbeitung der FMP-Aufgabenstellungen entwickelte Software besteht im wesentlichen aus Programmpaketen für Quick-Look-Filmerstellung, Datenaufbereitung, Bilderzeugung und aus Vorverarbeitungsprogrammen für solche Operationen, die während des Echtzeitprozesses der Band-Konvertierung oder Bilderzeugung nicht durchgeführt werden können. Diese Anwenderprogramme verwenden spezielle Treiber zur

Datenein/ausgabe und allgemein verwendbare Unterprogramme, wie z.B. einen Software-
Zeichengenerator oder Codekonvertierungsroutinen. Zusätzlich mußte ein Satz von
Dienst- und Hilfsprogrammen für Anlagenaufbau und Wartung entwickelt werden.

Das Quick-Look-Ausgabeprogramm bietet die Möglichkeit, einzelne Spektralbereiche
oder Auszüge aller 11 Spektralbereiche auf QL-Filmrecorder auszugeben. Der Quick-
Look-Film dient der ersten Kontrolle der FMP-Scanner-Daten und wird für die Freigabe
des anfallenden Bildmaterials benötigt.

Das Datenaufbereitungsprogramm sorgt für die Umsetzung der Analogbänder (HDDT's) in
rechnerkompatible Bänder (CCT's). Dabei werden Sensordaten und Zusatzinformationen
vom Analogband über den Scansynchronisierer byteweise korreliert im Wechselpufferbe-
trieb in den Datenkonvertierungsrechner eingelesen und nach Durchführung von Kali-
brierungen und Umformatierungen auf rechnerkompatible Magnetbänder geschrieben.
Während der Aufbereitung werden kanalspezifische Mittelwerte und Varianzen bestimmt
und die Werte werden mit ins Etikett aufgenommen. Ebenso werden Zusatzdaten (Funk-
tionsüberwachungsdaten, Navigationsdaten und Zeitinformationen) extrahiert, kontrol-
liert und auf Digitalplatte zwischengespeichert, um nach Abschluß der Aufbereitung
ein Fluglog auf Schnelldrucker erstellen zu können.

Die Aufgabe des Bilderzeugungsprogrammes besteht darin, die aufbereiteten Bänder zu
lesen und die Scannerdaten unter Verwendung des Bildausgabesystems in S/W-Bildmate-
rial umzusetzen. Dabei können beim FMP die Daten aller 11 Spektralbereiche inklusive
Filmbeschriftung und Graukeile in einem Durchgang auf 2 S/W-Transparente aufgezeichnet werden. Bei der Bildausgabe können unter Verwendung von Table-Look-Up-Verfahren
Grauwertmanipulationen, wie die Anpassung der Videodaten an die Eigenschaften des
Ausgabesystems (Lampenkennlinie, Filmgamma) oder verschiedene Möglichkeiten der Bild-
verbesserung, wie Kontrastverstärkung usw., durchgeführt werden. Für den freien
Kanal 12 des Planfilms 2 stehen den Nutzern Optionen zur Verfügung für die Ausgabe
von Meßwerten des Strahlungsthermometers (PRT5) als Kurvenzug aus den Zusatzinfor-
mationen und für Mittelwert-, Differenz- und Ratiobildausgaben jeweils einzelner
Kanäle. Ausgewählte Zusatzinformationen der Spur 12 des HDDT's und Daten aus dem
CCT-Etikett können auf Schnelldrucker protokolliert werden.

2.3 Datenformate. Das FMP-CCT-Format (Bild 2.2) basiert auf dem im Johnson Space
Center verwendeten Universal Imagery Format. Die Datenaufzeichnung erfolgt auf 9-Spur-
Bändern mit 800 / 1600 BPI und ungerader Parität. Die Bänder sind etikettiert, Grauwerte werden durch Bytes (8 Bit binär) dargestellt und Daten verschiedener Spektralbereiche sind zeilenweise nacheinander angeordnet und mit den Zusatzinformationen
(Spur 12 des HDDT) korreliert. Auf einem 1600 BPI-Band sind 3200 Zeilen aufgezeichnet
(ca. 10 KByte/Zeile).

Das <u>FMP-Bildformat</u> ist in Bild 2.3 aufgezeigt. Die Aufzeichnung erfolgt auf 2 S/W-Transparenten, auf denen je 6 Spektralbereiche nebeneinander dargestellt werden. Das Bildmaterial wird beschriftet und neben geometrischen Bezugsmarkierungen werden verschiedene Graukeile zur Qualitätskontrolle und als Referenz für densitometrische Auswertungen aufgezeichnet.

Parallel zu den Aufgaben im Rahmen des FMP wurde an der BKA ein Programmsystem entwickelt und integriert, das die Vorverarbeitung und Bilderzeugung mit Koordinatenberechnungen von LANDSAT-Daten ermöglicht, die von der italienischen LANDSAT-Bodenstation in Fucino aufgenommen werden und in Form rechnerkompatibler Bänder bezogen werden können. Dieses Programm wurde auf Wunsch vieler Anwender erweitert, so daß auch die Bilderzeugung von NASA-LANDSAT-Daten durchgeführt werden kann. Bei der Bildausgabe können Bildverbesserungen mit Hilfe von Table-Look-Up-Verfahren und Korrekturen der Erdrotation berücksichtigt werden, ebenso können die entsprechenden Histogramme auf Schnelldrucker ausgegeben werden. Bild 2.4 zeigt eine <u>Bildausgabe von LANDSAT-Daten.</u>

3. ARGUS – ein Programmsystem zur digitalen Bilddatenverarbeitung am Großrechner

3.1 Aufgabenstellung. Aus der Aufgabenstellung des Nutzers von Bilddaten aus der
Fernerkundung und den Möglichkeiten eines Prozeßrechnersystems, die unter Punkt 2.
umrissen wurden, ergibt sich ein Bedarf für Bilddatenverarbeitung am Großrechner.
Im FMP stellt z.B. eine Scanzeile in allen 11 Spektralbereichen einschließlich Zusatzinformationen einen Datenblock mit 10 KByte Länge dar. Wechselpuffer für Ein-
und Ausgabe belegen in diesem Fall bereits 40 KByte. Allgemein stellt das Handling
großer Datenmengen eine grundsätzliche Anforderung der Bilddatenverarbeitung dar.
Die Rechenzeitanforderungen sind so unterschiedlich wie die Verarbeitungsalgorithmen für eine einfache Kontrastverbesserung oder die geometrische Korrektur auf der
Grundlage von Paßpunkten.

Das Programmsystem soll geeignete Datenschnittstellen für die einzelnen Verarbei-
tungsroutinen aufweisen und eine modulare Programmstruktur besitzen. Die Verarbeitung ausgewählten Datenmaterials soll operationell durchgeführt werden, darüberhinaus muß das Programmsystem einen flexiblen Rahmen für die Entwicklung neuer Software und die Integration von Fremd-Modulen bieten. Eine problemorientierte Programmiersprache, wie FORTRAN oder PL/1, erleichtert generell den Programmaustausch.
Software-Entwicklung zur digitalen Bilddatenverarbeitung wird an verschiedenen Orten
betrieben, so daß inzwischen sogar schon komplette Programmsysteme verfügbar sind.
Die Übertragung solcher Systeme auf ein anderes Rechnersystem stellt in der Regel
eine hohe Anforderung an Personalkapazität, weil Rechnersysteme nicht kompatibel sind
und Assembler-Routinen ohnehin neu zu formulieren sind.
Aus dieser Erkenntnis wurde im GSOC der DFVLR das Programmsystem ARGUS entwickelt,
um im Rahmen des FMP die Anforderungen für Datenvorverarbeitung an zentraler Stelle
zu erfüllen und Vorarbeiten für meteorologische Bilddatenverarbeitung zu unter-
stützen.

3.2 Programm-Organisation. ARGUS besitzt ein Hauptprogramm, das den Ablauf von un-
tergeordneten Programm-Modulen parametergesteuert koordiniert. Kernspeicherresident
sind das Hauptprogramm, allgemeine Unterprogramme und COMMON-Bereiche für Parameter
und Daten. Die verschiedenen Verarbeitungs-Module und Ein-/Ausgabeprogramme werden
als Overlay-Routinen nach Maßgabe von Parametern nur im Bedarfsfall geladen. Auf diese Weise wird ein minimaler Kernspeicherbedarf für das Programmsystem realisiert.
Darüberhinaus besteht eine einheitliche Datenschnittstelle für alle ARGUS-Funktionen,
die Anpassung der Datenorganisation vom CCT-Format (z-B. Line / Pixel interleaving)
erfolgt in der Eingabe-Prozedur.
Der Ablauf des Hauptprogramms (s. Bild 3.1) beginnt mit der Parameterversorgung für
die Auswahl der Ein-/Ausgabe-Medien (Magnetband, -Platte) und -Formate (FMP, LAND-
SAT, usw.) und für die Spezifikation der Verarbeitungsfunktion. Auf Grund der vorliegenden Parameterspezifikationen werden vom Hauptprogramm die angezeigten Overlay-
Routinen geladen und zur Ausführung des Verarbeitungs-Moduls verzweigt. Innerhalb der

Verarbeitungsfunktion wird in einer entsprechenden Initialisierungsphase eine Parameterversorgung für funktionsspezifische Parameter durchgeführt. Danach erfolgt die
Ausführung der Verarbeitungsfunktion. Das Hauptprogramm durchläuft eine Schleife für
die beschriebene Schrittfolge, bis alle angezeigten ARGUS-Funktionen durchgeführt
sind.

Das Interesse des ARGUS-Nutzers besteht in der Fragestellung, was ist zu tun, um
einen ARGUS-Job für eine vorliegende Problemstellung vorzubereiten. Zum anderen ist
er daran interessiert, wie ist eine ARGUS-Funktion zu implementieren, um einen neuen
Algorithmus zu entwickeln. In diesem Fall sind die Daten- und Parameternahtstellen
von ARGUS zu beachten, das CCT-Datenformat ist nach der einmaligen Programmierung der
Ein-/Ausgabe-Prozeduren nicht mehr von Interesse.

Für die erste Fragestellung wurde in ARGUS eine Parameterversorgung auf der Grundlage
des FORTRAN-NAMELIST programmiert, die eine formatfreie Parameter-Spezifikation bedeutet. Das folgende Beispiel gibt die Parameter-Spezifikation für das READ NAMELIST
des Hauptprogramms:

```
&PARAM, FUNKTN='FMPPAN', CCTIN='FMPB', CCTOUT='FMPB',
        LABEL='BANDE1','BANDE2','BANDA1','BANDA2',
        FBAND=2,2, SL =1, LI=1, LL=3200, SS=1, SI=1, LS=803,
   &END
```

In der gleichen formatfreien Form werden funktionsspezifische Parameter durch ein
weiteres READ NAMELIST Statement in der Funktion aufgenommen.

3.3 <u>Ein-/Ausgabe-Programme.</u> Die ARGUS-Ein-/Ausgabe-Programme werden gemäß Parameter-
Spezifikation dem CCT-Format entsprechend als Overlay-Routinen geladen und führen den
Datentransfer vom/zum externen Medium (Magnetband, -Platte) zum/vom COMMON-Bereich
durch, der unabhängig vom CCT-Format organisiert ist. Der Aufruf erfolgt in der ARGUS-
Funktion in standardisierter Form 'CALL READ'/ 'CALL WRITE' für einen Datensatz (z.B.
eine Bildzeile). Mit Hilfe der Parameter-Spezifikation für den gewünschten Bildausschnitt (Starting Line / Sample, Last Line / Sample) und die Auflösung (Line / Sample
Increment) erfolgt die erforderliche Band-Positionierung intern in der Leseroutine,
für die aufrufende Funktion wird nur der gewünschte Datensatz in den COMMON-Bereich
übertragen.

Bisher stehen Leseroutinen für die CCT-Formate FMP, LANDSAT, NIMBUS, SMS, SKYLAB und
DIBIAS zur Verfügung. Magnetband-Schreibroutinen wurden für das FMP-CCT und das GSOC-
Standard-Format entwickelt, damit ist der Übergang zur Bildausgabe der manipulierten
Daten an der BKA möglich. Die Ergänzung dieser Liste von Ein-/Ausgabe-Routinen um
neue CCT-Formate ist im Bedarfsfalle leicht möglich.

3.4 <u>Verarbeitungs-Funktionen.</u> Eine ARGUS-Funktion stellt den Programm-Modul dar, in
dem die Datenmanipulation im Hinblick auf die Nutzer-orientierte Aufgabenstellung
durchgeführt wird. Die Funktion wird als Overlay-Routine geladen und steht über COM-

MON-Bereiche mit dem übrigen ARGUS-Rahmen in Verbindung. Der Programmablauf einer
Funktion geht aus Bild 3.2 hervor. Tabelle 3.1 gibt einen Überblick über die gegen-
wärtig verfügbaren ARGUS-Funktionen einschließlich der vorhandenen Optionen.
Es ist geplant, ein Programmpaket zur geometrischen Rektifizierung mit Hilfe von
Paßpunkten in ARGUS zu integrieren.
Die bisherige Programmentwicklung erfolgte auf einer TR440-Rechenanlage. Im Rahmen
des neuen DFVLR-Rechnerkonzeptes wird zukünftig die leistungsfähigere Anlage AMDAHL
470 V/6 zur Verfügung stehen. Für die Programmstellung ist angestrebt, bisherige
Assembler-Routinen durch PL/1-Prozeduren zu ersetzen. Für zukünftige Aufgaben im
Bereich Bilddatenverarbeitung, die am Großrechner durchzuführen sind, wird das GSOC
ARGUS weiter ausbauen und betreiben.

4. <u>Quellennachweis</u>

(1)   M. Wahl, A. Flasche
      The First Approach to Realizing a German Earth Resource Program.
      Proc. Remote Sensing of the Environment, Ann Arbor,
      Oct. 1975

(2)   F. Seige
      Sensor Equipment of the German Earth Scientific Airplane Program.
      Proc. NASA Earth Resources Survey Symposium, Houston / Texas,
      June 1975

(3)   BENDIX, Aerospace Systems Division
      Modular Digital Multispectral Data Acquisition and Data
      Processing Systems.
      Ann Arbor, Michigan,
      Oct. 1973

(4)   FMP-Nutzerhandbuch
      Beschreibung der GSOC-Anlagen und -Datenformate für Routine-
      Bildverarbeitung.

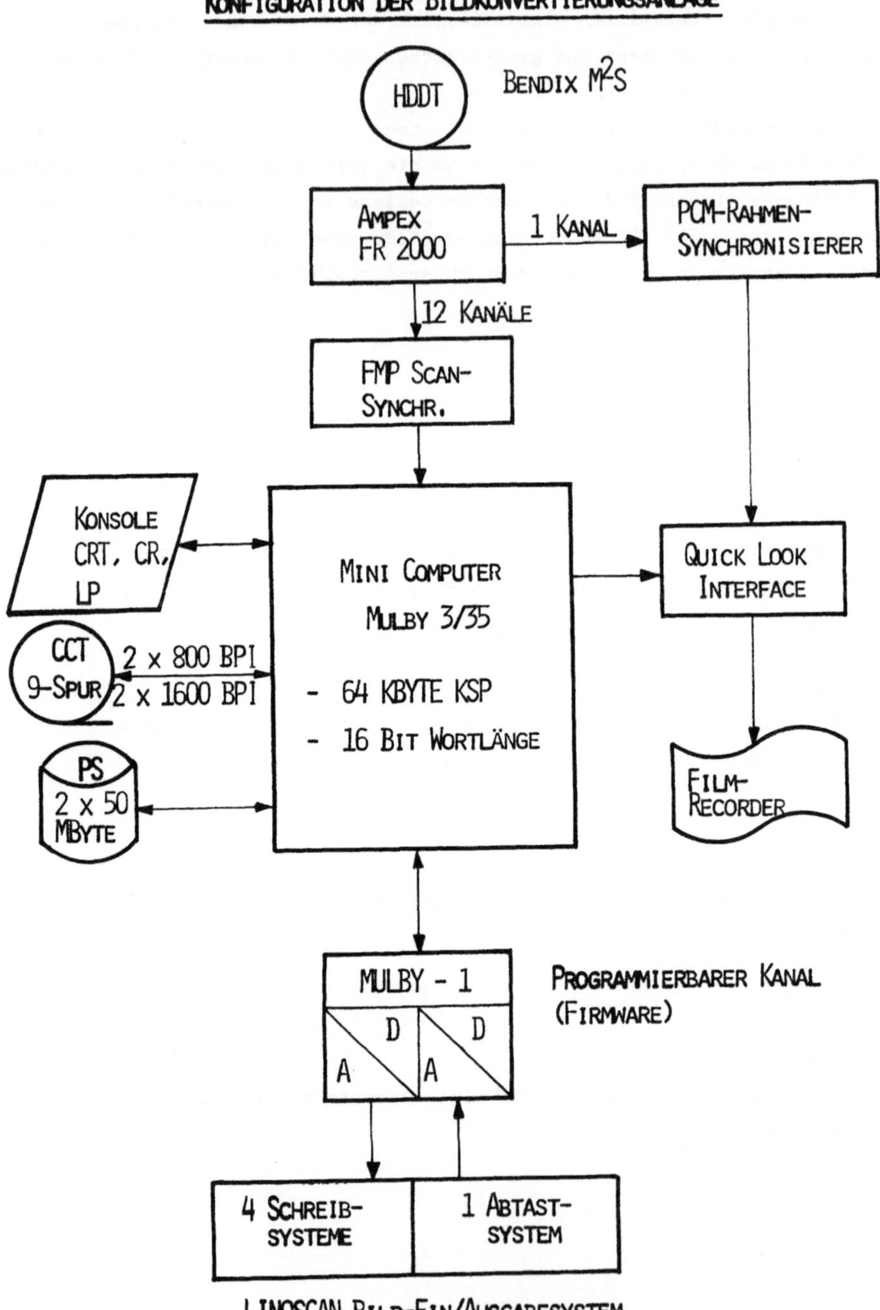

BILD 2.1
KONFIGURATION DER BILDKONVERTIERUNGSANLAGE
HDDT
BENDIX M²S
AMPEX FR 2000
1 KANAL
PCM-RAHMEN-SYNCHRONISIERER
12 KANÄLE
FMP SCAN-SYNCHR.
KONSOLE CRT, CR, LP
MINI COMPUTER MULBY 3/35
- 64 KBYTE KSP
- 16 BIT WORTLÄNGE
QUICK LOOK INTERFACE
CCT 9-SPUR
2 x 800 BPI
2 x 1600 BPI
PS 2 x 50 MBYTE
FILM-RECORDER
MULBY - 1
D
A
D
A
PROGRAMMIERBARER KANAL (FIRMWARE)
4 SCHREIB-SYSTEME
1 ABTAST-SYSTEM
LINOSCAN BILD-EIN/AUSGABESYSTEM

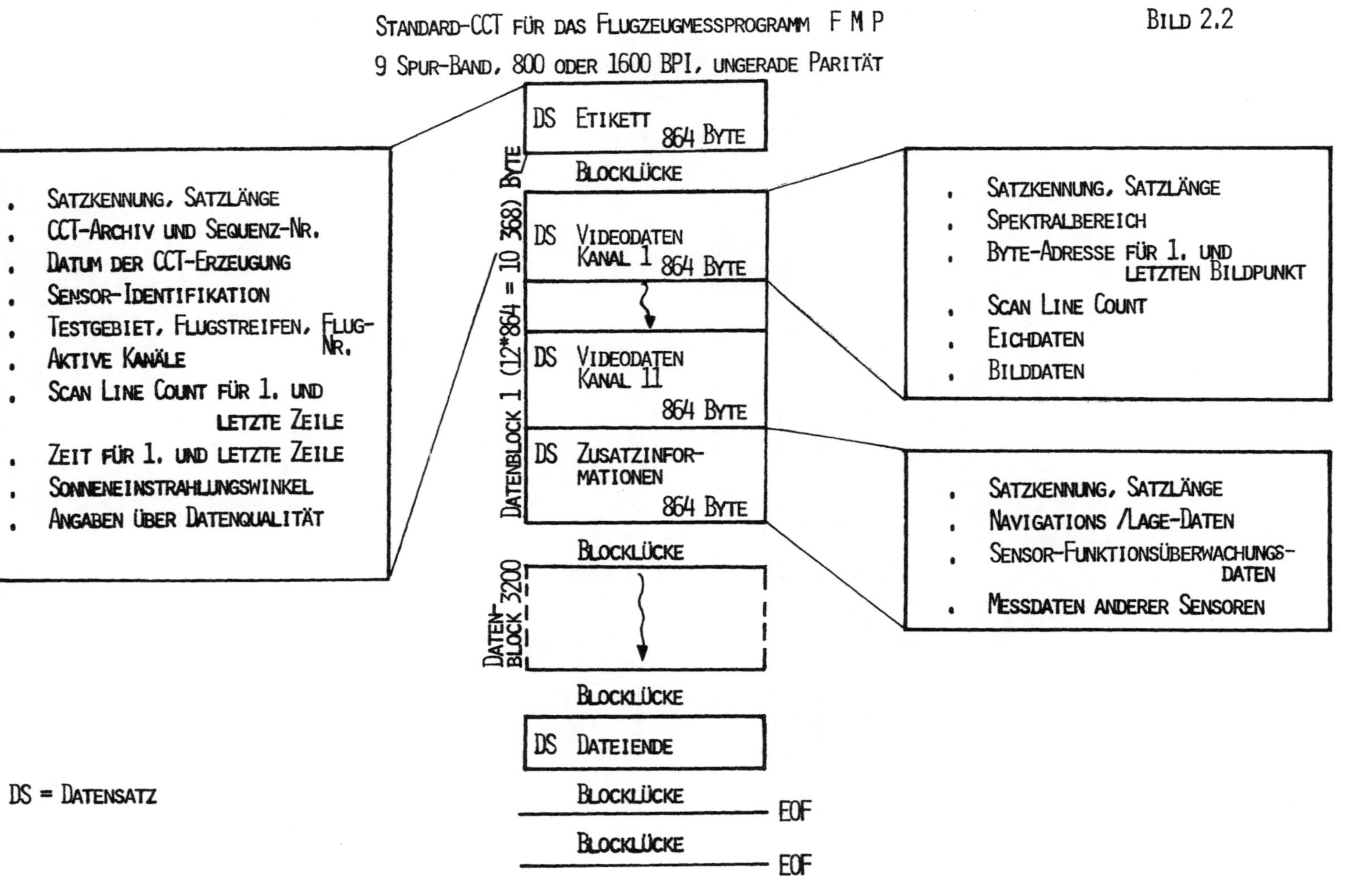

Standard-CCT für das Flugzeugmessprogramm F M P
9 Spur-Band, 800 oder 1600 BPI, ungerade Parität
Bild 2.2
303
DS Etikett 864 Byte
Blocklücke
DS Videodaten Kanal 1 864 Byte
DS Videodaten Kanal 11 864 Byte
DS Zusatzinformationen 864 Byte
Datenblock 1 (12*864 = 10 368) Byte
Blocklücke
Daten-Block 3200
Blocklücke
DS Dateiende
Blocklücke
EOF
Blocklücke
EOF
Satzkennung, Satzlänge
CCT-Archiv und Sequenz-Nr.
Datum der CCT-Erzeugung
Sensor-Identifikation
Testgebiet, Flugstreifen, Flug-Nr.
Aktive Kanäle
Scan Line Count für 1. und letzte Zeile
Zeit für 1. und letzte Zeile
Sonneneinstrahlungswinkel
Angaben über Datenqualität
Satzkennung, Satzlänge
Spektralbereich
Byte-Adresse für 1. und letzten Bildpunkt
Scan Line Count
Eichdaten
Bilddaten
Satzkennung, Satzlänge
Navigations /Lage-Daten
Sensor-Funktionsüberwachungs-Daten
Messdaten anderer Sensoren
DS = Datensatz

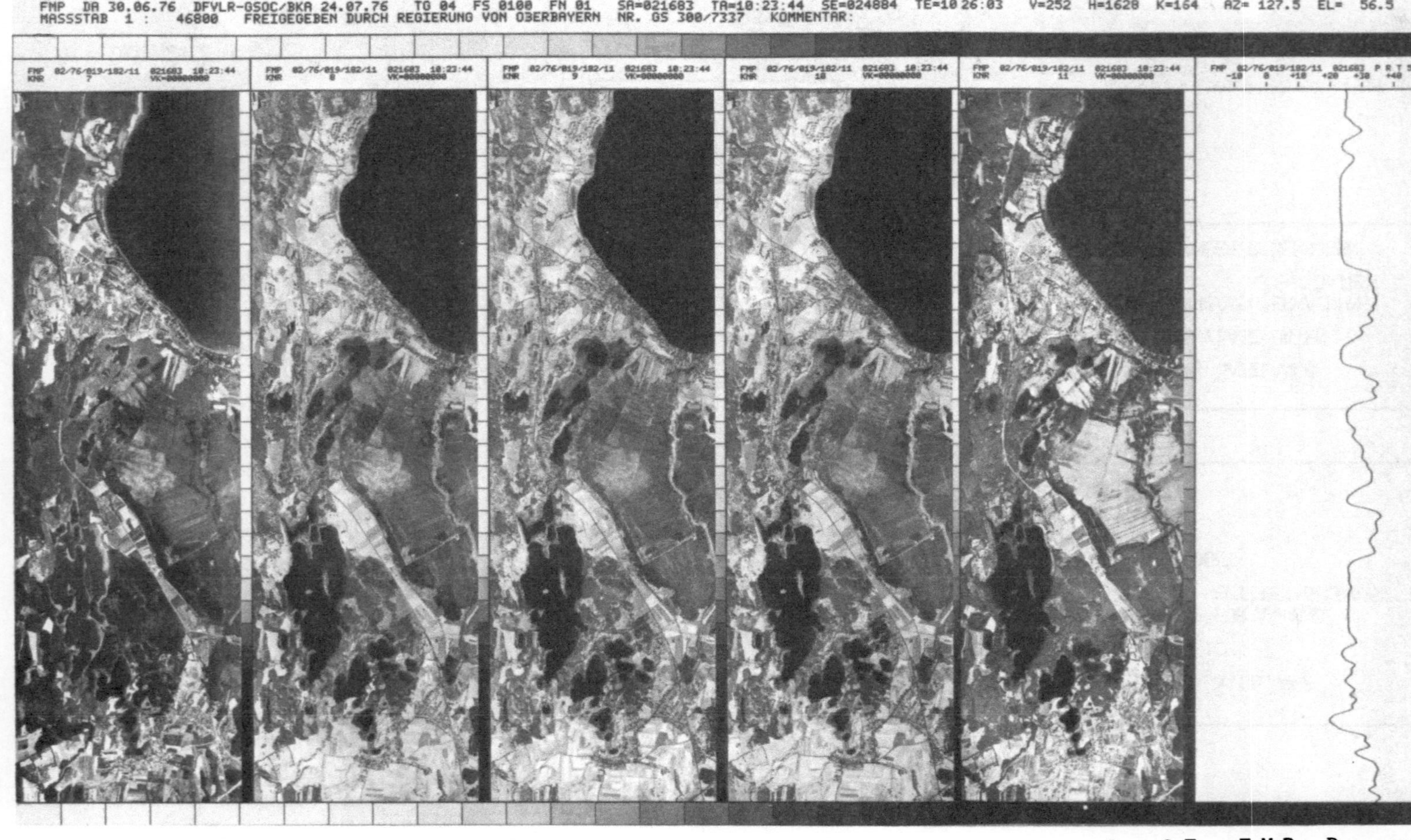

BILD 2.3: F M P - BILDFORMAT

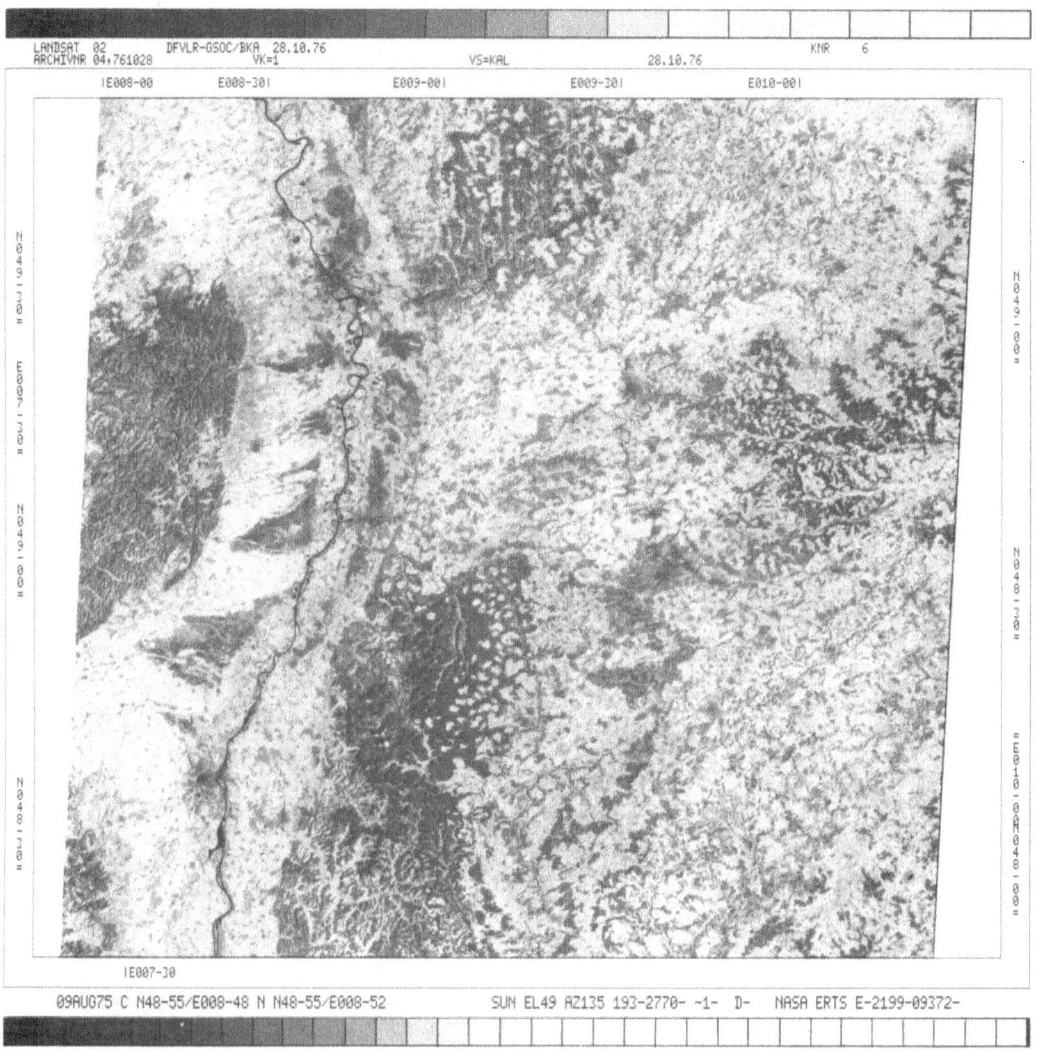

BILD 2.4:   BILDAUSGABE FÜR LANDSAT-DATEN

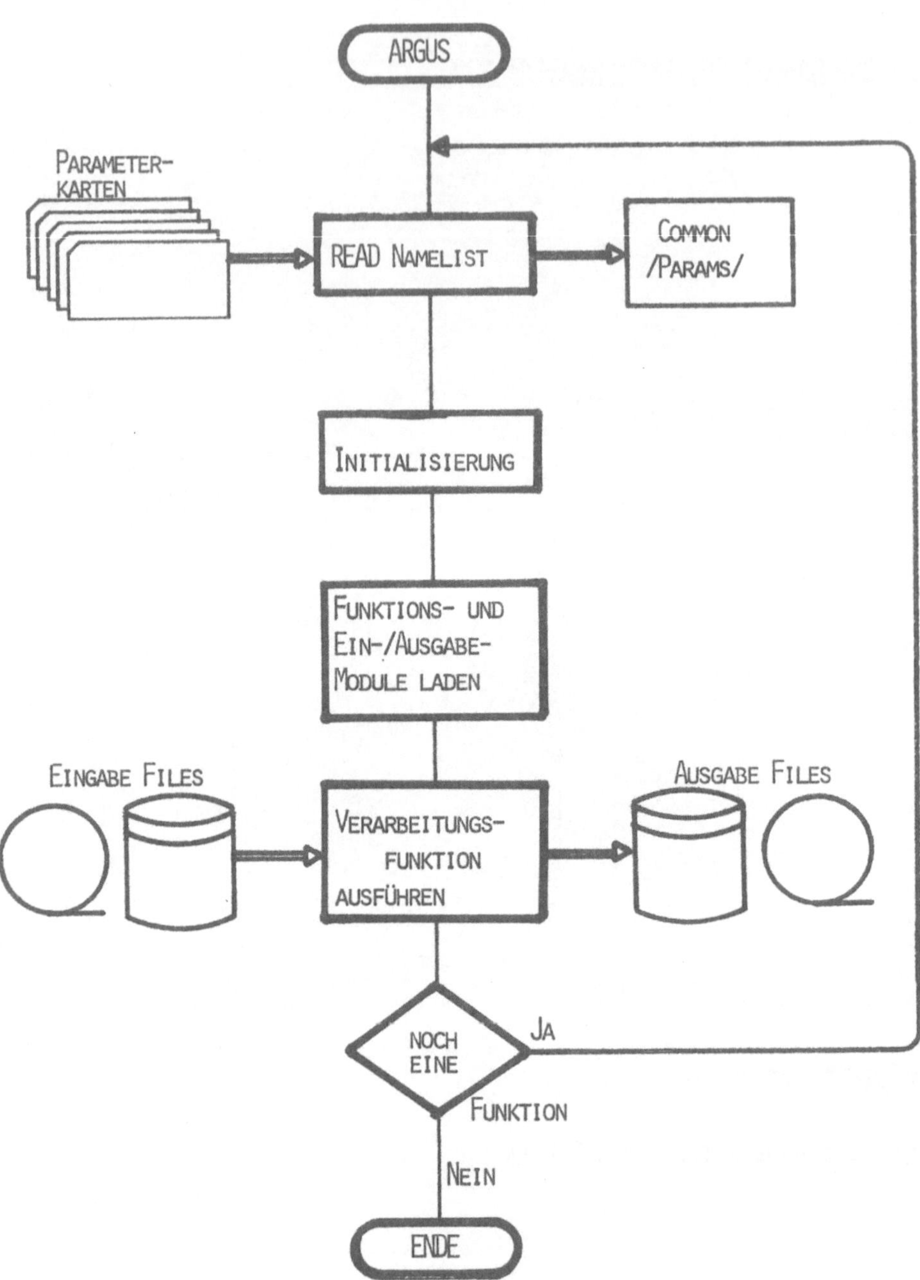

BILD 3.1: ARGUS-Programmablauf

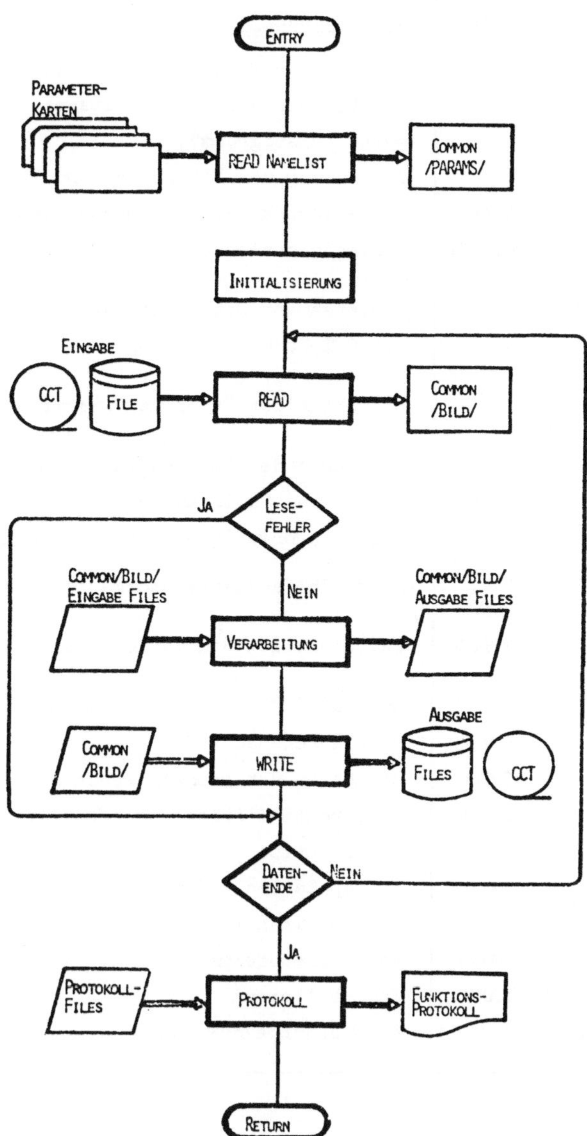

BILD 3.2: PROGRAMMABLAUF EINER ARGUS-FUNKTION

Tabelle 3.1: ARGUS-Funktionen (Stand 30.12.76)

Nr.	Funktion	Option	Beschreibung
1	QULOOK	DUMP	Numerisches Protokoll der Bilddaten
		HIST	Darstellung der Häufigkeitsverteilung der Grauwerte (Histogramm),
			Berechnung von Mittelwert und Streuung
		GRAU	Schnelldrucker-Bild-Reproduktion in 10 Graustufen
		HIST2D	2-dimensionales Histogramm für 2 Spektralbereiche
2	COPY		Kopieren von Daten auf Magnetband oder -Platte mit CCT-Formatumsetzung
3	FMPPAN		Korrektur der Panorama-Verzerrung für FMP-CCT's
4	FMPZUS		Protokoll der FMP-Zusatzinformationen
		FORM1	M^2S Source Calibration Data für Kanäle 1 bis 11
		FORM2	Zusatzinformationen Kanal 12 (komplett)
		FORM3 FORM4	} Ausgewählte Zusatzinformationen aus Kanal 12
		FORM5	Kamera-Zusatzinformationen protokollieren
5	COMDAT		Simulator für Bilddatenkompression
		WORT	Wortlängen-Reduktion
		GEOM	Reduktion der geometrischen Auflösung
		DPCM	Differential Pulse Code Modulation
		DELTA	-Modulation
		EXINT	Extrapolation - Interpolation
		FOUR	Fourier-Transformation
		WALSH	Walsh-Transformation
		KAMM	Kamm-Filterung
		LOEVE	Karhunen-Loéve-Transformation

Tabelle 3.1: <u>ARGUS-Funktionen (Fortsetzung)</u>

Nr.	Funktion	Option	Beschreibung
6	HSTMOD		Grauwert-Transformation durch Angleichung der Ist- an eine Soll-Häufigkeitsverteilung
		STANZ	Stanzen der Umsetz-Tabellen für BKA-Table-Look-up
		HIST	Protokoll der Histogramme
		TABAUS	Protokoll der Umsetz-Tabellen
		BLDAUS	Magnetbandausgabe der manipulierten Daten
		STANZ1	Zusätzlich zu BLDAUS Stanzen der Umsetz-Tabellen
7	KONTUR		Kontur-Verbesserung
		GRAD	Kontur-Verbesserung durch Gradienten-Verfahren
		HIST	Histogramm der GRAD-Ergebnisse
		GRAU	Graudruck der GRAD-Ergebnisse auf Schnelldrucker
		PLOT	Plot der GRAD-Ergebnisse für NIMBUS-Daten
		NMB5W	Magnetbandausgabe der konturverbesserten NIMBUS-Bilddaten
8	NMBPAN		Panorama-Entzerrung für NIMBUS-Daten
9	WINKOR		Radiometrische Korrektur der FMP-Scannerdaten bezüglich des Scannerwinkels (Sonneneinstrahlung, atmosphärischer Einfluß)
		MITTEL	Ausgleichung gemäß Spaltenmittelwerte für Trainingsgebiet
		STREU	Ausgleichung gemäß Spaltenmittelwerte und -Streuungen

Vorstellung des hybriden Bildverarbeitungssystems
ISI 47o für erdwissenschaftliche Auswertungen bei der
Zentralstelle für Geo-Photogrammetrie und Fernerkundung
(ZGF)

J. Bodechtel
R. Haydn
M. Seiderer, München

ZUSAMMENFASSUNG:

Das interaktive Bildverarbeitungssystem ISI 47o der ZGF
(eine Einrichtung der DFG) wird vorgestellt. Aufbau und
Funktionsweise des installierten Systems wird schematisch
dargestellt. Eine kurze Beschreibung des Software-Programm-
systems SWING, entwickelt für erdwissenschaftliche Auswertungen bei der ZGF, schließt sich an.

SUMMARY:

The interactive image processing system ISI 47o of the
central laboratory for remote sensing and geophoto-
grammetry (a institution of German Resarch Council) is
presented. The concept and operational function of the
system is pointed out schematically. A short description
of the software program system SWING, developed for earth
scientific evaluations on the ZGF finish this report.

1. Einführung

Die erderkundliche Datenauswertung konzentriert sich auf
die Analyse, die Interpretation und die Klassifikation von
Bilddaten, wie z.B. photographische Bilder, multispektrale
Bilddaten, Radarbilder.
Die Entwicklung halbautomatischer und automatischer Verfahren zur Bildverbesserung und Auswertung multispektraler
und multitemporaler Fernerkundungsdaten steht im
experimentellen Stadium.
Man unterscheidet im wesentlichen zwei Typen von Bildver-
arbeitungssystemen für erderkundliche Anwendungen

- **vorprogrammierte**, automatisch ablaufende
  Bildverarbeitung

- **interaktive** Bildverarbeitung

Ein bedeutsamer Nachteil der vorprogrammierten Bildverarbeitung, normalerweise durchgeführt im Rahmen der allgemeinen Benutzung von Großrechenanlagen, ist unter anderem
die geringe Eingriffsmöglichkeit des Benutzers beim Bild-
auswerteprozeß.
Zur Entwicklung operationell einsetzbarer Auswerte- und Bild-
optimierungsmodelle in verschiedensten Anwendungsbereichen
bietet sich ein interaktives System mit größtmöglichem Be-
nutzereingriff an. Die interaktiven Systeme dienen sowohl der
vom Anwender kontrollierten Datenauswertung wie der Entwicklung von automatisch ablaufenden Interpretationsmodellen.
Sie basieren zum Teil auf hybriden Anlagen, deren analoger Teil
häufig die Funktion der interaktiven Bildkontrolle übernimmt.
Die Durchsatzrate des Systems ist in der Regel bestimmt durch
die Anforderungen des Benutzers an die erforderliche Genauigkeit bei der Bildauswertung und Bildverbesserung und durch die
Komplexität der anstehenden Probleme.
Die verschiedenartigen Vorteile interaktiver, hybrider Systeme
hat die ZGF (eine Einrichtung der DFG) dazu veranlaßt, ein
solches Bildauswertungssystem für ihre erdwissenschaftliche
Aufgabenstellungen einzusetzen.

2. Das Bildverarbeitungssystem ISI 47o der Zentralstelle

Das interaktive, analog – digitale Bildauswertungssystem
ISI 47o der Zentralstelle wird für erdwissenschaftliche
Datenauswertung im Rahmen bestehender nationaler und
internationaler Fernerkundungsprogramme wie z.B. Flugzeugmeßprogramm (FMP), LANDSAT-Satelitenprogramm eingesetzt.
In diesem Zusammenhang steht es einem breiten Benutzer-
spektrum zur Verfügung. Während der analoge Teil des Systems
seit Oktober 1975 den Anwendern zur Verfügung steht, wird
das digitale Teilsystem gegenwärtig als Endstufe im Aufbau
des Gesamtsystems installiert.

Der Schwerpunkt der Anlage ISI 47o basiert auf interaktiver Bildaufbereitung und -verarbeitung, um den Benutzer ein hohes Maß an Eingriffsmöglichkeiten bei der
Bildauswertung zu gewährleisten. Darüber hinaus sollte
das System den Vorteilen bzw. Möglichkeiten analoger und
digitaler Bildverarbeitung für die erdwissenschaftliche
Datenauswertung gerecht werden. Diese Möglichkeiten voll
ausschöpfen zu können, war eine der Hauptaufgaben bei der
Konzipierung und Entwicklung des Bildverarbeitungssystems
ISI 47o.

2.1. Die Hardware-Konfiguration des Systems ISI 47o

Der schematische Aufbau des Systems ist in der Abb.1
dargestellt. Man erkennt die Gliederung in einem analogen
und einem digitalen Teil des Gesamtsystems.

2.1.1 Der analoge Teil der Anlage

Der seit geraumer Zeit eingesetzte analoge Teil des Systems
bildet eine in sich geschlossene Einheit. Die Ankopplung an
den digitalen Teil des Systems erfolgt über ein Interface
mit einem Analog-Digitalwandler.

Aufbau des analogen Teiles:

a) VP-8 Bildauswerteinheit
   bestehend aus
   - Leuchttisch mit montierter Fernsehkamera
   - eigentliche Auswerteeinheit, VP-8 Elektronik
   - Farbmonitor und XYZ-Monitor

   Funktionen des VP-8:

   Darstellung von Grauwerten und Grauwertverteilungen
   mit Äquidensiten, die auch farblich unterlegt sein
   können. Über ein Fadenkreuz kann ein beliebiger
   Bildpunkt auf dem Monitor angefahren und die Grau-
   wertintensität gemessen werden. Um feine Grauwertdifferenzen verstärkt sichtbar zu machen, kann
   über den XYZ-Monitor ein Grauwertrelief erzeugt
   werden.

b) AP-3 Bildauswerteeinheit

   Funktionen des AP-3:

   Gleichzeitige Überlagerung von maximal sechs
   Bildern. Die arithmetischen Operationen umfassen Summen, Differenzen, Produkt und Quotienten
   von ausgewählten Bildern. Diese, auf optischem
   Wege nicht durchführbaren Bildmanipulationen dienen
   als Grundlage für eine weiterführende Interpretation.
   Darüber hinaus kann durch geeignete Transformation
   der Ausgangsdaten ein verstärkter Kontrast zwischen
   spektral signitfikanten Oberflächenphänomenen erzielt werden.

c) Bildspeichereinheit
   bestehend aus
   - Videoplatte
   - Plattensteuereinheit (AD-41 C)

   Funktionen der Bildspeichereinheit:
   Vereinigt alle Komponenten, die für das analoge
   Abspeichern von Bildern notwendig sind.

Die Steuereinheit ermöglicht das kontinuierliche
Beschreiben der Speicherplatte mit den Bildern,
die über eine TV-Kamera nacheinander eingelesen
werden.

2.1.2 Der digitale Teil der Anlage

Kernstück des Digitalteils ist der Prozeßrechner PDP 11/4o
mit einem Kernspeicher von 28 K Worten, der mit dem Real-
time-Betriebssystem RSX-11M betrieben wird. Der Zentral-
einheit angeschlossen sind folgende peripheren Geräte:

- 1 Magnetbandgerät
- 1 Magnetplatteneinheit (Speicherkapazität 8o
  Megabyte)
- 2 Bedienungskonsolen
- Versatec-Matrixdrucker
- Lochstreifenleser

Die Konsolen dienen zur Eingabe von Kommandos und geben
die Möglich-keit des interaktiven Eingriffes in den ablaufenden Auswerteprozeß. Ein Terminal steht im wesentlichen für Gastwissenschaftler der DFVLR zur Verfügung,
die von der Zentralstelle im Rahmen einer Einführung in
die Bilddatenverarbeitung betreut werden.
Die Magnetplatte (8o Megabyte) dient sowohl zum Abspeichern der auszuwertenden Bildern, der verarbeiteten
Bilder, als auch der System- und Anwendungssoftware.
In der jetzigen Ausbaustufe besitzt das System einen
s/w Versatec-Matrixdrucker für die Ausgabe von Daten
und Bildern. Es ist geplant, die Bildausgabe durch
einen Filmrecorder   zu ergänzen.

2.2 Die Software-Konfiguration des Systems ISI 47o

Für die anstehenden Aufgaben in der Bildauswertung
wurde ein hoch modulares, benutzerorientiertes Soft-
wareprogrammpaket SWING (Software for interactive
graphics) entwickelt.System- und Anwendungssoftware
im Rahmen des Systems SWING sind in der Sprache FORTH
geschrieben, eine Sprache, die sich besonders für interaktive, on-line betriebene Kleinrechner eignet. Haupt-
merkmal von FORTH ist ein jederzeit erweiterungsfähiger
Satz von Kommandos, basierend auf einem anwenderorientiertem
Vokabular. FORTH verbindet extreme Kompaktheit mit hoher
Ausführungsgeschwindigkeit, interaktive Programmierung auf
höherer Ebene mit der Fähigkeit , Assemblerroutinen hinzu-
zufügen, falls sich dies als sinnvoll erweist.
Unter dem Programmsystem FORTH können mehrere Benutzer gleichzeitig zum Rechner zugreifen. In der jetzigen Ausbaustufe
erlaubt das System den Anschluß von zwei separat operierenden
Terminals. Neben FORTH besteht die Möglichkeit, unter dem
Betriebssystem RSX-11M Programme in Fortran IV und PDP-
Assembler zu rechnen.
Das Anwendungssystem von SWING beinhaltet sowohl Hilfs-
routinen für die Systemunterstützung als auch eine Anzahl
verschiedener Bildverarbeitungsoutinen.

SWING-ANWENDUNGSSYSTEM	
Systemroutinen	Bildverarbeitungsroutinen
Plattenfilesystem	Bildmanagement
DV-8-Bildplatte	Bildmanipulation
FORTH-Programm- system	Bildanalysis

Aufbauend auf dem FORTH-Programmsystem, als Basis des
Systems SWING umfassen die Systemroutinen unter anderem
Funktionen für File handling bei Bildfiles und Programm-
files und das Interface zwischen Analog-und Digitalteil
der Anlage (DV-8).

2.2.1 Die Prozeduren für die Bildverarbeitung im System SWING

Für die Bereitstellung und anschließender Verarbeitung von
Bildern bzw. Bildausschnitten stellt das System SWING eine
Reihe von Routinen zur Verfügung.
Im Rahmen des Bildmanagements bietet das System folgende
Möglichkeiten an:

- Directory- strukturierter Zugriff zu Bildern
  über Benutzernamen und (oder) Filenamen.
- Bildfiles variabler Größe (maximal 1o24 x 1o24
  pixel), variable Anzahl von Kanälen (maximal
  16) und variable Genauigkeit (1,4,8,16,32 bits/
  pixel).
- Fortschreiben der Bildgeschichte bei der Bildverarbeitung durch Zusatzinformationen
- Speicherschutz für Bildfiles
- Selektion von rechtwinkligen Bildausschnitten
  z.B. für Testgebiete
- Unterstützung aller Bildverarbeitungsroutinen
  während des Transfers der Bilder zwischen den
  vorhandenen Speicher- bzw. Ausgabemedien.

Im Bereich der Bildauswertung und Bildbearbeitung stellt das
System z.Zt. folgende Funktionen zur Verfügung:

- Bildmanipulation

  eindimensionale Datenmanipulation
- skalare Addition, Subtraktion,Multiplikation
  und Division
- logische skalare Operationen - AND, OR und

exklusives OR
- Quantisierung gleicher Intervalle und Wahrschein-
  lichkeiten
- Festlegung von Schwellenwerten und Zeichnen von
  Konturen

mehrdimensionale Datenmanipulation
- Array Addition, Subtraktion, Multiplikation und
  Division
- Array AND, OR, und exklusives OR
- Ratio von Spektralkanälen
- Lineare Kombinationen und Transformationen
- Laplace und Robert's gradient operator

<u>Bildanalysis</u>

statistische Funktionen
- Minimum, Maximum,Mittelwert und Standardabweichung
- Histogramme und Streudiagramme
- Kovarianzmatrix

Klassifikationsfunktionen
-"hyperbox"-Klassifikation

Die obengenannten Funktionen für die Bildverarbeitung stellen
die erste Ausbaustufe des Programmsystems SWING dar. Entsprechend den Anforderungen der Benutzer wird SWING weiter aus-
gebaut und ergänzt. Für die nahe Zukunft geplant ist die Entwicklung bzw. Eingliederung weiterer Anwendungsprogramme in
das FORTH-System wie

    - geometrische Korrekturprogramme
    - verschiedene " supervised" und "unsupervised"
      Klassifizierungsverfahren
    -- Orthogonaltransformationen (Fourier,Hadamard,usw.)

sowie die Entwicklung eines schnellen Fortran IV-Compilers in
FORTH.

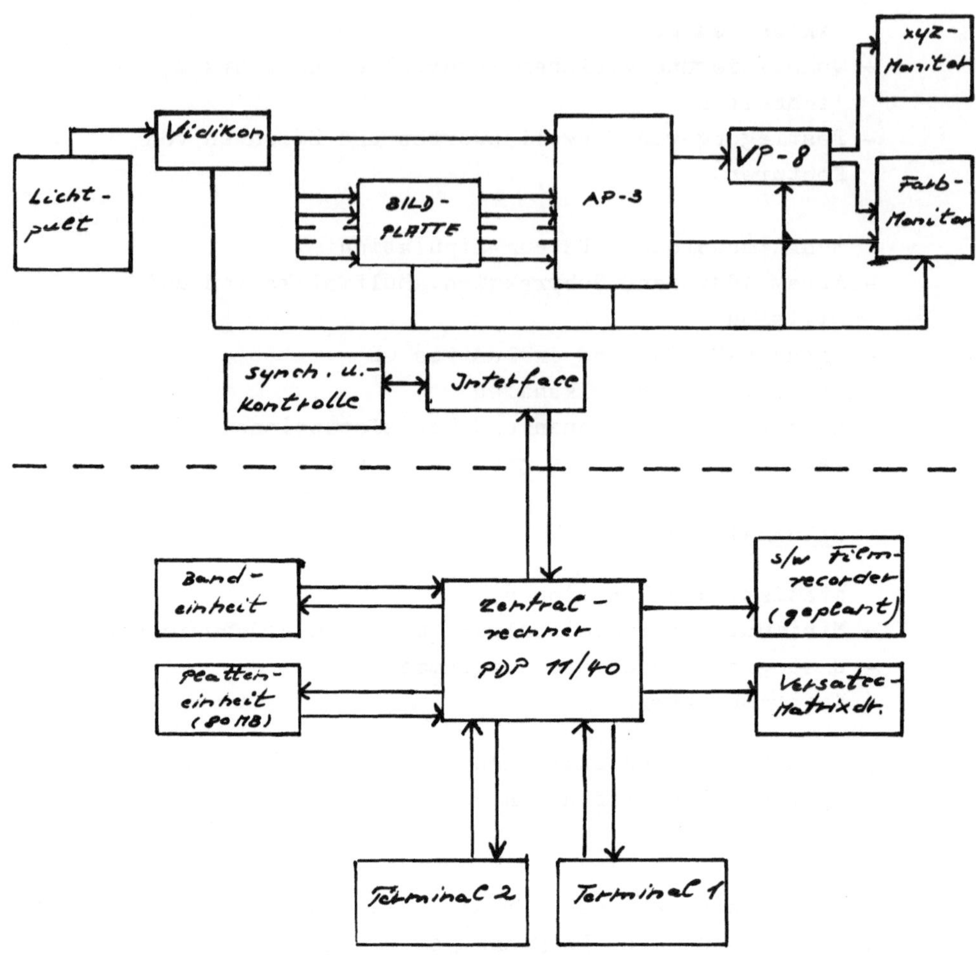

Abb. 1 Schematische Darstellung des Bildverarbeitungssystems
ISI 47o der ZGF

<u>DIBIAS - Das Digitale Bildverarbeitungssystem</u>

<u>der DFVLR</u>

P. Nowak
Institut für Nachrichtentechnik
Deutsche Forschungs- und Versuchsanstalt
für Luft- und Raumfahrt
8031 Oberpfaffenhofen, BRD

<u>Zusammenfassung:</u>

Es wird der aktuelle Stand der Arbeiten am digitalen Bildverarbeitungssystem DIBIAS in der DFVLR präsentiert. Nach einem Überblick über die
zur Zeit laufenden Verfahren werden an Hand von Bildbeispielen einige
Einsatzmöglichkeiten der digitalen Bildverarbeitung im Flugzeugmeßprogramm der BRD vorgestellt.

Abschließend wird ein Ausblick auf den weiteren Ausbau des Systems und
auf die in Zukunft geplanten Arbeiten gegeben.

Der Projektrahmen

Im Laufe der letzten Jahre hat der Einsatz von Fernerkundungstechniken
auch im zivilen Bereich in Europa stark an Bedeutung gewonnen. Die erzielten Ergebnisse lassen den praktischen Einsatz dieser Technologien
auch für Probleme der Landnutzung und des Umweltschutzes als angebracht
erscheinen.

Aus diesem Grunde führt die DFVLR ein Projekt unter der Leitung des
Bundesministeriums für Forschung und Technologie durch, dessen Ziel es
ist, Methoden der Fernerkundung zu erproben und Schlüsse für spätere
operationelle Einsätze zu ziehen.

Die folgenden Problemkreise werden durch dieses Projekt erfaßt:

- Datenakquisition,
- Bodenmeßtechnik,
- Datenaufbereitung und Datenmanagement,
- experimentelle und forschungsorientierte Bildverarbeitung,
- Erprobung der eingesetzten Verfahren für die Problemstellung ver-
  schiedenster Disziplinen.

Im Rahmen der digitalen Bildverarbeitung werden verschiedene Verfahren
auf deren Anwendbarkeit in geowissenschaftlichen Disziplinen untersucht:

- Grundlegende Bildverbesserungsmethoden,
- Multispektrale Klassifizierung,
- Filterung, Texturerkennung.

Ergebnisse dieser Entwicklungen sollen für die Bildauswertung zukünftiger
Fernerkundungsunternehmen (wie etwa Spacelab und künftige operationelle
Systeme) zur Verfügung stehen.

Dieses in der Bildverarbeitung angestrebte Ziel kann im wesentlichen auf
zwei verschiedenen Wegen erreicht werden:

1.) In Form der vollautomatischen Bildauswertung auf einem Großrechner,
2.) mithilfe eines interaktiven Bildverarbeitungssystems.

Die vollautomatische Bildauswertung geht von dem Grundsatz aus, alle
Entscheidungen dem Rechner zu überlassen. Im Gegensatz dazu strebt die
interaktive Bildauswertung eine Kopplung zwischen dem subjektiv erken-
nenden und interpretierten Menschen und dem schnell und objektiv arbeitenden Rechner an. Der Nachteil des geringeren erreichbaren Datendurch-
satzes der interaktiven Bildauswertung wird durch eine derzeit höhere
Qualität der erzielten Ergebnisse, verglichen mit denen der automatischen
Auswertung, kompensiert. Auf dem gegenwärtigen Stand der Technologie erbringt nämlich der synoptisch erkennende und interpretierende Mensch
immer noch bessere Ergebnisse gegenüber dem seriell und völlig objektiv
urteilenden Rechner. Die Ergebnisse und Erkenntnisse aus der interaktiven Bildverarbeitung können zu einer schrittweisen Automatisierung
der Bildverarbeitung durch den Großrechner führen.

Aus diesen Gründen wurde bei der DFVLR im Rahmen des Flugzeugmeßprogrammes primär zugunsten eines interaktiven Bildauswertungssystems entschieden; parallel dazu fließen in weiterer Folge Ergebnisse und Erkenntnisse aus der interaktiven Bildauswertung in ein automatisches Bildverarbeitungssystem am Großrechner ein. Auf diese Weise kann für künftige Fernerkundungsprojekte eine schrittweise Automatisierung der Bildauswertung erreicht werden.

Das Systemkonzept

Für das Konzept und den Aufbau des beschriebenen Systems war folgende

Zielsetzung vorgegeben:

- DIBIAS mußte ein experimentelles, forschungsorientiertes Bildverarbeitungssystem sein, und sich dem Benutzer so präsentieren, daß auch
  der EDV-unerfahrene Fachwissenschaftler bereits nach kurzer Einarbeitungszeit die Möglichkeit hat, selbständig mit dem System zu arbeiten,
  und die zur Verfügung gestellten Verfahren auf sein Bildmaterial sinnvoll anwenden kann.

Eine wesentliche Stärke des Systems ist auch die sofortige Darstellbar-
keit der jeweiligen Ergebnisse nach einem Bildverarbeitungsprozess. Somit kann der Geowissenschaftler sofort beurteilen, ob ein eingesetztes
Verfahren die von ihm erwünschten Ergebnisse erbringt oder nicht. Dies
ist ein wesentlicher Vorteil des beschriebenen Systems gegenüber Bild-
verarbeitungssystemen, die etwa auf einem Großrechner in einem Rechenzentrum betrieben werden.

Die wichtigsten Merkmale sind:

- Durch den Einsatz moderner Bildverarbeitungsgeräte und entsprechender
  Programmierung hat der Benutzer die Möglichkeit, interaktiv die gewünschten Bildverarbeitungsprozesse zu aktivieren, zu steuern und zu
  überwachen.

- Der Benutzer kann nach kurzer Einarbeitungszeit das System bedienen,
  ohne tief in die "Geheimnisse der Datenverarbeitung" eindringen zu
  müssen, da sich alle Systemteile dem Benutzer im Klartext präsentieren.

- Die gesamte DIBIAS-Software ist streng modular gegliedert. Vor allem
  sind die Ein- und Ausgabeprogramme für Bildinformation von den eigentlichen Bildverarbeitungsprogrammen getrennt.

- Das System läßt die Simultanarbeit verschiedener Bildverarbeitungsprogramme zu, wodurch ein optimales Ausnützen der gebotenen System-
  leistungen möglich ist.

- Der Benutzer hat sofort nach dem Ende eines Bildverarbeitungsprozesses
  die Möglichkeit, das erzielte Ergebnis auf einen Farb-Bildschirm zu
  beurteilen.

- Das System ist jederzeit auf sehr einfache Weise um neue Bestandteile
  erweiterbar, wobei großes Gewicht auf die einfache Integrationsmöglich-

keit neuer Bildverarbeitungsprogramme gelegt wurde.

Die Geräte

Die Hardware-Konfiguration von DIBIAS ist in Bild 1 schematisch dargestellt. Das Kernstück der Anlage ist der Prozessrechner INTERDATA M 85,
der aufgrund seiner Geschwindigkeit in Hinblick auf die oft sehr rechen-
intensiven Programme der Bildverarbeitung ausgesucht wurde. Um den speziellen Anforderungen der Bildverarbeitung gerecht zu werden, ist der
Rechner neben der üblichen Peripherie mit folgenden Geräten ausgerüstet:

Ein Datensichtgerät (Bild 1,1) ist für den Benutzer die Bedienungskon-
sole zur Kommunikation mit dem Bildverarbeitungssystem DIBIAS. Es sind
folgende Kategorien von Benutzerinteraktionen möglich:

- Aktivierung von einzelnen Bildverarbeitungsprogrammen,
- Eingabe von modulspezifischen Parametern,
- Kontrolle des DIBIAS-Systemstatus,
- DIBIAS-Systemmeldungen an den Benutzer.

Ein Farbbildschirm (Bild 1,2) bietet dem Benutzer die Möglichkeit die
Ergebnisse von einzelnen Bildverarbeitungsschritten sofort zu kontrol-
lieren und zu beurteilen. Damit wird die zeitraubende und kostspielige
Belichtung und Entwicklung von Papierbildern oder Filmmaterial vermieden.
Außerdem ist die direkte Beeinflussung der Bilddaten über eine Rollkugel
mit Lichttarget am Bildschirm und über das Sichtgerät möglich.

Ein graphischer Bildschirm (Bild 1, 3) dient zur Darstellung graphischer
Information (z.B. Histogramme, Verteilungsfunktionen), die zur Beurteilung und Beeinflussung der Bildverarbeitungsprozesse herangezogen werden können.

Zur Abtastung von schwarz-weiß Papierbildern wird ein mechanischer
Trommel-Scanner verwendet. Dieses Gerät gestattet die Abtastung von
schwarz-weiß-Vorlagen bis zu einer Größe von 20 x 20 cm (Bild 1, 5).
Ein entsprechendes Gerät steht für die Belichtung von schwarz-weiß-
Papierbildern desselben Formats zur Verfügung (Bild 1, 6).

Zur Verarbeitung von schwarz-weiß- und Farbfilm-Material wird ein so-
genannter Flying-Spot-Scanner eingesetzt (Bild 1, 7). Es können 35mm
und 70mm Filme und Diapositive abgetastet werden.

Zur Belichtung von schwarz-weiß- und Farbfilmmaterial wird ein soge-
nannter Film-Recorder eingesetzt (Bild 1, 8). Bei der Belichtung eines
Bildes werden vom Rechner her die Koordinaten des zu belichtenden Punktes
angegeben, dann der Bildpunkt einer Elektronenstrahlröhre positioniert,
über eine Optik auf die Filmebene projiziert und anschließend proportional zum eingespeicherten Grauwert belichtet. Farbfilme werden in drei
Druchgängen unter Zwischenschaltung entsprechener Filter belichtet. Es
können auch direkt Schwarz-weiß und Farb-Polaroid-Bilder erstellt werden.

Die Programme

Die Einsatzmöglichkeiten und die Effektivität eines solchen Bildverarbeitungssystems hängen im wesentlichen von der Flexibilität des zum Betrieb der Geräte erstellten Software-Paketes ab. Unter den Gesichtspunkten der Benutzerfreundlichkeit und der Effektivität des Mensch-
Maschine-Dialogs wurde in den Jahren 1974 und 1975 das folgende Konzept
verwirklicht.

Das Grundkonzept der DIBIAS-Software ist in Bild 2 schematisch dargestellt. Der Benutzer hat die Möglichkeit mit Hilfe von Steueranweisungen
(Kommandos) und den entsprechenden Eingabegeräten Bildinformation in das
System einzugeben. Diese Bildinformationen können durch Zusatzinformationen (z.B. Daten aus Bodenmessungen) ergänzt werden. Durch die Eingabe weiterer Kommandos kann der Benutzer nun Prozesse aktivieren, die
die vorhandene Bildinformation nach seinen Wünschen modifizieren. Dabei wird er vom System durch Interpretationshilfen (z.B. Histogramme,
Verteilungen, Tabellen), durch Zusatzinformationen (z.B. Bildgeometrie,
Bildgeschichte) und durch Systemmeldungen (z.B. erfolgreiches Ende eines
Verarbeitungsprozesses) unterstützt. Wenn der Benutzer nach einer Reihe
von Bildverarbeitungsprozessen ein für ihn zufriedenstellendes Ergebnis
erzielt hat, kann er durch Belichtung von Farbfilm ein Bild anfertigen,
das dann vom System automatisch mit Zusatzinformationen versehen wird.
Damit wird sichergestellt, daß eine Sequenz von erfolgten Verarbeitungsschritten eindeutig reproduzierbar ist.

Zur Zeit (Anfang 1977) besteht das beschriebene Bildverarbeitungssystem
DIBIAS aus etwa 130 verschiedenen Programmen, die einen Arbeitsaufwand
von insgesamt etwa 10 Mann-Jahren darstellen. Die Programme selbst umfassen etwa 60.000 Lochkarten. Die Programme lassen sich in folgende
Gruppen aufteilen:

- Ein- und Ausgabeprogramme für verschiedene Bildformate,

- grundlegende statistische Programme,

- elementare Programme zur Bildverbesserung,

- Programme zur interaktiven Bearbeitung von Bildern mit Hilfe des Farbbildschirmes,

- Programme zur multispektralen Klassifizierung,

- Programme zur Filterung.

Es wird laufend an der Verbesserung bereits installierter und an der Erstellung neuer Verfahren gearbeitet.

<u>Die Einsatzmöglichkeiten</u>

DIBIAS kann dann optimal und im Sinne seiner Zielsetzung verwendet werden, wenn der Experimentator mit vorausgewähltem Bildmaterial an das System herantritt. Bei Bilddatenmaterial in der Größenordung bis zu typisch 512 x 512 Bildpunkten (in mehreren Spektralbereichen) benötigen einfache Verfahren Rechenzeiten von einigen Minuten. Dies erlaubt rasches Arbeiten und oftmaliges experimentieren an ein und demselben Bild. Mathematisch aufwendigere Verfahren wie etwa Fouriertransformation oder multispektrale Klassifizierung beanspruchen natürlich mehr Rechenzeit, was dann in einer längeren Verarbeitungsfolge einen gewissen Engpaß darstellt. Dieser Nachteil kommt daher, daß DIBIAS als umfassendes, experimentelles Bildverarbeitungssystem konzipiert wurde, das die verschiedensten Gruppen von Verarbeitungsverfahren enthalten sollte. Im Gegensatz dazu stehen manche industriell gefertigte amerikanische interaktive Bildverarbeitungssysteme, die zwar sehr schnell Klassifizierungen durchführen können, dafür aber viele andere Verfahren, die in DIBIAS integriert sind, nicht anbieten.

Zur Abgrenzung gegen analog arbeitende Bildverarbeitungssysteme ist zu sagen, daß diese zwar in manchen Verfahren erheblich schneller sein mögen, niemals aber die Flexibilität eines digitalen, frei programmierbaren Systems erbringen können. Einen gewissen Kompromiß stellen hier sogenannte hybride Systeme dar, die aus einer Kombination eines analogen und eines digitalen Verarbeitungsteiles bestehen.

Obwohl in DIBIAS die Möglichkeit besteht, auch große Datenmengen zu verarbeiten, sollte das System nicht dafür verwendet werden, da dies dem ursprünglichen, interaktiven Konzept zuwiderläuft, und bei Verarbeitung großer Datenmengen die Eigenschaften und Geräte, die die wesentliche Stärke des Systems ausmachen, ungenützt bleiben.

Unter Berücksichtigung der wissenschaftlichen Zielsetzung des Flugzeug-
meßprogramms werden zur Zeit zusammen mit den Experimentatoren die Pro-
blemstellungen folgender sechs Testgebiete mit Hilfe von DIBIAS bearbeitet:

1.) Ostfriesisches Wattengebiet mit Teilen der Nordsee, Schwerpunktauf-
    aufgabe Wechselwirkung Land-Wasser im Küstenbereich.

2.) Ein Meeresgebiet in der Deutschen Bucht, ozeanographische Unter-
    suchungen.

3.) **Ein Meeresgebiet in der Kieler Bucht für ozeanog**raphische
    Fragestellungen.

4.) Ein Testgebiet im Bereich des Unter-Mains mit Taunus und Wetterau
    mit der Schwerpunktsaufgabe: Biosphäre eines Ballungsgebietes
    für Fragen der Landesplanung und des Umweltschutzes.

5.) Oberrheintal-Bruch und Schwarzwald bei Freiburg i.Br.,
    der Schwerpunkt liegt auf der Bearbeitung von Vegetations- und
    Landnutzungsformen.

6.) Ein Alpenrandgebiet südlich von München mit der Schwerpunkt-
    aufgabe der Ökologie eines Hochgebirgsrandgebietes.

Die Experimente in den einzelnen Testgebieten (Flugeinsätze, Bodenmessungen) werden in enger Zusammenarbeit mit dem angeschlossenen Forschungs-
und Hochschulinstituten durchgeführt. Ebenso erfolgt die Auswertung des
aufgenommenen Datenmaterilas in enger Zusammenarbeit mit den einzelnen
Fachwissenschaftlern.

Bei der aktuellen Verwendung von DIBIAS im erdwissenschaftlichen Flugzeugmeßprogramm wurden und werden viele Verfahren erst in enger Zusammenarbeit mit den einzelnen Geowissenschaftlern erarbeitet, sei es nun, daß
erst eine gewisse Abfolge von Einzelschritten erarbeitet werden muß, sei
es, daß ein völlig neues Programm erstellt und in das System integriert
wird, was in der erforderlichen Geschwindigkeit nur an einem programmierbaren, digitalen System möglich ist.

Zur Zeit wird das System im erdwissenschaftlichen Flugzeugmeßprogramm
hauptsächlich für Fragestellungen der Erdfernerkundung eingesetzt.

Dies bedeutet aber keine Einschränkung; ebenso kann das System, wie einige Anwendungsbeispiele schon gezeigt haben, für medizinische und wehrtechnische Belange eingesetzt werden.

Bis Ende 1977 wird DIBIAS hauptsächlich für die Belange des Flugzeug-meßprogramms eingesetzt; parallel dazu läuft ab Anfang 1977 ein Forschungsprojekt des BMBau zur Anwendung der digitalen Bildverarbeitung in der Raumplanung. Zukünftige Einsätze sind sicher auch im Rahmen des SFB 149 (Fernerkundung von Küsten und Meeren) zu erwarten.

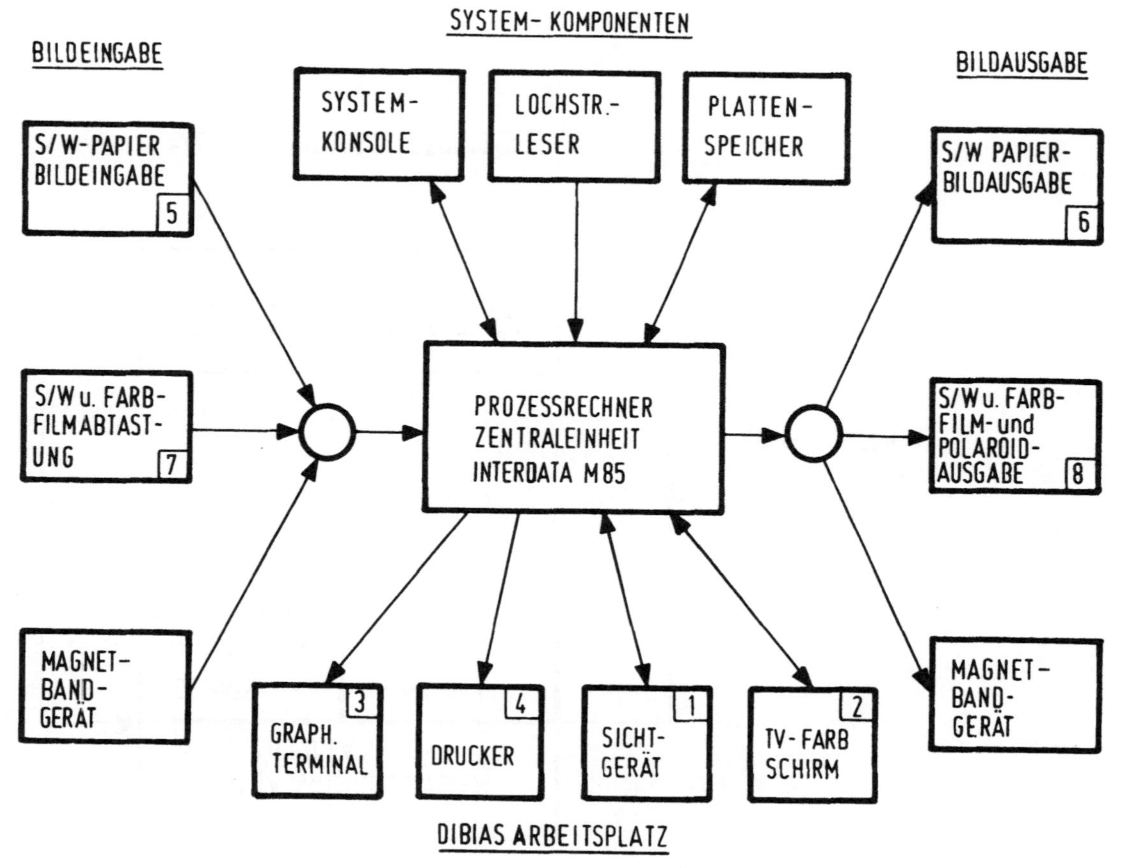

BILD 1)   DIBIAS GERÄTEKONFIGURATION

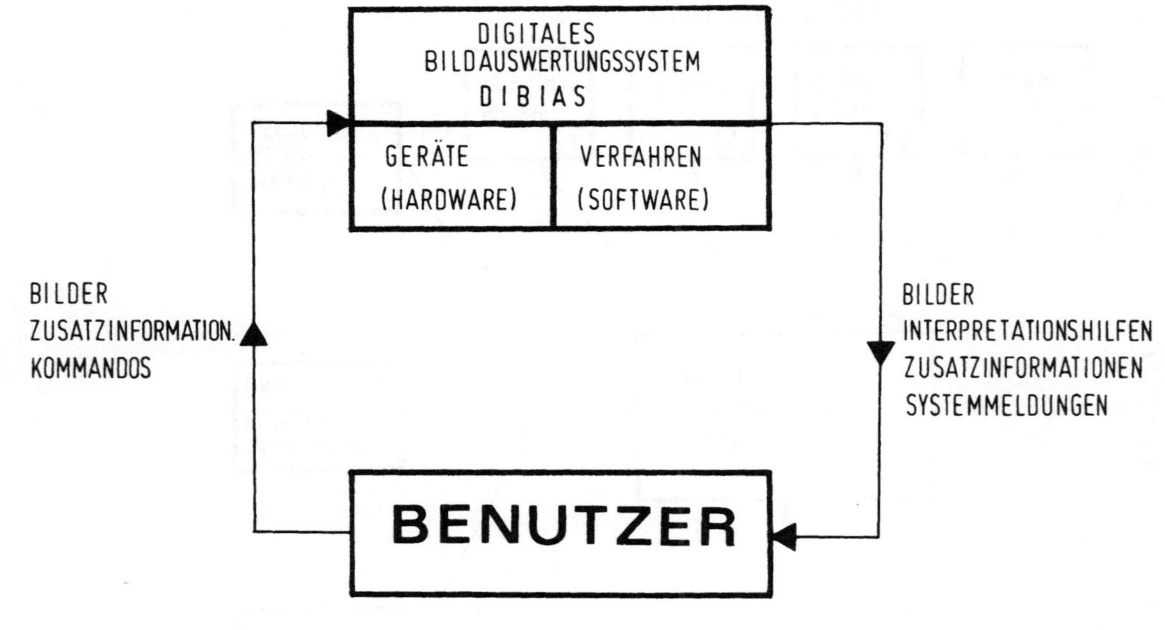

BILD 2)   DIBIAS   GRUNDKONZEPT

Informatik – Fachberichte